# Training

## for

# E C D L

*Editors*

**John Brennan**

**Tom Mac Mahon**

Blackrock Education Centre
2001

© Blackrock Education Centre

ISBN   0 9512465 9 3

*Published by*
Blackrock Education Centre
Kill Avenue, Dún Laoghaire
Co. Dublin, Ireland

Tel. (+353 1) 2 300 977   E-mail. bec@blackrock-edu.ie   Web.  www.blackrock-edu.ie

| First published | 1999 |
| Reprinted (5 times) | 1999 |
| 2nd edition | 2000 |
| Reprinted with additions | 2001 |
| Reprinted (minor updates) | 2001 |

"European Computer Driving Licence" and "ECDL" and Stars device are registered trade marks of the European Computer Driving Licence Foundation Limited in Ireland and other countries.  Blackrock Education Centre is an independent entity from the European Computer Driving Licence Foundation Limited, and not affiliated with the European Computer Driving Licence Foundation Limited in any manner. 'Training for ECDL' may be used in assisting students to prepare for the European Computer Driving Licence Examination. Neither the European Computer Driving Licence Foundation Limited nor Blackrock Education Centre warrants that the use of this 'Training for ECDL' manual will ensure passing the relevant Examination.  Use of the ECDL-approved Courseware Logo on this product signifies that it has been independently reviewed and approved in complying with the following standards:

Acceptable coverage of all courseware content related to ECDL Syllabus Version 3.0. This courseware material has not been reviewed for technical accuracy and does not guarantee that the end user will pass the associated ECDL Examinations.  Any and all assessment tests and/or performance based exercises contained in this manual relate solely to 'Training for ECDL' and do not constitute, or imply, certification by the European Driving Licence Foundation in respect of any ECDL Examinations.  For details on sitting ECDL Examinations in your country, please contact the local ECDL Licensee or visit the European Computer Driving Licence Foundation Limited web site at **http://www.ecdl.com**.

References to the European Computer Driving Licence (ECDL) include the International Computer Driving Licence (ICDL).  ECDL Foundation Syllabus Version 3.0 is published as the official syllabus for use within the European Computer Driving Licence (ECDL) and International Computer Driving Licence (ICDL) certification programme.

Microsoft® Windows®, Microsoft® Office, Microsoft Word, Microsoft Access, Microsoft Excel, Microsoft PowerPoint®, Microsoft Internet Explorer and Microsoft Outlook® are either registered trademarks or trademarks of the Microsoft Corporation.

Other products mentioned in this manual may be registered trademarks or trademarks of their respective companies or corporations.

The companies, organisations, products, the related people, their positions, names, addresses and other details used for instructional purposes in this manual and its related support materials on the Web are fictitious.  No association with any real company, organisations, products or people are intended nor should any be inferred.

# Blackrock Education Centre

**Director/Stiurthóir**: Séamus Cannon/Séamus Ó Canainn
Phil Caulfield (Chairperson), Patrick Fox, Siobhán Cluskey, Dóirín Creamer,
Walter Cullinane, Nóirín Daly, Kieran Griffin, Deirdre Keyes, Thérèse McPhillips,
Alan Monnelly, Mena O'Leary, Peter O'Loughlin, James O'Neill, Michael O'Reilly.

# Credits

*Original Text*
John Brennan, Ursula Hearne, Deirdre Mathews,
Tom Mac Mahon, Denis O'Connor, Damien O'Sullivan

*Design and Layout*
Tom Mac Mahon

*Editorial Consultant*
Roberta Reeners

*Cover Design*
Vermillion

*Line Drawings*
Helen Mac Mahon

# Acknowledgements

The contributions of Cyril Drury (former head of the Centre's ECDL project),
Paula Curran, Mary O'Donoghue and Paul Landers to an earlier edition are acknowledged.
Con O'Doherty was a valued member of the project team for this edition.

The assistance of the following staff members is also acknowledged:
Lil Lynch, Evelyn Logan, Siobhán McStay, Chris Murphy, Phil Halpin,
Monica Dowdall, Adela Fernandez, Joan Bauerle, Aileen Benson, Tomás Ó Briain

# Contents

# About This Book

## The Manual

'Training for ECDL' offers a practical, step-by-step guide for any person who wishes to use the Microsoft Office software suite (either Office 97 or Office 2000) and Internet Explorer on Windows PC computers. It has been designed primarily as a study aid for students of courses for the European Computer Driving Licence (the International Computer Driving Licence – ICDL – outside Europe).

The manual has been approved by the ECDL Foundation as suitable for use with the new ECDL/ICDL Syllabus, Version 3. It incorporates the content of our previous ECDL Ireland-approved manual for ECDL Syllabus Version 1.5.

## Design

Every use has been made of the expertise we have gained from working closely with ECDL over the last several years. Additionally, the knowledge and skills of our substantial pool of trainers hugely influenced the content and layout of the material.

We use plain English, not computer jargon. We take you point by point through detailed explanations and action sequences. We pay particular attention to relating what you see on the pages of the manual to what you see on the computer screen. Where necessary, we include small amounts of additional information to enhance your understanding of very important topics.

You will also find that the A4 size of the manual, the side-by-side layout of graphics and text, and the spiral binding all combine to make it an ideal *desk-top friendly* training manual.

## Exercises

At the end of each module, there are two kinds of exercises. Self-check questions (with answers supplied) are designed to jog your memory of important details. The practical exercises (also with solutions) have been designed to revise some of the more important skills associated with using the applications.

In successfully completing a set of exercises, you can be confident of your progress in learning to use a given skill or application.

## Web Support

Support material is available on the Internet at **www.ictlearning.ie** – a sister site of Blackrock Education Centre (**www.blackrock-edu.ie**). Should there be any minor amendments to the ECDL syllabus in the future, updates and/or additional material will be posted there.

*This manual was produced – design and layout – using only the Microsoft Office suite of programs and the skills described in the manual. The screen shots were captured using a small utility program and most were inserted directly onto the page.*

**The Editors**

# Foreword

Blackrock Education Centre provides support services to teachers and to partners in education under the auspices of the Department of Education and Science in Ireland. For many years the Education Centre has provided training for teachers in the use of Information and Communications Technology. While introductory courses were always popular, we frequently experienced difficulties in progressing beyond the basics. There was a large gap between the introductory course and what was being offered at university, with little in between that was both comprehensive and practical. There was a need for a training programme that measured progressive development of competency across a range of skills.

The European Computer Driving Licence – ECDL (ICDL outside Europe) – provides a very good framework for such a training programme. Blackrock Education Centre tested it on a pilot basis in 1997 and subsequently opened it up to larger numbers. The response was very encouraging. The demand for teacher training in Ireland increased dramatically with the launch of *Schools IT2000* – the national programme launched by the Department of Education and Science – and the Blackrock initiative was supported by the National Centre for Technology in Education.

The key attractions of ECDL are the focus on practical competency and the flexible syllabus, independent of platform or software. These enabled us to tailor our training while maintaining standards that are recognised internationally. It is the experience of Blackrock Education Centre that completing the ECDL programme gives the user confidence in using the computer, a significant level of practical skill and an excellent preparation for further study.

In the Information Age, all of us are required to engage in continuous lifelong learning. We have been aware that many of the schools we work with want to offer a programme to parents and to other members of the community. Increased access to learning opportunities, through libraries and other community institutions, is more and more the norm. Our training programme has encouraged this development and many schools have themselves become accredited ECDL test centres offering local training. In addition, *Training for ECDL* has come to be used extensively in the commercial and corporate training sectors, both in Ireland and abroad.

These training materials have been written and tested by teachers and incorporate many new ideas since the first edition. All the authors and others who worked on the project deserve great credit. Particular thanks are due to Director Séamus Ó Canainn, to editors John Brennan (who also managed the project) and to Tom Mac Mahon. Cyril Drury was the inspiration behind our entire ECDL project. These training materials are a testament to the thoroughness with which they have addressed the requirements of lifelong learning in the Information Age.

Phil Caulfield
*Chairperson*

Blackrock Education Centre
August 2000

# E C D L

## The European Computer Driving Licence
## (ICDL outside Europe)

The European Computer Driving Licence is a means of indicating that you have acquired the basic skills to use a computer in a wide variety of applications, just as your standard Driving Licence indicates that you have acquired the skills necessary to drive a car on public roads.

As with learning to drive a car, a variety of skills has to be learnt before the licence is issued. Also, it is important that these skills be acquired by actually using the computer: one does not expect to have a vehicle Driving Licence issued just by reading all about it and answering questions in a written examination.

The ECDL concept originated in Finland in 1988 and has spread all over Europe since then, with headquarters now established in Dublin. In each country, ECDL operates under the auspices of and in association with the national computer society. In Ireland, this is the Computer Society of Ireland.

The success of ECDL throughout Europe has been due to the well thought out and structured modular approach which allows training establishments to provide flexible training in basic computer skills with varying degrees of emphasis according to the candidates' needs, while at the same time maintaining uniformly high standards.

ECDL has now spread beyond European borders and attracted the attention of trainers and training establishments in many parts of the the world. It is now becoming known internationally as ICDL – the International Computer Driving Licence.

At present there are seven modules in the ECDL syllabus. On enrolling for an ECDL course, candidates are issued with an ECDL Skills Card on which their progress is recorded with an authorised stamp after the successful completion of each module. The modules can be studied and tested in any order. Individual modules can be completed at different training centres or even in different countries.

The tests are each of 45 minutes duration. All tests, except the Module 1 test, are practical hands-on tests at the computer. The Module 1 test is the only written test as it teaches concepts rather than skills. On successful com-pletion of all seven tests, the Skills Card is returned to the national ECDL office which then issues the ECDL certificate.

The issue of the certificate – the European Computer Driving Licence – is administered in Ireland by ECDL Ireland, which controls accreditation and provides tester training on a national level. It also monitors very closely the standards under which ECDL training and testing are carried out at the hundreds of accredited training centres throughout the country.

Training and training materials for the ECDL are the responsibility of the individual training establishment. Blackrock Education Centre has over twenty years' experience in Information Technology training and has been closely associated with ECDL Ireland from the beginning, organising and administering one of the first ECDL pilot projects in this country.

# Before
## You Begin

BYB

# Before You Begin

# Section 1      The Computer Workplace

## 1.1     Introduction

The Microsoft Office Suite of Applications, i.e. Word, Access, Excel, PowerPoint, Outlook and Explorer, share many common features.  How you open an application, how it looks on the computer screen and how you work with it on the computer are similar across the whole suite.

This chapter describes a number of the most common features that are important for the effective use of the computer and it explains how to use them.  The features and skills described in this preliminary module are important elements of the course.

This chapter is best read with two purposes in mind. The first is for you to gain an overview of the common elements and skills that you will be required to use during the course.  The second is that in being aware of them before you begin to study any module, you will be better prepared to understand and use the specific skills and features required for each Module as you come to it.

## 1.2     Where You Work

The first thing you see when the computer has finished its starting up is the **Desktop** screen.  It is referred to as the desktop because you will be using it as you would the top of a real office desk.

You will place new or previously created work here, as you would place a writing pad, a sheet of paper or a calculator on top of your real desk. You will do this electronically, of course, on the computer.

Items on the desktop are represented by small pictures, or **icons**, with their names underneath.

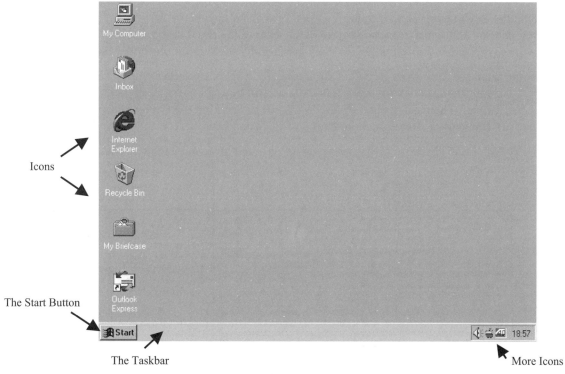

The Computer Desktop

## 1.3    The Taskbar

The **Taskbar** is a bar (or strip) that appears along the bottom of the **desktop**. It is usually visible no matter what program you are using, although it can be hidden if you want to make more space available for your work.

The taskbar contains a number of icons in the form of **buttons**. A button is an icon that you can click on to perform an action. Some buttons are always on the taskbar while others appear on it from time to time, depending on what work is in progress.

You can think of the items on the taskbar as being like drawers in a real desk where things can be put out of the way when they are not being consulted or used. Here are some examples as they may appear on the part of the taskbar in the illustration.

The **Start** button is permanently in position at the left of the taskbar.

The **Microsoft Word** button represents a document, named Letter.

The **Calculator** button represents a calculator on which you can make calculations.

The **Printers** button represents a folder that contains information about printers.

When a button has a **pressed in** appearance like the Calculator button above, it indicates that the Calculator is the item that is currently displayed and being used in the main part of the desktop. It is the **active** item, the one you are working on at the moment. The other items may or may not be visible on the desktop but the buttons on the taskbar remind you of their presence.

Clicking a button on the taskbar makes the object it represents the active item and, if it has been hidden, it will now be displayed.

## 1.4    The Keyboard

The computer **keyboard** is similar to the standard typewriter keyboard. Most computer keyboards, however, have an additional numeric keypad to the right of the usual keys. There is also an extra row of keys at the top, called **Function** keys, which are used by some programs or applications.

In addition, there are some extra keys that are frequently used in computer work. The **arrow** keys, for example, can control the cursor on the screen and the **Tab** key can move from box to box when forms have to be filled in. The most commonly used of the extra keys are the **Ctrl** (Control), **Alt** (Alternative), **Backspace**, **Delete** and the **Return** (or **Enter**) keys.

Familiarity with basic keyboard skills – simple typing – will be an advantage if you are going to use the computer a lot.

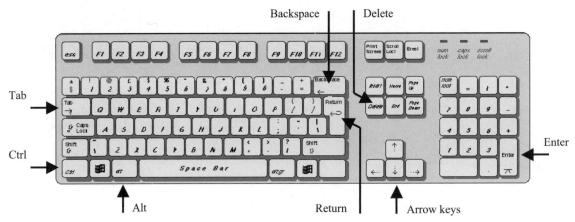

## 1.5    The Mouse

The **mouse** is a small box that you move around on a pad called a **mouse mat**. The usual mouse has two buttons, on the left and right.

As you move the mouse on the mat, a **cursor** (or **pointer**), usually in the shape of a small arrow, moves on the screen in the same way as the mouse.  Move the mouse to the right and the cursor moves to the right, and so on.

The **cursor** or **pointer**

When the pointer is placed in a particular position, over an icon for example, pressing a button causes the computer to perform an action related to the icon.

 The mouse is the principal means of controlling the computer.  While appearing deceptively simple at first, it is very important to learn how to use it properly in order to be able to use the computer with ease and confidence.

You perform three actions with the mouse – **Point**, **Click** and **Drag**.

1    When you **point** to an object on the desktop, you move the mouse until the **tip** of the pointer rests on, or inside, the object.

Example: Point to the **Start** button.

2    To **click** on a object, first point to it and then **quickly press and release** the left mouse button. Unless otherwise stated, it is usually the left-hand button that is clicked. **Left-click** and **Right-click** are often used to describe which button to use.

- A **single click** selects an object or performs an action.
  Example:    Click on the **Recycle Bin** icon.  It darkens, or becomes highlighted, meaning that you have selected it.
  Click on the **Start** button.  A menu is displayed.

- A **double-click** (clicking twice in rapid succession) performs a different action, such as opening a folder or starting a program or application.
  Example:    Double-click on the **Recycle Bin**.  A window opens to display the contents of the bin.  (If the bin has nothing in it, neither will the window.)

3    To **drag** means to move an object on the desktop with the mouse.
  Example:    Place the tip of the **pointer** on an icon on the desktop, hold down the left mouse button and move the mouse.  An outline of the icon moves with the mouse.
  Release the button to 'drop' the icon in its new position.  (It may spring back to its original position, however, depending on how your computer has been set up.)

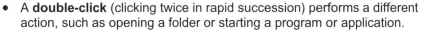

**Point** to
the Recycle Bin.          **Press** the button.          **Move**          **Release** the button.

## 1.6    Pointers

The **Pointer** (or **mouse pointer** or **cursor**) can have different shapes. Different pointers are used for different purposes. The different shapes appear automatically, according to the action being performed, and the shapes give the user a visual indication of their purpose.

Some of the more common pointers that you will encounter in your work are described here.

- The Arrow pointer is probably the most common. It is used most frequently to select objects, to click buttons, to choose options in menus and on toolbars and so on.

- The **Busy** pointer (or **Hourglass**) appears when the computer is engaged in an activity that will take a few moments to complete. You should wait until the action is completed and the pointer resumes its former shape.

- The **Help** pointer appears when you click the **Help** icon on the toolbar. When you point to an object or menu with this pointer, a pop-up explanation is displayed.

- The mouse pointer on a **text** document – called the I-beam – has a tall thin shape to enable it to be placed between letters in the text.

- The flashing vertical line you see on a text page is *not* a mouse pointer. It is the **Insertion Point** at which the next thing you type or insert will appear. Do not confuse it with the mouse pointer above.

- Click with the mouse pointer to place the Insertion Point where you want to type, make corrections or insert text. (Then move the mouse pointer away to avoid confusion.)

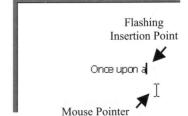

When you are using an application such as a word processor, the action you are engaged in or the function you choose determines which mouse pointer appears. Some other pointers and their functions are described below.

- The **Crosshair** pointer is used as a drawing tool or to select a specific area of a graphic.

- The **Resize** pointer can be vertical, horizontal or diagonal, depending on where you place it. It appears when you select shapes or graphics to be resized.

- The **Move** pointer is used to move graphics from one position to another on the desktop or on a page.

- This pointer appears when you are trying some option that is not available. It may appear momentarily when, for example, you are dragging an object from one location to another and the object cannot be 'dropped' until you reach the new location.

## 1.7    Office 2000 Pointers

The **I-beam** pointer in Office 2000 is associated with the way the text will be aligned on the page. (Aligning text is described in Module 3, Section 3.5, page 133.)  The alignment icons appear beside or under the I-beam to indicate how the text will be aligned.

Left aligns the text

Centre aligns the text

Left aligns the text
and applies a left indent

Right aligns the text

You can place text anywhere in the document by double clicking the position and then typing the text. This process is known as **Click and Type**. Click and Type automatically applies the alignment and/or indentation.  To disable Click and Type:

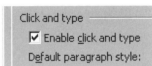

- Select **Options** in the **Tools** menu.

- Click the **Edit** tab in the window that appears.

- Click to remove the tick from the **Enable click and type** box.

## 1.8    Windows

The documents and other work you produce on the computer are recorded electronically and cannot normally be seen.  To make them visible to the user, they are represented by icons as part of the graphical user interface (see Module 1, Section 4.4, page 42).

**Windows** are used to enable the user to 'see' what is on the computer.  A window is a panel that appears on the desktop – itself a window – to give the user a visual indication of what is essentially an invisible electronic storage medium.  A window enables the user to relate the (invisible) electronic files on the computer to objects in the real world.

The illustration shows, as an example, the **Control Panel** window of the computer. The control panels allow access to various settings that may be adjusted according to the user's requirements.  (Do not open or make any changes to control panels until you have learnt how to use them.)

When you are using the computer, various windows appear on the desktop from time to time.  Many windows are similar to that in the illustration, serving to show the contents of a folder or disk, for example.

A special window – called a **dialogue box** – allows you to make choices, such as how many copies of a document are to be printed.  Other dialogue boxes present information for your attention and require you to click an **OK** button before you can continue.

Working with windows is described in detail in Module 2, Section 2, page 72.

# Section 2        Opening an Application

## 2.1        Introduction

Before you begin your work, you must open the application, such as a word processor, that you will need to produce the work.  You can open an application in a number of ways.

The two most usual ways to open an application are:

- Using the **Start** button on the left of the taskbar at the bottom of the desktop.

- Using the **Office Toolbar**, if it is displayed on the desktop.

The Taskbar

## 2.2        Using the Start Menu

Click once on the **Start** button to display the **Start** Menu.

Point to or click on **Programs** to display the **Programs** sub-menu.

The individual applications may be displayed separately, as in the illustration, or there may be a further sub-menu for **Microsoft Office**.

To open an application, click the name of the application in the menu.

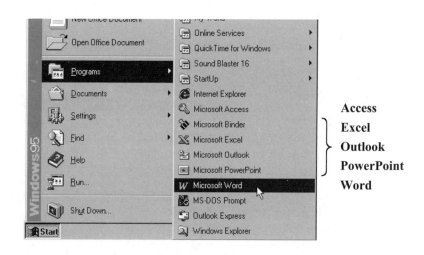

Access
Excel
Outlook
PowerPoint
Word

## 2.3        Using the Office Toolbar

The **Office Toolbar** is a special small toolbar that usually appears at the top of the screen. (It may not be visible on some computers.)

There are usually buttons for the four Office applications, Word, Excel, PowerPoint and Access.  Other buttons may also be present.

To open an Office application, click once on its icon on the toolbar.

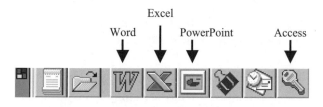

The Office Toolbar

# Section 3      Selecting

## 3.1      Selecting Text

From time to time you will want to change the look of your document. You may want to make a particular piece of text larger than the rest, colour it, underline it and so on.

The first step in making changes to a piece of text or an image is to **select** it.  It must be selected so that the Application knows what you want to apply the changes to.

When text is selected, a black colour appears over it to **highlight** it, just as you would use a highlighter on text on a sheet of paper.

Text can be selected in many different ways, depending on your requirements.  These are described in Module 3, Section 2.4, page 126.

From time to time you will **want to change** the look of your document.

Highlighted text

## 3.2      Selecting Graphics

A **graphic** or **image** is an **object**, as distinct from a piece of text.  Text continues down the page line after line until it fills the page.  An object can be placed on the page independently of text or other objects and can be moved about at will.  The graphics (illustrations) used in this manual are objects.

To select an object, click once inside the object.  When an object is selected, it is not highlighted in the same way as text.  Instead, a series of square dots, called **handles**, appear around it as in the illustration.

The size of an object can be changed, as can the way text flows around it.  See the section on **Graphics** in Module 3, Section 9, page 161, for detailed information.

A selected graphic

## 3.3      Selecting in Tables

A **table** presents information in rows and columns.  The table appears on the page as a **grid**.

The columns are identified across the top by letters of the alphabet. The rows are numbered down the left-hand side.  The individual boxes in the grid are called **cells**.

To select a number of cells, drag through them, from side to side, from top to bottom, or diagonally.  The selected cells are **highlighted** as with text.

A whole column can be selected by clicking the letter at the top of the column.  A row can be selected by clicking the number of the row on the left.

To select the whole table, click **Select Table** in the **Table** menu.

Tables are described in detail in Module 3, Section 8, page 153.

| | A | B | C | D | E |
|---|---|---|---|---|---|
| | Munster Office Returns | | | | |
| 1 | Munster Office First Quarterly Report | | | | |
| 2 | | | | | |
| 3 | | | | | |
| 4 | | | September | October | Novembe |
| 5 | | | | | |
| 6 | | | | | |
| 7 | | Telephones | 116 | 79 | 56 |
| 8 | | Answer Mach. | 47 | 50 | 35 |
| 9 | | Calculators | 9 | 38 | 17 |
| 10 | | Shredders | 297 | 225 | 120 |
| 11 | | Laminators | 79 | 56 | 34 |
| 12 | | Binding Mach. | 83 | 88 | 38 |
| 13 | | Mini Recorders | 57 | 69 | 7 |
| 14 | | Transcribers | 57 | 69 | 36 |
| 15 | | | 745 | 674 | 343 |
| 16 | | | | | |
| 17 | | | | | |

# Section 4        Copy, Cut and Paste

## 4.1     Copying and Cutting

**Copy**, **Cut** and **Paste** are common to most applications and are listed in the **Edit** menu.

Before you can copy or cut an item, it must first be **selected**.

When a piece of text or an object is **copied**, the original stays in position in the document and the copy is stored in a part of the computer's memory called the **Clipboard**.

When a piece of text or an object is **cut**, a copy is stored on the Clipboard, but the original is deleted.

The Clipboard is normally invisible to the user. So, when you copy a piece of text, for example, nothing appears to happen.

The Clipboard can only hold one item at a time. When you copy or cut something, anything previously on the Clipboard is discarded and is no longer available.

## 4.2     Pasting

A copy of what is on the Clipboard can be **pasted** into another part of the same document, or into a different document.

It can also be pasted into a document in a different application.

If required, copies can be pasted repeatedly – to place a row of graphics across a page, for example.

The illustration on the right shows part of a spreadsheet copied and pasted into a Word document.

| | A | B | C | D | E |
|---|---|---|---|---|---|
| 1 | Munster Office First Quarterly Report | | | | |
| 2 | | | | | |
| 3 | | | | | |
| 4 | | | September | October | Novembe |
| 5 | | | | | |
| 6 | | | | | |
| 7 | | Telephones | 116 | 79 | 56 |
| 8 | | Answer Mach. | 47 | 50 | 35 |
| 9 | | Calculators | 9 | 38 | 17 |
| 10 | | Shredders | 297 | 225 | 120 |
| 11 | | Laminators | 79 | 56 | 34 |
| 12 | | Binding Mach. | 83 | 88 | 38 |
| 13 | | Mini Recorders | 57 | 69 | 7 |
| 14 | | Transcribers | 57 | 69 | 36 |
| 15 | | | 745 | 674 | 343 |
| 16 | | | | | |
| 17 | | | | | |

Spreadsheet

Word →

| | September |
|---|---|
| | |
| | |
| Telephones | 116 |
| Answer Mach. | 47 |
| Calculators | 9 |
| Shredders | 297 |
| Laminators | 79 |
| Binding Mach. | 83 |
| Mini Recorders | 57 |
| Transcribers | 57 |
| | 745 |

## 4.3     Toolbar Buttons

Cut, Copy and Paste buttons are also available on many Toolbars.

Cut, Copy and Paste are described in detail in Module 3, Section 2, pages 128 and 129.

Cut   Copy   Paste

# Section 5      Toolbars

## 5.1    Tools for Work

A **Toolbar** is a strip, or **bar**, that stretches across the top (usually) of the desktop. It contains buttons and icons for menus, commands and tools needed by the user to work on a document.

Some commands and tools, such as **Save** and **Print**, are common to most applications. Others are specific to certain applications or parts of applications. A word processor will need commands for use with text, while a database or spreadsheet program will need to deal with numbers, for example.

When there are very many commands, tools and buttons available, they will not all fit on a single toolbar, so several toolbars may be necessary. Toolbars occupy space on the desktop, so only those needed for the purpose in hand are usually displayed.

## 5.2    The Menu Bar

The most commonly used toolbar in applications is the **Menu Bar**. It contains a number of menus which, in turn, contain lists of commands for use with the application. Some menus, such as the **File** and **Edit** menus, are common to almost all applications. Most of the other menus are specific to the particular Application. The **Word** Menu Bar is shown here.

File   Edit   View   Insert   Format   Tools   Table   Window   Help

Click on a menu name to display the menu. Click on an item in the menu to perform an action. The action may be to save a document, for example, or to open a window that gives access to other options or choices.

Many of the commands in the menus can be duplicated at the keyboard. These **Keyboard Shortcuts**, if available, are shown at the right of the menu item. Pressing the **Ctrl** key and the letter **S**, for example, **saves** the current document.

## 5.3    Office 2000 Menu Bars

The menus in Office 2000 differ from the menus in earlier versions of Office in that only the more frequently used items are displayed at first.

To display the full menu, click the chevron symbol.

The additional items are then displayed against a lighter background.

Note also that many buttons may not be displayed on the toolbars (see following Sections) at first. When Office 2000 detects the user accessing these 'hidden' buttons, it automatically places them on the toolbar for future use.

Chevrons

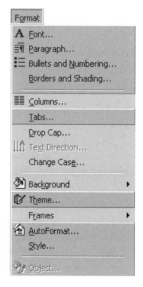

## 5.4    Other Toolbars

A toolbar with commonly used items in an application is called its **Standard Toolbar**. The **Word Standard Toolbar** is illustrated here. Commonly used word processing functions are accessed by clicking the appropriate button on the toolbar.

Clicking a button allows the user to open a new document, save, copy, paste, print, and much more. Clicking the **ABC** button, for example, checks the spelling of the current document.

The **zoom** tool is used to alter the size of the document as it appears in the window. Click the arrow to display a menu. Then click on the magnification you want to use, or type your own preferred size in the box.

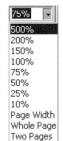

Note that the size of the document as displayed on the screen is independent of the size that will be printed by the printer.

Another example of a toolbar is the **Formatting Toolbar**. It has menus and buttons for some of the most frequently used tools needed to change the appearance of text.

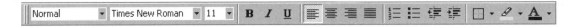

Selecting text and clicking a button on this bar allows you to change the font type, its size, make it bold, make it italic, align it on the page and much more.

## 5.5    Displaying Toolbars

Most applications do not display all their toolbars. This leaves the maximum amount of workspace available for the document you are working on.

A list of available toolbars can be displayed in a **sub-menu** of the **View** menu. This allows you to display an additional toolbar or remove one that is currently displayed.

When there is a **tick** beside a toolbar name in the menu, the toolbar is currently displayed in the application window.

To **remove** a toolbar from the window, click the name in the menu again. The tick is removed and the toolbar is hidden.

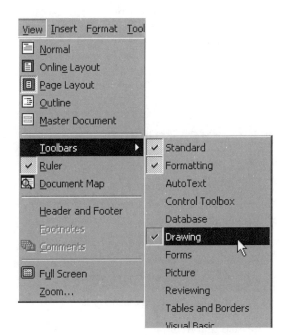

**To display** the **Drawing** toolbar in Word, for example, do the following:

- Select **Toolbars** in the **View** menu.

- Click **Drawing** in the **Toolbar** menu.
  The Drawing toolbar appears at the bottom of the Word window.

You can create your own toolbars, customise the ones already there, and place your own buttons on a toolbar. Instructions are given in the **Help** system (see Section 7, page 16).

## 5.6    Moving Toolbars

Toolbars normally appear at the top of the application window but they may, however, be placed elsewhere according to personal preferences.

To move a toolbar, click on a blank space on the toolbar and drag it to its new position.

If there is no blank space, drag the **slider handle**, the ribbed area at the left of the toolbar.

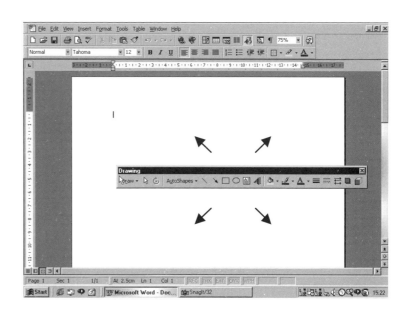

To return a toolbar to its normal place, drag it back to its original position.

## 5.7    Hidden Buttons

Chevron symbols (») on toolbars in Office 2000 indicate that there are hidden buttons. To display the buttons, click the chevrons.

*Alternatively*, move the toolbars to a new position on the desktop to view the wider range of buttons.

If a toolbar is obscured by another, use the **slider handle** to reposition either one.

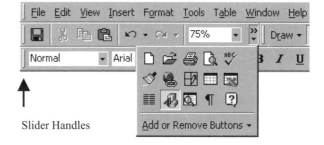

## 5.8    Adding Buttons

Buttons may be added to, or removed from, an Office 2000 toolbar.  To add a superscript button, for example, do the following.

- Display the toolbar you want to modify, if it is not already displayed.

- In the **View** menu, select **Toolbars** and then **Customise** in the sub-menu.

- Click the **Commands** tab and select **Format** in the **Categories** panel.

- Scroll to find **Superscript** in the **Commands** panel and click on it to select it.

- Drag **Superscript** on to the toolbar. (The mouse pointer changes to a toolbar pointer during this process.)

To remove a button, drag it off the toolbar until an **X** appears in the mouse pointer.  Then release the mouse button.

# Section 6    Saving

## 6.1    Saving a Document

It is very important to save a permanent copy of your document.  If you don't, it will no longer exist when you turn off the computer and all your hard work will have been wasted!  You can save your document on the computer's hard disk, on a floppy disk, on a Zip disk or other media.

The procedure for saving a document for the first time is different from saving changes to it afterwards.  The first time you save a document, the computer needs to know certain details.

To save a document for the **first time**, do the following.

- Click **Save** in the **File** menu.
  *Alternatively*, click the **Save** button on the toolbar.
  The **Save As** window opens.

- Type a name for the document in the **File Name** box.
  Use a name that will easily identify the document for you later.
  What you type will replace anything that is already in the box.

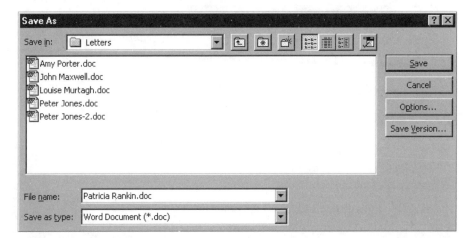

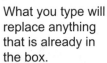

**Save As** window

- Make sure that the folder or disk where you want to save the document appears in the **Save in** box.

- Click the **Save** button to save the document.

When you save a document, the name you have given it appears in the Title Bar at the top of the screen. (An unsaved file usually has a name such as 'Document 1'.)

See Module 2, Section 4, page 84, for detailed instructions on how to save your work.

## 6.2   Saving Changes to a Document

As you work on a document, you should save your work from time to time as you proceed. If the computer 'crashes' or if there's a power failure, you will lose any unsaved work. When you save regularly, only the work done since the last save will be lost and any inconvenience will be minimised.

There are two methods you can use:

Save

- Click the **Save** button on the toolbar.

- Click **Save** in the **File** menu.

As the computer already has the information you typed in when you first saved the document, the **Save As** window does not appear again and your work is saved with the minimum of disruption.

> Use **Auto Recover** to save files automatically after a set time interval, e.g. every 10 minutes. Then only work done since the last Auto Recovery save will be lost if there is a major problem. See Module 2, Section 4.10, page 89, for details.

## 6.3   Good Saving Practice

Save soon and save often. It is good practice to name and save a document from the earliest stage of its creation. Do not wait until you have finished the document before saving it. If a problem should occur before the document is saved, you may lose your work.

On beginning a new document in Word, for example, you should name and save it immediately.

As you continue to work on the document, you should click the **Save** icon on the toolbar at regular intervals. *Alternatively*, select **Save** in the **File** menu. In the event of serious mishap, this will ensure that only the most recent work is lost. Previously saved work will not be affected.

# Section 7    The Help System

## 7.1    On-Line Help

While you are using the computer, there are comprehensive **Help** systems available on the screen to assist you with problems that may arise in the course of your work.

**System Help** assists you with using the computer. It is available in the **Start** menu.

**Application Help** assists you with using an application. It is available in the **Help** menu on the **Menu** bar in each application.

In both cases, there are different types of help available, depending on the task. Step-by-step instructions are also available for procedures with which you may not be familiar.

As both help System help and Application help are similar, and are used in the same way, the following examples apply to both.

System Help (Computer)

Application Help (Word)

## 7.2    Using Help

The **Help** systems can be used for general information as well as for specific queries.

- To use the **System** help, select **Help** in the **Start** menu.

  To use **Application** help, select **Contents and Index** in the **Help** menu.

  The Help window opens.

- Check that the **Contents** tab at the top of the window is clicked.

  A list of **books** is displayed according to topic.

- Double-click a book to 'open' it and display further books or topics.

  When you open the book with the information you are looking for, a list of subject headings is displayed with **question mark** buttons on the left.

A **question mark** button means that this is the actual help topic itself.

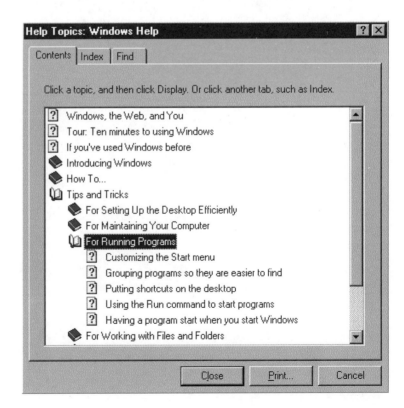

- Double-click a question mark button – or click it once and then click the **Display** button at the bottom of the window – to display detailed help or instructions on the topic.

  The Help appears in a new window (see right). The main Help window closes and you can now carry out any instructions given in the new Help window as you read them.

- If the window gets in the way of your work, move it to another location on the desktop by dragging its title bar.

- Minimise the window to hide it temporarily if you want to refer to it again later.

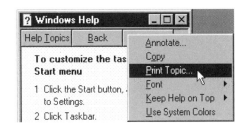

  This saves the trouble of searching for it afresh.

- To print out the help, select **Print Topic** in the help window **Options** menu.

- Click **Help Topics** to return to the main **Help** window.

## 7.3    Searching for Help by Topic

The **Index** is probably the most convenient way of finding help if you know what you are looking for.

Click the **Index** tab in the main Help window for help on a specific topic. The index gives a wider choice of topics than are listed under the **Contents** tab.

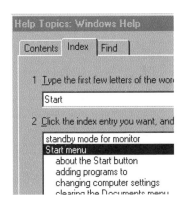

To search for help on a subject or topic, type a word or words in the box at the top of the window.  As you type, a list – or index – of related topics appears in the box underneath.  You may have to scroll to see them all if the list is very long.

Double-click the appropriate index entry to display a Help window as before. Alternatively, click the topic to select it. Then click the **Display** button at the bottom of the window.

Click the **Find tab** to look for specific words or phrases.  Use this option if you can't find the topic you are looking for under the **Contents** or **Index** tabs.

Type the word in the top box. Some related words are shown underneath to help you narrow your search.  The Help system is searched for occurrences of the word you typed in.

Click on a topic and then click the **Display** button to display it.

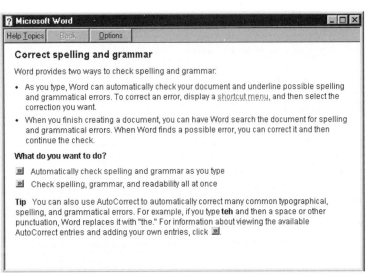

A Word Help Window

## 7.4    Using the Help Windows

The Help window has the ususal
**minimise**, **maximise** and **close** buttons
as well as its own buttons.

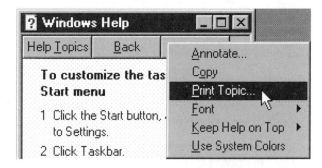

- Click the **Back** button to move back to
  the previous topic you looked at.

- Click the **Help Topics** button to return
  to the **Contents** window.

- Click the **Options** button to display a
  menu.

Some of the facilities available in the
**Options** menu are described below.

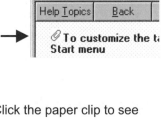

- Click **Annotate** to write your own note and add it to
  the Help system.

  A small window opens.  Type your comments and
  click the **Save** button in the window.

  The next time you look up the topic you will see a **paper clip** before it.  Click the paper clip to see
  your comments.

- **Copy** makes a copy of the topic on the Clipboard.  You can then paste it into a Word or other
  document, but you may have to adjust the formatting.

- **Print Topic** prints out the topic, as described earlier.

- **Keep Help on Top** prevents other windows from obscuring the Help window so that you can follow
  the instructions as you work.  (This is the default.)

Small arrow buttons often appear in the text in the Help window.

- More detailed instructions are available when this button appears.
  Click the button to display step-by-step instructions for the task.

More info

- Some instructions have a **Show Me** button
  Click the button to display step-by-step instructions.

Show me.

Close the Help window by clicking the **Close** button in the normal way.

## 7.5    ScreenTips

**ScreenTips** displays information about different objects on the screen.   Use ScreenTips to find
information about Toolbar buttons or Menu commands, for example.  ScreenTips can also be used to
provide information about objects in the various
windows that appear from time to time.

To see a ScreenTip for a menu command, toolbar
button or screen region, do the following.

- Select **What's This?** in the **Help** menu.

  The cursor changes to an arrow with a question mark.

- Click the item about which you want information.

  A **Help** box which describes the selected element appears.

- To **close** the Help box, click anywhere else on the screen.

ScreenTips are useful when you are asked to select preferences or make decisions in a window called a **dialogue box**. (A dialogue box is a window in which you can select preferences or enter information, such as the Save As window.)

- Click the **Question Mark** button at the top right of the title bar of the window.

- The cursor changes to an arrow with a question mark.

- Click the part of the window or the object for which you want help.

  A **Help** box appears, as before.

- If there is no question mark button in the window, click the item for which you want help and then press the **Shift + F1** keys on the keyboard instead.


## 7.6    The Office Assistant

One of the items in the Help menu is the **Office Assistant**. It appears in Word as **Microsoft Word Help**, in Excel as **Microsoft Excel Help**, and so on. The Office Assistant can answer your questions, offer tips and provide help for a task that you may want to carry out.

To use the Office Assistant, do the following.

- Click the **Office Assistant** button on the toolbar or press the **F1** key on the keyboard.

  Alternatively, select **Microsoft** (*Name*) **Help** in the **Help** menu.

  The Assistant appears as a small window with a paper clip 'character'.

  A **speech bubble** contains a box where you can type a question or key words for help on a specific topic.

- Click **Search** when you have typed your request.

  A list of relevant topics appears. Click the one you require.

- A **Tips** option in the speech bubble box provides hints on using some of the features of the application or details of keyboard shortcuts.

  A tip is also available when a yellow **light bulb** appears in the Assistant. Click the light bulb to see the tip.

- Click the **Close** button to close the speech bubble or tips box at any time.

  Note that this doesn't close the Office Assistant itself, just the speech bubble.

- If the Assistant is still on the screen, the speech bubble can be re-opened at any time by double-clicking the Assistant **title bar**.

- The Office Assistant sometimes gives **Suggested Help** automatically. It senses what you are doing and appears when it thinks you might like some assistance, whether you do or not.

  The help it offers is relevant to the specific task you are performing.

- To close the Office Assistant, click the **Close** button as usual.

Office
Assistant

Close

   In Office 2000, a 'lightbulb' may appear on the screen when you are performing a task. Click the lightbulb to display help related to the task.

## 7.7    Wizards

**Wizard** is a term used to describe a set of instructions that lead you through the steps of performing a task.  The wizard asks you various questions about the available options.  When you make your choices, the wizard then performs the task for you.

Wizards are usually available for complex tasks that involve many steps, such as creating a table or performing a Mail Merge.  (See Tables, Section  8, page 153 and Mail Merge, Section 14, page 180, in Module 3.)

The advantage of using a wizard is that it simplifies a complex procedure – you just follow the steps. Automating the task also saves time.  The disadvantage of using a wizard is that you may have less control over the final result, as your choice of options may be limited.

We shall see some examples of using wizards later in the course.

# Section 8      Settings

## 8.1      Default Settings

When the computer is switched on, it presents its information and screen displays in a certain manner. The colour scheme of the desktop, the arrangement of the icons, the size of the display font, the behaviour of the mouse and much more, are all preset. These preset values for the different features are referred to as the **default** settings, or **defaults**.

Defaults are used by the computer when the user does not specify any other values. Individual users, however, can change the defaults to suit individual preferences or for specific purposes.

The original defaults remain available at all times and can be restored by either cancelling the new settings or choosing the default options, as explained below.

## 8.2      Application Display Settings

An application can usually display a document in a number of ways.

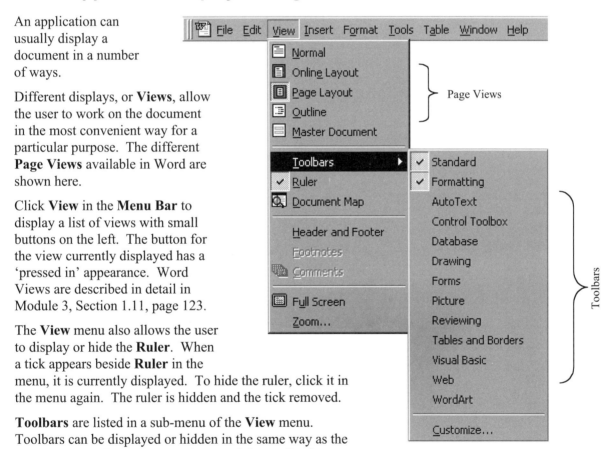

Different displays, or **Views**, allow the user to work on the document in the most convenient way for a particular purpose. The different **Page Views** available in Word are shown here.

Click **View** in the **Menu Bar** to display a list of views with small buttons on the left. The button for the view currently displayed has a 'pressed in' appearance. Word Views are described in detail in Module 3, Section 1.11, page 123.

The **View** menu also allows the user to display or hide the **Ruler**. When a tick appears beside **Ruler** in the menu, it is currently displayed. To hide the ruler, click it in the menu again. The ruler is hidden and the tick removed.

**Toolbars** are listed in a sub-menu of the **View** menu. Toolbars can be displayed or hidden in the same way as the ruler. Most toolbars appear at the top of the application window when they are displayed. An exception is the **Drawing** toolbar, which appears at the bottom. (See Section 5 of this Module, page 11, for more information on toolbars.)

Selecting **Header and Footer** in the **View** menu displays the Header and Footer toolbar in the centre of the window. Any text on the page is 'grayed out' and the (small) header area at the top of the page is displayed for you to work in. Click the button on the toolbar to change to the footer. When you return to the main page, any text in the header and footer is grayed out as it is no longer available to work on. Headers and footers are described in detail in Module 3, Section 7, page 149.

A special window in which choices may be made is called a **Dialogue Box**, as mentioned before.

- Select **Zoom** in the **View** menu to display the Zoom window.
  The **Zoom** window gives a greater choice of options than the **Magnification** menu on the toolbar.

A document's magnification on the screen can be selected, or you may type in a specific magnification of your own.

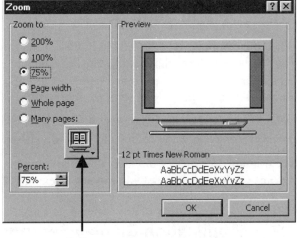

- Click the desired magnification in the **Zoom to** panel.

- Alternatiively, type your own requirement in the box lower down. (You can also click the small arrors in the right of the box to enter a size.)

A button, just above the **Percent** box, allows you to select the number of pages that are displayed on the screen at the same time.

Button

A preview of the display is shown in the **Preview** panel on the right.

The various display options allow the user to use the settings that are most convenient for his or her way of working. The many rulers, toolbars and other aids take up valuable document space on the desktop, however, and the less space you have for your actual work. A larger monitor is one way of solving this problem. This is why you will invariably find large monitors in design and publishing establishments.

To increase the amount of space available on the screen for your document, especially if you are using the usual 15" or 17" monitor, select **Full Screen** in the **View** menu. This hides the rulers and toolbars etc., and enlarges the document window to full screen size.

A mini window then appears on the screen. so that you can restore the usual display when required. The mini window can be dragged to any convenient part of the screen. Click **Close Full Screen** to restore the original display.

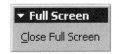

## 8.3    Application Default Settings

When you use an application to open a new document, all the document settings, such as font, text size, page layout and so on appear with preset values. These are the application **default** settings.

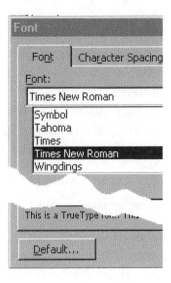

If these default settings are not convenient, they can be changed. The way in which they are changed, however, varies from one application to the next.

The default font size for a new document in Word is **10 point**, for example. If you find this too small, you can make **12 point** the default.

Select **Font** in the **Format** menu, set the font size to 12 point and click the **Default** button at the bottom of the window. Click **Yes** to confirm this in the following window.

Now every time you open a new document, the font size will be set to 12 point.

# Section 9      Checking Spelling

## 9.1      Checking Spelling Automatically

Many computer users think of the **spell check function** as only being useful (and available) for word processing.  In the Office Suite, it is available in all the applications.  You can use it to check a single word, a selected section of text or the whole document.

Word automatically checks your spelling as you type. Zig-zag red lines appear under unrecognised words. A word is not recognised if it is incorrectly spelled or if it does not appear in the Word dictionary.

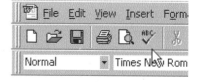

As you type, zig-zag red lines appaer under unrecognised words.

Automatic Spelling Check

In the illustration, **zig-zag** is not in the dictionary, **appaer** is not spelled correctly and **unrecognised**, although correctly spelled, is questioned because the dictionary used is an American English one, which spells the word with 'z' rather than 's'.

As you type, you can make corrections to marked words – and the red markers disappear – or you can choose to ignore them.  The zig-zag markers are shown on the screen only.  They do not appear if you print out the document.

## 9.2      Checking Spelling Manually

Click the **Spelling and Grammar** button on the toolbar – indicated by the pointer in the illustration – to check spelling manually.  Normally, the whole document is checked.  If you only want to check a piece of text, or even a single word, select it first.

When an unrecognised word is found, the Spelling and Grammar window opens.

The suspect word appears in red with its context in the upper **Not in Dictionary** box. There will usually be a list of suggestions in the lower box, with the first, most likely, suggestion highlighted.

Buttons on the right allow the user to make changes, ignore the word, or add it to the dictionary. This is described in detail in Module 3, Section 4, page 140.

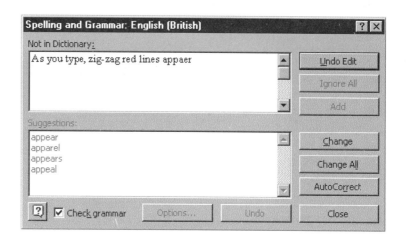

## 9.3      Checking Your Work

Using the spell checking facility to correct spelling mistakes does *not* guarantee that the document is free of errors.  'I want to meet her' will not be questioned, for example, even though you meant to write 'I want to meet here'.  You must still read through your work to make a final check.

# Section 10    Closing Down

## 10.1    Closing a Document or Application

There are a number of steps to be followed when you have finished your work and want to close the document, the application, the computer, or all of them.

First, you should save your work unless you have no further use for it.

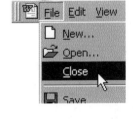

**To close a document**, click the document **Close** button. Alternatively, select **Close** in the **File** menu.

If you have not saved the document, you will be reminded and given the choice of saving it or not.  The document disappears from the desktop but the application stays open for you to work on other documents if you wish.

**To close an application**, click the application **Close** button (see below). Alternatively, select **Exit** in the **File** menu.

If you have not saved your work, you will be reminded and given the choice of saving it or not.  The application disappears from the screen but the computer is still operational and the desktop appears.

Notice that there are **two sets of buttons** at the top right-hand corner of the application window when a document is open in Office 97.  The upper buttons control the application while the lower set controls the document.  Don't close down the application when you only want to close the document! Office 2000 may have only one row of buttons or just a single button on the lower row.

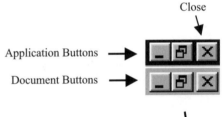

Close

Application Buttons ➔

Document Buttons ➔

Minimise

It is not necessary to close a document or application when you want to use or open another one.  Several documents and applications can be open at the same time and you can switch between them as needed.

To temporarily hide a document or application, click the **Minimise** button to reduce it to an icon on the **taskbar**.  Click its icon on the taskbar when you want to see it or use it again.

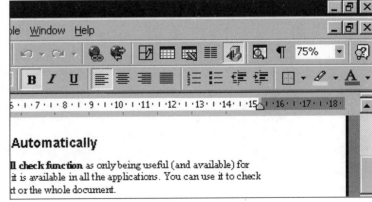

Working with more than one window is described in Module 2, Section 2, page 75.

Working with more than one document is described in Module 3, Section 6, page 146.

# Module 1

## Basic Concepts
of
### Information Technology

1

Module 1

# Basic Concepts
of
# Information Technology

# Introduction

> ## Syllabus Goals for Module 1
>
> **Basic Concepts of Information Technology** (IT) requires the candidate to know about the basic physical make-up of a Personal Computer and understand some of the basic concepts of Information Technology (IT), such as data storage and memory, the context for computer-based software applications in society and the uses of information networks within computing. The candidate shall also appreciate how IT systems are found in everyday situations and how personal computers can affect health. The candidate shall be aware of some of the security and legal issues associated with computers.

## Basic Concepts

Computers are information processing machines. No matter how small or how large and no matter how simple or sophisticated they are, they perform three basic functions. They accept information. They process it according to predefined instructions. And they produce results based on their work.

Knowing how your computer does these things will make it easier to interact with the machine and to use it productively. This module sets out to explain the basic concepts associated with the computer and its operation, and it deals with issues that relate to information processing.

## Computers and Society

Computers are not just machines sitting on office desks. Computer control is a matter of everyday life, from the operation of traffic lights to setting the video recorder, from playing music on your CD player to paying your bills and withdrawing money from the bank by inserting a plastic card in the Automatic Teller Machine (ATM).

We tend to take familiar technology for granted. Take, for example, the hundred-year-old system of communication now in every home in the land. Invented long before the computer, it is now controlled by it and sometimes described as the largest computer network in the world – the humble telephone.

Knowing how computers are used and how they affect our lives will help you to put the computer in context as you work your way through the various modules of the ECDL.

## Legal Restraints

Computers make it possible to access information from all over the world and to send and receive messages with an ease and facility that is astonishing. With this new technology, however, there are accompanying legal considerations. These range from knowing how to position your computer to avoid stress and health problems, to being aware of your rights in connection with personal information about you that is stored on computers by businesses and government departments.

The programs that make the use of computers possible, such as word processors, drawing programs, games and so on, are also subject to various legal constraints, as are their users and the owners of the computers on which they are used. It is important to be aware of them.

# Section 1    Getting Started

## 1.1    Hardware, Software and IT

There are two principal components of computer use in the field of **Information Technology**. They are **hardware** and **software**.

- **Hardware** refers to the physical parts of the computer such as the screen, system box, keyboard, cables which come in the large heavy box or boxes when you buy a computer.

  The word 'hardware' can describe the complete computer, a part of it, the printer, or any other such items.  The hardware, however, can do nothing without software.

- **Software** refers to the sets of instructions, or programs, which tell the computer (the hardware) to do something and how to do it.  Software can be loaded into a computer from, for example, a CD or a floppy disk.

  Word Processors, Graphics Programs, Encyclopedias and Computer Games are examples of software frequently used on the computer.  Without software, the computer would be like a TV set without any TV programs.

- **Information Technology** is a term commonly used to describe the use of computers and computer-related equipment to produce, store, manipulate, print, receive and transmit information in electronic form, whether it is text, pictures, sound, video or other data.

  The ease with which large amounts of information can be processed electronically, and the speed and convenience with which it can be routed from place to place or even around the world, has given rise to the phrase, **the Information Superhighway**.

## 1.2    Types of Computer

Different types of computer are used for different purposes.  The principal categories are listed here.

**Mainframe Computers**

These room-sized computers are used by major organisations such as banks, supermarket chains and government departments. They can handle vast amounts of information at high speed and they have correspondingly large storage capacities.  The cost of installing, running and maintaining such computers runs into hundreds of thousands of pounds or more.

Mainframe computers are usually connected to a large number of terminals – screens and keyboards – such as you may see in banks and in travel agents' offices.  Some terminals are known as 'dumb' terminals.  They cannot operate on their own as all the processing is carried out by the mainframe. Other terminals, while still relying on the mainframe, have a certain amount of processing power themselves that can be used locally by the user.  These are known as 'intelligent' terminals.

**Minicomputers**

A minicomputer does much the same job as a mainframe but on a smaller scale.  They are used where a larger mainframe computer would be needlessly expensive but where smaller personal computers would be inadequate.

**Personal Computers**

The personal computer is commonly know as a **PC**.  When first introduced, PCs allowed a complete, self-contained computer to be placed on an office desk.  PCs are manufactured under different brand names throughout the world.  They are also referred to as **IBM-compatible** computers.  This indicates that although brand names may differ, they can run the same programs and applications as similar computers made by **IBM**, the American company whose PCs became the business standard.

PCs are also distinguished from **Macintosh** computers, which use a completely different operating system and which are only made by **Apple**.

PCs can be connected together, or **networked**, to share programs and information between users. In some fields of work, networking makes the complexity and expense of minicomputers or mainframe computers unnecessary. Since the PC has become a universal office and home machine, prices have dropped from thousands of pounds to as low as five hundred pounds for a basic machine. The PC is now the most widely used small computer.

## Laptop Computers

These are small, portable, briefcase-sized computers that can be carried around and used, as the name suggests, on your lap. They are characterised by small screens and small keyboards. Some laptops can be connected, either directly or through a **docking station** – a connecting device – to a standard monitor and keyboard. In this way, the disadvantages of working in miniature for extended periods may be overcome. Laptop computers can be as powerful as desktop machines but they are typically 50% more expensive than a comparable desktop computer because of the miniaturisation and relatively smaller market.

## Palmtop Computers

Palmtop computers are small, hand-held computers and are sometimes referred to as **Notepads**. The very small size of the screen and keyboard has obvious limitations but they are becoming increasingly popular. Palmtops can offer some of the functionality of the laptop in a much reduced size. Files can be transferred from palmtops (and laptops) to desktop machines. Prices are generally very low when compared with the larger laptop and desktop computers.

## Computers in Networks

**Networked** computers are computers that are linked together. In a business with many PCs, it becomes necessary for work done on one computer to be available to other workers in the business. The PCs are connected by cable, and files and documents can then be shared between them.

Each PC is a self-contained 'normal' computer that can be used independently. It has its own processor, hard disk and other facilities. Documents and files can be prepared and stored on the hard disk. These can be made available to other computers as required.

Most networked computers make use of a server (see below). The server is typically used to store common files. A list of customers' names and addresses stored on the server, for example, may be added to or edited by anyone on the network. The updated list is then instantly available to all the other computers on the network.

## Network Computers

The term **Network Computer** should not be confused with **networked** PCs described above.

The use of network computers is effectively a miniaturisation of the mainframe idea. Instead of the mainframe, a large PC-type computer called a **server** is connected to the smaller network computers, called **terminals** or **clients**. The server holds all the applications and data which it 'serves' to the clients.

A client – the network computer – is a monitor and keyboard with an accompanying small box of specialised circuitry that replaces the usual PC system box. Clients usually have no independent or local hard disk storage. They download programs and data from the server into their memory. Any work done or changes made to the information is then stored back on the server.

In a network computer system, all the computing power and resources are concentrated in the server. This allows for cheaper, less powerful, less resourceful client machines to offer the same facilities as a normal PC but with lower installation and maintenance costs.

## 1.3    The Parts of a Computer

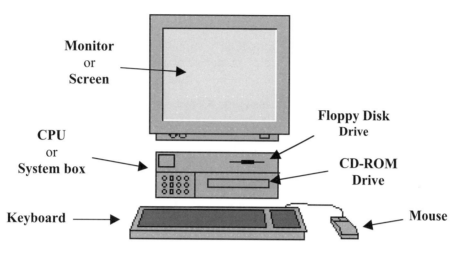

A Desktop Computer

A computer has three basic parts.

*   The **System** or **CPU** box houses the **Central Processing Unit** and the system software that controls it.  This is the 'works' of the computer.

    The box also houses the power supply, hard disk and floppy disk drives, the CD-ROM drive and other items.  The system box may be either horizontal (known as a **desktop** case), as in the illustration, or vertical (a **tower** case).

*   The **Keyboard** and **Mouse** enable the user to input data and tell the CPU what to do with it.

*   The **Monitor** is a display unit (also known as a **VDU – Video Display Unit**) that shows the user what the CPU is doing and thus monitors what is happening.  Early computers had no such display units and the user had no visual assistance.

Other items – printers, scanners, modems and so on – which can be added to the basic computer for different purposes are known as **Peripheral Devices** or, more commonly, **Peripherals**.

## 1.4    Input and Output

The user enters data which the computer then processes in some way, such as putting text on a page or finding and listing information.  After processing, the new data has to be made available for the user.

*   The keyboard and mouse, with which data is input to the CPU, are **Input Devices**.

*   The monitor and printer, which display or print the output from the CPU, are **Output Devices**.

Input and Output devices are described in more detail in Section 2 of this Module, page 32.

# Section 2      Hardware

## 2.1      The Central Processing Unit

The **Central Processing Unit (CPU)** is the brain of the computer. It is also called the **microprocessor**. The CPU is an electronic 'chip' an inch or two square that contains millions of electronic components. It interprets and executes the instructions contained in a software program.

The CPU chip is installed with other components in the **System** or **CPU box** as already described in Section 1.3 on page 31.

A common PC microprocessor is the **Pentium** but there are several other types made by different manufacturers.

The three main parts of a CPU are the **Arithmetic Logic Unit (ALU)**, the **Immediate Access Memory** and the **Control Unit**.

- The **ALU** carries out arithmetical, comparative and logical processes (the processing).
- The **Immediate Access Memory** is where the data used by the ALU is stored.
- The **Control Unit** ensures that the program instructions are followed in the correct sequence.

## 2.2      Input Devices

The computer works on information (**data**) which is entered by the user. Various devices enable the user to enter data, depending on the kind of data to be entered.

**Keyboard**

A keyboard has keys with the same arrangement as a typewriter. The standard keyboard is known as a **Qwerty** keyboard (from the first five letters on the top row of letter keys). Most keyboards have a numeric keypad on the right-hand side, as well as extra keys that may be used for other purposes.

**Mouse**

The mouse is a small hand-held device. It is mouse-shaped and connected to the computer by a cable (the mouse's tail). As the mouse is moved on the mouse mat, a rolling ball on the underside transmits information to the computer which moves a cursor in sympathy on the screen. The standard PC mouse has two buttons. When a button is pressed or clicked, the computer performs an action.

**Trackball**

This is essentially a mouse turned upside down. The user rotates the ball with a finger to move the cursor about the screen. The trackball saves the space normally taken up by the mouse and the mouse mat. There are usually buttons beside the trackball which duplicate the buttons on the mouse.

**Touchpad**

A touchpad is a touch-sensitive device, an inch or two square, which replaces the mouse. When a fingertip is moved over the surface, the result is similar to using a mouse or trackball. Touchpads are common on laptop computers but may also be seen on some keyboards as an alternative to the mouse.

**Touch Screen**

A touch screen enables the computer to be controlled by a finger directly touching the screen. No mouse or other device is needed. Touch screens are used in information booths for public access where a mouse or other device would be impracticable.

### Light pen

A light pen looks like a conventional writing pen but it transmits electronic information to the computer. It can be used to move the cursor and select objects on a display screen by directly pointing to them. A light pen can also be used to read bar codes. Moving the pen over the bar code inputs information. Scanners have now largely replaced light pens.

### Scanner

A scanner is an input device that converts images, graphics, pictures or text into electronic information that can be used by the computer. A common type of scanner is used in shops and supermarkets to read the bar codes on merchandise and enter the details into a computerised cash register.

Another type of scanner resembles a small photocopier. It is used to input graphics or text to a computer where they can then be edited and used in documents and publications.

### Joystick

A joystick is a hand-lever that can be moved in all directions to control movement on the screen. Most joysticks include a number of buttons that can be pressed to perform various actions. Joysticks are commonly used for playing games on the computer or to control computer-operated machines.

### Microphone

As well as allowing sound to be recorded on the computer, a microphone can also be used to allow speech to control the computer or to input spoken text directly into a word processor, when the appropriate software is installed.

### Disk Drives

Data can also be input from floppy disks, CD and DVD disks, as well as from a variety of removable drives that can be connected to the computer.

## 2.3    Output Devices

The work the user does on the computer is of limited use if it cannot be extracted and used.

There are various output devices to suit different purposes.

### The Monitor

This is also known as a **Video Display Unit** (**VDU**). It is a screen similar to a television screen but with a much sharper picture. It displays the work being done by the CPU – and by the user – in graphical form so that the user can **monitor** what is happening. (Remember that early computers were not equipped with monitors. Information was typed on a keyboard and output on punched tape.)

#### Construction

The standard computer monitor used a **cathode ray tube** (CRT) similar to that used in a television set but capable of displaying a much sharper and clearer picture. CRT monitors are large and heavy. They take up a large amount of space on the desk.

**Liquid crystal displays** (LCD) are commonly used in laptop computers where CRT displays are impractical. LCD displays for desktop computers are small and light. They take up little space on the desk, being only an inch or two deep. Their widespread introduction has been delayed, however, by manufacturing difficulties and the consequent high cost.

#### Size

Monitor size is measured diagonally, between opposite corners of the screen. Common sizes are 15" and 17". Larger sizes, usually 19" to 21", are used for graphics and page layout work where one or more pages can be shown full-size on the screen.

### Resolution

The monitor's resolution is the number of dots or **pixels** that can be displayed on the screen. For many years, the usual display was 640 pixels across the screen and 480 pixels from top to bottom. This is known as VGA (Video Graphics Array) resolution.

The present standard is 800 x 600 pixels, or SVGA (Super VGA). A higher resolution of 1024 x 768 pixels or XVGA (Extended VGA) is also available. Resolutions higher than XVGA are also used for specialist purposes.

A monitor with higher resolution will display more of a document than one with a lower resolution on the same size screen, but the print will appear smaller. A monitor that can display different resolutions is called a **Multiscan** (or **Multisync**) monitor.

### Colour

The quality of the colour displayed by a monitor depends on the construction of the monitor itself as well as the electronic circuitry in the computer. It is common to describe colour quality by the number of colours that can be displayed.

Early computer monitors could only display 4 or 16 colours, but 256 colours gradually became a standard used in software. Computers and their monitors are now able to display thousands or even millions of colours, giving photographic quality to the display.

## LED Displays

Light Emitting Diodes (LEDs) are small light sources commonly used to indicate the equipment is switched on. There is usually one on the front of the monitor and the CPU box. LEDs are also used to indicate a level of activity – on modems, for example – where they flash on and off to show what is happening.

## Printer

A printer allows documents produced on the computer to be printed on paper (or other material). Such documents are often known as **printouts** or **hard copy**. **Inkjet** and **laser** printers are the most widely used. Different kinds of printers are described in Section 2.4, page 35.

## Plotters

A plotter is a special type of printer used principally by architects, engineers and scientists in conjunction with **Computer Aided Design (CAD)** and **mapping software**. The machine uses actual pens to draw directly on the paper. Plotters can select pens and colours, as directed by the computer, to produce complex technical drawings.

## Loudspeakers

Multimedia applications have made the use of loudspeakers or headphones with computers essential. Loudspeakers are standard equipment in modern computers used in the home. In education, headphones are often more appropriate in the classroom. Small loudspeakers are usually supplied but the computer can be connected to an external amplifier and larger loudspeakers, if required.

## Speech Synthesis

Software, when installed on the computer, can produce sound that resembles human speech. This can be used to assist people with disabilities or used in areas where verbal feed-back may be preferable to visual. The computer can read out documents and can also 'speak' to the user to confirm commands.

## Removable Media

Data can be output to floppy disks, tape, data cartridges, compact disks and other removable media for transfer to remote computers, for back-up storage and for other purposes.

## 2.4    Printers

There are many different kinds of printers.  They are generally used to print on paper but transparencies or other media may also be used.

- **Daisy Wheel:** The characters are raised on a piece of metal or plastic which strike a ribbon placed between them and the paper, thus imprinting the shape of the character on the paper. Being an impact printer, it is possible to produce carbon copies.  Daisy wheel printers are generally slow and noisy.

  The Daisy Wheel mechanism is now used only in electric typewriters.

- **Dot matrix** printers are also impact printers.  They use a print head with pins that produce dots on the page by striking through an inked ribbon.  The greater the number of pins, and the greater the number of times they strike a particular area, the better the quality of the print, but the slower the printing speed.  Carbon copies can also be produced with these printers.  Dot matrix printers produce a characteristic whining noise.

  Dot matrix printers are now used only where small printouts are needed, such as in ticket machines or at supermarket checkouts.

- **Inkjet** printers work by shooting minute jets of ink directly onto the paper. They use different coloured inks to produce high-quality colour images.  Most inkjet printers use separate black ink for ordinary text.

  Inkjet printers are inexpensive but running costs are high, with cartridges having to be replaced after a few hundred copies.  When a printer uses a single cartridge containing all the colours, the whole cartridge has to be replaced when one of them runs out.  Some printers use separate cartridges for the different colours, up to six in some cases, but then several cartridges have to be replaced on a regular basis.  For maximum print quality, special paper has to be used, adding to the expense.

  Carbon copies cannot be produced by inkjet printers as there is no mechanical striking action involved.  Inkjet printers are quiet in use but are slower than laser printers.

- **Laser** printers work in the same way as photocopiers.  Instead of a lens, they use a laser to place an electrical charge in the shape of the text and/or graphics to be printed on a rotating drum.  The charged area of the drum attracts fine black powder (toner) to itself and the powder is pressed onto the paper as the drum rotates.  The paper is then heated to seal the image onto the paper.

  Laser printers produce high-quality images, usually only in black and white (or greyscale) because of cost.  Colour laser printers cost typically twice or three times as much as an equivalent black and white model.

  An office-quality laser printer is much more expensive than a small inkjet printer but it is of more robust construction and it is designed for heavy use. It is also much faster than an inkjet printer and running costs are lower, a toner cartridge producing typically 5000 or more pages before having to be replaced.

  As with inkjet printers, carbon copies cannot be produced.  Laser printers are very quiet in use.

# Section 3     Memory, Storage and Performance

## 3.1     Storing Data

When the computer is switched on, the programs you use are loaded into **RAM** (Random Access Memory) from the hard disk. Any work you do is also held in RAM until you choose to save it or not. The computer uses RAM because anything contained in RAM is instantly available to it. It does not have to look for the information on the Hard Disk. Think of the knowledge you hold in your head. You do not have to look something up in a book every time you want to remember something.

RAM can only store data when the computer is switched on. Everything in RAM vanishes when the power is switched off. RAM is sometimes referred to as **primary memory** because another kind of memory, called **secondary memory**, is used when the computer is switched off.

## 3.2     Memory

The computer must be able to 'remember' the information with which it is working, just as people do. The information is 'remembered' by being stored, either temporarily or permanently. All information processed by the computer is handled and stored in digital form using only two digits, 0 and 1.

A number system that only uses two digits is called a **binary system**. We normally use a number system that uses ten digits, 0 to 9. This is called a **decimal system**. Here is how you and a computer count from 0 to 10.

| **You:** | 0 | 1 | 2 | 3 | 4 | 5 | 6 | 7 | 8 | 9 | 10 |
|---|---|---|---|---|---|---|---|---|---|---|---|
| **Computer:** | 0 | 1 | 10 | 11 | 100 | 101 | 110 | 111 | 1000 | 1001 | 1010 |

A single digit, **0** or **1**, is called a **bit**. Bits are grouped together, typically in sets of 8, to make **bytes**. Computer memory is measured in bytes – in the same way as the length of a newspaper article is measured in words – as follows:

| 1 Bit | 1 Byte | 1 Kilobyte (Kb) | 1 Megabyte (Mb) | 1 Gigabyte (Gb) |
|---|---|---|---|---|
| A single digit: 0 or 1 | 8 Bits Can represent (e.g.) the letter 'A' | 1,024 Bytes (One thousand) | 1,048,576 Bytes (One million) | 1,073,741,824 Bytes (One thousand million) |

The number of bytes per Kb, and so on, is a little more than the names would suggest because the computer counts in twos while people count in tens – but it's easier to remember round numbers.

## 3.3     Memory Chips

Memory such as **RAM** is manufactured on **microchips** ('chips'). The chips are then assembled on small cards that can be inserted into slots inside the systems box. These cards are described as **DIMMs** (Dual Inline Memory Modules) or **SIMMs** (Single Inline Memory Modules). They are usually supplied in 16, 32, 64, 128Mb and larger sizes.

Extra memory (RAM) can be added to a computer by purchasing the required modules and inserting them in the appropriate slots. There are many different types of memory, so it is important to purchase the type that is suitable for the particular computer. Memory chips are sensitive to static electricity and special precautions should be taken when handling and inserting them.

## 3.4    Kinds of Memory

**Random Access Memory (RAM)** is the main working memory of the computer. A computer may have 64Mb or more of RAM. RAM is empty when the computer is first switched on. The system software is loaded into it so that the computer can carry out all the functions that make it work. If you are using a word processor to produce a document, the word processor is first loaded into RAM and the document you are preparing is also stored in RAM as you work on it. Should the computer be switched off before your document is saved, or should there be a power cut, everything in RAM is lost and you will have to start all over again when the power is restored.

This kind of memory is called **Random Access** because the computer can place data in it – the text of your document, for example – and retrieve it when it is needed, without restriction.

**Read Only Memory (ROM)** is also stored on 'memory chips' but data is burnt into it permanently at manufacture and cannot be altered afterwards. The data is there before you turn the computer on and it is still there when the power is off. Unlike RAM, the computer cannot place data in ROM. It can only read from it, thus giving it its name.

This kind of memory is used to store the instructions which the computer needs to start up and which must be available immediately when the computer is switched on. Only small amounts of data such as this are stored in ROM, compared with the large amount of RAM that is needed.

**Cache Memory**: This is a special type of memory linked to the processor (CPU). Frequently used processor data is stored here to be used as and when necessary, thus saving time and effectively speeding up the computer. The amount of cache memory used by the CPU may be as little as 512Kb.

## 3.5    Storage Devices

The programs you use and the work you produce must be stored before the computer is switched off so that they are available for future use. The next time you turn on the computer, they can be loaded into RAM again and you can continue with your work. This kind of mechanical storage is often referred to as **secondary memory**.

The usual storage device is a mechanical unit in the form of a spinning disk on which data can be recorded – in much the same way as music is recorded on magnetic tape. Common examples are:

**Hard disk.**   The hard disk is located within the computer system box. It is usually composed of several metal (hard) magnetically coated disks in a single unit and encased in a sealed metal box. The capacity of a typical hard disk is 10Gb or more. Larger sizes are readily available. Extra hard disk units can be added to the computer, either internally or externally.

**Floppy disks** are small, portable versions of the hard disk which use a magnet-ised plastic (floppy) disk in a compact plastic case $3^1/_2$ inches square. A floppy disk has a nominal capacity of 1.4Mb. They are commonly used to transfer files from one computer to another, particularly when the computers are not linked in any way. A variation of the floppy disk, the Super Disk or Smart Disk, has a nominal capacity of 120Mb but needs a special drive unit.

**Compact Disks**   While floppy and hard disks are magnetic, a compact disk is an optical disk which uses a laser to read the information. It can store very large amounts of data, typically 650Mb. CD-R and CD-RW are compact disks that can be recorded on by the user who has a suitable CD writer. CD-ROM is a pre-recorded compact disk that cannot be recorded on.

Compact disks are most suitable for storing large files and for programs that mix text, graphics and audio, i.e. **multimedia**, such as illustrated encyclopedias, interactive games, computer-based training programs and so on.

**Zip Drives** and similar units are small, portable versions of the hard disk that use **cartridges**. The cartridges are slightly larger than floppy disks but they have a much larger storage capacity, 100Mb or 250Mb according to type.

**DVD** (Digital Versatile Disk) is a high-capacity development of the CD-ROM that can store Gigabytes of information. While the CD was originally designed for recorded music, DVD has had many uses from the beginning. It may replace the standard video cassette, for example, as it can store an entire feature film with very high picture quality. Like CD-ROM, DVD disks can not be recorded on by the user but DVD-R, a recordable version, is now beginning to appear.

---

**Drives**:  A **disk drive** – often called a drive – is a unit that makes use of a disk.

- A floppy drive uses floppy disks.

- A hard drive uses a hard disk (usually only one).

- A Zip drive or similar uses cartridges.

- CD-ROM and DVD drives use CD-ROM or DVD discs.

The illustration shows how different drives are represented on the computer screen.

---

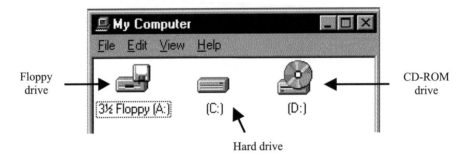

Floppy drive → ... ← CD-ROM drive

Hard drive

## 3.6  Stored Data

As data is used and stored by the computer using only the digits 0 and 1 (bits), it has to use various combinations of these to represent everything that can be processed.

- **Bits** combine to make **bytes**. Bytes combine to describe a **character** such as a letter of the alphabet or a number. Series of characters make up a word, a number of words, a sentence and so on. The entire document is a **file**. Because of the large number of bits required, even a simple document uses many thousands of bits.

Here is another way of looking at it.

- A set of **data,** such as information about the pupils in a school or employees in a company, is a **file**. The file contains **records**. The records are divided into **fields**. Each field is composed of a series of **characters**. Each character is made up of a number of **bytes**, and each byte in turn is made up of a number of **bits**.

A picture or graphic is stored in a similar fashion, with bits and bytes making up the picture elements and colours. The picture, graphic or other object is also a file. A number of documents and pictures, or a combination of both, can also be combined into a single file. A number of files can be stored in a **folder** (also known as a **directory**).

The size of a file – document, graphic etc. – is measured by the number of bytes it uses, usually in Kb or Mb. See Module 2, Section 7, page 98, for more information.

---

## 3.7    Computer Performance

The CPU is governed by a clock – in much the same way a piece of music is governed by a metronome or an orchestra by its conductor. Along with the processor and other factors, the clock speed determines how fast the computer carries out the instructions it receives.

- **Clock Speed:** In general terms, the faster the clock speed, the more efficient the computer. Just as with an orchestra, however, the speed at which a particular CPU can operate has a limit.

  The clock speed of current computers ranges from 500Mhz to over 1000Mhz (millions of cycles per second).

- **Memory:** The amount of memory (RAM) installed on the computer may affect the speed at which it operates. The system software takes up an appreciable part of the available memory. So, if there is not enough RAM available for what the user wants to do, the computer uses some space on the hard disk as **temporary** or **virtual memory**.

  It takes much longer to access data in virtual memory on the hard disk than it does to access data in RAM. This slows the computer down.

- **Hard disk:** The speed at which the hard disk can save and access information has an effect on the overall speed of the computer when it is using the hard disk. This is connected with the speed at which the disk rotates, commonly 5,000 to 10,000 rpm. The faster the speed of rotation, the faster the computer can save, or gain access to, the data.

  The storage capacity of the hard disk also affects access speed. A 9Gb hard disk, for example, has a faster access speed than a 4Gb one due to the type of mechanism used.

  To illustrate the speed difference between the hard disk and other media, it takes the computer perhaps 10 times longer to access data from a CD-ROM than from a hard disk and even longer to access data from a floppy disk.

- **Bus speed:** A further factor in the speed of a computer is the speed at which data is sent from one part of the system in the CPU box to another. The **System Bus** transfers data like a bus moving passengers between a railway station and an airport. (It is usually the slowest part of your journey.) System Bus speeds are typically 50 to 100Mhz, much slower than the CPU (500Mhz or more) which thus has to 'wait' for data.

- **Graphics Acceleration:** As well as performing all the calculations for the user's work in progress, the CPU also has to calculate and display information graphically on the monitor. So it has a double task. By using a **graphics acceleration card**, which has its own processor and memory for the display, the CPU is relieved of a large part of its workload. The overall apparent speed of the computer as seen by the user is thus increased, according to the type of graphics card and the amount of memory on it.

# Section 4    Software

## 4.1    System and Applications Software

Computer software can be divided into two broad categories – software used by the computer itself, called **system software**, and software used by the user, called **applications software**.

- **System software** is the **Operating System** that holds all the instructions that make the computer work, e.g. the start-up procedure, monitor display and the use of hard or floppy disks etc. for storing data.

  The Operating System manages programs such as word processors, games and Internet browsers. It accepts instructions from them, passes them to the CPU, arranges the display on the monitor, takes the results from the CPU, sends them to be stored on the hard disk or to the printer for printing. It is permanently stored in the computer and is automatically started when the computer is switched on. Without an Operating System, the computer would be like a car without an engine.

  Two common examples of system software are the Mac OS (Macintosh) and Microsoft Windows (PC). Examples of other operating systems are MS-DOS, UNIX, OS/2 and Linux. Various versions of Windows (95, 98, NT, 2000) are the most commonly used Operating Systems on PCs today.

- **Applications software** is all the other software that runs on a computer, e.g. Word Processor, Spreadsheet, Database, Payroll programs, Presentation tools, Desktop Publishing software, Games and Multimedia programs.

  This is the software most users recognise as the **applications** with which they do their work. The Microsoft Office suite of programs, which you are learning to use as part of this course, is an example of applications software.

## 4.2    Types of Software

Thousands of software programs are available from a wide variety of sources, from computer shops, to supermarkets, to remote access over the Internet. Some common examples are described here.

### System Software

System Software is supplied with the computer. It has already been installed on the hard disk when you purchase the computer. When you use the computer for the first time, you may need to enter certain information to **configure** it. This could mean telling the computer what printer is connected, whether there is a connection to the Internet and similar details.

Additions can be made to the system software as the need arises. If you change your printer, for example, you may have to install some extra software so that it will work with your computer.

### Commercial Software

Any software that you buy is commercial software. The Microsoft Office suite of programs is an example. Commercial software is available for thousands of different uses including graphics, accounts, business management and video editing.

Commercial software is usually licensed to the user rather than 'sold' in the accepted sense. Various terms and conditions are connected with its use, as explained in Section 8, page 55.

### Shareware

Many computer programmers and hobbyists write software programs which they allow to be distributed freely as **shareware**. Distribution may be via the Internet or on the CDs distributed with magazines. Shareware is copyrighted software that allows you a try-it-out period before you make the purchase. Payment for shareware is based on an honour system. If you wish to continue using the software after the trial period, you are required to send a payment (usually nominal) to the author.

To encourage payment, many shareware programs will only function for a limited period, or some functions may be disabled. Paid-up users may get additions and free updates. The quality of shareware is variable but some programs, such as early versions the popular image editing program, Paint Shop Pro, are of professional standard. (Current versions are no longer shareware.)

### Freeware

Freeware is similar to shareware. It is also distributed freely, but no payment is expected. Some authors may ask for feedback or for a reciprocal action ('Do something nice for someone', or 'Send me a postcard.') As with shareware, freeware comes in an 'as is' condition. Some developers may freely distribute the first version of their product so that they can benefit from users' reactions in the development of the program. Freeware authors often retain all the rights to their software under copyright legislation. Copying and distributing further copies of the material may not be allowed.

### Public Domain Software

This is software in which ownership has been relinquished to the public at large. It is freely available, can be copied and/or modified, and no payment is involved.


## 4.3    Programs and Applications

A **program** is a set of detailed instructions that tells the computer how to do something, such as detecting or removing a virus. (The spelling 'program' has come to indicate a computer program rather than a programme of events at a festival, for example.)

- You can also think of a program as a set of instructions written in a language that the computer understands. (Computers do not understand English or other human languages. Anything the user types at the keyboard is converted into binary numbers [binary code] before the computer can do anything with it.)

- The computer acts on the instructions, processes data and outputs information in a format understood by the user, usually on the monitor or printed on paper by a printer.

**Applications** are programs such as word processors that are used in everyday work. If you are working with graphics, you will use various graphics applications; if you are working with music, you will use music applications. Desktop Publishing, Payroll and Presentation programs are widely used in business. There are programs for every conceivable purpose.

The terms 'programs' and 'applications' are interchangeable.

Microsoft Word, Excel, Access and PowerPoint are examples of applications (or programs) that you are using in this course. Adobe Photoshop is a widely-used graphics program. Quark Xpress and In Design are desktop publishing programs. Macromedia Director is an application for producing multimedia presentations. Adobe Premier and Apple's Final Cut Pro are video-editing applications.


## 4.4    Interfaces

An **interface** is required to enable two-way communication between the user of an application and the computer. An interface accepts information in one format, such as the typed word, and translates it into another, such as the binary code used by the computer – much as a translator is the interface between business people who speak different languages.

Early computers used a **command line interface** – as in MS-DOS – where commands had to be typed in at the keyboard. The user typed a command as a line of text to which the computer responded. This was a slow process and required a high degree of computer knowledge.

A **Graphical User Interface (GUI)** uses pictures, or **icons** – as in Windows 95 – to represent objects or information on the monitor. The GUI, introduced by Apple Computer in the early 1980s, is now universally used. The icons can be clicked and manipulated with the mouse to make the computer perform actions or carry out instructions. Users can relate the work they are doing to the real life objects and concepts represented by the icons, thus making the computer an easy-to-use tool.

## 4.5   Systems Development

**Systems development** involves the design, development and implementation of computer operations to replace or update some process within an organisation. A manual payroll system, for example, could be replaced by a computerised version. There are many stages in the development of such a system, ranging from identifying the organisation's requirements to the implementation of the new system and staff training.

In organisations such as banks, insurance companies and multinational corporations, system design teams comprised of analysts, programmers and engineers collaborate to develop the hardware and software facilities required to meet the organisations's needs.

The steps involved in the development of a system are much the same as for any design project. Whether it is a car, a house or a company organisation, the same careful research, analysis and evaluation must be carried out.

The diagram illustrates the possible steps in developing a computer system.

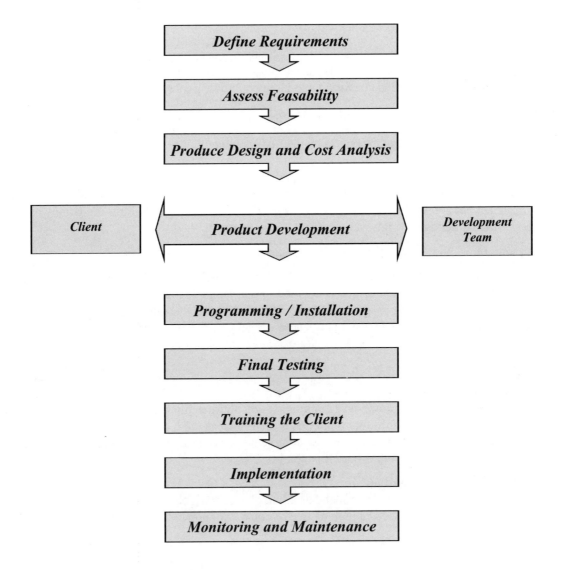

## 4.6    Multimedia

**Multimedia** is the use of different media in a computer program: text, graphics, audio, video and animation. Multimedia is particularly suited to presentations, educational and self-study learning programs and games, and it is used for many commercial purposes.

In recent years, with the advent of more advanced and faster processor chips, both the speed of operation of computers and their capacity to hold information has increased greatly. This coincided with the use of the Compact Disc to store large amounts of computer data and opened new possibilities.

Combining the CD's large storage capacity with fast processors and their ability to deal with greater amounts of data than before led to the development of multimedia technology.

The term 'multimedia' as it applies to software refers to programs that can use text, images and sound simultaneously or in a sequenced fashion.

- **Images** can range from the simplest drawings and charts to reproductions of great masterpieces on the computer screen.

- **Sound** can be anything from simple voice, music and sound effects to actuality recordings from real life.

- **Animation** can refer to moving text, drawings, images or cartoon sequences to illustrate a point or to attract the viewer's attention.

- **Video** can be used on screen as the occasion demands, from historical film clips in an on-screen encyclopedia to full-length feature films.

## 4.7    Multimedia Computers

A **multimedia computer** is one that is capable of using multimedia programs. The standard office computer was designed principally for text processing, storing data and producing documents. It did not require colour or sound, or very great processing power.

The demands of the home user for more powerful and versatile machines, particularly in the area of entertainment, accelerated the development of multimedia machines. These developments are now being reflected in improvements in office computers as workers begin to expect the facilities they already use at home.

- Before the advent of multimedia, a typical processor speed was 33MHz, the memory installed in the computer was perhaps 8 or 16Mb of RAM and the hard disk could store a few hundred Mb of data.

- In a modern multimedia computer, processor speeds of over 750MHz are normal, 128Mb or more of RAM is common and hard disk capacity is 20Gb or more. The computer is also supplied with a range of other devices, either installed in the CPU box or externally.

- Peripherals include CD drives, sound cards, microphones, loudspeakers and modems.

- Larger monitors with the capacity to display millions of colours are replacing the smaller and more limited monitors of earlier years, where 16 colours were deemed sufficient.

A more recent development has been the introduction of **DVD** (**Digital Versatile Disk**). These have a greatly increased storage capacity and make it possible to have a full-length feature film on a single small disk with standards superior to broadcast quality. With the appropriate video card installed, the film can be shown on a normal television set as well as on the computer screen.

## 4.8    Multimedia Programs

A wide range of activities is available to the user of a multimedia computer.

You can have a guided tour of the Louvre museum in the language of your choice or learn a foreign language, with the computer recording your pronunciation and comparing it with that of a native speaker.  You could also play a game, tour the planets of the solar system, simulate living as a Viking, or even produce your own multimedia software.

Many of these applications are termed **interactive**, given their facility to respond **intelligently** to the uscr's actions.

## 4.9    Computer Based Training

**Computer Based Training (CBT)** uses interactive programs and modern multimedia computers to enable people to acquire skills and knowledge in a way that may be more convenient, more practical or less expensive than traditional training methods.

A simple example of CBT is a computer typing tutor that teaches keyboard skills.  Such a program is able to sense the learner's skill level and to adjust the exercises appropriately.  It can demonstrate the correct placing of the fingers on the screen, monitor the learner's progress, detect where mistakes are made, provide encouragement and set additional exercises in problem areas.

More elaborate CBT programmes make use of text, video, sound and simulation.  Such programs can be used to train operatives of complex machinery, for example, on screen without the risk of damaging expensive industrial plant in the event of an incorrect decision being made.

An aircraft flight simulator used for training pilots can be seen as a sophisticated example of CBT. The learning takes place in a replica of an aircraft cabin.  Computer-generated video is projected onto the 'windows'.  The whole cabin is moved by external machinery with appropriate engine noises and sound effects.  A virtual reality situation is created in which the pilot's actions give an accurate impression of flying a real aircraft but without the catastrophic consequences that a major error might produce in real life.

Computer Based Training enables large numbers of people to be trained without them necessarily having to travel to a training venue.  The training can take place at the individual person's desk – or even at home, a situation commonly referred to as distance learning.  However, the learner then often does not have the benefit of a tutor to answer questions or to advise when difficulties arise.  The training may also be so rigidly controlled that unforeseen problems may occur in actual 'real life' situations.

Web Based Training (WBT), also known as On-line Training, is a form of CBT in which the training material is accessed over the Internet rather than being located primarily on the individual learner's computer.

---

**Interactive**  programs exchange inputs and outputs with the user.
Typically, the user views a display or listens to an instruction
and then avails of choices to pursue some action or activity.

**Intelligent**  programs can monitor interactions with a user and take
appropriate action in response to the user's input.

---

# Section 5    Information Networks

## 5.1    Workgroup Computing

Workgroup computing means that people who are working on aspects of a common task can each use their own computer or terminal but they can also share documents, files and resources with other workers over a network.

Workers can communicate by means of a **LAN** (see below) or telecommunications network. Resources can be shared and messages can be sent to all members of the group at once.

Documents can be produced with a common format or similar content.  The same word processing file, for example, can be accessed and edited as necessary by different people in different locations.

## 5.2    Local Area Networks

In a **Local Area Network (LAN)**, a number of computers are **networked** – linked together – by means of cabling within a limited area, often in the same building or group of nearby buildings. Company offices are often networked in this way.

In a **server/client** network, a computer called a **server** stores common data which it 'serves' to the other computers, called **clients**. The client computers store data on the server which is then available to the other clients.

For example, a single copy of a stock or customer database on the server can be used by everyone on the network.  Any updates or changes made by one user are immediately available to the others.

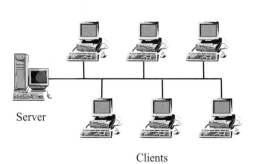

Server

Clients

 A **peer-to-peer** network does not use a server. Instead, individual computers share data directly with other computers.

## 5.3    Wide Area Networks

In a **Wide Area Network (WAN)**, computers, as well as computer networks, are linked together over a large area.

The WAN operates in the same way as a Local Area Network, but on a much larger scale.  Many organisations operate Wide Area Networks to link their offices in different parts of the country or even in different parts of the world.

Worldwide coverage is provided largely by satellite communications.  Data is transmitted from one part of the world to a satellite in orbit around the Earth. The satellite re-transmits the data which can then be received in a distant location without the need for extensive land lines or undersea cables.

Satellite Communication

A bank **ATM** machine is an example of a computer on a WAN. It enables you to access your account not only from almost anywhere in your own country but also from ATMs in other countries as well.

The international telephone system is another example of a WAN. Now virtually all computer controlled, it is probably the largest WAN in the world. The **Internet** is a high-profile WAN. Millions of computers are connected, often via smaller networks, to provide an extraordinary revolution in communication worldwide.

## 5.4    Data Communications

An important requirement of the Information Society is the facility to transfer data to remote locations quickly and conveniently. **Data communication** can involve many different types of data, from numbers to text to graphics to sound to video or the whole lot together. The data is transferred by means of the telecommunications networks provided by governments and private organisations.

Government organisations in Europe, such as Eircom in Ireland, BT in the United Kingdom, France Telecom in France and Deutsche Telecom in Germany, traditionally provide data communications in their countries.

In recent years, increased competition from private companies has led to a lowering of charges and an expansion of services. The use of mobile phones has become commonplace and some of them can now be used to provide Internet access in conjunction with portable computers in areas without a mains electricity supply. Internet access itself is being offered free of join-up or monthly charges. The customer pays only for use of the telephone line, and even here, special low-rate 'Internet access' telephone numbers reduce costs further.

## 5.5    The Telephone System

The telephone system we are all familiar with is called the **Public Switched Telephone Network (PSTN)** or **Public Switched Data Network (PSDN)**. It was originally designed for voice, and sounds are transmitted in **analogue** format – a continuously varying electrical signal. PSTN is increasingly used for the transmission of data but is limited in the speed at which data can be transmitted.

- To transmit **digital** computer information over normal **analogue** telephone lines, the data has to be converted from its digital format (a series of zeroes and ones) to analogue format (a varying voltage) by a device called a **modem**.

  At the other end of the line, another modem converts from analogue back to digital for the receiving computer.

- The maximum processing speed that can be achieved by modems is about 56Kb (thousands of bits) per second. This is sometimes referred to as the **baud rate**.

  This connection speed is only a tiny fraction of the speed that the computer itself is capable of, so the transfer of data via a modem is very slow compared with the transfer of data within the computer to and from the computer's hard disk. Noise and interference on the telephone lines slow the signal further and the claimed maximum speed is rarely achieved consistently.

- The **Integrated Services Digital Network (ISDN)** was designed for the transmission of digital signals, the kind that computers use, and so modems are not required.

  ISDN is much faster than normal PSDN telephone lines although still much slower than the speed the computer is capable of. The basic speed is 64Kb per second. 128Kb is available but often at extra cost. Additional ISDN lines can be combined to give increased speed.

- An older method of transmitting data is the **Telex** machine, a kind of electric typewriter that can send or receive typed messages to similar machines. Telex is still used in many countries.

- A **Fax (facsimile)** machine is a simple scanner with an integrated modem that is used to send scanned copies of documents to similar machines over normal telephone lines.

## 5.6    The Internet

The **Internet** is a network of computers and computer networks around the world that are linked by means of the telecommunications network. It can be accessed by any computer that has the facilities outlined below. The computer on your desk can be – and probably is – one of them. A computer with an Internet connection gives the user access to large amounts of information on practically every subject imaginable on a scale that was not possible before.

- The first transfer of data between two remote computers took place in the USA just over 30 years ago, the beginning of what is now known as the Internet. Only text could be transmitted and a high degree of computer skill was needed to use the system. However, it gradually grew into a valuable research tool, used mainly by universities and other large organisations.

- A simplified way of connecting to other files, especially on remote computers, by just clicking on a word on the screen was developed in the 1990s and is known as **Hypertext**.

- Later, methods of transmitting graphics, sound and video over the Internet were developed. This 'multimedia' branch of the Internet is now known as the **World Wide Web** (**WWW**). It has become synonymous with the Internet for many people.

- The introduction of the World Wide Web increased use of the Internet by ordinary people.

- The computers linked to the Internet store vast amounts of information that can be accessed or transferred around the world to users as needed. Governments, universities, organisations and individuals all over the world publish information on the Internet.

## 5.7    Using the Internet

The following are needed to connect to and use the Internet with a single computer.

- **A computer**. All modern and many older computers can be used for Internet access.

- **A modem.**   A modem is built-in to most modern computers. It can be fitted either internally or externally to older ones.

   In an organisation with a large number of computers, Internet access may be available over a network and a modem is not required for individual computers.

- **A telephone line**. A single telephone line can be shared between normal telephone use and modem use but you will not be able to use it for both simultaneously. If anyone telephones you while you are using the modem, they will hear an engaged tone. If you use the Internet and e-mail a lot, you may want to install a second telephone line.

- **Internet and e-mail software**. This is already installed on most computers as part of Windows.

- **An e-mail address**. Your e-mail address is allocated to you when you sign up with an Internet Service Provider.

- **An account with an Internet Service Provider**. Free accounts are now available, as mentioned in Section 5.4 above. It may not be necessary to install software from 'free offer' CDs with most modern computers as the necessary software is usually pre-installed. Seek advice if you are not sure what to do.

## 5.8    Search Engines

There is so much information available on the Internet, it would be very tedious and take an enormous amount of time to search for information manually. A **search engine** is a program that helps you find information on the Internet.

Different search engines use different methods to search for information on the Internet and they can retrieve information in seconds that would otherwise take weeks or months of manual searching. Search Engines are described in more detail in Module 7, Section 4, page 352.

## 5.9    Electronic Mail

**Electronic mail**, or **E-mail** as it is commonly known, is a method of sending and receiving mail messages over the Internet.  In order to use e-mail, you must have Internet access as described in Section 5.7 above.  As with the Internet, access is available free of cost other than the reduced rate Internet Access or local call telephone charges.

E-mail has revolutionised communication between individuals, businesses and organisations.

- It allows fast, low-cost communication around the world. An e-mail message or document can usually be sent to any destination in the world for the cost of a local call.

- You can send and receive messages or documents in electronic form, edit them and forward them to someone else.

- You can correspond with friends easily and quickly.

- An e-mail message can be sent to a number of people simultaneously.

- You can request and receive information by e-mail.

- E-mail speeds communication.  A reply can be sent to a message by typing a few words and clicking a button on the screen.

- E-mail has a writing convention that is generally friendlier and more informal in use than traditional written communication.

# Section 6    Computers in Everyday Life

## 6.1    Computers in the Home

In the home environment, you might expect to find:

- **A multimedia computer** with loudspeakers, microphone, modem and printer.  Home users may also use other peripherals such as a scanner and a digital camera.  You might also expect to find computers designed for playing games only.

- **Software** might include word processing, educational programs for use with school projects and homework, an on-screen encyclopedia and atlas, general interest programs, hobby related programs, household accounts programs, games, Internet access and e-mail facilities.

- The use of computers to **work from home** is increasing, with many people communicating with the office over the Internet.

## 6.2    Computers at Work

There are many different types of business activity, each requiring different systems to meet their needs.  Here are some examples.

- **Manufacturing** industries employ computer control of machines for automation and assembly line processes, as well as stock control, accounting systems and payroll programs.  Transport and other companies employ scheduling and tracking systems.

- **Medical** establishments and hospitals have complex analysis, monitoring and life-support systems.

- **Governments** use computers in virtually all departments, such as vehicle registration, police, taxation, employment and social services.

In general, you might expect to find:

- **Hardware** that includes computers without many of the multimedia elements you would see in a home computer.  Their principal use is for processing data as functional tools rather than for general-purpose home use and entertainment.

  The principal programs would most likely be stored on a central server and the printers would most likely be networked rather than be connected to individual computers.  Other items of hardware might include printers, scanners, bar code readers, modems or Internet servers and touch screens for customer use.

- **Software** would include word processor, spreadsheet, database, graphics, presentation, publishing, telecommunications, e-mail.  Business programs and tools would include statistics, diary, planning/simulation, decision-making, calendars and project management.  Computerised accounting systems are also widely used throughout business and industry.

See also CAD, CAM, CRM, DSS, EIS and MIS in the Glossary for further information.

## 6.3    Computers in Education

In education, computers are used in universities, colleges and schools for training, teaching and research, as well as for administration.  There would be separate requirements for administration and classroom use. You might expect to find:

- **Networked** or **stand-alone** computers with multimedia facilities, i.e. CD-ROM and sound cards, printers, modems, scanners, graphics tablets and specialised keyboards for younger and special needs children.

- **Software** for administration would include word processing, an administration database, accounts packages and so on as for business.

- For **classroom use** you would expect to find educational packages, multimedia authoring, Internet and e-mail applications, computer-based instruction/training programs, word processing, spreadsheets, desktop publishing programs, and presentation and graphics packages.

## 6.4    Computers in Daily Life

In our everyday lives, we engage with computers in many different settings. Some examples follow.

- **Supermarkets** use computers coupled to bar-code scanners to identify and itemise purchases and payments at the checkouts. The checkout data is also linked to stock control and ordering systems.

- **Libraries** use computers to record book lending and return. Computers, bar-code readers, database and telecommunications record transactions and link to other libraries and resources. Readers can search for book titles and availability. Video lending libraries use computers in a similar way.

- **Banks** use computers to enable their customers to access their accounts through roadside ATM machines, not only locally but internationally. Customers can access their accounts, make enquiries and pay bills from home using the Internet banking facilities provided by their banks.

- **'Plastic' cards** of all description, such as credit cards, company loyalty cards, and smart cards such as mobile phone cards, telephone call cards and so on could not exist without the use of extensive networked computer systems. Credit card companies handle millions of transactions every day and keep track of their customers using world-wide computer and telecommunications networks.

- **E-commerce**, the use of the Internet for business, is expanding constantly as more and more people realise the convenience of doing business electronically. Shopping, airline bookings and holiday arrangements can all be done over the Internet using the computer.

- **Touch-screen** information kiosks in public places such as airports and tourist areas allow easy access to information by unskilled users.

- **Doctors and hospitals** keep patients' information on computer. The computer can assist in diagnosis by comparing the symptoms of thousands of patients, and analysing the treatment prescribed for them and the results obtained.

- A modern **aircraft** with computer guidance systems, carrying hundreds of people, can fly thousands of miles without the intervention of the pilot and even land unaided at its destination. It may even alert the pilot in the case of a potentially unsafe manoeuvre.

- **Cars and other vehicles** are being fitted with computer-operated positioning systems that can plan journeys and assist navigation down to the smallest detail – displaying maps and giving instructions to the driver: 'Turn left at the next roundabout', for example.

> **Magnetic Strip Cards** have a characteristic dark brown strip along the back. They are used for many purposes. Information can be saved on and read from the magnetic strip. Examples are credit cards, security access cards and bank ATM cards.
>
> **Smart Cards** may contain a processor and/or memory. They can interact with computers in a more complex way than magnetic strip cards. An example is the telephone callcard used in many countries, where the location of the 'chip' is clearly visible. The SIM card in a mobile phone is another example.

# Section 7     IT and Society

## 7.1    Computer Use

Computers play an increasingly important role in society. In almost every aspect of our daily lives, we come in contact with them – from household appliances to smart cards to work environments. Computers can make life easier for people. They can eliminate the drudgery of repetitive tasks and provide greater efficiency and reliability in processing information. Computers can also provide new employment opportunities in creating a demand for skills and jobs that did not exist before. However, in replacing people, computers can also cause unemployment. They may also lead to less personal contact in business or commercial dealings.

In their homes, people can use their computers to book a holiday, hire a car, do their banking business or order a pizza, as well as accessing information on the Internet and using e-mail for communication. With the development of better telecommunications and better security software, many people can – and choose to – work from home.

In business, firms can sell directly to people in their homes without having to pay the large overheads involved in maintaining shops in expensive locations. An architect can prepare projects and drawings and send them electronically to clients anywhere in the world. A local bookshop can have a world-wide market. The use of electronic information technology in commerce has given rise to the term **E-commerce**.

Employees of some companies may now only visit their office for meetings. As **ISDN (Integrated Services Digital Network)** and other high-speed lines and satellite communications become more available, it is also becoming possible to conduct these meetings through **video conferencing**.

This growth in the use of computers allows for greater efficiency, more rapid development, higher standards of living, better communications and more leisure time. The increasing role which technology now plays, both at work and at home, has implications for the acquisition of new personal skills, re-training, education and the use of leisure time. It is important that as many people as possible benefit from, and use, computers in their daily lives.

## 7.2    The Information Society

Society relies heavily on the processing of information that generates wealth, just as agriculture, fishing, industry and services have done in the past. Today, the processing of information occurs in almost every aspect of life – in the area of leisure as well as work.

Many people are employed in information processing businesses and many more are engaged in information processing in non-commercial ways. Accessing information, shopping, booking holidays, reading news, sending messages and many other activities are all being done with computers in homes all over the world by people who are not particularly technically minded. Thus we refer to our society as the **Information Society** and the facility for the rapid interchange of information as the **Information Superhighway**.

The rapid developments that are occurring due to the Information Society and its demand for efficiency can have their drawbacks. Machines now do many tasks that were previously carried out by people. There is a danger of reduced social contact and poorer social skills. As information processing involves mainly mental work, physical development can be neglected, causing illness. The increasingly technical demands of lifelong learning, which is necessary for society, may place a burden on some people and reduce opportunities for others.

## 7.3    Computers and People

Computers are good for tasks that are repetitive or monotonous, those that require accuracy, speed and calculation.  They are good at combining data from different sources, for sorting data, for dealing with tasks that require long-term memory or large volumes of data.

People are good for tasks that require creativity, imagination, and where instructions cannot be pre-written.  People are better for tasks that are 'once-off' or different each time, and for tasks that require a personal touch or where feelings need to be considered.

Computers play an ever-increasing role in the lives of people all over the world, but there will always be areas where no machine, however sophisticated, can replace person to person contact.

The Computers and People debate has now developed in the context of information and communications technology being an integral part of everyday life.  The debate is taking place at an international level.  The **European Commission**, for example, in a discussion document on the Information Society, posed the following questions:

- Will the technologies destroy more jobs than they create?

- Will people be prepared to adapt to the changes in the way they work?

- Will the cost and complexity of the new technologies not widen the gap between the industrialised and less developed areas, between the young and the old, between those in the know and those who are not?

*Living and Working in the Information Society: People First,*
Bulletin of the European Union, Supplement 3/96

The considered opinion of the Commission was that computer literacy skills have become as important as the traditional skills of reading, writing and arithmetic in enabling people to avail of opportunities in work and to participate fully in all other aspects of living.

## 7.4    Opportunities Offered by Computers

Computers have become commonplace and they have uses in almost every sphere of modern life in developed countries.

- Computers facilitate the automation of many industrial processes.

- Business, industry, hospitals, etc. requiring precision measuring and monitoring use computers.

- Travel systems such as rail and air use computers to monitor and guide trains and planes.

- Computers enable people all over the world to communicate quickly and reasonably cheaply.

- Business can be easily and efficiently carried out on a world-wide scale. This creates more wealth and can help to create a better standard of living.

- People can access large volumes of information using computers. This has enormous possibilities for business and education and enables people who work in these areas to be more efficient and competitive.

- The greater use of computers reduces the need for heavy manual labour in labour intensive processes such as vehicle assembly.  It can bring down labour costs and improve services that can be offered.

An example of the opportunities offered by computers can be seen in the growth of **Desktop Publishing**, or **DTP**.  This is the production of documents, papers, newsletters, or other material on a desktop computer rather than using traditional publishing methods.

The modern desktop computer, with large storage capacity, excellent graphics, sophisticated software, and high-quality printing, facilitates this process.  It allows the user to produce such material more quickly, more conveniently and with more control than was possible in the past.

## 7.5    Computer Use and Care

It is important to develop good practice and habits when using computers. They should always be switched on and, in particular, shut down according to the correct procedures. Some other things to be borne in mind include:

- Keep the equipment clean. A slightly damp cloth with a dab of mild soap or cleaning agent should be used regularly. (Switch off the computer first!) Pay particular attention to the keyboard, mouse and the screen.

- The mouse requires regular attention and will become erratic in use if not cleaned regularly. Open the cover on the underside, take out the ball and use a wooden cocktail stick to remove the accumulated dirt from the internal rollers.

- As with all electrical equipment, make sure that power and other cables are correctly wired and in good order. They should also be safely secured and kept neat and tidy.

- Place, store and use equipment in well-ventilated areas with adequate temperatures.

- Make back-up copies of your data regularly to guard against computer breakdown.

## 7.6    Health and Safety

Prolonged use of computers, or their use in poor lighting conditions, with bad positioning, or with bad posture, can lead to health problems such as upper limb disorder and eye fatigue.

Do not have food or drink near the computer. Liquid spilled on the keyboard or on other parts of the computer can cause serious damage. It can also be a serious health hazard.

Being too close to the monitor is a common cause of eye-strain. Reflections of room or window lighting on the screen should be avoided. The monitor should be positioned to avoid such reflections. The user should not have a strong light source, such as a bright window, behind the monitor.

A particular problem associated with the use of computers is **Repetitive Strain Injury (RSI)** where muscular strain or damage is caused by repeated use of the same muscles over a long period. Having to look up at a monitor that is too high, for example, and/or using the mouse at the wrong level over a long period, can cause pain or stress in the hand or fingers or in the muscles in the neck and back. Sensible precautions can help prevent prevent the incidence of RSI, as explained in the next section.

## 7.7    Ergonomics

Ergonomics is the study of the interaction of people with equipment and machines so that people can work with them more efficiently.

Stress-related illness can result from improper working conditions and practices. To avoid these and other problems, simple precautions should be taken.

Some of these include:

- Take regular breaks.

- Make sure the work area is comfortable and that adequate temperature is maintained.

- Ensure that there is adequate ventilation.

- To avoid visual fatigue, make sure that there is adequate lighting.

- Examine plugs, sockets and leads for defects and have any necessary repairs carried out by qualified personnel.

- Keep pathways clear.

- Comply with local fire and safety regulations.

Computer systems should be logical and easy to use. Users should be instructed or trained in the use of all new hardware and software.

Check the health and safety requirements of your local authority. They may be legally binding.

The illustrations here are given as examples of a good monitor positioning and user posture.

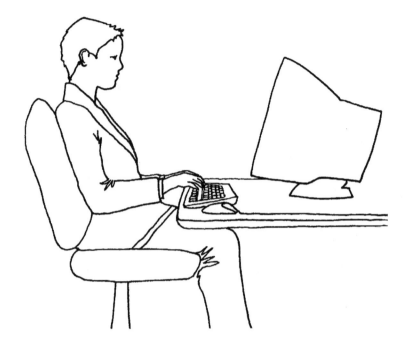

- Look down, not up, at the monitor.

- Place the monitor on the desk, rather than on top of the CPU box, for correct viewing and to avoid neck strain.

- Set the monitor back on the desk to avoid eye strain.

- Position the monitor to avoid glare from lighting or from windows behind it.

- Fit windows with adjustable blinds to remove any reflections from the screen.

- Use a document holder beside the screen and at the same level to minimise head and eye movements.

- Have the keyboard and mouse at the correct level for the individual user.

- Use a chair with adjustable height and backrest facilities.

- A footrest should be provided if required by individual users.

- Knee and thigh clearances should be adequate for different users.

- The elbow angle should be from $70°$ to $90°$.

- Use a desk lamp to provide local illumination where necessary.

# Section 8      Security, Copyright and the Law

## 8.1    Software

Commercial software is covered by **copyright**, similar to printed media such as books.  You are obliged to look after your software and not allow others to copy it.  You should purchase and register your own software for your own use.

- Program or application disks should be copied only for the purposes of back-up and safe-keeping as specified in the licence agreement.

  If the original disks are damaged or become corrupted, the back-up copies can be used to reinstall the software.

- Sharing or lending program disks may be in breach of licensing agreements.  It is also a common cause of the spread of viruses which can cause inconvenience, damage and the corruption of data.

- Transferring or copying software over a network should only be carried out under the terms of the software license agreement.

- **Software piracy**, the illegal duplication, distribution, sale and use of software, is a criminal offence.

- Copyright legislation may also apply to Shareware and Freeware.  See Section 4.2, page 40.

## 8.2    Licensing

When you purchase a software package, you are not paying for ownership but for the right – a **licence** – to use the product.  It is important to read the **licensing agreement** displayed on the carton or in the documentation.  It is also common practice among software companies to display the agreement on screen at some stage when the software is being installed on the computer.  No matter where the licence agreement is displayed, you are legally obliged to adhere to it if you use the software.

Most copies of software are **single-user** copies.  This means that the purchaser may only use the software on one computer.  A **site licence** can be purchased if the software is to be installed on a number of computers.  Only one copy of the software is supplied but the site licence legally entitles the purchaser to install it on a specified number of computers.  The cost of a site licence is generally much lower than the cost of buying individual copies of the software for each machine.

## 8.3    Back-ups and Storage Capacity

Information on a computer is stored electronically. Because of this, there is always a possibility that it can be lost due to a malfunction in the system, human error, accidents or through carelessness.  It is important to have copies of all your important files, called  **back-ups** or **backing store**.

Back-ups can be made in several ways, e.g. by copying the information onto floppy disks, zip disks or external hard disks.  The data from some files could be kept as hard copy, i.e. printed onto paper.  These back-ups should be kept in a safe and secure place – for example, locked away in fireproof containers, with further copies off the premises in a remote location.

- The storage capacities of floppy disks, zip disks and hard disks are outlined in Section 3.5, page 37.

- Floppy disks and other storage media should always be clearly labelled and stored in a dust-free, safe and secure place.

  Floppy disks should not be exposed to sunlight or magnetic fields.  In addition, any program disks should be write-protected (see Module 2, Section 8.3, page 101).

## 8.4    Personal Data

In the current Information Age, it is common for personal details and other data to be entered and stored in computers.  It has been estimated that personal data about each individual in developed countries now appears, on the average, in 300 different databases.  The following list is only a small selection of examples that could lead to your personal details being added to a computer database.

- Bank accounts
- Supermarket loyalty cards
- Service providers such as electricity, water, the Internet
- Electoral rolls and local government records
- Credit cards
- Magazine subscriptions
- Medical records held by doctors and hospitals
- Payrolls
- Employment agencies
- Insurance companies
- Application or other forms that you fill in

In business and commerce, there is a continuing demand for up-to-date personal information.  Many companies and organisations that hold such information may use it as a commodity to be sold to other interested parties.   The information can be used for market research, direct mail marketing, surveys and so on.

Data held on computers is easily and quickly sorted, copied, distributed and manipulated.  Thus, the customer information held by a credit card company will be of interest to other financial institutions.  A database of supermarket customers will be of interest to other retail organisations.  Database analysis can identify potential customers and locate the parts of the city or country where they live.  Advertising campaigns, marketing, publicity and direct mail can then be directed at the target group.

Before you discard the next batch of 'junk mail' you receive, whether through the letterbox or by e-mail, spend a moment trying to work out how it came to you.


## 8.5    Data Protection Legislation

In the Republic of Ireland, for example, a Data Protection Act was passed on 13th July 1988 and came into force on 13th April 1989.  The following is an extract from *IRELAND The Data Protection Act, 1988, A Summary from the Data Protection Commissioner.*

> 'The Act gives a right to every individual, irrespective of nationality or residence, to establish the existence of personal data, to access any such data relating to him, and to have inaccurate data rectified or erased. It requires data controllers to make sure that the data they keep are collected fairly, are accurate and up-to-date, are kept for lawful purposes, and are not used or disclosed in any manner incompatible with those purposes. It also requires both data controllers and data processors to protect the data they keep, and imposes on them a special duty of care in relation to the individuals about whom they keep such data.'
>
> *The Data Protection Commissioner, Dublin*

Similar legislation has been passed by other governments.  You should contact the appropriate authority regarding the legislation that applies in your own country.

## 8.6    Privacy

It is essential that any data relating to individuals that you store or to which you have access on a computer, be adequately protected.  There are certain legal obligations relating to this in many countries.

The following points illustrate the importance of protecting privacy and of knowing the procedures that may be in place governing your work with such information.

They are taken in part from the *Guidelines for Data Controllers* issued by the Data Protection Commissioner for the Republic of Ireland.

- **Use of Data:** '... the data... shall be kept only for one or more specified and lawful purposes...'

- **Not Excessive:** '... the data... shall be adequate, relevant and not excessive in relation to that purpose or purposes...'

- **Retention of Data:** '... the data... shall not be kept for longer than is necessary for that purpose or purposes...'

- **Disclosing Information:** '... the data... shall not be used or disclosed in any manner incompatible with that purpose or purposes...'

- **Security:** '... appropriate security measures shall be taken against unauthorised access to, or alteration, disclosure or destruction of, the data and against their accidental loss or destruction...'

- **Right of Personal Access:** 'Every individual about whom a data controller keeps personal information has a number of rights under the Act, in addition to the Right of Access.  These include the right to have any inaccurate information rectified or erased, to have personal data taken off a direct mailing list, and the right to complain to the Data Protection Commissioner.'

## 8.7    Security

Security involves not only the physical security of the computer equipment, but also the security of the data contained on the hard disk, floppy disks and other storage media.

- **The computer** should be protected from damage as far as possible.  PCs are expensive, as is software, and they should be looked after accordingly.

- **Data** contained on the computer as software or files should be backed up and suitably protected from viruses and other damage.

- **Passwords** are a good way of protecting both equipment and software.  Passwords should not be obvious: mix letters and numbers.  They should be changed from time to time and they should not be widely distributed.

- **Back-ups** are essential for the protection of data.  Files and/or disks should be backed up regularly, i.e. daily or weekly.  Back-ups can be made on floppy disks, external hard disk, zip drives, tape units, remote servers and so on.  Backup programs can be set to carry out the backing up process automatically at pre-set times or at times when the computer is not in normal use.

## 8.8    Viruses

**Viruses** are software programs written with the intention of causing inconvenience and disruption or even serious damage.  This can involve destroying anything from files to whole operating systems and networks by corrupting their data.  Unless precautions are taken, a computer user may be unaware that there is a virus on the computer until its effects become apparent.

Viruses can be spread from one computer to another by files on floppy disks or on other media. They can also be spread across a network or via e-mail and the Internet.

Many viruses are specific to a particular kind of file, such as a word processing file.  When an 'infected' file is opened on the computer, the virus attaches itself to other similar files and so the virus spreads within the computer.  If an infected file is sent to a different computer, the virus can infect that computer too and so the process continues.

Other viruses, called **Worms**, can operate independently and spontaneously.  Another kind of virus, called a **Trojan Horse**, can be carried onto a computer by other files to perform its illegal objective.

## 8.9    Anti-Virus Measures

It is important to guard against viruses by installing software that checks for viruses before they enter the system.  Anti-virus software is available from software vendors.  It can detect and remove viruses found on the computer and it can automatically check floppy disks and e-mail attachments.  When such software has been installed, it is important to keep it up-to-date by installing updating information on a regular basis as new viruses appear all the time.  If you detect a virus, you should inform the provider or sender of the infected file or files who may be unaware of the problem.

If up-to-date anti-virus software is not installed on your computer, you should take certain precautions:

- Avoid using floppy disks from unreliable or unknown sources.
- Use only reputable registered software.
- Never open an e-mail attachment unless you are sure that it is from a reliable source.
- Keep regular back-ups of your data to minimise any disruption caused by virus infection.

## 8.10   The Y2K Problem

The Year 2000 (Y2K) problem, also known as the **Millennium Bug**, caused a lot of concern as the year 2000 approached.  In the early days of computers when memory was very expensive, programmers saved space by using only two digits to record the year when they were writing system software – the software that controls the computer and is essential to its working.  Thus the system software saw the year 1984 as 84, 1999 as 99 and so on.

The problem arose with the approach of the year 2000.  The computer would see this as 00.  This was of no consequence to most home users but presented major problems to business and industry.  Would the electricity company's computers, for example, think that the bills for January 2000 were actually for January 1900 and had therefore already been sent out – resulting in millions of customers not being billed from January 2000 onwards?  Would a computer-controlled life-support machine in a hospital, programmed to run over the new year, turn itself off at the stroke of midnight on New Year's Eve?

Millions of pounds were spent by organisations and governments to ensure that all their computers and systems were prepared for the change and the term **Y2K Compliant** became widely used.

If you are buying a computer today, it may still be wise to ensure that it is Y2K compliant.  You should also ensure that any software you intend to use is also Y2K compliant.  In a business or home situation where documents or other data span the 1999/2000 divide, the Y2K problem may still be relevant.

# 8.11   Power Cuts

If there is a power cut while the computer is in use, any unsaved information will be lost and files on the computer may be corrupted.  When you restart the computer after the power has been restored – or after the computer has not been shut down properly – a program called **Scan Disk** runs automatically to check the system.  If errors are found, you will be asked to make some decisions about how they are to be treated.

- In the event of a power cut, the computer should be turned off and unplugged until the power is restored.  A **power surge** when the current is restored may cause damage.

  Power surges are brief irregularities in the mains supply that can cause damage in certain circumstances.  Data may be corrupted or the computer may crash.  In severe cases, physical damage may be caused to the equipment.

- Computers can be protected from power surges and power cuts by using **surge protectors**.

  A surge protector is a small filter unit designed to protect against variations in the electricity supply.  It is often built into the mains power socket.

- An **Uninterruptible Power Supply** (**UPS**) is a battery-powered back-up power supply that will keep the computer running in the event of a mains failure.

  A battery is kept fully charged while the mains supply is on.  If the mains fails, the UPS takes over instantly, allowing the user to save work in progress and shut down the computer properly.

  The time given by a UPS after a mains failure depends on its size (and cost): it may be from a few minutes to several hours.

# Section 9      Exercises

# Self Check Exercises

**1** Which of these is not an input device?

- ☐ Touchscreen
- ☐ Scanner
- ☑ Monitor
- ☐ Touchpad

**2** Tick the terms that could apply to a computer in a network.

- ☑ Client
- ☑ Peer
- ☑ Server
- ☑ Station

**3** What is the number system used by computers?

- ☐ Decimal
- ☑ Binary
- ☐ Natural
- ☐ Primary

**4** Tick the correct statement.

- ☑ 8 bits make 1 byte.
- ☐ 8 bytes make 1 bit.

**5** Which of these refer to an area for storing data? Tick all correct answers.

- ☐ Data
- ☑ File
- ☑ Record
- ☑ Field

**6** In which of the following are the instructions to start up the computer stored? Tick.

- ☐ RAM
- ☑ ROM
- ☐ Cache

**7** Are the terms 'Application' and 'Program' interchangeable?

- ☑ Yes
- ☐ No

**8** One of these devices does not normally affect the performance (speed) of the computer. Which one?

- ☑ Monitor
- ☐ RAM
- ☐ Graphics accelerator
- ☐ Hard disk

**9** Tick the peripheral/s or device/s you would not expect to find on a multimedia computer.

- ☐ Microphone
- ☐ Loudspeakers
- ☐ Floppy Disk Drive
- ☐ VGA Monitor

**10** In a Web page, what is most likely to be used to link you directly to another page or Web site?

- ☑ Hypertext
- ☐ A Search Engine
- ☐ E-mail
- ☐ An Account

**11** Which of these terms refer to viruses your computer may 'catch'? Tick.

- ☑ A Trojan Horse
- ☐ A Drop
- ☐ A Maggot
- ☑ A Worm

**12** Tick the terms that refer to equipment.

- ☑ Hardware
- ☐ Shareware
- ☐ Software
- ☑ Peripheral

**13** Tick the terms you would associate with computer networks.

- ☑ WAN
- ☑ Dumb terminal
- ☑ LAN
- ☑ Client

62

# Module 2

## Using the Computer
and
## Managing Files

2

# Module 2

# Using the Computer
### and
# Managing Files

Module 2

# Introduction

---

**Syllabus Goals for Module 2**

**Using the Computer and Managing Files** requires the candidate to demonstrate knowledge and competence in using the basic functions of a personal computer and its operating system. The candidate shall be able to operate effectively within the desktop environment. He or she shall be able to manage and organise files and directories/folders and know how to copy, move and delete files and directories/folders. The candidate shall demonstrate the ability to work with desktop icons and to manipulate windows. The candidate shall demonstrate the ability to use search features, simple editing tools and print management facilities available within the operating system.

---

## The Computer

This module begins with instructions about how you turn on the computer. From this starting point, you will progress through descriptions of the various ways of working with the computer. You will learn how to manage and manipulate what you see on the screen. The purpose of this module is not just to assist you in getting around but to provide you with the skills to be in control, to know where you are going and what you are doing when you interact with the computer.

In computer terms, this module will provide you with the operational skills and knowledge to work effectively with the Windows operating system.

## Files and Filing

In a traditional office, all your work is produced on paper and can be seen, stored, filed and retrieved relatively easily. The computer can be thought of as storing files in exactly the same way as traditional office filing systems, but it does this electronically.

But where are all your documents? How are they stored? Will you be able to find them again the next time you switch on the computer? The work you have produced with the computer and the information you have stored in it may also be retrieved. When you need it again, the computer locates the stored information that you wish to use and places it on the screen for viewing.

It is important to understand where and how the computer stores the information so that you can access it with the same ease and facility you have with paper files. In this module, you will learn to relate electronic files to 'real world' files so that you can organise and use them efficiently.

---

# Reference Table

Should you begin your studies with this module, it is important to note that related material is dealt with in other sections of the manual. This reference list will assist you to locate the material conveniently.

| Skill | Task | Module | Page |
|---|---|---|---|
| **First Steps** | | | |
| | Close a document | Before You Begin | 24 |
| | Help | Before You Begin | 16 |
| **Adjusting Settings** | | | |
| | Change page display modes | Before You Begin | 21 |
| | Page magnification | Before You Begin | 22 |
| | Page orientation | Module 3 | 149 |
| | Page margins | Module 3 | 149 |
| | Toolbars | Before You Begin | 11 |
| **Basic Functions** | | | |
| | Alignment and justification of text | Module 3 | 133 |
| | Autoshapes | Module 3 | 164 |
| | Copy, Cut, and Paste | Before You Begin | 10 |
| | Deleting text | Module 3 | 127 |
| | Formatting text | Module 3 | 131 |
| | Images, graphics and objects | Module 3 | 161 |
| | Printing | Module 3 | 143 |
| | Preview a document | Module 3 | 143 |
| | Printers, choosing | Module 3 | 145 |
| | Selecting | Before You Begin | 9 |
| | Spell Check | Before You begin | 23 |
| | Symbols and special characters | Module 3 | 124 |
| | Templates | Module 3 | 189 |
| | Undo | Module 3 | 135 |

# Section 1    Getting Started

## 1.1    Switching On

Most computers have two switches, one on the computer 'box' and another on the monitor. There may be another switch for the loudspeakers, if any. Each of these switches must be in the 'on' position, usually indicated by a coloured light.

The switches and lights on your computer may be in positions different from those in the illustration.

*Do not* touch the keyboard or mouse until you see the desktop screen (illustrated below), as this may interrupt the start-up process.

In business or training centres, you may have to enter a password before you can use the computer. Your instructor will tell you what to do.

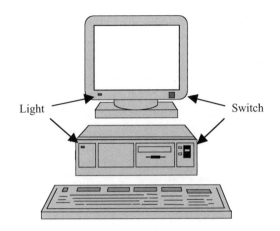

Light                                    Switch

## 1.2    The Desktop

Various items appear briefly on the screen while the computer is starting up.  Eventually the **desktop** appears.  This is a screen with a number of **icons** arranged vertically on the left and a bar, called the **Taskbar**, along the bottom.

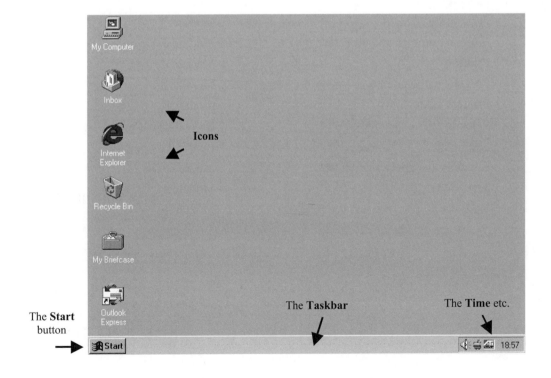

The **Taskbar** along the bottom of the screen displays various items, with the **Start** button at the left.

# 1.3    Arranging Icons

The icons on the desktop are usually arranged in a vertical line down the left side of the screen but the user can change the arrangement to suit his or her individual preferences.

- Right-click anywhere on a blank area of the desktop. A **menu** is displayed. Select **Arrange Icons** to display a sub-menu.

- Click on the different options and observe the effect as the icons are arranged by **Name**, by **Type** and so on.

- When there is a tick by **Auto Arrange** at the bottom of the menu, the computer will arrange the icons automatically.

- With **Auto Arrange** ticked, drag an icon to a different position on the desktop.

  Notice that it is always brought back to the vertical arrangement at the left of the screen.

- Click **Auto Arrange** to remove the tick, if there is one. With the tick removed, you can drag icons to any position on the desktop and they stay there. This enables you to have your own icon arrangement on the desktop.

- Clicking **Auto Arrange** again restores the tick and the icons are arranged automatically as before.

# 1.4    The Start Menu

Click the **Start** button once with the left mouse button to display the **Start** menu.

A **menu** is a list of **commands** for the computer. You can choose from a menu by moving the **pointer** over an item on it or by clicking an item with the mouse.

When you select a menu item, the computer performs an action.

A small arrowhead to the right of a menu item leads to a further sub-menu when you move the cursor over it, as illustrated here.

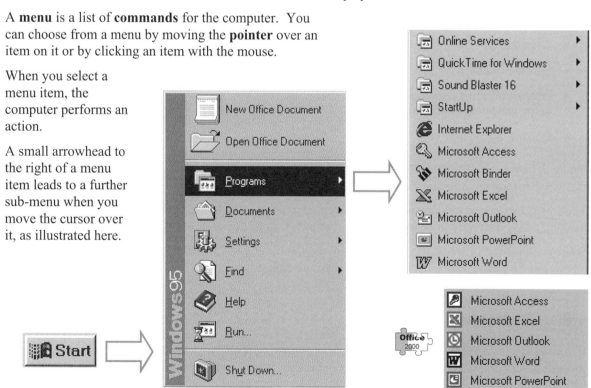

Clicking the **Start** button displays the Start menu. Moving the pointer over **Programs** – or clicking on it to hold it open – displays the **Programs** menu, a list of the programs on the computer. Items in the sub-menu may have further sub-menus. Click on the item you require to open it.

The principal items in the **Start** menu are described in this table.

| Menu item | Function |
| --- | --- |
| **Programs** | Displays a list of the programs installed on the computer. |
| **Documents** | Displays a list of the documents you have recently used. |
| **Settings** | Displays sub-menus from which you can alter various computer and printer settings. |
| **Find** | A program to help you find documents, files, folders, shared computers or mail messages. |
| **Help** | Displays a Help screen to assist you in using the computer. |
| **Run** | Manually starts a program when you type in a command. |
| **Shut Down** | Shuts down, restarts or allows you to 'log off' the computer. |

## 1.5    Shutting Down

When you have finished using the computer, you must follow a special **Shut Down** procedure.

If you switch off the computer without going through the Shut Down procedure, there will be problems the next time you switch it on. You will also lose any work that was not saved prior to switching off.

If the computer is connected to a network, you may have to disconnect from the network before shutting down. To shut down the computer, do the following.

- Click the **Start** button.

- Select **Shut Down**.

- Check that **Shut Down** is selected in the window that appears.

- Confirm by clicking **Yes**.

You will be prompted to save any work you have been doing that you have not already saved.

The computer then takes a few moments to prepare itself to be switched off. When you see the message, '**It is now safe to switch off your computer**', you can switch it off.

Some computers will automatically switch off and the message is not displayed. In most instances, the monitor and loudspeakers must be switched off separately.

## 1.6    Switching On Again

If you want to switch on the computer again after switching it off, you should wait for *at least ten seconds* before doing so. This allows all the electrical circuits in the computer to discharge completely before you switch it on again. Switching on too soon may cause problems.

Remember to wait for the desktop screen to appear before using the keyboard or mouse.

## 1.7    Restarting

Occasionally a problem may arise where the computer 'freezes' or ceases to respond to the mouse or to the keyboard.  In this case, it is necessary to force it to end the task it is engaged in or to reset itself completely.

The keyboard shortcut, pressing the keys **Ctrl + Alt + Delete** together forces the computer to end its current task if a serious problem, as outlined above, should occur.  Click **End Current Task** in the window that appears.  If more than one task is in progress, you may have to click the button repeatedly.

When the tasks have been ended, pressing **Ctrl + Alt + Delete** again restarts the computer.  Restarting the computer resets it completely.

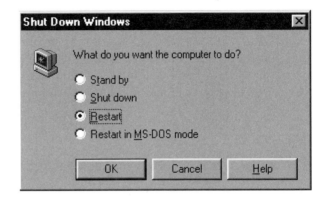

*Alternatively*, instead of selecting **Shut Down** via the **Start** menu, select **Restart** to switch off the computer momentarily and to reset it.

Remember to save your work regularly to avoid losing work when there are computer problems.

# Section 2     Windows

## 2.1     What is a Window?

A folder on the computer resembles a manila folder in real life. It is used to store documents or other items. Double-clicking the folder opens it so that we can see what is inside. What actually happens is that a panel opens on the desktop in which the contents of the folder – represented by icons – are displayed. This panel is called a **Window** – it is a 'window' through which we can see into the folder.

## 2.2     Parts of a Window

The illustration shows the **Control Panel** folder on a computer as an example of a window. The main part of the window displays the contents of the folder, only some of them in this case. Around the window, there are various aids to assist you in using the window effectively.

The **Title Bar** displays the name of the window on the left. On the right are three buttons for changing the size of the window and for closing it.

The **Menu** bar contains a number of menus that provide various options. Click on a menu name to display the menu. Click on an item in the menu to perform that particular action.

The **Scroll Arrows** appear when a window is too small to display all of its contents (as in the illustration). Click on a scroll arrow to move the contents of the window so that you can see more. Hold down the mouse button on a scroll arrow for continuous movement.

The **Slider** indicates what part of the window is presently displayed. If it is at the top, the top of the window is visible, and so on. It can be dragged to move quickly to another part of the window.

The **Status Bar** at the bottom of the window shows how many objects are in the window, whether or not they are all visible.

## 2.3    Other Windows

Computers using Windows 98 can display extra features that may be selected in the **View** menu. Here, the **Web Page** option in the menu has been selected.

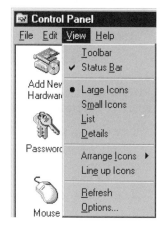

The **Address** bar displays the location – the directory path – of the file or folder (see Section 3.9, page 82).

A panel at the left of the window displays the icon for the window, as identified in the Address box, and a title in large print.

When an object in the window is selected, information about it is displayed in the panel on the left.

A toolbar displays a number of buttons, including **Cut**, **Copy**, **Paste** and **Delete**. There are also **Back** and **Forward**  buttons.

An **Up** button enables you to go to a previous level in the directory structure (see Section 3.9, page 82). You can use the Back and Forward buttons to move through the various folder levels you have already viewed.

## 2.4    Viewing Windows

The contents of a window can be displayed and arranged to suit your personal preferences.

- Click the **View** menu to display a list of options.

- The tick beside **Status Bar** indicates that the Status bar is currently displayed (at the bottom of the window).

- The bullet (large dot) beside **Large Icons** indicates that the contents of the window are currently displayed as large icons.

- Click **Toolbar(s)** to display a toolbar at the top of the window.

- In Windows 98, select in the sub-menu the items you want displayed, the Buttons and the Address bar, for example.

- Click **List** to display the contents of the window in list format, arranged – with small icons – alphabetically in columns.

- Point to **Arrange Icons** to display a sub-menu with further options. Arranging icons is described in Section 1.3, page 69.

Toolbar displayed

List View

## 2.5 Moving Windows

To reposition a window on the desktop:

- Drag the **Title** bar. Place the tip of the pointer in the Title bar, hold down the mouse button and drag. When you release the mouse button, the widow assumes its new position.

## 2.6 Resizing Windows

You can change the size of a window to suit your work. If you have several windows open at once, you may want to have the principal one large enough to work in and the others smaller so that, while you can still see their contents, all of them are visible together on the desktop.

- To change the size of a window, move the pointer slowly over the bottom right-hand corner of the window.

- When the pointer changes to a double-ended arrow, as in the illustration, drag diagonally to change the size. When you release the mouse button, the widow assumes its new shape.

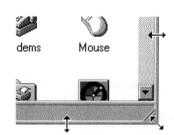

- You can drag the sides of the window in the same way to change the width or depth of a window.

## 2.7 Window Buttons

When a window is too small to display all of its contents, you can enlarge or **Maximise** it to fill the whole desktop area. This is useful where scrolling would be too tedious.

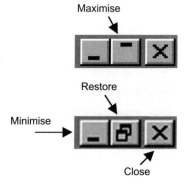

- Click the **Maximise** button at the right of the Title bar to enlarge the window to full screen size.

- When a window is maximised, the **Maximise** button becomes the **Restore** button.

- Click the **Restore** button to return the window to its previous size.

If you want to temporarily remove a window from the Desktop, you can reduce or **Minimise** it. The window closes and a button representing it appears on the Taskbar.

- Click the **Minimise** button to temporarily close a window and reduce it to a button on the Taskbar.

- To open a minimised window again, click its button on the Taskbar.

- To close a window completely, click the **Close** button.

Two sets of buttons appear in the top right-hand corner of the desktop when there is both an application open and also an open document in the application. In the illustration, there is a document open in Microsoft Word.

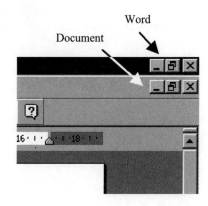

The top row of buttons controls Microsoft Word. Clicking the **Close** button will close Microsoft Word and also the document.

The lower row of buttons controls the document. Clicking the **Close** button will close the document but leave Microsoft Word open for other work. Note that in Office 2000 documents, there may be only a single **Close** button, or no lower row at all.

## 2.8    More Than one Window

It is common to have several windows open on the desktop at once but you can only work with one window at a time, although they may all be visible on the desktop.

The window you are working with is called the **Active** window.
The Title bar of the active window is in colour (usually blue) while the Title bar of an inactive window is gray.

The **My Computer** window is the active window in the illustration. It is in front of the other windows and obscures them.

- Click on a window to bring it to the front. It is then the active window.

- If you want to see the contents of two or more window at once, move them so that they do not obscure each other or resize them so that you can see the parts that you want to work with.

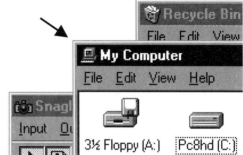

## 2.9    The Application Window

When you open an **application**, it appears on the desktop in its own window, which normally covers the whole desktop area.

A **blank document** – a 'sheet of paper' in the case of a word processor, for example – usually appears in the window when it opens.

The appearance of the window varies, depending on whether or not a document is displayed.

If there is no open document in the application window, a blank gray area appears where the document would normally appear (see page 76).

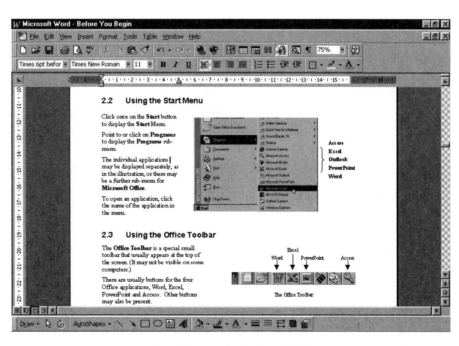

Open Document – Tools available

A selection of **menus**, **buttons** and other **tools** appears around the window.

Only some tools are displayed on the screen at any particular time although many more may be available. This makes more screen space available for your work. The hidden tools may be accessed as required by, for example, displaying more toolbars.

Notice that most of the tools are **grayed out** when there is no document displayed, as in the illustration on the right. This means that they are not available for use – you cannot use tools if there is nothing to use them on!

The document in the illustration on the previous page does not quite fill the window but it can be **enlarged** or **reduced** as required.

A smaller size lets you see more of the page but the print will be smaller. A larger size lets you see the print more clearly but not as much of the page at the same time. As you work through the course, the many features, tools and options available for different applications will be described as they are needed.

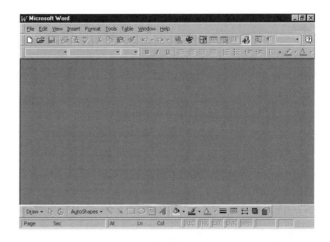

No Document – Tools grayed out.

## 2.10 More than One Document

Several documents can be open in an application window at the same time. Each document appears in its own window. Usually, only one of them is visible. The others are hidden behind the first document, like a pile of papers on a real desk.

Hidden documents can be brought to the front as required. All open documents are listed in the **Window** menu. Clicking the name of a document in the Window menu brings that document to the front.

It is also possible to have more than one document visible in the application window at the same time, but at reduced size to make them fit. In this case, they each appear in their own smaller windows.

These smaller windows, depending on their size, may overlay each other, partly or completely hiding the ones behind. A single click on the window of your choice brings it to the front. You can move in this way from window to window as your work requires.

In the illustration, there are three open documents. The selected document, **Overview**, is the document currently at the front.

With several documents open in separate windows like this, you can compare and edit the documents, transfer material from one to another, and so on.

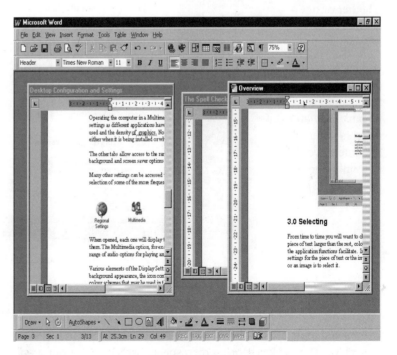

Document Windows

# Section 3        Files and Folders

## 3.1        Introduction

A **file** is an organised collection of information used by the computer, just as the files stored in the office filing cabinet are used by the office staff. The work you prepare on the computer, such as documents and so on, are files. The applications that you use to prepare your work are stored in the computer as files. The instructions the computer itself needs in order to operate are files. The user creates and adds many more files.

A **folder** in the computer is an electronic container in which files can be stored, just as manila folders are used to store files in the office filing cabinet. Folders are used to store files in an organised way. The files used to operate the computer are stored in folders. Applications, such as word processors that are used when working on the computer, are stored in folders. A folder may contain both files and other folders, just as a folder in the office filing cabinet may have other folders inside it.

When the computer needs to use a file, for its own purposes or for the user, it must find where it is stored, open it and do whatever is required. If files and folders are stored in a disorganised fashion, this will result in a slower, more disorganised computer. When the files are stored in an organised manner, the files are easier to find and the computer (and the user) can work faster.

## 3.2        Icons

Files and folders are represented on the desktop by **icons**. Icons are small pictures that identify the type of object, file, document or folder that is stored in the computer.

**File icons**

Table 1.doc        Sales Report.ppt        Order.wri

**Folder icons**

Tours        Practice        Program Files

## 3.3        Making a Folder on the Desktop

A folder can be created on the hard disk, on a floppy or other disk or in an existing folder. Here we shall make a folder, called **My Folder**, on the **desktop**. The procedure is as follows.

- Click the right mouse button in a blank area of the desktop.

- Click **New** in the menu that appears and then **Folder** in the sub-menu.

- A new folder appears on the desktop with the words **New Folder** highlighted.

- Type the name you want to give the folder. For this exercise, type **My Folder**. What you type replaces 'New Folder'.

- Press **Return** or click on the desktop when you are finished.

New Folder

To make a folder **inside** an existing folder, first open the folder. Follow the same procedure, starting with a click in a blank area in the folder window.

Do not put too many folders on the desktop as it soon becomes cluttered.

My Folder

## 3.4    Renaming a Folder

To rename a folder:

- Click the folder once to select it.  Then click once on the **name** under the folder (*not* on the folder itself).  After a brief delay, the name is highlighted.

- Type the new name, **Helen's Folder**, for example.

- Press **Return** or click on the desktop when you are finished.

Here is another way to rename a folder.

- Right-click on the folder. A menu appears.

- Click **Rename**.  The name of the folder is highlighted.

- Type the new name, for example **Helen's Folder**.

## 3.5    Making a Folder using My Computer

Clicking the **My Computer** icon on the desktop opens a window that displays the disk drives and some folders.  You can use My Computer to make a folder anywhere on the computer, for example on one of the disks.  Double-click **My Computer** to open its window.

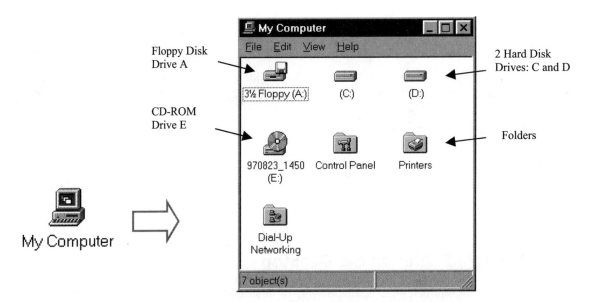

To make a folder on the hard disk (C:), double-click the (C:) icon.  A window opens in which the contents of the disk are displayed.  (The contents of your window may be different.)

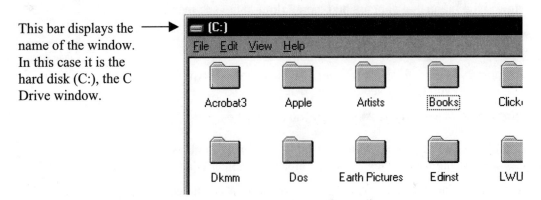

This bar displays the name of the window. In this case it is the hard disk (C:), the C Drive window.

Create a new folder called **Office** on the hard disk (C:). The process is similar to making a folder on the desktop, as described already.

- Right-click in a blank area of the hard disk window.

- Point to **New** in the menu that appears.

- Click **Folder** in the next menu, the **New** menu.
  A new folder icon appears in the window.
  The words **New Folder** are highlighted, which means that you can type a new name over them if you wish.

- Type **Office** as the name for the folder.

- Press **Return** or click on the desktop when you are finished.

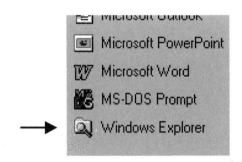

### Practise

Rename the folder you have just created as **My Work**.


## 3.6    Windows Explorer

**Windows Explorer** is a program that gives you a more comprehensive view of the computer's contents than My Computer. You should become familiar with it.

To open Windows Explorer:

- Click **Start.**

- Point to, or click, **Programs** to display the Programs menu.

- Click **Windows Explorer** (it is usually at the bottom of the menu).

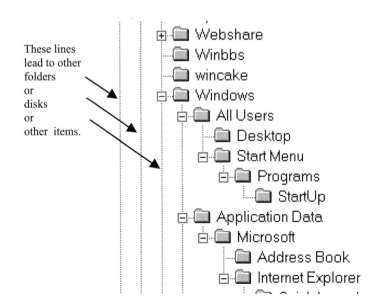

The illustration below shows a set of folders in the **Windows Explorer** window, some of which have been opened to show other folders inside (branching out to the right).

Notice the + and − signs in the little boxes.

When a folder is preceded by a plus (+) it indicates that there are more items inside it.

- Click the plus box (**+**) to display the contents of the folder.

- Click the minus (**−**) box to close an open folder.

Notice the lines that join the folders vertically and horizontally. These help the user to navigate the structure of the hard disk, like a family tree.

These lines lead to other folders or disks or other items.

Double-click a folder to display its contents in the right-hand part of the window. It is then possible to see any files or other folders it contains and to make new folders there, if required.

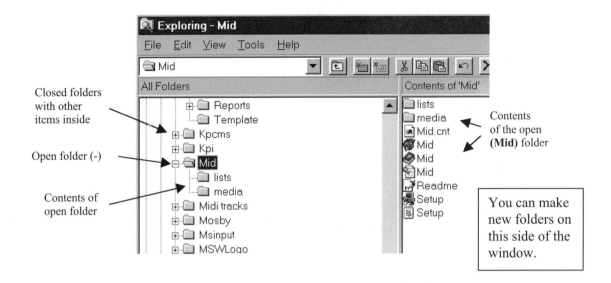

Closed folders with other items inside

Open folder (-)

Contents of open folder

Contents of the open (**Mid**) folder

You can make new folders on this side of the window.

# 3.7    Making a Folder using Windows Explorer

To make a folder named **Income Tax** on the **hard disk**, follow these steps.

- Open **Windows Explorer** as described above. Check that the contents of the hard disk are displayed. (Your computer may be different from the illustration.)

- Click with the right mouse button in the right (Contents) side of the window.

- Click **New** in the menu that appears.

- Click **Folder** in the **New** menu.

  A new folder appears, with the words **New Folder** highlighted. This indicates that you may type your own title to replace **New Folder**.

- Type **Income Tax**. It will replace **New Folder.**

- Press **Return** or click on the desktop when you are finished.

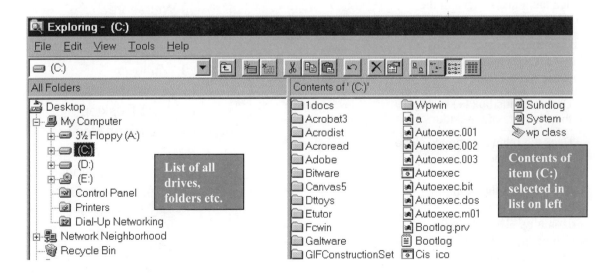

List of all drives, folders etc.

Contents of item (C:) selected in list on left

## 3.8    Making a Folder from within a Program

You may sometimes need to make a new folder while you are working on a project.  In this section, we shall open **Notepad**, a simple word-editing program.  We shall type a few words and save the file in a folder that we will create on the hard disk.

Proceed as follows.

- Click the **Start** button and go via Programs and Accessories to Notepad.

- Click on **Notepad** to open it.

- Type a piece of text such as your name and address.

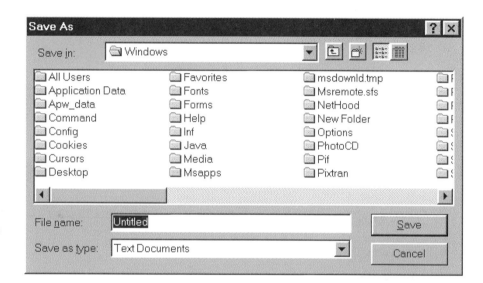

This document must now be saved as **My Details**.

It will be placed in a folder named **Myself** which we shall first create on the hard disk.

To create the **Myself** folder, follow these steps.

- Select **Save** in the **File** menu.
  The **Save As** window opens.

The **Save As** window in Office 2000 has a panel on the left containing buttons for frequently used items.

- The folder in the **Save in** box  (**Windows** in the Ilustrations) is very often *not* where we want to save the document.

- Click in the **Save in** box to display a menu to help you select where you want to save the file.

  In Office 2000, you can click the **Desktop** button in the panel on the left.

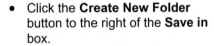
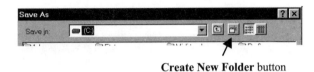

- Click the hard disk **(C:)** icon in the menu that appears.

- The hard disk icon now appears in the **Save in** window.

- Click the **Create New Folder** button to the right of the **Save in** box.

  A new folder icon appears.

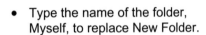

**Create New Folder** button

- Type the name of the folder, Myself, to replace New Folder.

- Double-click on the new folder, **Myself**, to open it.

- The **Myself** folder icon now appears in the **Save in** box.

- Type **My Details** in the **File name** box.

- Click the **Save** button.

- The file **My Details** is now saved in a new folder named **Myself** on the hard disk.

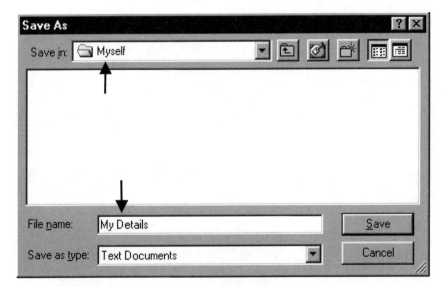

- Close **Notepad** if you do not want to prepare any more documents. (Saving is described in detail in Section 4, page 84.)

## 3.9    The Directory Structure

The **folders** on the computer's hard disk are also known as **directories**. Although they are all on the same hard disk, you can think of them as being on different levels, something like a family tree.

The first level is the hard disk (C:) itself – one big folder that contains everything else. For this reason it is referred to as the **root** directory.

When you make a folder or save a file directly on **C:**, you are placing it in the root directory – on the first level.

When another folder or file is **inside** a folder on the root directory, it is on the second level.

An item inside a second-level folder is on the third level, and so on.

When you use **Windows Explorer**, the levels are displayed as illustrated here. The vertical lines represent the different levels, branching out – left and right – from C:, the root directory.

The directories **Webshare**, **Winbbs**, **wincake** and **Windows** all branch out from C:, which means that they are *in* the root directory.

The directories **All Users** and **Application Data** branch off to the right – to the next level – from the **Windows** directory. This means that the are *in* the Windows directory.

The **All Users** directory contains two other directories (on the next level), **Desktop** and **Start Menu**, and so on.

The route from C: to a folder or file is called the **directory path**. It is a way of describing exactly where the folder or file is on the hard disk.

The path from **C:** to the **Start Menu** folder, for example, is written as follows (a backward slash separates the levels):

**C:\Windows\All Users\Start Menu**

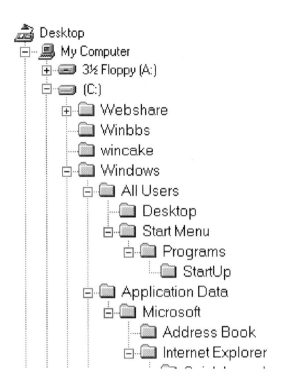

Module 2

# Section 4      Saving

## 4.1     Saving a Document or File

Any work you produce on the computer must be saved or it will cease to exist when the computer is switched off.   You normally save your work on the computer's hard disk.  The hard disk is the central storage area of the computer and is generally the safest and most reliable place for your work.  You can also save your work on a floppy disk, on a Zip disk or other media.

The names **document** and **file** are used interchangeably.  A **file** is any kind of work you produce on the computer, whether it is a one-page letter or a database with thousands of records.  You might prefer to reserve **document** for something that can be printed out – but remember that a document is also a file.

The procedure for saving a document or file for the first time is different from saving changes to it afterwards.  The first time you save a document (or file), the computer needs to know two important pieces of information:

- What is  the name of the file?

- Where do you want to save the file?

In the following parts of this Section, we shall prepare a document, give it a name and save it in a particular location.  Begin by completing Exercise 4A.

## Exercise 4A

Use the skills you have learnt above to do the following.

- Make three folders on the hard disk, **Letters**, **Bank** and **Business**.

- Make three other folders, **National Bank**, **Equity Bank** and **Bahamas Bank** inside the **Bank** folder.

- Prepare a short letter in **Notepad**, addressed to the **Equity Bank**.  (A few words will do.)
  How to save the letter is described step-by-step in the following sections.

## 4.2     Giving a File a Name

The Save Button

To save a document or file for the **first time**, begin by using **one** of the following.

- Click the **Save** button (the one with the floppy disk icon) on the toolbar.

- Select **Save** in the **File** menu.

- Use the keyboard shortcut.
  (Hold down the **Ctrl** key while you press the letter **S** on the keyboard.)

Whichever method you use, the **Save As** window opens.

- The appliciation may have already inserted a name in the **File name** box.

  This is rarely suitable and it is already **highlighted** so that you can change it by typing a new name.

  (You do *not* have to click in the box first.)

  For this exercise, type **Equity Letter**.

  Whatever you type will replace anything that may be in the box.

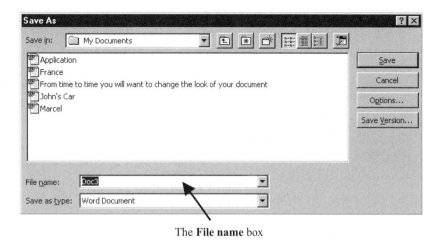

The **File name** box

(If you do click in the box first, you will have to delete what is there before you start typing.)

- **Tip:** Use **meaningful** file names that you will remember when you want to find them again later.

## 4.3    Where are Files Saved?

If you click the **Save** button after you have given the file a name, the computer saves it for you… but where?  If you do not know where the computer saves your file, you will have trouble finding it again when you want to re-open it.

There are two areas where the computer might save your file, in a folder called **My Documents** or in whatever **folder that was last used** to save files in.

**The first area** – the **My Documents** folder – is intended as an 'easy' option for beginners.
The computer is set to save everything in it unless instructed to do otherwise.

**The second area** where the computer might save your file is the folder used the last time a file was saved.  This may have been the **My Documents** folder, but it may just as well have been **any other folder** on the hard disk – whatever was chosen by the last user.

To save your work in an organised way, you should set up folders for the principal subject areas of your work.  For this exercise, we have already set up the various Bank folders.

> Saving everything in the **My Documents** folder is equivalent to saving all your work and documents in a single drawer in your office desk instead of using the filing cabinet.  It may suffice while you have only a few documents, but it will become chaotic very quickly as your work accumulates.

## 4.4    Finding Where to Save

The Save in box

The area where *the computer* is set to save your file is shown in the **Save in** box at the top of the **Save As** window (**My Documents** in the illustration).

To save in another location, you must first find the area or folder in which you want the file to be saved.

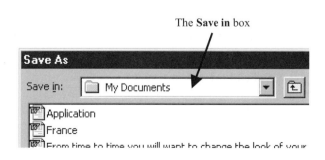

- Click once in the **Save in** box to display a menu of possible locations.

  In Office 2000, you can also click the **Desktop** button in the panel on the left of the window to display a similar menu in the main part of the window.

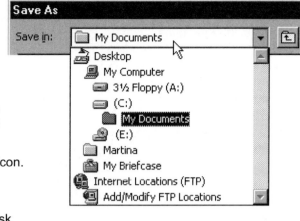

- Among other icons listed in the menu are those for the **Desktop**, the **Floppy** disc drive (A:) and the **Hard Disk** (C:).

  - To save on the **Desktop**, click the Desktop icon.

  - To save on a **Floppy** disc, click the Floppy icon (A:).

  - To save on the **Hard Disk**, click the Hard Disk icon (C:).

  The location you select will appear in the **Save in** box.

- As the **Bank** folder is on the hard disk, click the **Hard Disk** icon.

  The **Hard Disk** icon now appears in the **Save in** box.

  The contents of the hard disk appear in the main part of the window underneath.

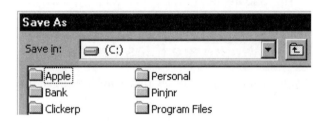

- Scroll through the folders on the hard disk, if necessary, to find the **Bank** folder.

- Double-click the **Bank** folder to open it.

  The **Bank** folder icon now appears in the **Save in** box with its contents displayed in the main part of the window underneath.

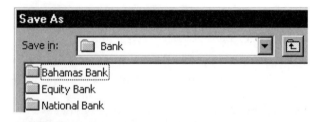

- Double-click the **Equity Bank** folder.

  The **Equity Bank** folder now appears in the **Save in** box with its contents (if any) displayed in the window.

  This is where we want to save the **Equity Letter**.

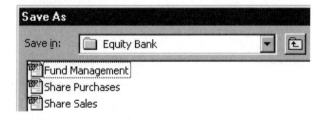

## 4.5   Pressing the Save Button

Before you press the **Save** button, you should ask yourself these two questions:

- Have I given my file a name?

- Is the location where I want to save my file shown in the **Save in** box?

If the answer to both these questions is **Yes**, you can click the **Save** button at the top right (bottom right in Office 2000) of the **Save As** window.

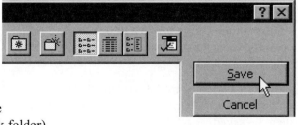

Your file is then saved with the name **you** have give and in the location of **your** choice (the **Equity Bank** folder).

## 4.6    Saving Again

When you save a document for the **first** time, you have to give it a name and tell the computer where you want to save it, as described above.

As you work on a document, you need to **save** it at regular intervals.  To save the document **again** after you have added to it or made other changes, use one of the same methods as before.

- Click the **Save button**.
- Select **Save** in the **File** menu.
- Use the **Keyboard shortcut** (Ctrl + S).

This time, however, the **Save As** window does not appear.  You have already given the document a name and told the computer where it is to be saved, so it does not need to ask you for this information again.  Your document is saved without disturbing you and your work is not interrupted.

If the document or file is very large, however, you may see a **Progress bar** on the screen telling you that it is being saved.  You will then have to wait a moment or two for it to finish saving before you can continue using the application.

## 4.7    Using Save As

**Save As** is used when you want to save a **copy** of a document or file under a different **name**, in a different **location** or in another **format**.

A notice for a meeting in May – called **Meeting May**, for example – may require only minor changes for the June meeting.  To save time typing out a new notice, you can edit the old one, as follows.

- Open **Meeting May**.
- Make the changes.
- Select **Save As** in the **File** menu.  The **Save As** window opens.
- Change the name in the **File name** box to **Meeting June**.

  (If you want to save the document in a different location, select the new location in the **Save in** box as described in Section 4.4 above, page 85.)

- Click **Save**.

A new copy of the document is saved with the name **Meeting June** and the new name appears on the **title** bar.  Any further work you do is now done on the new **Meeting June** file.

The original **Meeting May** document remains unchanged where it was originally saved.

## 4.8    Saving in Different Formats

When you send a document or file to another person, they may not be able to use it if they are not using the same kind of computer and software that you used to prepare it.  You should check with the recipient in advance.  Then, if possible, you can save your work in a format they can use.

- Go through the **Save** process as before until the **Save As** window appears.

- Click in the **Save as type** box to display a list of available formats.

  **PowerPoint** Save options are shown on the right as an example.

  (The list on your computer may differ from those in the illustration.)

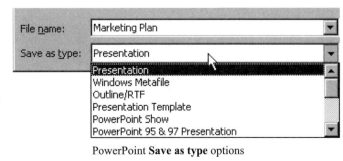

PowerPoint **Save as type** options

- **Word** options are shown here.
  For word processing documents, select the word processor your recipient uses, if it appears in the list.

  - For someone with Microsoft Office 95, using Word 6.0, select **Word 6.0/95**.

  - Select the appropriate **Word Perfect** option for a Word Perfect user.

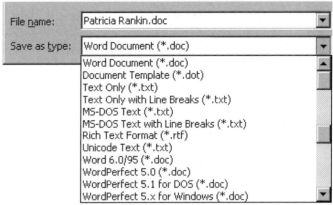

Word **Save as type** options

Some other options are described here.

**Rich Text Format** (RTF) can be used by most word processors. It preserves common formatting options such as text size, bold, italic and so on but will not be able to reproduce some more advanced formatting.

**Text Only** saves the file as plain text. Any formatting in the original document is discarded but the recipient will at least have access to the text that can then be inserted into other documents and reformatted if necessary. This format can be used by any word processor.

Select **Template** (Document, Presentation etc.) to save a document in a format that preserves its formatting for further use. Word templates are described in detail in Module 3, Section 16, page 189.

## 4.9    Saving for the World Wide Web

Documents intended for publication on the **World Wide Web** – on the **Internet** – have to be saved in a special format. The computer language used for documents on the Web is called HTML (see Module 7, page 336). Microsoft Office allows you to save simple documents in this format and they can then be made available to other people on a Web site.

Documents may be saved in HTML format in two ways.

Using the **File** menu:

- Select **Save as HTML** in the **File** menu.
  You are asked to give the file a name and say where it is to be saved.
  You are also advised to save the document first as a Word file, as some formatting may be lost in the conversion process.

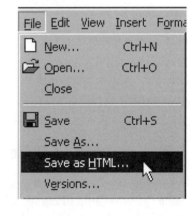

Using **Save As**:

- Select **Save As** in the **File** menu.
  The **Save As** window opens.

- Select **HTML Document** (**Web Page** in Office 2000) in the **Save as type** box.
  You are asked to give the file a name etc, as above.

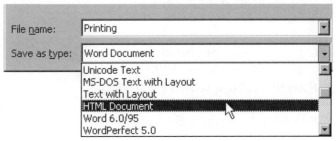

# 4.10    Saving Options

Various options for saving your work are available to suit individual preferences.

- Select **Options** in the **Tools** menu.
- The Options window opens.
- Click the **Save** tab to display the **Save options**.

Select an option you require, by clicking it to place a tick in the box. To turn off an option, click it to remove the tick.

Some of the options available in Word are described here. Similar options are available in the other Office Applications.

**Always create backup copy** saves a second copy of your work every time you save. If the original copy is damaged, your work is not lost.

**Allow fast saves** speeds up the saving process. Instead of saving the whole document every time you save, the program only saves the additions or changes you made since you last saved and adds them to the previously saved version. This causes the size of the file to increase every time you save. For most users, this can be switched off.

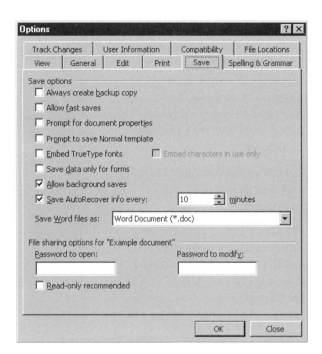

**Allow background saves** enables you to continue using the computer while your work is being saved. For most users, this will be of little significance but more memory is needed to allow background saving. Switching this off will make more memory available to the work in hand.

**Save AutoRecover info every** automatically saves your work at intervals, as specified in the box. In the event of a computer crash or a power cut, only work done since the last AutoRecover save is lost.

# 4.11    Opening a Saved Document or File

To open a saved document or file, do *one* of the following.

Open

- Click the **Open button** on the toolbar.
- Select **Open** in the **File** menu.
- Use the **Keyboard shortcut**.
  (Hold down the **Control** key while you press the letter **O** on the keyboard.)

The **Open** window appears, similar to the **Save as** window used when you were saving the file.

Find the file you want to open in the same way as you found the folder to **Save** in, as described in Section 4.4, page 85.

The **Open** window

- When the file is displayed in the main part of the **Open** window, double-click it to open it.
  *Alternatively*, click it once to select it and then click the **Open** button.

## 4.12   Office 2000 Windows

The **Open** window in Office
2000 is similar to the **Save as**
window used when you were
saving the file with the same
buttons in a panel on the left.
(See the **Save As** window on
page 81 and the similar button
bar below).

The last folder used appears in
the **Look in** box at the top of
the window.

The **Open** button (and the **Save**
button in the **Save As** window)
is at the bottom right instead of
at the top right in earlier
versions of Office.

A panel at the left of the window has a number of large buttons.
Click a button to display information in the main part of the window.

> The **History** button lists the most recently used files and folders.
> File details, such as size, when last modified and so on are displayed.

> My **Documents** is the folder in which the computer saves your work
> unless you decide to save it elsewhere.

> The **Desktop** button displays what is on the Desktop.  You may find this
> more convenient than clicking in the **Look in** or **Save in** box at the top of
> the window.

> The **Favourites** and **Web Folders** icons relate directly to work being
> prepared or exchanged between the various Office and Web applications.

# Section 5      Finding Files

## 5.1      File Names and Extensions

The name of a file is in two parts, the **name** itself and the **extension**. They are separated by a dot (full stop) with no spaces. An extension is a set of three letters that tells the computer the **kind** of file it is.

The **File Name** is the name you give the file when you save it. The extension is usually added automatically when you save a file. You do not have to type it in.

Each application has its own extension. The extension for a PowerPoint file is **.ppt** and the extension for an Access database file is **.mdb**, for example. The extension **.doc** in the illustration means that this is a Microsoft Word file – a document.

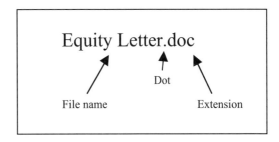

File Name and Extension

When you double-click a file icon, the computer uses the extension to identify the application it needs to open the file. Thus **.doc** files are opened by Microsoft Word, **.ppt** files are opened by PowerPoint and so on.

Note that extensions, while always present, may not always be displayed by some computers.

## 5.2      Lost Files

It is easy to forget where you saved a document or file in your computer. A program called **Find** lets you use various search criteria to find 'lost' files or folders.

Open the **Find** program as follows.

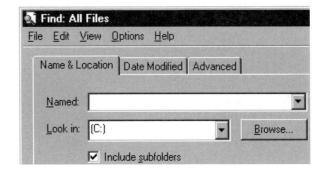

- Click on the **Start** button, select **Find** and then **Files and Folders** in the sub-menu.

- The **Find: All Files** window opens.

Part of the **Find** window is shown here.

It is possible to search for files in many ways, depending on your requirements.

## 5.3      Searches

To search for a file by name, you need to know the name of the file you are looking for. (Remember to give your files meaningful names when you are saving them.)

Type the name of the file you want to find in the **Named** box. If necessary, you can specify a particular area for the search in the **Look in** box. Click the **Find Now** button to start the search. The files found during the search are displayed at the bottom of the search window. The number of found files is shown on the Status Bar (see the illustration in Section 5.5, page 93).

Each search is unique. After your first search, you must click the **New Search** button to perform other searches.

## 5.4    Wildcard Searches

If you cannot remember the exact name of the file, you can use a **wildcard** search.  This means that you can type in the letters you know and use the wildcard character – a single asterisk – to represent the other letters.

Here are some examples of wildcard searches.  Try them on your computer.  Ensure that **Include subfolders** at the bottom of the window is ticked.  This includes folders inside other folders in the search.

- Type **\*.doc** in the **Named** box.

  The **\*** symbol is a **wildcard** symbol meaning 'anything'.

- Click the **Find Now** button.

  The program searches the entire hard disk for all files with the extension **.doc**.

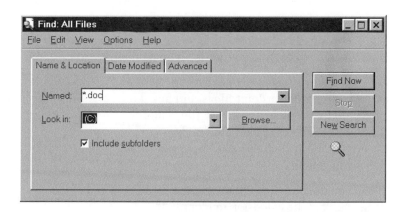

As .doc is the extension used by Microsoft Word, the search finds all the Word documents on the computer.

- Click the **New Search** button.

- Type **win\*.exe** in the **Named** box.

- Click **Find Now**.

This searches for all files that start with **win** and have the extension **.exe**.

It finds files with names such as windows, winston, winifred and so on, with the **.exe** extension.

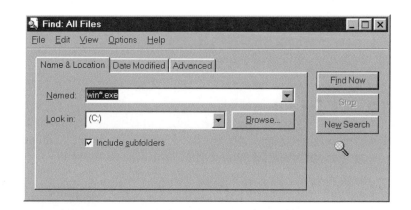

When searching for a file or folder, you may not always need to search through everything on the computer.

- Click the **Browse** button in the **Find** window to confine your search to a particular folder, drive or other area.

  Use the scroll arrows if necessary.

- Click the item to which you want to confine the search to select it.

- Click **OK**.

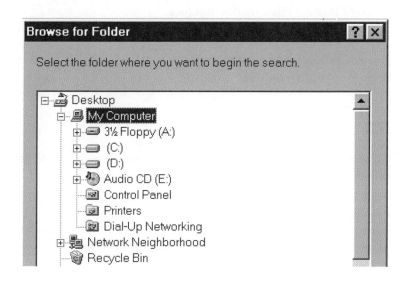

## 5.5    Advanced Searches

The **Advanced** feature in the **Find** window allows you to be more specific in your searches.

This example searches for the location of files that contain the word **multimedia.**

- Click the **Advanced** tab in the **Find** window.

- Type **multimedia** in the **Containing text** box.

- Click **Find Now**.

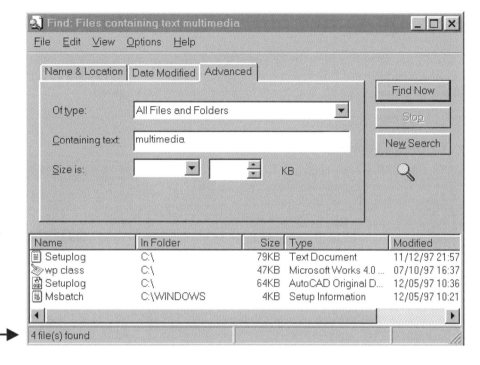

Number of files found → 4 file(s) found

The next example finds all the files created or changed between 9th October 1997 and 7th January 1998.  This kind of search is useful when you cannot remember the name of a file but you know approximately when you worked on it.  (The small round buttons are known as **radio buttons**.)

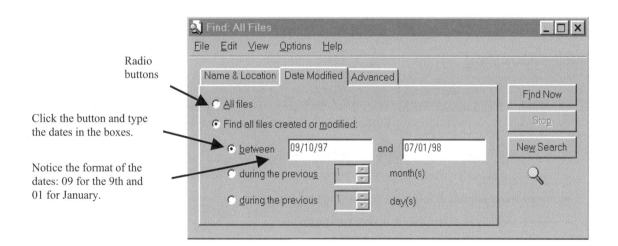

When a file has been located by any of these searches, it may be opened from inside the window.

For example, double-clicking on **wp class** in the list of found files above would open the appropriate application and display the file.

# Section 6      Working with Files and Folders

## 6.1    Selecting

Before you can work with a file or folder on the desktop or in a window, you must select it first. This tells the computer that this object (file or folder) is the one with which you now want to do something. When an item is selected, its icon changes colour or is **highlighted**.

You can select a single object or several objects at once.

- To select a single object, click on it once.

- To select several objects anywhere in a window or on the desktop, hold down the **Ctrl** key while you click on them in turn.

- To select several files or folders that are beside each other, you can **lasso** them to save time.

  Hold down the mouse button, click in a blank space and drag to make a rectangular lasso over the icons. Note that the lasso does not have to enclose the objects: anything it touches will be selected.

- To select all the files and folders in a window, click **Select All** in the **Edit** menu or use the keyboard shortcut, **Control + A**.

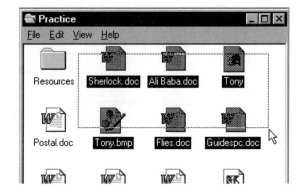

Lasso selection

When more than one file or folder has been selected, they can all be copied, moved, deleted, and so on, together. Dragging any one of the selected items moves them all.

- To deselect a group of items, click in a blank space.

## 6.2    Copying

From time to time, you may need to make a copy of a file or folder – to place a copy of a document in another folder, for example. In this section, we will copy the file **My Details** – in the **Myself** folder on the hard disk **C:** – to the folder **My Folder** that you created earlier on the desktop. Follow these steps.

- Open **My Computer** and locate the **Myself** folder.

- Open the **Myself** folder and find the file to be copied (**My Details**).

- Open the destination folder by double-clicking **My Folder**.

- Right-click on **My Details**. A menu appears.

- Click **Copy** in the menu.

- Place the pointer in the **My Folder** window and right-click.

- Click on **Paste** in the menu that appears.

- A copy of the file should now be visible in the **My Folder** window.

> When a file is **copied**, the original remains where it is and a **copy** is placed in the new location. This means that there are now two copies of the file on the disk.

## 6.3    Moving

In this section, you will move the folder **My Folder** from the desktop and place it in the folder **Myself** on the hard disk (C:). Follow these steps.

- Locate the folder to be moved, **My Folder**.
- Use **My Computer** to locate and open the **C:** window.
- Double-click the **Myself** folder to open it.
- Right-click **My Folder**. A menu appears.
- Select **Cut** from the menu.
- Place the pointer in the hard disk window and right-click.
- Choose **Paste** from the menu that appears.
- The file now appears in the hard disk window.

> When a file is **moved**, the original is **removed** from its old location and placed in a new location. There is only **one** copy of the file on the disk.

## 6.4    Moving with Drag and Drop

Another method of moving a file or folder is **Drag and Drop**. This involves using the mouse to drag the item to its new location (see **Before You Begin**, Section 1.5, page 5).

Here you will drag the folder **Myself** from the hard disk window to the **desktop**.

- Use **Windows Explorer** to locate the **Myself** folder that is to be moved.
- Click on the **Myself** folder icon *and keep the mouse button down*.
- Keeping the left mouse button pressed, move the mouse so that the folder moves out of the window onto the desktop as you move the mouse.
- Release the mouse button. The file appears on the desktop.

## 6.5    Shortcuts

A **shortcut** is a special kind of icon that allows you to perform an action without having to go through the usual procedure, such as opening menus and sub-menus.

If you have a folder on the hard disk that you use often, you can make a shortcut to it on the desktop, as follows.

- Use **My Computer** to find the folder on the hard disk (C:).
- Right-click on the folder icon. A menu appears.
- Click **Create Shortcut**. A copy of the icon – the Shortcut – appears.
- Drag the icon onto the desktop.

Notice that the Shortcut icon has a little arrow in the bottom left-hand corner to indicate that it is a Shortcut, not the original item. Also, the name is **Shortcut to...**.

Double-click the shortcut icon to open the folder directly from the desktop.

Practice    Shortcut to Practice

## 6.6    Renaming

A file or shortcut may be renamed in the same manner as a folder, as described in detail above.

> **File Names:** Files should have unique names. Two files with the same name will cause problems and you may lose data. Be careful not to duplicate names when renaming files.

## 6.7    Deleting

If a file or folder is no longer required, it can be removed from the computer. There are two methods you can use:

- **Drag and Drop** can be used as described above.
  To delete, drag the item to the **Recycle Bin**.
- Select the file or folder and press the **Delete** key.

Recycle Bin

In the following exercise, we shall delete the folder **Myself** from the desktop.

- Click the **Myself** folder icon to select it.
- Press the **Delete** key on the keyboard. A window appears.
- Click **Yes** to answer the **Are you sure...** question.

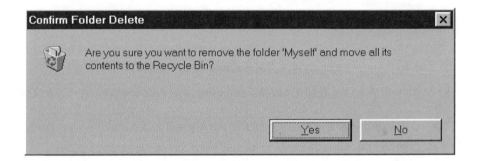

(Note that the folder itself is discarded when its contents are moved to the recycle bin.)

> **Deleting:** Deleted files and the contents of folders are not actually removed from the computer immediately – they are placed in the **Recycle Bin** and remain there until it is emptied.
>
> Even though the folder **Myself** and its contents have been 'deleted', the contents are actually in the Recycle Bin. This gives you one last chance to retrieve them before emptying the bin.
>
> Note that files deleted from a floppy disk are discarded immediately and cannot be retrieved.

## 6.8    Retrieving and Restoring

If you find that you still need something that you have deleted or dragged to the recycle bin, you can retrieve it if the recycle bin has not been emptied.

To retrieve an item from the recycle bin:

- Double-click the **Recycle Bin** icon to open it.
- Locate the file you want.
- Drag it out of the recycle bin onto the desktop or into an appropriate folder.

Another way to retrieve deleted items is to use the **Restore** command. To retrieve the **Myself** folder from the **recycle bin**, follow these steps:

- Double-click the **Recycle Bin** icon to open it.
- Locate the file **My Details** in the window. (Notice that the folder **Myself** does not appear.)
- Click on **My Details** to highlight it.
- Click **Restore** in the Recycle Bin **File** menu.
- The folder reappears on the desktop with the file **My Details** inside.

You can use restored files immediately in the normal manner.

## 6.9    Emptying the Recycle Bin

Items placed in the recycle bin remain there until it is emptied.

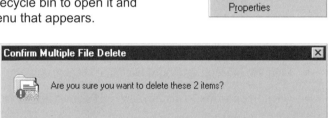

- To empty the recycle bin, right-click on it and select **Empty Recycle Bin** from the menu that appears.
- *Alternatively*, you can double click the recycle bin to open it and select **Empty Recycle Bin** from the menu that appears.
- An **Are you sure…** window asks you to confirm that you want to delete the contents of the bin.
- If you wish to change your mind at this stage, click **No** and you can retrieve files as described above.
- To empty the bin, click **Yes**.

## 6.10   Deleting and Security

Even when you empty the recycle bin, the data is **still** not removed from the computer although it is lost to the normal user. What the computer does is to change its hard disk contents list and now marks the area where the data is stored as 'empty'.

The data remains in the 'empty' area until the computer is looking for space on the hard disk to store new data. If it decides that the 'empty' area is suitable, it will replace the old data with the new. It is only then that the old data is erased.

> Imagine having an old music tape that you are no longer interested in. You mentally mark it as being blank – available for taping new material when the occasion presents itself. It is only when you tape new music over the old that the original is erased. Even then, some of the old music may remain, depending on the amount of new music you recorded.

Special recovery programs and utilities may be used to retrieve data even when the recycle bin has been emptied. These may be able to rescue important data that has been accidentally deleted or that has been made unavailable because of a major computer breakdown. They can also be used by police and security services to recover information that may help them in their investigations.

For security-sensitive work, programs are available that wipe the 'blank' areas of the hard disk by recording random material over all 'deleted' data, thus ensuring that the information no longer exists.

# Section 7    Looking at Files and Folders

## 7.1    File and Folder Information

A file or folder occupies space in the computer's memory or on a disk. The space is measured in **bytes**. The larger the file or document, the more bytes are used.

Each file or folder created on a computer contains extra identifying information unique to itself. You can see this information by right-clicking the file or folder icon.

The illustration below shows details of a Microsoft Excel file – the school timetable described in Module 4 – that was saved on the hard disk. You can use this or any other file that you have saved to see how information about the file is displayed. (The **.xls** or other extension may not be displayed on some computers.)

- If the file is on the desktop, skip the next two steps.

- Double-click the **My Computer** icon.

- Double-click the **hard disk** (**C:**) icon (or other icon depending on where you saved the file).

- Find the file icon and right-click it to display a menu.

- Click **Properties** to display the file **Properties** window.

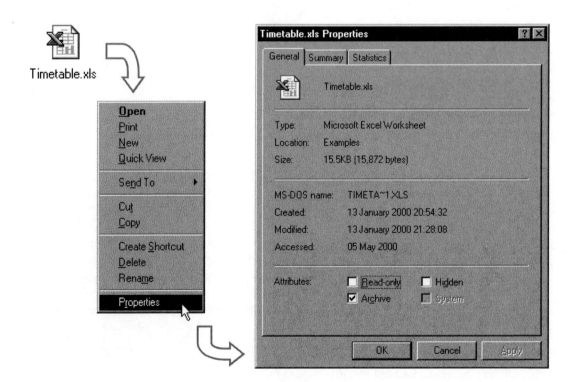

The name and size of the file are shown, as are the creation and modification dates. (The details on your computer may be different.)

Click the tabs at the top of the window to display other information.

Right-click on any other file or folder and select **Properties** to display a similar window for that particular file or folder.

This table describes some of the details displayed in the **Properties** window.

| Type | Identifies the kind of file. |
|---|---|
| **Location** | Shows the disk drive and folder where the file is located. |
| **Size** | The size in bytes (or Kilobytes, if applicable). |
| **MS-DOS name** | The MS-DOS name used by the computer. |
| **Created** | The date and time the file was first created. |
| **Modified** | The date and time the file was last modified. |
| **Accessed** | The date the file is being accessed. |

Click the tabs along the top of the window for more information.

Different information will be displayed for different files.

The illustration below shows the top of the **Properties** window for a **Microsoft Word** file. Find a Microsoft Word file on your computer and open the **Properties** window. Then click the **Summary** and **Statistics** tabs in turn to display information unique to that particular file.

## 7.2    File Icons

Files are displayed graphically on the screen by small icons. Each program or application has a unique icon for its files so that you can recognise the kind of file immediately.

The names underneath are those give by the users. 'Birthday', for example, would perhaps be the name given to a birthday letter. Office 2000 icons are on the right in left-hand group.

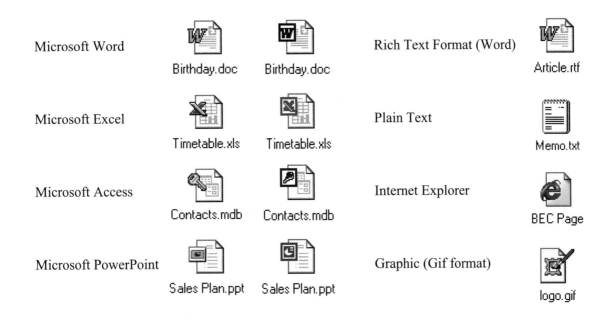

---

# Section 8      Floppy Disks

## 8.1    Formatting

Before a floppy disk can be used for the first time, it must be **formatted** to suit the computer's operating system.  This prepares the disk for use with the particular type of computer you are using.  The two common formats are IBM-compatible and Macintosh.

Disks can be purchased pre-formatted.  If you buy unformatted disks, the following procedure should be used to format them before they can be used.

- Double-click the **My Computer** icon to open the My Computer window.

- Click the $3^1/_2$ **Floppy (A:)** icon once to select it.

- Click **Format** in the *My Computer* **File** menu.

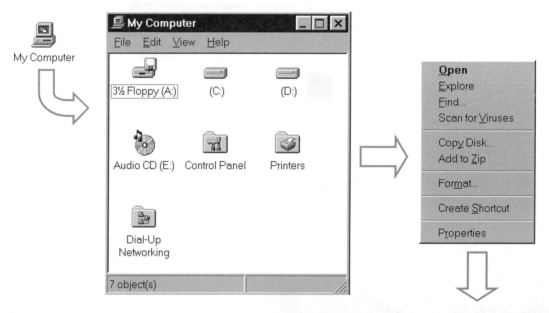

- The **Format** window gives a choice of format types.

  - **Quick (erase)** deletes data from disks that have already been formatted.  Use it when you want to recycle previously used floppy disks.

  - **Full** formats new (unformatted) disks so that you can use them in the computer.  (The computer will not recognise unformatted floppy disks.)

  - **Copy system files only** copies certain computer files, ignoring data. (Not commonly used.)

- Click the **Format type** you require.

- Click the **Start** button in the window to format the disk.

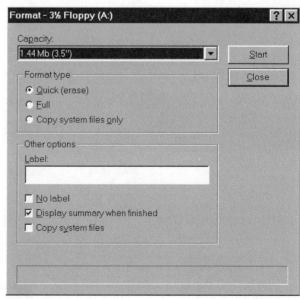

The Options in the lower part of the Format window are described in this table.

| Label | Type a name for the disk here. |
|---|---|
| No label | Click if you do not want a label. |
| Display summary when finished | Show the results of the formatting process. |
| Copy system files | Copies certain files in addition to data files. |

The **Format Results** window displays the result of the formatting process.

Formatting divides the disk into a large number of electronic areas – called **sectors** – in which the computer can store data.

In the formatting process, all data (if any) previously on the disk is erased. Be sure that you do not need any existing data if you are reformatting a used floppy disk.

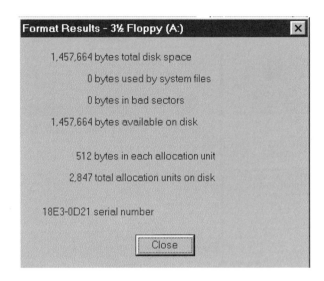

**Warning**

Do not format your hard disk – all the System and other files will be deleted and the computer will be unusable.

## 8.2    Floppy Disk Care

Floppy disks should be looked after properly or data can be lost and/or corrupted. Proper care will help to prevent problems. Remember the following when handling floppy disks.

- Keep disks away from things that have magnets or magnetic fields such as radios, TV sets, loudspeakers, mobile phones etc.

- Keep disks away from sources of extreme temperatures, moisture or dust.

- Do not touch the magnetic disk contained inside the plastic casing.

- Before inserting a disk into the drive, check it for damage.

- Always keep disks in a box designed for disk storage.

## 8.3    Security

Use the **security tab** to prevent data being accidentally erased from a disk. The tab is a small plastic slider on the underside of the disk, beside one of the two small square holes in the corners.

When the tab is closed – you **cannot** see through the hole – you can use the disk normally.

When the slider is open – you **can** see through the hole – the disk is locked and data on the disk cannot be altered by the computer, nor can you save on the disk. The disk is now **write protected**.

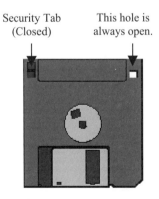

Security Tab        This hole is
(Closed)            always open.

**Warning**:  Floppy disks are easily corrupted and may fail at any moment for no apparent reason. Never work with, or store, important data on floppy disks **only**. Always save on the hard disk first.

## 8.4    Disk Information

From time to time, it may be necessary to find out how much free space is left on a disk.  To check a disk, right-click the disk icon and click **Properties** in the menu that appears.

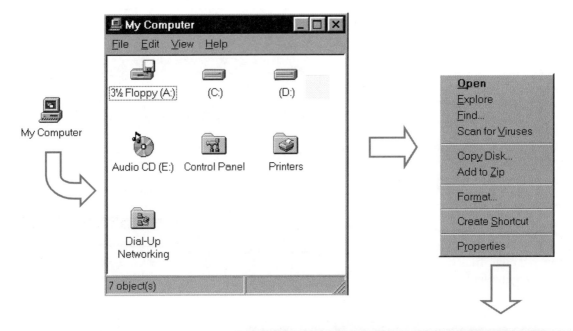

The **Properties** window shows the amount of used space, free space and other information.

The pie diagram gives you an instant visual indication of the used and free space.

You can change the name (label) of the disk here by clicking in the **Label** box and typing a new name.

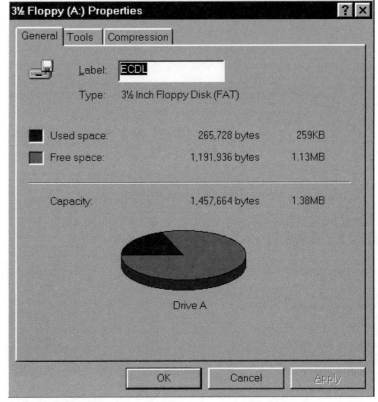

# Section 9    Information and Settings

## 9.1    System Information

Information about your computer is readily available.

Proceed as follows.

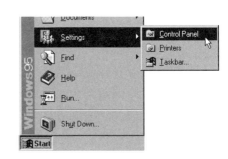

- Select **Settings** in the **Start** menu.

- Select **Control Panel** in the sub-menu.
  The Control Panel window opens.  It contains a large number of controls, represented by icons, with which you can adjust various computer settings and set defaults.

- Scroll through the Control Panel window if necessary to find the **System** icon.

- Double-click on the **System** icon to open the **System Properties** window.

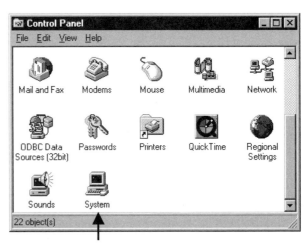

- A row of tabs across the top of the **System Properties** window gives access to system information under different headings.

- Click the **General** tab if it is not clicked already.

- Details of the version of the Windows System used by the computer appear at the top of the window.

- In the illustration, it is **Windows 95** and the version number is **4.00.950 B**

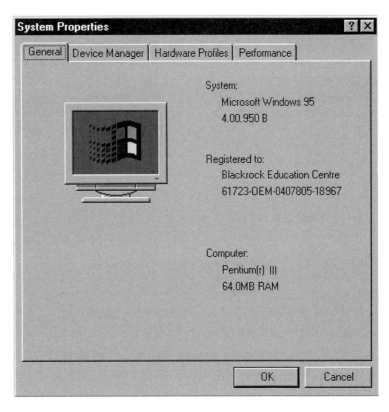

- Underneath are details of the registered user and the registration number.

- The type of processor in the computer is given in the lower part of the window.
  The processor here is a **Pentium(r) III**.

- The amount of RAM in the computer is shown underneath the processor information – here **64Mb**.

Click the other tabs to display more specialised information – probably of interest to expert users only!

## 9.2    Display Settings

The appearance of the desktop, the screen area, the range of colours displayed, and many other settings can be selected to suit the individual user or the requirements of particular software.

**Important:**  Be aware that changing these Display – and other – Control Panel settings will effect how your computer operates. Do not change any settings if you are not sure about them.

Proceed as follows.

- Select **Settings** in the **Start** menu.

- Select **Control Panel** in the sub-menu. The Control Panel window opens.

- Scroll through the Control Panel window if necessary to find the **Display** icon.

- Double-click on the **Display** icon to open the **Display Properties** window.

To make adjustments to the display, click the **Settings** tab.

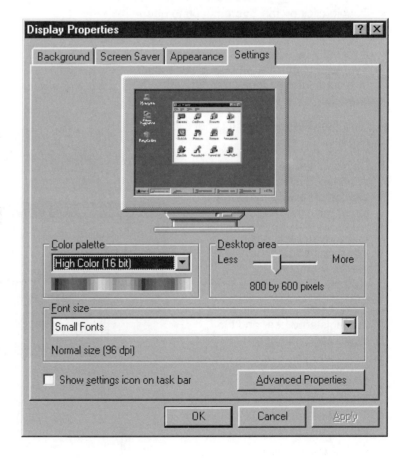

- Select the number of colours to be displayed from the menu in the **Colour palette** area.

- To set the screen area, drag the slider in the **Desktop area** panel.

  Drag towards **Less** to show a smaller part of the desktop but at increased magnification.

  Drag towards **More** to show more of the desktop but at reduced magnification.

- Click **Apply** to make your new settings effective.

- You may be asked to **verify** that the settings are correct, or to **restart** the computer.

  Follow the instructions on the screen.

---

The number of colours that can be displayed may vary, depending on the computer and monitor.

**256 colors** is still used by some multimedia programs.

**High Color (16 bit)** can display thousands of colours for superior quality.

**True Color (24 bit)** can display millions of colours for photographic quality.

See Module 1, Section 2.3, page 33, for more information on monitors.

---

## 9.3    Appearance

To adjust the appearance of the desktop:

- Click the **Appearance** tab in the **Display Properties** window.

- Select the scheme you want from the menu in the **Scheme** box.

- Click **Apply** to make your new settings effective.

- Click **OK**.

Examples of the scheme you select are displayed in the panel at the top of the window.

**Windows Standard** is shown in the illustration.

The menu in the **Item** box allows you to set the font and colour for individual items. Select the size and colour in the small boxes to the right of the Item box.

## 9.4    Background

The background – the main area of the desktop – can be adjusted as follows.

- Click the **Background** tab in the **Display Properties** window.

- To display a pattern on the desktop, select from the menu in the **Pattern** panel.

- To display 'wallpaper' on the desktop, select from the menu in the Wallpaper panel.

- Select **None** in either case if you do not want a pattern or wallpaper.

Your choice is displayed on the 'monitor' in the upper part of the window.

- Click **Apply** to make your new settings effective.

- Click **OK**.

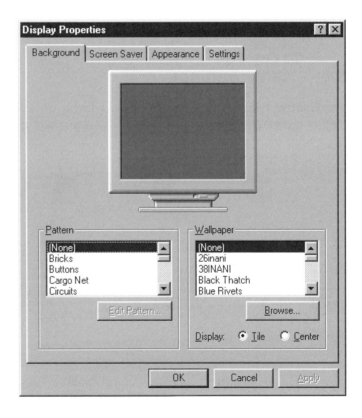

**Note:** Some versions of Windows only display the **Wallpaper** choices on the **Background** tab.
Then a **Pattern** button beside the Wallpaper choices opens the Pattern window.

## 9.5    Screen Saver

A **Screen Saver** replaces the display on the screen with an animated graphic after a set time interval when the computer is unattended.

- Click the **Screen Saver** tab in the **Display Properties** window.

- Select the screen saver you want from the menu in the **Screen Saver** box.

  If you do not want a screen saver, select **None**.

Your choice is displayed on the 'monitor' in the upper part of the window.

- Set the time before the screen saver appears in the **Wait** box.

- Click **Apply** to make your new settings effective.

- Click **OK**.

When the screen saver is in operation, touch the mouse or press any key on the keyboard to restore the original display.

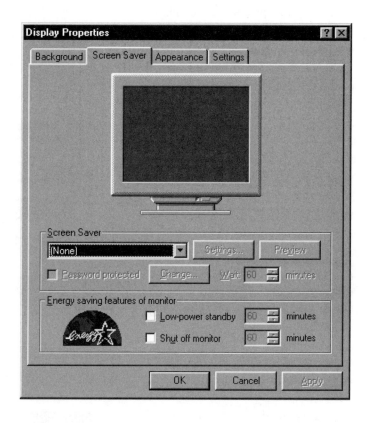

## 9.6    Other Settings

The **Control Panel** window contains icons which enable you to control many other settings in a similar manner to those described above. Some of them are shown here.

Regional Settings       Multimedia       System       Date/Time       Add/Remove Programs

When opened, each one displays the current settings and provides the facility to make changes if required. The Multimedia option, for example, displays the volume settings and allows a range of audio options for playing and recording sound.

> **Remember:** Changing Control Panel settings will effect how your computer operates. If you are not sure about any settings, do not make any changes. Click the **Cancel** button and seek expert advice.

# Section 10    Printing

## 10.1    Setting Up

Before a printer can be used for the first time, it must be **set up** so that the computer knows that it is there and that it is able to use it.

This involves running a **Setup** program that installs details of the printer on the computer. You would begin the process by double-clicking the **Add Printer** icon.

Unless you have just bought a new computer or a new printer for your present computer, you will **not** need to run the **Setup** program.

To check which printers are available to your computer, click the **Start** button, select **Settings** and then **Printers**.

The **Printers** window opens and displays icons for the available printers. Where there are a number of printers available, you can select a particular printer to be your normal – default – printer.

Click the printer you want to use and then click **Set as Default** in the Printers **File** menu so that a tick appears beside it.

The computer will now use this printer by default, unless you select a different one when you are printing a document.

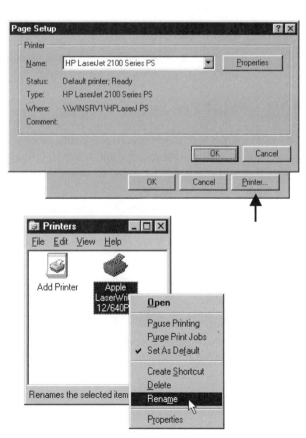

Another way to check which printers are available to your computer is to open a program such as **Notepad** and click **Page Setup** in the **File** menu. The **Page Setup** window appears.

Click the **Printer** button at the bottom right of the window to show the printer that is currently selected.

Click the name box to display a list of other printers, if any. Any one of them may be chosen by clicking it to select it and then clicking **OK**.

You can give the printer a name to personalise it. Right-click on the printer icon in the **Printers** window and select **Rename** in the menu that appears.

Type the new name, **Office Printer** or **Paul's Printer**, for example.

## 10.2   Printing a Document

When a document is ready for printing, it is sent from the computer to the printer. This process may vary slightly according to the software you are using. First, check that the printer is switched on.

To try out printing, type a few words in **Notepad**. Then click **Print** in the **File** menu. The page is sent directly to the printer and should print out after a short delay. Notice that Notepad is a simple no-frills program and the user cannot set the number of copies to be printed or make any other choices. The only preferences that can be set are those in **Page Setup** as shown in the previous section.

Now print a document in **Microsoft Word** by selecting **Print** in the **File** menu, as before. Notice that a window appears allowing the user to select page size, orientation, number of copies, and so on.

The **Print** window displays numerous options.

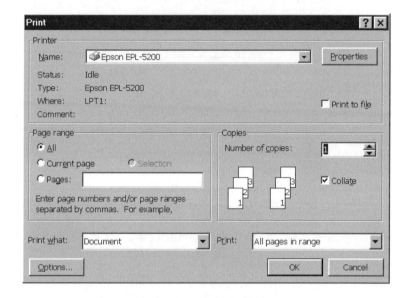

- A different printer can be selected, if one is available.

- All or only some of the pages can be selected for printing.

- The number of copies to be printed can be set.

- The printed copies can be collated.

- Further choices can be made by clicking the **Properties** button.

- The document can be 'printed to' (saved as) a file instead of being printed. The file is a special kind of file that can be used by commercial printers.

When any special options you need have been selected, click the **OK** button to start printing.

**N.B.** If you have no special requirements, it is usually only necessary to click the **OK** button.


## 10.3   Print Preview

The view on the screen as you are preparing a document is not always a completely accurate representation of what will appear on paper. Using **Print Preview** can help you to avoid potential problems.

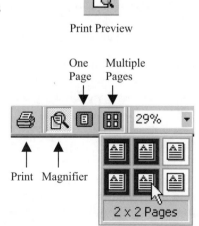

Print Preview

- Click the **Print Preview** button on the toolbar or select **Print Preview** in the **File** menu.

  The document is displayed in reduced format *exactly* as it will appear when printed.

- Click the **Multiple Pages** button and drag to display several pages at once in a long document.

- Use the **Magnifier** to enlarge a page.

- Click the **Print** button to print the document or **Close** to return to the main display.

---

**Save:**  It is good practice to save your work *before* printing.

---

# 10.4 Monitoring Printing

When a document is sent to a printer, a **printer icon** appears on the taskbar at the bottom right-hand corner of the screen. You can use this icon to examine print progress and to make necessary changes.

Printer

- Right-click on the **Printer** icon to display a printer menu.

- Click on the name of the printer you are using. The Printer window opens.

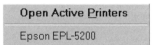

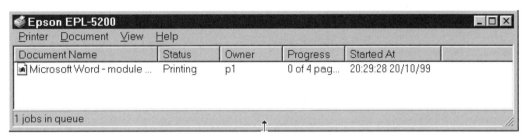

The Printer Window

Documents waiting to be printed appear in a **queue** in the window and details of progress are displayed. (You do not have to wait for one document to be printed before sending another to the printer.)

You can pause printing by clicking **Pause Printing** in the **Printer** menu. This stops any more work being *sent* to the printer but any documents already in the printer's memory will continue to print out.

Click **Pause Printing** again to resume printing.

Click **Purge Print Jobs** to clear the Print queue. When the Print queue is cleared, the **list** of items waiting to be printed is deleted. The actual documents themselves remain untouched on your computer and can be printed out again later, if necessary

The Printer window can also be opened by clicking the **Start** button and selecting **Printers** in the **Settings** menu.

# Section 11 Exercises

# Self Check Exercises

**1** To shut down your computer, which menu would you select?

- ☐ File
- ☐ View
- ☐ Settings
- ☑ Start

**2** From the list below, select the items that may be represented by an icon.

- ☐ File
- ☑ Folder
- ☑ Object
- ☑ Disk drive

**3** What is another name for a folder?

- ☐ File
- ☑ Directory
- ☐ Menu
- ☐ Icon

**4** The Return key may also be known as which of the following?

- ☐ Shift
- ☐ Delete
- ☐ Backspace
- ☑ Enter

**5** In which of these may you store a folder?

- ☑ Hard disk (C:)
- ☐ Folder
- ☑ Floppy Disk (A:)
- ☐ My Documents

**6** When searching for a file or a folder with the Find function, which sign may precede the name in some cases?

- ☐ +
- ☐ -
- ☑ *
- ☐ /

**7** A file name has two components. The first is the actual name you give the file. What is the second?

- ☐ The suffix
- ☐ The address
- ☑ The location
- ☐ The extension

**8** Place the following in order of size, starting with the smallest.

- 4   Megabyte
- 1   Bit
- 2   Byte
- 5   Gigabyte
- 3   Kilobyte

**9** Which of these is the usual representation of the computer's hard disk?

- ☐ A:
- ☑ C:
- ☐ D:
- ☐ E:

**10** Which of these functions would be used in the process of replacing a damaged or corrupted file?

- ☐ Backup
- ☐ Format
- ☑ Restore
- ☐ Insert

**11** What happens when you delete a file from a floppy disk (A:)?

- ☐ It is temporarily deleted.
- ☐ It is placed in the Recycle Bin.
- ☑ It is permanently deleted.
- ☐ It is placed in My Documents.

**12** What happens when you format the computer's hard disk (C:)?

- ☑ Files essential to operating the computer are erased.
- ☐ Only temporary files are erased.

Module 2

# Practical Exercises

**Exercise 1**

Create a new folder on the desktop and name it 'Master'.

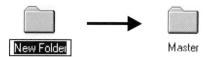

**Exercise 2**

Create a file in Word or Notepad by typing your home and work addresses on a blank page. Save it with the name 'Addresses' in the Master folder.

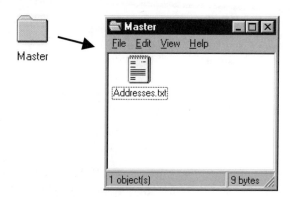

**Exercise 3**

Create a file in Paint by drawing a very simple house, using colour as appropriate. Save it with the name 'My House' in the Master folder.

**Exercise 4**

Create a file in Word by typing a half page of text from any page of this module (ignore graphics, tables etc.). Save the file with the name 'Information' in the Master folder.

**Exercise 5**

Create a file in Word by inserting any piece of Clip Art (no need to add any text) on a blank page. Reduce the Clip Art to postage-stamp size. Save the file with the name 'Small Clip Art' in the Master folder.

**Exercise 6**

Repeat Exercise 5 but resize the Clip Art to fill the whole page. Then save it in the Master folder with the name 'Big Clip Art'.

**Exercise 7**

Create a new folder within the Master folder and name it 'Slave'.

**Exercise 8**

Place all the files that are not Word documents in the 'Slave' folder.

Now answer the following questions.

*(You will need to access* <u>*Properties*</u> *to find the answers.)*

1. What is the difference in file size between 'Small Clip Art' and 'Big Clip Art'?

2. List the files in order of size.

3. What is the difference in Location between the files 'Addresses' and 'Information'?

4. Which is the biggest file?

5. What size is it?

6. How many different file types have you altogether?

**Exercise 9**

Insert a floppy disk and, using Windows Explorer…

1. View the contents of the 'Master' folder.
2. Copy the 'Slave' folder to the floppy disk.
3. Copy the remaining files separately to the floppy disk.

Now answer the following questions.

4. What is the capacity of the floppy disk?
5. How many folders are there on the floppy?
6. What free space is left for storing further information on the floppy disk?

**Exercise 10**

Move the 'Master' folder from the desktop to the Recycle Bin.

# Module 3

## Word Processing

3

# Module 3

# Word Processing

Module 3

Module 3

# Introduction

---

**Syllabus Goals for Module 3**

**Word Processing** requires the candidate to demonstrate the ability to use a word processing application on a personal computer.  He or she shall understand and be able to accomplish basic operations associated with creating, formatting and finishing a word processing document ready for distribution.  The candidate shall demonstrate competence in using some of the more advanced features associated with word processing applications such as creating standard tables, using pictures and images within a document, importing objects and using mail merge tools.

---

**Module 3**

## What is Word Processing?

Word processing has replaced typing. With a typewriter, you had to be a skilful typist to produce accurate, attractively laid-out work.  There was only one typeface - the one used for this paragraph - and one size.  If you made mistakes, it was annoying and tedious to make corrections.  Even then, the amount of correction you could make was very limited.  Major corrections meant typing out the whole page all over again.

The document you are reading now was prepared entirely on a word processor.   The type does not always have to have the 'typewriter' appearance of the paragraph above.  You will have noticed that the titles, text and paragraph headings are in different typefaces, sizes and styles.  The text can be lined up neatly at both left and right margins.  Illustrations can be included and lines can be drawn.  This kind of presentation would have been impossible to do on a typewriter.  And it is easy!  Typists who change over to the computer find that their typing speed increases.  The extra facilities of the computer have led to the adoption of the term **word processing**.

---

The computer has replaced the typewriter for all kinds of work because it is far more versatile.  You still have to know how to type.  The computer keyboard has replaced the typewriter keys and has given rise to a new word: keyboarding!  With the computer, words and pictures can be added or deleted, paragraphs can be interchanged, and the text can be arranged on the page much more attractively than when using the typewriter.   In the event of changes to parts of the text, the whole document does not have to be typed out again.

---

A word processor application allows the computer to be used as a super-duper typewriter with many more facilities than any typewriter could ever have.  The major software companies have developed word processors for both PC and Macintosh computers.  Widely-used word processing applications include Microsoft Word and Word Perfect.  Integrated packages such as AppleWorks and Lotus Office Suite also include word processors.

---

# Reference Table

Should you begin your studies with this module, it is important to note that related material is dealt with in other sections of the manual. This reference list will assist you to locate the material conveniently.

| Skill | Task | Module | Page |
|---|---|---|---|
| **First Steps** | | | |
| | Save a new document | Module 2 | 84 |
| | Save changes to an existing document | Module 2 | 87 |
| | Close a document | Before You Begin | 24 |
| | Help | Before You Begin | 16 |
| **Adjusting Settings** | | | |
| | Change page display modes | Before You Begin | 21 |
| | Page magnification | Before You Begin | 22 |
| | Toolbars | Before You Begin | 11 |
| **Document Exchange** | | | |
| | Save a file in a different format | Module 2 | 87 |
| | Save for Web posting | Module 2 | 88 |
| **Basic Functions** | | | |
| | Copy, Cut, and Paste | Before You Begin | 10 |
| | Selecting | Before You Begin | 9 |
| | Spell Check | Before You begin | 23 |

# Section 1     Word Documents

## 1.1     Opening Microsoft Word

Open Microsoft Word by clicking the **Word** button on the
Microsoft Office **Shortcut Bar** on the Desktop.

*Alternatively*, click the **Start** button and select **Microsoft Word**
in the **Programs** menu or sub-menu.

## 1.2     A New Document

When you open Word, it usually creates a new blank document called **Document 1**.  The document
appears on the screen as if it were a sheet of blank white paper.  If there is no document open, blank or
otherwise, the main part of the screen where the document would normally appear is gray.

If Word doesn't create a new blank document, you can create one yourself.

- Click the **New** button at the left of the Toolbar.  The button represents a blank
  sheet of paper.

  A blank document opens, ready for you to begin.

New

- *Alternatively*, select **New** in the **File** menu.

  The New window opens with the **Blank
  Document** icon already selected.

  Click **OK** and a new blank document
  appears.

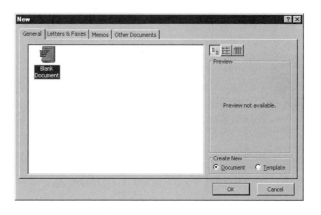

## 1.3     Templates

A **template** is a document with various
preset design and layout features which save
you having to set them yourself.

When using a template, you type your own
text to replace the text on the template.
Your text then assumes the design features
of the template.

You can alter or adapt a template to suit
your own particular needs.

- Click the tabs at the top of the **New**
  window to display a selection of
  **Templates** that you can use.

- **Letters and Faxes** templates are shown
  in the illustration.  Notice the example of
  the selected template in the **Preview** box
  at the right of the window.

- To use a Template, click on an icon to
  select it and then click **OK**.

Templates are covered in detail in
Section 16 of this Module, page 189.

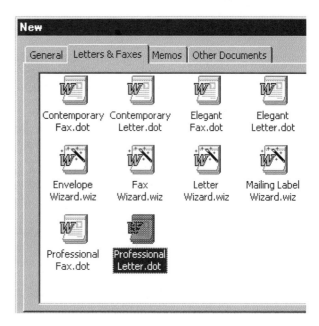

Module 3

## 1.4    The Word Window

The window that appears when a WORD document is opened is similar to the windows used in other Microsoft applications.  The main features of the Word window are shown here.  (The Windows Taskbar – with the Start button – is shown at the bottom of the Word window.)

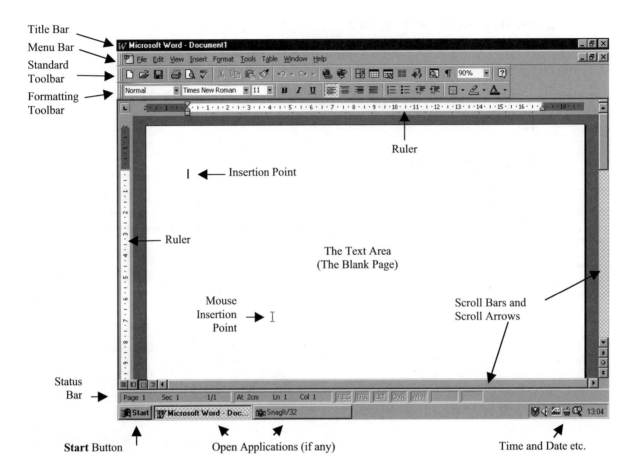

## 1.5    Word Window Features

The principal features of the Word window are described here.

- The **Title Bar** displays the name of the document that you are using.

- The **Menu Bar** contains menus of actions that can be performed by the computer.  Click on a menu to display a list of options.  As you point to a menu item, it is coloured or **highlighted**.  Some items have a sub-menu that appears beside the first menu.  Click once on an item to select it.

- **Scroll Bars and Arrows** are used to move left and right or up and down over a document in the window when it is too large to see all at once.

- The **Toolbars** contain buttons that you click to perform an action.  Common actions are grouped together on separate toolbars, such as the Standard and Formatting toolbars described below.  The user can select the buttons to be displayed to suit individual requirements.

    **The Standard Toolbar** has buttons for the most commonly used actions, e.g. Opening, Saving and Printing.  To see a description of a button, hold the pointer over it **without clicking**.  You will learn how to use the buttons as you progress through the course.

    **The Formatting Toolbar** has buttons that are used to change the appearance of text, e.g. bold, italics, font and font size.

- The **Rulers** are used as guides.  The horizontal ruler is also used for placing tabs and indents and for changing margins.

- The **Text Area** is the 'blank sheet of paper' on which you type your document.

- The **Text Insertion Point** or Cursor is a flashing vertical line ( | ) that appears in the text area. Any text that you type will begin at this point.  Don't confuse it with the Mouse Insertion Point.

- The **Mouse Insertion Point** is an I-shaped bar – the I-beam – that shows the position of the mouse pointer on the page.  Don't confuse it with the Text Insertion Point (see above).  When the mouse is moved out of the text area, the mouse cursor changes to a different shape, usually an arrow.  It can also be used to select objects.  (See **Before you Begin**, Section 1.6, page 6.)

- The **Status Bar** displays the page number and other information, such as the line number on which the cursor is currently placed.

- **Other items** may be displayed on occasion in separate windows.

## 1.6    Displaying Toolbars

If toolbars are not visible on the screen, you can display them.  If they are visible, you can hide them. Hiding unnecessary toolbars gives you more space on the screen for your text.

- Select **Toolbars** in the **View** menu.  A list of toolbars appears, with a tick beside those that are displayed on the screen.

- Click on the toolbar you want to display.  If a toolbar has a tick beside it, click on it to hide it.

See **Before you Begin**, Section 5, page 11, for more information on toolbars.

## 1.7    Saving a Document

The procedure for saving a document for the first time is different from saving changes to it later. The first time you save it, you must give it a name and choose the location in which it is to be saved.

To save a document for the **first time**, do the following.

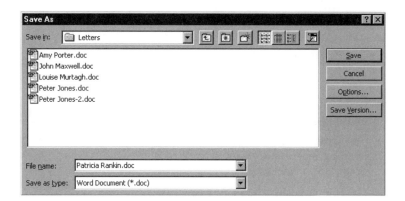

- Click the **Save Button** on the toolbar or select **Save** in the **File** menu.

  The **Save As** window opens. (See page 14 for the Office 2000 **Save As** window.)

- Type a name for the document in the **File Name** box.

- Make sure that the Folder, area or floppy disk where you want to save the document appears in the **Save in** box.

- Click the **Save** button.

When you have saved a document, the name you have given it appears in the Title Bar at the top of the screen.  (An unsaved file usually has a name such as **Document 1**.)

If you reopen the document later to edit it or make other changes, the altered version will need to be saved again.  This time, however, the **Save As** window does not appear, as the computer already knows the document name and the location where it is to be saved

Saving is described in detail in Module 2, Section 4, page 84.  Instructions for saving in different formats, including HTML format for the World Wide Web are also described there.

## 1.8    Closing a Document

To close a document:

Close

Word Processor Buttons

- Click the Document **Close** button on the top right of the document window (the **X** button).

  The Document Close button is always the *lower* one In Office 97. Be careful not to click the **Word** Close button above it.

Document Buttons

Close

- *Alternatively*, select **Close** in the **File** menu.

- If you haven't saved the document or if you have made changes since you last saved it, you will be reminded.

  You will normally click **Yes** in the reminder window to save the document.

- When a document is closed, it disappears from the screen.

Closing is described in more detail in **Before You Begin**, Section 10, page 24.


## 1.9    Closing Microsoft Word

To close the Word Processor:

- Click the Word **Close** button at the top right of the screen, the *upper* one.

- *Alternatively*, click **Exit** in the **File** menu.

- If you have unsaved work, or if you have made changes since you last saved it, you will be reminded.  Click **Yes** in the reminder window to save the document.


## 1.10   Opening a Document

Find the document you want to open in the same way as you found the folder in which to **save** it, as described in Module 2, Section 4.4, page 85.

Open

A summary of the procedure follows:

- Click the **Open** button on the **toolbar** or select **Open** in the **File** menu.

  The **Open** window appears. (See page 90 for the Office 2000 **Open** window.)

- Find the location of the document you want to open in the **Look in** box.

- Double-click the document icon in the main part of the window to open and display it.

  *Alternatively*, click on the document icon to select it. Then click the **Open** button to display the document.

The **Open** window

You can open more than one document at a time.  They will appear on the Desktop in separate windows.  You can move between the different documents by selecting them in turn in the **Windows** menu on the Toolbar, or by dragging and resizing the windows to view them together.

## 1.11   Viewing Documents

There are several ways in which Word documents can be displayed (and viewed) on the screen.

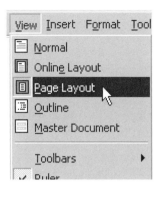

Select the required format in the **View** menu. *Alternatively*, click a **View Button** at the bottom left-hand corner of screen.

The most commonly used views are **Page Layout** and **Normal**.

- **Page Layout** view displays the document as it appears on the page. You can see the actual 'page', any graphics you have inserted, headers and footers and so on. As you work on a document, you see it taking shape.

- **Normal** view displays only the text. Graphics do not appear. The document looks like one continuous piece of text with dotted lines representing breaks or divisions between pages.

Use **Page Layout** view when you need to see the layout of the page, including any graphics and the margin areas.

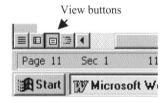

Use **Normal** view if you have a lot of text to type in. You have more space on the screen and it is less cluttered.

Use the **Zoom** control to change the size of the document on the screen. Note that changing the size of the document on the screen does not affect the size at which it will be printed.

See **Before You Begin**, Section 8, page 21, for more information on viewing options.

In Office 2000, **Print Layout** view corresponds to **Page Layout** in earlier versions of Office.

## Exercise 1A

To put the document handling information you have learned into practice, do the following:

- Create a new document.

- Save it in your chosen location with the name **My Word 1**.

- Close the file, not **Word** itself.

- Open the file again in Word.

- Save the file on a floppy disk, naming it **My Disk File 1**.

- Close both the file and Word.

# Section 2     Managing Text

## 2.1     Entering Text

Once you've mastered the basics of opening, closing and saving a file, you can start typing in some text to prepare a simple document.

- Check that the text cursor is positioned where you want to place your text. (If it's not, click there with the mouse to insert the cursor.)

- Start typing.  When you come to the end of a line, the text will automatically continue on to the next line.

## 2.2     Useful Keys

You must learn the positions of some imporant keys on the keyboard.  (See Before You Begin, Section 1.4, page 4, for more information on the keyboard.)  Some of the keys may be different on your keyboard, as may the symbols printed on them.

- For capital letters, hold down the **Shift** key and then press the key of the letter.  (There are two shift keys, one at each side of the keyboard.)

- If you want to type a lot of capitals together, press the **Caps Lock** key once, then type the letters: they will all be in capitals.  To return to small letters, press the **Caps Lock** key again.

- To start a new paragraph or line, or to insert a blank line, press the **Return** key on the right of the keyboard (sometimes called the **Enter** key).  It's the one with an arrow like this ⏎.
Do *not* press the **Return** key when you reach the right-hand side of the screen – **Word** will automatically go on to the next line as you type.

- To type the characters above the numbers on the number keys, e.g. the **£** sign, hold down the **Shift** key and then press the key for the character.

- To move to a particular place in your document, use the mouse to place the cursor, as already described.  *Alternatively*, you can use the arrow keys (←, ↑, →, ↓) at the bottom right of the keyboard.  There are 4 arrow keys, one for each direction.  Pressing an arrow key  moves the cursor from its current position in the direction shown by the arrow.

- Use the scroll bars at the bottom and side of the text area to move up or down or across the document.

## 2.3     Symbols and Special Characters

A word processing program is not confined to the letters or characters that appear on the keyboard keys, as in a traditional typewriter.  Many special characters and symbols are also available.  These include accents for different languages, special typesetting characters, copyright and registered symbols.

To insert symbols or special characters, do the following:

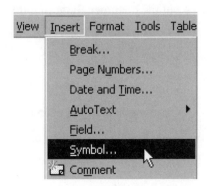

- Place the **Typing** cursor in the document where you want the symbol or special character to appear.

- To insert a symbol or character, select **Symbol** in the **Insert** menu.  The Symbol window opens.

- Click the **Symbols** tab at the top of the window, if it is not already selected, to display the full set of characters available.

- Click in the **Font** box and select **(normal text)**, if it is not already selected.

- Click on a character to display a magnified view, as in the illustration.

- Click the Insert button to insert the selected character.

  It is inserted at the position of the **Typing** cursor in the document.

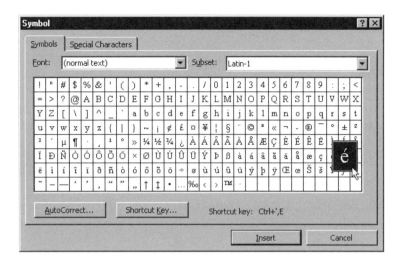

Note the **Shortcut key** (*not* the Shortcut Key *button*) at the bottom of the window for inserting the character directly from the keyboard. For the selected character é in the illustration – e with an acute accent – the shortcut key is **Control + Apostrophe, then e**. To insert the character é, hold down the **Control** key and press the apostrophe key ('). Then release both keys and press the letter **e**. An accented e – é – is inserted.

**Control** key

It will save time if you learn the shortcut key combinations for common symbols and characters. The Shortcut Key **button** allows you to set your own shortcut key combinations.

Different fonts have different symbols and special characters. Click in the **Font** box to display the fonts available and look at the different characters available in each one.

Click the **Special Characters** tab to display the special characters. Note that **En** and **Em** dashes should be used instead of a hyphen in certain circumstances – as here. The En dash is longer than a hyphen and the Em dash (—) is longer again. The widths of the letters 'n' and 'm' will help you to remember which is which.

Note also the **non-breaking space** that prevents awkward breaks at the end of a line, such as in **6 Alperton Road**. Using a non-breaking space prevents the awkward break after '6' and places **6 Alperton Road** all together on the next line, as demonstrated here.

## Exercise 2A

**1** Open the **My Word 1** document which you created earlier. Type the text in the box below. (The box itself is not part of the exercise!)

Don't try to set out the text *exactly* as in the sample. There's no need to move your words onto new lines or to use extra spacing.

**2** Save and close the file.

---

*Here is an example of the work of Charles Dickens.*

They turned into the wine-shop which was closed (for it was midnight) and where Madame Defarge immediately took her post at her desk, counted the small moneys that had been taken during her absence, examined the stock, went through the entries in the book, made other entries of her own, checked the serving man in every possible way, and finally dismissed him into bed.

Then she turned out the contents of the bowl of money for the second time, and began knotting them in her handkerchief, in a chain of separate knots, for safe keeping through the night.

---

## 2.4    Selecting Text

Sometimes, you'll want to manipulate the text that you have typed in.  You might want to move it, delete it or change its appearance in some way.  To do this, you must first select the text you want to alter so that Word knows which piece of text to change.  The methods described below use the mouse to select text.  This is usually the easiest way, although you can also use the keyboard.  (Later, when you learn how to use the Word Help system, you can look this up yourself.  For now, we'll use the mouse.)

### To Select Text with the Mouse

Place the cursor in front of the first letter of the text you want to select.  Then use one of the following methods.

- Hold the left mouse button down and drag the mouse towards the end of the text you want to select.  You will see the text being highlighted (coloured over) as you drag.  When all the text you want is highlighted, release the mouse button.

- *Alternatively*, place the cursor in front of the first letter of the text to be selected.  Hold down the **Shift** key while you click after the last letter of the required text.  The entire text in between will be highlighted.

- When you are finished working on the selection, click anywhere outside the selected text to deselect, i.e. anywhere there is white space on the page.

### Shortcuts

- To select one word only, double-click on the word.

- To select one line of text on the screen, move the mouse to the left margin of the text: the mouse pointer will change to a white arrow.  Click once.  The line will be highlighted.

- To select an entire paragraph, move the mouse to the left margin as above and double-click to select the paragraph.

### Selecting all the text in a document

If you want to select all the text in the entire document:

- Click the **Edit** menu.

- Click on **Select All**.

## Exercise 2B

**1**  Open the **My Word 1** document and practise selecting different sections of text using the above techniques.

## 2.5    Inserting Text

Sometimes, you will want to make changes to text in a document that you have already created. You may want to insert new text or delete some existing text.

To **replace** existing text with new text:

- Select the old text.

- Type in the new text directly.
  What you type will replace the selected text.

To **insert** new text into the middle of a previously typed line
(e.g. if you forgot to put in a word):

- Place the cursor where you want to insert the new text.

- Start typing.
  The existing text moves to the right to make room for the new text as you type.

To **overwrite** existing text with new text:

- Place the cursor where you want to insert the new text.

- Press the **Insert** key.
  The status line will now display the letters **OVR** in black print. This means that Word is in **Overwrite** mode.

- Type the new text.
  You will see the new text *writing over* the old text.

- When you are finished, press the **Insert** key again to leave Overwrite mode.

## 2.6    Deleting Text

To delete one character at a time:

- Place the cursor to the **left** of the character to be deleted and press the **Delete** key on the keyboard.  Be careful when pressing the Delete key. If you hold it down too long, it will delete more characters.

Delete

- *Alternatively*, place the cursor to the **right** of the character to be deleted and press the **Backspace** key (above the **Return** key).

To delete a word or a block of text:

- Select the text you want to delete.

- Press the **Delete** key.

Backspace

# Exercise 2C

**1** Open the **My Word 1** document.  Insert and delete text (as appropriate) as shown in the box below. (Don't worry about having the same words on each line exactly as in the example.)

**2** Don't forget to save the changes to your file.

---

Below is an extract from *A Tale of Two Cities* by Charles Dickens, p179.

They turned into the wine-shop which was closed (for it was midnight) and where Madame Defarge immediately took her post at her desk, counted the small moneys that had been taken during her absence, examined the stock, went through the entries in the book, made other entries of her own, checked the serving man in every possible way, and finally dismissed him into bed.

Then she turned out the contents of the bowl of money for the second time, and began knotting them in her handkerchief, in a chain of separate knots, for safe keeping through the night. All this while Defarge, with his pipe in his mouth, walked up and down, complacently admiring, but never interfering; in which condition, indeed, as to the business and his domestic affairs, he walked up and down through life.

---

## 2.7    Cut and Paste

You can move text around a document by **cutting** it from one place and **pasting** it into another.  You don't have to retype the text into its new position.

First select the text you want to move.  Then **Cut** the selected text using one of the following methods.

Cut

- Click the **Cut** button on the toolbar (the scissors).

- *Alternatively*, select **Cut** in the **Edit** menu.
  You can also use the keyboard shortcut, **Control + X**.  Hold down the **Control** key and then press the letter **X** key.   (It doesn't have to be a capital 'x'.)

**Control** key

The cut text is removed from its original position and stored on the **Clipboard** – a part of the computer's memory.

Now **Paste** the text, i.e. insert it into its new position. First, use the mouse to place the **Typing** cursor where you want the text to appear.  Then use one of the following methods.

Paste

- Click the **Paste** button on the toolbar.

- *Alternatively*, select **Paste** in the **Edit** menu.
  You can also use the keyboard shortcut, **Control + V**.  (Using 'V' may not seem sensible but 'P' is already used for another keyboard shortcut.)

- The text appears in its new position.

---

**The Clipboard**

The clipboard is an area of the computer's memory where items are stored temporarily. The clipboard can hold only one item at a time in Office 97. Text placed on it by *cutting* or *copying* is available to you *only* until you cut or copy something else.  When you *paste*, you put a **copy** of what is on the clipboard into your document. Thus you can paste the same item many times – into the same or different places – if you want to.

---

## 2.8    Copy and Paste

While cutting **removes** text and stores it on the Clipboard, copying makes a **copy** of the text without removing it.  Cut or copied text is available to you until you cut or copy something else.  Thus you can paste it into a new position.

You might want to repeat the same text in a document – e.g. the chorus of a song.  You don't have to type the whole thing again.  First select the text you want to copy.  Then copy it using one of the following methods.

- Click the **Copy** button on the toolbar.

- *Alternatively*, select **Copy** in the **Edit** menu.
  You can also use the keyboard shortcut, **Ctrl + C**.

Copy

You won't actually see anything happening, but a copy of the selected text is placed on the clipboard.

Next **Paste** the text using the same techniques used in Cut and Paste.

- Click the **Paste** button on  the Toolbar.

- *Alternatively*, select **Paste** in the **Edit** menu.
  You can also use the keyboard shortcut, **Control + V**.

Paste

The copy now appears where you had placed the **Typing** cursor.

You can paste the same text several times without having to copy it again (as long as you don't place anything else on the Clipboard) by using **Paste** repeatedly.

Module 3

## Exercise 2D

**1**  Open the **My Word 1** document.  Make changes to the text until it appears approximately as it does below.  The length of the lines and the number of words in them will be different on your computer.  The box is not part of the exercise.

---

Below is an example of the work of Charles Dickens.


They turned into the wine-shop which was closed (for it was midnight) and where Madame Defarge immediately took her post at her desk, counted the small moneys that had been taken during her absence, examined the stock, went through the entries in the book, made other entries of her own, checked the serving man in every possible way, and finally dismissed him into bed.

Then she turned out the contents of the bowl of money for the second time, and began knotting them in her handkerchief, in a chain of separate knots, for safe keeping through the night. All this while Defarge, with his pipe in his mouth, walked up and down, complacently admiring, but never interfering; in which condition, indeed, as to the business and his domestic affairs, he walked up and down through life.

*A Tale of Two Cities*, Page 179

---

**2**  Copy the entire text and paste it below the original text so that you have two copies on the same page.

**3**  Save the document.

**4**  Now save the same document on a floppy disk, calling it **My Disk 1**.  You now have two copies of the same document, one called **My Word 1** and the other called **My Disk 1**.

**5**  If a message tells you that **My Disk 1** already exists, this is because you have already saved a document earlier with the same name.

**Word** asks if you want to replace the existing document.  In this case you do, because you want to save the new version that contains the text you used for Questions 1 and 2 above.

Always read messages that **Word** gives you in cases like this: if you replace an existing document with a new one, then the older document is gone.

**6**  Save and close the document.

# Section 3    Changing the Appearance of Text

## 3.1    Formatting Text

Formatting text means changing its physical appearance. Many different aspects of the text's appearance can be changed, e.g. the size of the letters, the font, whether it's in **bold type**, *italicised* or underlined. You may want to format only some of the text or set a format for the whole document.

### The Formatting Toolbar

Using the Formatting Toolbar is the easiest way to change the appearance of text. The toolbar usually appears as in the illustration below. It may appear differently on your computer as it is possible to specify what buttons are displayed according to individual requirements.

If the Formatting Toolbar is not visible, select **Toolbars** in the **View** menu and click **Formatting** in the submenu that appears. If there is a tick (✓) beside **Formatting**, it means the toolbar is already on your screen. See **Before You Begin**, Section 5, page 11, for more information on toolbars.

### Formatting Text

This is the general method for formatting text.

- If you want to set formats for the entire document, do so before you begin to type anything.

- If you want to format specific text, first select the text you want to format.

- Click the appropriate button on the Formatting Toolbar or use the Format menu to make the changes you want. The different types of formatting are described in the following sections.

## 3.2    Fonts and Font Size

**Font** (or typeface) is the name given to the physical design and appearance of letters. The same letter appears differently in different fonts. There are many different fonts installed on most computers. Two of the most commonly used are **Times New Roman** (this typeface) and **Arial** (this typeface). They are used throughout this manual.

The font and font size currently in use appear on the Toolbar.

Font box ➡  ⬅ Font size box

To use a different font, first select the text you want to change. If you want to set a font for the whole document, select the font before you begin typing. Use either of the methods below.

### 1 – Using the Toolbar

The quickest and easiest way to change fonts is to use the Formatting Toolbar.

- Click the little arrowhead to the right of the font name. A list of the fonts available on your computer is displayed.

- Click on the name of the font you want. Its name appears in the font box.

- To change the font size, click the arrowhead in the font size box to display a list of sizes. Font size is measured in **points**, with 72 points (pt) to an inch.

- Select the size you want. If your preference is not listed, select the size displayed in the **Size** box and type in the value you require. It will replace what was in the box.

## 2 – Using the Format Menu

Using the **Format menu** gives you many more options. It also displays a preview of the font.

- Select **Font** in the **Format** menu.

  The Font window opens.

  In the top left of the window, the name of the current font appears in the **Font** box.

  Underneath is a list of available fonts.

  Use the scroll bar on the right of the box, if necessary, to see the complete list.

- Click on the font you want to use. Its name appears in the box above.

- Select the size you want in the **Size** area at the top right of the window. 10pt or 12pt are usually used for normal text.

- The **Preview** panel at the bottom of the window gives an example of the Font in its selected size and style.

- Select any other options that you require.

  (In Office 2000, the **Animation** tab becomes **Text Effects**.)

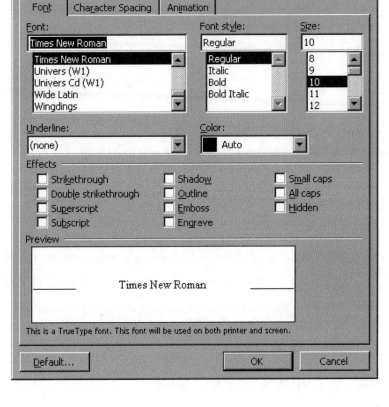

- Click **OK** when you have selected all the options you want.

- If you decide that you don't want to change anything, click **Cancel**.

## 3.3     Bold, Italics and Underline

Either the Formatting Toolbar or the Format Menu can be used.

### 1 – Using the Toolbar

- Select the text you want to format.

- Click the appropriate button on the toolbar, i.e. the **B** button for **bold**, the *I* button for *italics* and the U button for underline.

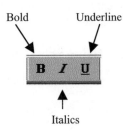

### 2 – Using the Format Menu

- Select **Font** in the **Format** menu and click on the **Font** tab (see previous page) to display the Font window.

- In the **Font style** section of the dialogue box, click on the appropriate option, e.g. **Bold**.

- Click on **Regular** for plain text.

- In the **Underline** section of the window (under the list of fonts), click the arrowhead to display a list of Underline styles.  There are more options here than given by the Underline button on the toolbar.

- Don't forget to look in the **Preview** panel to see the effects of the changes.

- Click **OK** to close the Font window as before.

## 3.4    Special Effects and Colour

The Font window can be used to apply other effects to text, e.g. ~~strikethrough~~, SMALL CAPITALS, superscript ($^{\text{Superscript}}$) and subscript ($_{\text{Subscript}}$).  These options are not usually available on the Formatting Toolbar.  You can also add a shadow effect and change the text colour.

- Select **Font** in the **Format** menu to open the Font dialogue box (see previous page).

- Select an option in **Effects** by clicking the small box to the left of the option.  If a tick mark (✔) is in the box, that option is already selected.

- If you're not sure what an option means, select it and look in the **Preview** box.  If you change your mind, click the option again to de-select it.

- To change the text colour, click the arrow on the right of the **Colour** box and select the colour you require.
  *Alternatively*, use the text colour button on the Formatting Toolbar. Click the little arrowhead on the right of the button and select a colour in the palette that appears.

Text Colour

## 3.5    Alignment or Justification

**Alignment** or **Justification** defines the way in which the text is lined up against the margins.

**Left-aligned** text is lined up along the left margin and is jagged on the right.

**Right-aligned** text is lined up along the right margin and is jagged on the left.

**Centre-aligned** text is centred between the margins.

**Fully justified** text has text lined up along both the left and right margins.  There are no jagged edges at either side.

To set or change the alignment, use one of the methods below.   If you are aligning text you have already typed, select the text first.

### 1 – Using the Toolbar

- Click the appropriate button on the Toolbar.  The 'lines of text' on the alignment buttons indicate their effect, as shown in the illustration.

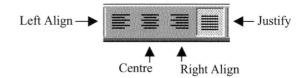

## 2 – Using the Format Menu

- Select **Paragraph** in the **Format** menu.

  The Paragraph window opens.

- In the **Alignment** section on the top left, click the arrow in the right of the white box to select the required option.

- Look in the **Preview** box to see the effect of your selections.

- Click the **OK** button to apply your selections to the text.

- Click **Cancel** if you change your mind.

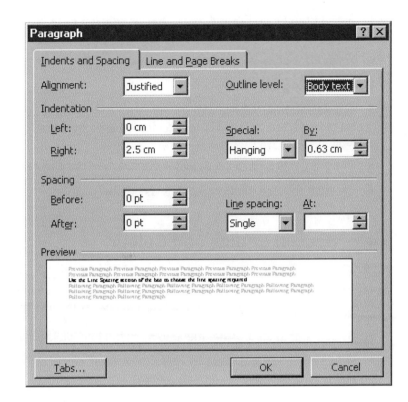

## 3.6    Line Spacing

**Line spacing** refers to the amount of space between lines of text, relative to the size of the text itself. Most documents use single-line spacing.  Sometimes you might want more space between lines to make the text easier to read, for example.  Double-line spacing gives the effect of an extra blank line between two lines of text. You can't change the line spacing for only a few lines in the middle of a paragraph: any change will affect the whole paragraph.

First select the paragraphs you want to change.  If you only want to change the spacing for one paragraph, click anywhere in the paragraph.   Then use the **Format** menu to change the line spacing as follows.

- Select **Paragraph** in the **Format** menu.

  The Paragraph window appears (see above).

- Make sure that the **Indents and Spacing** tab is clicked.

- Use the **Line spacing** section to select the required spacing.

  (Click the arrowhead to display a menu.)

  You can use the **Single**, **Double** or **1.5 line** spacing.

- Select **Exactly** in the Line Spacing menu to make finer adjustments.

  When you select **Exactly**, the spacing is measured in **points** (as for the font size).

  This allows for much finer adjustment of line spacing than is possible with line-size spacing.

- Use the **Preview** box to see the effects of the changes.

- Click **OK** to close the window.

## 3.7    Paragraph Spacing

Space can be added before or after a paragraph.  This is useful for inserting extra space between a heading and the main text, as used throughout this manual.  Paragraph spacing only affects the space before the first line or after the last line of the paragraph, not the spacing between the lines in the paragraph itself.

To change the paragraph spacing, first select the paragraphs.  If you only want to change the spacing for one paragraph, just click anywhere in that paragraph.  Then proceed as follows.

- Select **Paragraph** in the **Format menu**.
  The Paragraph window appears as before.

- Make sure that the **Indents and Spacing** tab is clicked.

- In the **Spacing** section, select a size for the spacing before and/or after the paragraph.
  6pt spacing is about half the size of a normal line of text, for example.
  Use the arrows to the right to choose higher or lower values, or type in your own.

- Don't forget to look in the **Preview** box.

- Click **OK** to close the dialogue box.

Module 3

## 3.8    Copying Formatting

When you want to apply the selected formatting  (line spacing, font size and style etc.) to another piece of text, it is not necessary to go through all the formatting options described above every time.  You can save time by using the **Format Painter** button on the Standard Toolbar.

Format
Painter

- Select the text with the formatting you want to copy.

- Click the **Format Painter** button on the Standard Toolbar.  Move back onto the page and the cursor is now in the shape of the  Format Painter **Tool** – a typing cursor with the Format Painter brush in front of it.

- Drag the Format Painter tool through the new text and release the mouse button.

Format
Painter
Tool

- To apply the formatting to several pieces of text, double-click the Format Painter button first.  The button will stay selected.  When you have finished formatting, click the button again to de-select it.

## 3.9    Undoing Formatting

When a button on the Formatting Toolbar appears 'pressed in', that option is active.  Clicking the button again will de-activate it.  For example, if text is bold and you want it in plain text, first select the text.  The **bold** button will have a 'pressed in' appearance.  Click it to remove the bold formatting. If you had just made the text bold a moment before, you can use the **Undo** button.

**Undo and Redo**

If you make or mistake, e.g. delete text accidentally, you can usually undo your mistake by clicking the **Undo** button.  Word lets you undo several previous actions by continually clicking the Undo button.  Note, however, that there are some actions that can't be undone, so don't rely absolutely on this button!

Undo

**Redo** is used to undo **Undo**.  For example, if you undo something, then realise you should have left it the way it was, click Redo to restore the previous version.

Redo

## 3.10   Using Styles

A **Style** is a selection of formatting options that determines the appearance of text.  When you open a new document in Word, the default Style is usually Times New Roman, 10 point, left-aligned, with single-line spacing.

Style menu

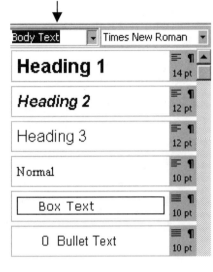

A selection of other Styles is available in the **Style** menu at the left of the Formatting Toolbar. You can use them to vary the appearance of your text without having to go to the trouble of setting up the formatting yourself.

The **Style Name** is displayed in the Style menu as it will appear in the document.  The font size is given in the box to the right of the name of the Style. Symbols indicate the alignment and whether the Style will affect the whole paragraph (¶) or selected characters only (**a**).

- To type in a particular Style, select the Style from the **Style** menu before you start to type.

- To apply a Style to an existing paragraph, click anywhere in the text and then select the Style in the **Style** menu.  (A **Character Style** will only affect the character or text you have selected.)

You can add a new style or modify an existing style by selecting **Style** in the **Format** menu.

## 3.11   Themes

In Office 2000, **Themes** can be used when documents are to be saved as Web pages.

Themes are used to give a uniform appearance to the pages by imposing various styles:

- The font, colour, size, and so on, of text.

- The images used for bullets.

- The appearance of horizontal lines.

- The colour of table borders.

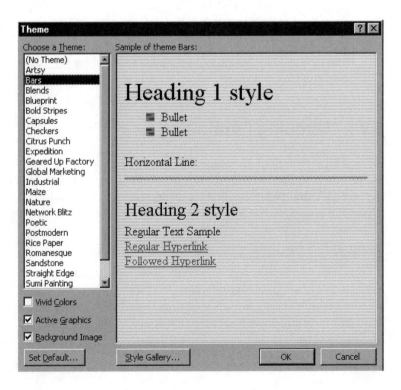

Other styles – seen only when **Web Layout** is selected in the **View** menu – are also set:

- The page background

- The colour of text hyperlinks

- The positioning of graphics

To apply a Theme:

- Select **Theme** in the **Format** menu.
  Select **No Theme** if preferred.

- Click on a Theme in the **Choose a Theme** panel.

- Click **OK**.

# 3.12  Adding a Border

You can add a **border** to a whole page, to a selected paragraph or to a piece of text.  To add a border to a paragraph or page, do the following.

- Select the paragraph or text to which you want to add the border.

- Select **Borders and Shading** in the **Format** menu.

  The Borders and Shading window opens.

- To apply a border to a whole page, click the **Page Border** tab at the top left.

- Click the type of border you want in the **Borders Setting** list on the left.

- In the centre of the window, select the **Style**, **Colour** and **Width** (line thickness).

  Use the menus and scroll bars to display the various options.

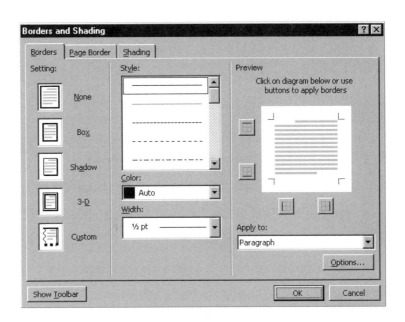

- Look at the **Preview** panel to see the effect of your choices.

  The four buttons, to the left of and below the **Preview** panel, allow you to place or remove the border individually on the top, bottom, left or right.

- Click the **Options** button to set the distance of the text from the border.

  It is a good idea to have some space between the text and the border.

- Click **OK** in each window to return to the page.

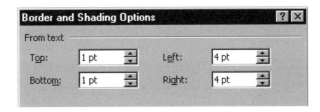

# 3.13  Adding Page Numbers

Page numbers are usually inserted in **Headers** or **Footers**.

See Section 7.3, page 150, for details.

## Exercise 3A

1   Open the **My Word 1** document.
    You should have 2 copies of the same text from an earlier exercise.

2   Format the original copy of the passage as described below.
    An example of what the finished text might look like is given in the box.

3   Set the font to Times New Roman.

4   Set the text size to 10 pt.

5   Add a title as below in 14 pt.

6   Make the first sentence italic and centre-align it.

7   Set a paragraph spacing of 6 pt above and below the first sentence.

8   Insert a blank line before the start of the main text.

9   Justify the rest of the passage.

10   Place the last sentence in a separate paragraph.

11   Right-align and italicise the name of the book.

12   Right-align the page number.

---

### Charles Dickens

*Below is an example of the work of Charles Dickens.*

They turned into the wine-shop which was closed (for it was midnight) and where Madame Defarge immediately took her post at her desk, counted the small moneys that had been taken during her absence, examined the stock, went through the entries in the book, made other entries of her own, checked the serving man in every possible way, and finally dismissed him into bed.

Then she turned out the contents of the bowl of money for the second time, and began knotting them in her handkerchief, in a chain of separate knots, for safe keeping through the night.

All this while, Defarge, with his pipe in his mouth, walked up and down, complacently admiring, but never interfering; in which condition, indeed, as to the business and his domestic affairs, he walked up and down through life.

*A Tale of Two Cities,*
page 179

---

## Exercise 3B

Format the second copy of the text so that it appears approximately as below. All the formatting options you need are in the Font dialogue box or on the Formatting Toolbar.

This exercise will help you to practise the formatting methods covered in this section. It is not meant to be an example of a well laid-out document!

Begin as follows.

1   Change the font to 14 pt Times New Roman for the title and 10 pt Arial for the rest.

2   Set the line spacing to 1.5 lines.

3   Practise other effects such as changing the text colour.

4   Save and close the document.

---

### Charles Dickens

*Below is an example of the work of CHARLES DICKENS.*

They turned into the wine-shop which was closed (for it was midnight) and where Madame Defarge immediately took her post at her desk, counted the small moneys that had been taken during her absence, examined the stock, went through the entries in the book, made other entries of her own, checked the serving man in every possible way, and finally dismissed him into bed.

Then she turned out the contents of the bowl of money for the second time, and began knotting them in her handkerchief, in a chain of separate knots, for safe keeping through the night.

~~All this while~~, Defarge, with his pipe in his mouth, walked up and down, complacently admiring, but never interfering; in which condition, indeed, as to the business and his domestic affairs, ***he walked up and down through life***.

*A Tale of Two Cities,*

*page 179*

---

# Section 4        Spelling and Grammar

## 4.1    Spelling

A built-in **Spell Check** in Word automatically checks the spelling in your documents.  However, it may not recognise some words such as local place names or words in a language other than English. Also, there are different versions of English, so if Word is set up for US English, it won't recognise English spellings such as 'colour', spelt 'color' in the US.  See Section 4.2 below for more details on the language used by the Spell Check.

It is important to remember that the Spell Check does not alert you to an incorrect word that is correctly spelt – 'there' instead of 'their', for example.  You still have to read through your work.

To use the Spell Check:

- Click the **Spell Check** button on the toolbar.
  *Alternatively*, Select **Spelling and Grammar** in the **Tools menu**.
  The Spelling and Grammar window appears.

Spell Check

- If all your spellings are correct (according to Word), a box appears telling you that the spell check is complete.

- When an incorrect spelling or an unrecognised word is found, it appears coloured red in the **Not in Dictionary** box.

  A list of suggestions appears in the **Suggestions** box underneath, with the first one selected as being the most likely.

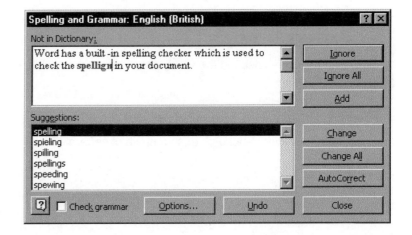

- Click on **Change** if the suggestion is appropriate.

- Click **Change All** to change all similarly incorrect spellings throughout the document.

- If the suggested word is not the right one, click on the correct word. (Scroll down if necessary.)
  Then click the **Change** or **Change All** button, as appropriate.

- If no suggestions are offered, you can type in your own correction.  Select the incorrect word in the **Not in Dictionary** box and type the correction.  Then, click **Change** or **Change All**.

- Sometimes the word is correct but not recognised by the Spell Check, e.g. a placename.
  Click **Add** to add the word to the Spell Check dictionary and it will not be questioned again.
  Click **Ignore** or **Ignore All** if you do not want to add a word to the dictionary.

- Note that clicking the **AutoCorrect** button will replace any incorrect word with what Word thinks is the correct spelling, <u>without asking you</u>.  This can be unpredictable so AutoCorrect should be used with care.

## 4.2    Language

If Word uses American English as the **default** language, you will have to change to a different version of English if you live elsewhere.  To change the default language, do the following.

- Select **Language** in the **Tools** menu.

- Click on **Set Language** in the window that opens.

- Click on the language version you want to select.

- Click the **Default** button.  This sets your chosen language as the default.  Click **Yes** if you are asked to confirm your choice for the whole document.

- Click **OK** in the original dialogue box.  The default language is now the one of your choice.

You may select a different language for parts of the document by selecting the text in the other language list and following the above procedure.  Then click **OK**, *not* Default.  This will result in the new language being used for the selected text in all future spelling checks.

Languages such as French and German, though listed, are not usually installed with Word and cannot be chosen for the Spell Check unless you have a disk containing those dictionaries.  Dictionaries for various languages and specialist subjects may be obtained on disk from your software supplier.

## 4.3    Find and Replace

Use the **Find** and **Replace** tools in the **Edit** menu to find all occurrences of a piece of text in a document and replace it, if necessary, with other text.  You may have used the wrong name in a document, for example.

Use **Find** to locate the word or text you are looking for.  If you want to change a particular occurrence, click the Replace button.

Use **Replace** when you know that you want to replace a word or phrase, not just find where it occurs in the document.

To use Find and Replace, do the following.

- Select **Find** or **Replace** in the **Edit** menu

- In the **Find what** box, enter the text you want to search for.

- Click **Find Next** to let Word find the next occurrence of the text so you can see it before deciding whether to replace it or not.

- Enter the replacement text in the **Replace with** box. (Click the **Replace** tab if you selected **Find** in the **Edit** menu.)

- Click the **Replace** button to replace it.

- Click **Replace All** to replace all occurrences of the word in the document.

## 4.4    Grammar

Word can check the grammar in a document, but you may not always agree with its advice!  Grammar can be checked automatically each time you run the Spell Check.  The same window is used. Questionable grammar appears in green.  The procedure for using the **Grammar Check** is similar to that used for spelling.

When the **Check Grammar** box at the bottom left corner of the Spelling and Grammar window is ticked, the Grammar Check is turned on.  To turn it off, click the box to remove the tick.

## 4.5    Counting Words

The number of words in a document can be
counted as follows.

- Select **Word Count** in the **Tools** menu.
  The Word Count window appears.
  It shows the number of words, individual
  characters, pages and so on.

- Click the **Close** button to close the
  window.

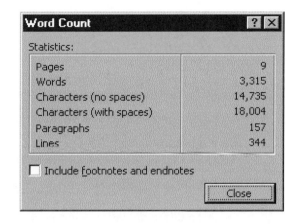

## 4.6    Using the Thesaurus

Use the **Thesaurus** to find the
right word.

- Select the word you want to
  look up.

- Select **Language** in the
  **Tools** menu and click on
  **Thesaurus**.

- The Thesaurus dialogue box
  appears.

- **Meanings** of the selected
  word appear on the left with
  a list of **synonyms** on the
  right.
  (A synonym is a word with a
  similar meaning.)

- To replace the word with a
  synonym, select the
  synonym and click **Replace**.

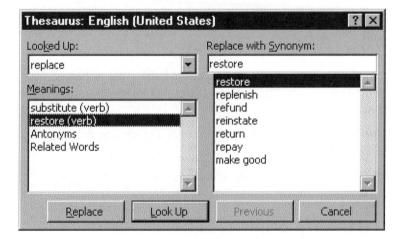

- Click **Cancel** if you don't want to replace the selected word.

- To look up alternatives for one of the synonyms, select it and click **Look Up**.

- **Antonyms** and **Related Words** may sometimes be listed by clicking on those options in the
  **Meanings** box.

## Exercise  4A

1   Open the **My Word 1** file.

2   Check the spelling and grammar.

3   Check the word count.

4   Look up some of the words in the Thesaurus.

5   Find all occurrences of **her** and replace it with **Madame's**.

# Section 5    Printing

## 5.1    Previewing a Document

When you've prepared your document, you will want to print it.

As the document has been prepared on the screen, not on paper, it is a good idea to make a final check before printing begins.

You can **Preview** the document on screen to see what it will look like on paper when it is printed.  This allows you to make any last-minute adjustments that may be necessary.

Print Preview

- Click the **Print Preview** button on the toolbar.

  *Alternatively*, select **Print Preview** in the **File** menu.

  A small preview of the full page is displayed on the screen as it will appear on the paper.

- To see the next page, press the **Page Down** key on the keyboard. Press **Page Up** to see the previous page.

  *Alternatively*, use the **Scroll Bars** on the screen.

- Click the **Magnifier** button on the toolbar if the text is too small to read.

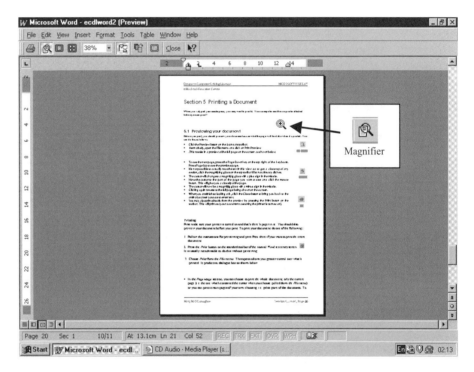

- The cursor changes to a magnifying glass with a plus (+) sign in the middle.

- Move the cursor to the part of the page you want to enlarge and click the mouse button.

  A magnified view of the text is displayed.

  The magnifying glass now has a minus sign (–) in the middle to indicate that it will reduce the size of the document if clicked.

- Click on the page with the minus (–) magnifier to return to the full-page view on the screen.

- Click the **Print** button on the toolbar to print directly from the preview screen.

Print

- Click the **Close** button on the **Preview** toolbar when you are finished looking at the preview to return to the ordinary screen.

## 5.2    Printing a Document

The computer must be connected to a printer – and there must be paper in it!
Make sure the printer is turned on.

Print

- Click the **Print** button on the Toolbar of the normal Word document screen.

- *Alternatively*, select **Print** in the **File** menu.

The **Print** window opens.

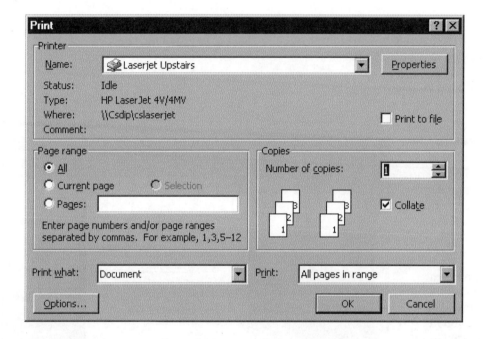

- Click the **OK** button at the bottom right of the window to print a single copy of the document.

- To print more than one copy, enter the number you require in the **Number of copies** box.

## 5.3    Printing Part of a Document

When a document consists of several pages, you may not need to print it all.  To print only the pages you need, follow these steps.

- Click the **Print** button on the toolbar or select **Print** in the **File** menu as before.
  The **Print** window opens.

- Click **Current page** to print the page you are working on.
  (The Current page is the one with the cursor on it when you clicked on **Print**.)  It is usually the one displayed on the screen.

- Click the **Pages** button to print a selection of pages.
  Enter the numbers of the pages you want to print, separated by commas of hyphens.
  **Use commas** to print individual pages.  2,5 prints page 2 and page 5 but not pages 1,3 and 4.
  **Use a hyphen** to print a range of pages.  2-5 prints pages 2,3,4 and 5.

- To print more than one copy, enter the number you require in the **Number of copies** box.

- Click the **OK** button to print the pages.

## 5.4    Choosing a Printer

The printer in use is displayed in the **Name** box at the top of the **Print** window. A single stand-alone or home computer will have a single printer connected directly to it.

In an office situation where there are many computers connected on a network, there may also be several printers, in different locations. Select the printer to use by clicking in the **Name** box to display a list of printers available and click on your choice. The selected printer's name then appears in the Name box.

In the illustration on page 144, the selected printer is Laserjet Upstairs.

## 5.5    Print to File

**Print Files** are used by commercial printers. In some ECDL tests, candidates are given the option of saving their work as a Print File if a printer is not available.

Although no printout is produced, the presence of the Print File on the candidate's test disk is evidence that the candidate is familiar with Print procedures.

To save your work as a Print File, proceed as follows.

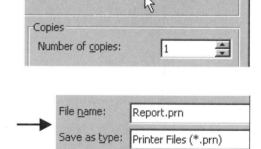

- Select **Print** in the **File** menu.
  The Print window opens (see page 144).

- Click the **Print to File** box to place a tick in it.

- Click **OK**. The **Print to File** window appears.
  It is similar to the Save As window.

- Give the file a title and select where it is to be saved, in the usual way. in the case of an ECDL test, you will save it on your candidate disk.
  The extension **.prn** is added to the title of your document (but it may not be displayed on some computers).

- Click **Save**.
  The file is saved. Its icon may be a Word icon or a generic one.

Report.prn      Report.prn

**Important:**  If there is no Print to File facility in the Print window that appears, select another printer or seek help from the test supervisor.

## Exercise 5A

**1**  Open the **My Word 1** document.

**2**  Preview it.

**3**  Make sure that your printer is turned on and has paper in it.

**4**  Print the document

**5**  It is a good idea to make a copy of your document on a floppy or other disk, so that you will have a separate back-up copy.

**6**  Close the document.

# Section 6     Adding and Importing Text

## 6.1     Adding Text

**Adding** or **appending** text means placing it in an existing document. You can add text to a document that you have open on the Desktop. If you have already saved and closed a document, you can open it again at any time and add more text.

You can also add or append text from another document without having to retype it. You can insert a whole document (also called a **file**) into another document or you can select and insert just part of it.

## 6.2     Opening More than One Document

It is possible to have two or more documents open at the same time.

- Use the **Open** button or select **Open** in the **File** menu to open the first document.
- Open the second document in the same way. The second document hides the first document on the screen but the first one is still there underneath.
- Open further documents if you need to. All the documents will be open, but you must switch between them to work on the individual documents.

See Module 2, Section 2.10, page 76, for more information.

## 6.3     Switching Between Open Documents

Only one document can be **active** at a time. The active document is the one you are working on.

- The open documents are listed at the bottom of the **Window** menu.
- Click the document in the **Window** menu that you want to use.
  The document is displayed on the screen and hides any other open documents.

*Alternatively*, do the following.

- Use the **Minimise** button to minimise the active document. Be careful not to minimise **Word** by clicking the upper button.
  A button for the document appears on the **Taskbar** at the bottom of the screen.

Minimise

- Another open document is now visible on the screen

- The second document can also be minimised to make a similar button for it on the Taskbar.

- One of the document buttons on the Taskbar is highlighted, usually in blue.
  In the illustration, the **Agenda** document is the one highlighted – you can see the **3 window buttons** to the right of its name on the Taskbar button.
  Click the document's **Maximise** button to view the document again.

Maximise

- To highlight the other document, click its button. The document window buttons appear.
  Click the **Maximise** button to view this document.

## 6.4    Viewing Two Documents at the Same Time

When you switch between open documents, you normally see them displayed full size on the Desktop. It is also possible to see two documents displayed together. Because they then both share the Desktop, a much smaller part of each document is displayed. However, it can be useful to see and compare parts of different documents at the same time.

- Make sure that the two documents you want to see are open and that both of them are maximised.
  Click the **Maximise** button on each if you are not sure.

- Select **Arrange All** in the **Window** menu.
  The two documents appear in the window, one above the other.

- Click in the document you want to work with.

- Click in the other document when you want to work in that one.

- To return a document to full screen size, click its **Maximise** button.

You can use a similar technique to have two different parts of the same document on the Desktop.

- Make sure the document you want to examine is open.

- Select **Split** in the **Windows** menu.
  The document is split into two parts, one above the other.

- Scroll through each part of the document separately, as required.

- To remove the split, select **Remove Split** in the **Windows** menu.

## 6.5    Inserting One Document into Another

Sometimes you may want to combine two documents.

- Open the document into which you want to insert the second document.

- Place the cursor in the first document at the point where you want to insert the second document.

- Select **File** in the **Insert** menu.
  The **Insert File** window appears. It is similar to the **Open** window that appears when you want to open a document or file.

- In the **Insert File** window, find and select the document that you want to insert.

- Click **OK** to insert the document.

## 6.6    Inserting Part of One Document into Another

Sometimes you may need to insert some text, a paragraph or topic from one document into another.

The process used to do this is **Copy and Paste**. In this instance, you are copying and pasting between two separate documents instead of within the same one.

- Open both documents. You can have them full size or displayed together, as you prefer.

- In the first document, select and copy the text you want to use.

- Click in the second document, placing the cursor where you want the copied text to appear.

- Paste the text in the usual way.

## 6.7    Importing a Spreadsheet

When you are writing a report, it may be appropriate to include, for example, an expenses sheet that you have already created on a spreadsheet. It can be imported to your Word document as follows.

- Select **File** in the **Insert** menu.

- Find the Spreadsheet file you want to insert.

- (You may have to select **All Files** in the **Files of Type:** box.)

- If the file contains more than one sheet, the **Open Worksheet** window appears.

- Click **OK** to insert the entire worksheet.

- To select a particular sheet, click in the **Open document in Workbook** box to display a list of the sheets in the Spreadsheet.

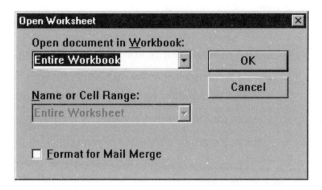

- Double-click the sheet you wish to insert.

- The sheet now appears in your Word document as a working spreadsheet that you can edit if necessary.

- A **chart** or **graph** can be imported by following the same procedure.

# Section 7     Layout, Headers and Footers

## 7.1     Page Setup

The size of the page, its orientation, the width of the margins and so on can all be selected according to your personal preferences and to suit the paper you use in the printer.  To set your own preferences, proceed as follows.

- Select **Page Setup** in the **File** menu.

  The Page Setup window appears.

- Tabs along the top of the window display various options.

  If the **Margins** tab is not already selected, click it to display the Margins settings window.

- Enter the margin sizes you require.

  A good margin size is 2cm all round the page.

  If your document is to be bound in a ring binder, increase the left margin to 3cm or more.

  The **Preview** panel on the right shows the page with the settings.

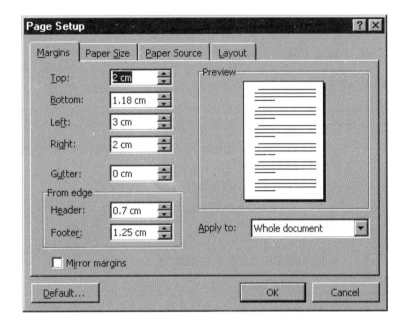

- Click the **Paper Size** tab to set the paper size.  The standard size in Europe is **A4**.

  To set the **Orientation** – the way the page will be printed – click **Portrait** (vertical) or **Landscape** (horizontal).  Portrait is used for the majority of documents.

- Click **OK** to apply your settings to this document only.

> You may change from the default settings for individual documents, but when the next new document is created, Word will again revert to the defaults.
>
> Click the **Default** button if you want your new settings to become the defaults for all future new documents.

## Exercise  7A

1  Open the **My Word 1** document that you created earlier.

2  Change the top and bottom margins to 3 cm and the left and right margins to 2.5cm.

3  Make sure that the paper size is A4 and the orientation is Portrait.

4  Do not set the above as the default settings.

5  Save the changes to the document.

## 7.2    Page Breaks

When you have finished a piece of text before the end of a page, you might prefer the next piece of text, such as a new chapter, to begin on a new page. Insert a **Page Break** to do this.

- Select **Break** in the **Insert** menu. The Break window opens.

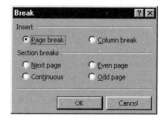

- **Page break** is already selected. Click **OK**. Word creates a new page and positions the cursor on it, ready for you to begin typing.

Using a page break means you can edit the page before the page break – as long as there is space enough for you to do the additional work – add or delete text or make other changes, without effecting the layout of text and graphics on the following page or pages.

## Exercise 7B

1   Open the **My Word 1** document if it is not already open.

2   The document should contain two pieces of text titled **Charles Dickens**. Insert a page break between the two pieces so that they are now on two separate pages.

3   Select **Print Preview** to make sure that there are now two pages in your document, each containing a piece of text.

4   Close the Print Preview window (without printing).

5   Save the changes to the document.

## 7.3    Headers and Footers

**Headers** and **Footers** contain text or graphics that automatically appear at the top or bottom of each page, as in this manual. They are usually used for document, author or chapter names (**Header**) and page numbers (**Footer**). To create a Header or Footer, proceed as follows.

- Select **Header and Footer** in the **View** menu.

- The Header and Footer Toolbar appears, usually in the centre of the screen.

- A **Header** area, outlined with a dashed line, appears at the top of the page.

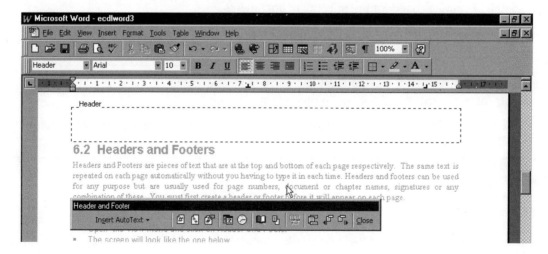

Any text on the actual page is 'grayed out', as you will be unable to work on it until you close the Header and Footer Toolbar.

# 7.4    The Header and Footer Toolbar

Some of the buttons on this toolbar are described below.  Remember that pointing to (*not* clicking on) a button will display a description of what it does.

The Header and Footer Toolbar

- Click **Insert AutoText** at the left of the toolbar to display a menu of items that can be automatically inserted.  See Section 7.5 on page 152 for details.

- The **Insert Page Number** button places a page number on each page.  The page number is automatically increased or decreased as you add or delete pages.

  Click to place the cursor where you want to insert the page number.  Then click the **Insert Page Number** button.

Insert Page
Number

- The **Insert Number of Pages** button inserts the total number of pages in the document.  It can be used with the Page Number button to insert such text as **Page 1 of 10**.  (You must type the words 'Page' and 'of' yourself, with spaces.)

  *Alternatively*, select **Page X of Y** in the **Insert AutoText** menu (see page 152).

Insert Number
of  Pages

- The **Format Page Number** button allows you to set the type of number to be used, ordinary, Roman numerals etc.

  The start number can also be set so that the numbering is continued from another document.  Chapter 2 of a book, for example, could begin at page 25.

Format
Page Number

- Clicking on the **Date** or **Time** buttons inserts the current date or time.

Date   Time

- The **Page Setup** button can be used to change the setup as described in the **Page Setup** section (Section 7.1, page 149).

  It also allows you to have a different, or no, header on the first page, e.g. if the first page is a title page.

Page Setup

- The **Show/Hide Document Text** button allows you to show or hide the main text on the page while you are inserting a Header or Footer.

- The **Same as Previous** button is normally selected by default as Word assumes that all your headers and footers are going to be the same.  You can, however, have different headers or footers for different sections of a document.

Show/Hide
Document Text

- Click the **Switch between Header and Footer** button to move between the Header and Footer.

Same as Previous

- The **Show Previous** and **Show Next** buttons display the next or previous Headers or Footers (if any).

- Click the **Close** button at the right of the toolbar when you are finished.

  You are returned to the main text page.

Switch  between
Header and Footer

Note that when you return to the main page, any text in the **Header** and **Footer** is 'grayed out' and unavailable.

To edit a Header or Footer, select **Header and Footer** in the **View** menu.

Previous / Next

## 7.5    Using Headers and Footers

Type the text or insert the graphics that you want in the Header or Footer.  The usual text formatting options can be applied, e.g. Font, Size, Alignment and so on.

- Click the **Switch between Header and Footer** button to move from Header to Footer and back.

- Click the **Close** button to return to the normal text page.

Word can automatically insert information in headers or footers with a facility called **AutoText**.

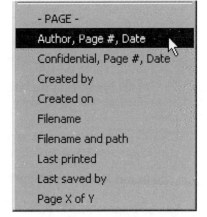

- Display the Header or Footer as required.

- Click **AutoText** in the **Insert** menu.
  A sub-menu appears, as shown on the right.

- Click the item you want to insert.
  It appears in the Header or Footer.
  (Word assumes that the author is the registered user of the software, as shown in the example below.)

```
 _Footer_ _ _ _ _ _ _ _ _ _ _ _ _ _ _ _ _ _ _ _ _ _ _ _ _ _ _ _ _ _ _ _ _ _ _ _ _ _
｜Blackrock Education Centre        Page 1                        29/02/00｜
```

Note that Headers and Footers are displayed in the **Page Layout** and **Print Preview** views but not in **Normal** view.


## Exercise 7C

**1**   Open the **My Word 1** document if it's not already open.

**2**   Insert a Header and a Footer as shown below.

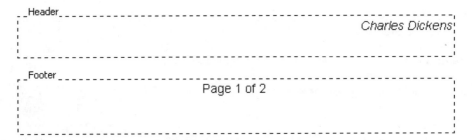

**If you need some help, try the following**.

**1**   For the Header, type the text, then right align it and make it italics.
      Do not use the space bar to move the text to the right-hand side of the page.

**2**   For the Footer, type the word 'Page '.  (Don't forget the space.)
      Then use the **Insert Page Number** button.
      Then type the word ' of ' (spaces before and after) and click the **Insert Number of Pages** button.
      Centre the text.

**3**   Close the Header and Footer Toolbar and check the Header and Footer in **Print Preview**.

**4**   Print the document and close it.

# Section 8    Tables

## 8.1    Creating a Table

A **table** is a grid of rows and columns with **cells** in which you can insert text and graphics.  It is useful for many different purposes in word processing, e.g. when you want neat columns of text or numbers across the page.  The table doesn't even have to look like a table, if you don't display the lines that form the grid.

To create a table, position the insertion point on the page where you want to place the table.  Then use one of the following methods.

### 1 – Use the Toolbar

This method is useful for creating small Tables.

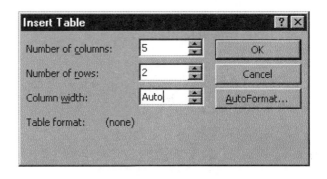

- Click the **Insert Table** button on the toolbar.
  A grid appears below the button, as shown in the illustration.

- Drag the mouse across the grid to select the number of rows and columns you want in the table.
  In the illustration, 2 rows and 5 columns have been selected.

- Release the mouse button and the table appears in the document.

### 2 – Use the Table menu

This method gives more options than using the Insert Table button.  It is useful for creating larger tables.

- Select **Insert Table** in the **Table** menu.
  The Insert Table window appears.

- Use the arrow buttons or type in the number of columns and rows you want.

- You can specify exact measurements for the width of columns but leaving the width as **Auto** is usually sufficient.

- Click **OK**.  The table appears in the document.

If a blank outline of the table does not appear when you create the table, the outline has been set to be hidden.  Select **Gridlines** in the **Table** menu to display it.

In Office 2000, the **Insert Table** window offers additional choices.

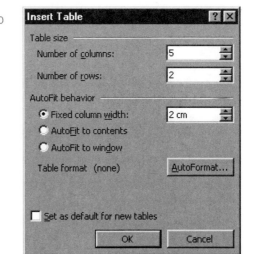

**Fixed column width** allows a specific width to be set.

**AutoFit to contents** adjusts the width according to what is in the cells.

**Autofit to window** adjusts the width of the table to the window in which it appears.

## 8.2    Entering Text

When Word inserts an empty table in a document, it positions the insertion point in the first cell. You can start typing in text right away.

When you reach the end of the cell as you type, the text automatically goes on to the next line and the height of the cell changes automatically to accommodate the text.

To insert text in a different cell, click with the mouse in the new cell and type the text. *Alternatively*, use one of the following.

- To move to the next cell, press the **Tab** key.

- To move to the preceding cell, press **Shift** + **Tab**.

- To move to the next row, use the **Arrow** keys, *not* the **Return** key.

- To go on to a new line in a cell, use the **Return** key.

- To move to any cell, click with the mouse in that cell.

## 8.3    Aligning Text in Tables

Text is aligned left in table cells by default.  To centre or right-align text, use the alignment buttons on the toolbar.  Text can also be orientated vertically (see the illustration).

To re-orientate text, proceed as follows.

- Select the cell(s) you wish to modify.

- Select **Text Direction** in the **Format** menu.
  The **Text Direction** window opens.

- Click the direction you require in the **Orientation** panel.

- Click **OK**.

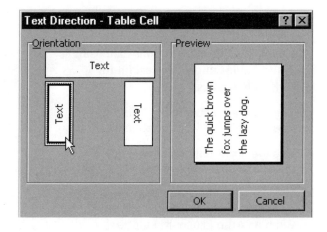

Text can be aligned vertically as well as horizontally in cells.

- Select the cell(s) you wish to format.

- Select **Cell Alignment** in the **Format** menu.

- Click the alignment you require in the sub-menu that appears.

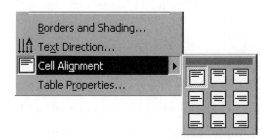

# Exercise 8A

**1** Create a new document and call it **Table 1**.

**2** Create the Table shown below in the document.  Use Times New Roman, 10 pt.
   The table on your computer may look slightly different from the illustration.

**3** Don't forget to save the document.

| Student Name | September Test | October Test | November Test |
|---|---|---|---|
| Jean Martin | 78 | 56 | 89 |
| John Hoyt | 34 | 75 | 65 |
| Clare Stone | 69 | 91 | 47 |
| Ted Wells | 48 | 69 | 98 |

## 8.4    Working with Text, Rows and Columns

### Formatting Text

You can format text in a table – in cells, rows or columns – in the same way as you format normal text, i.e. by first selecting it and then using the buttons on the **Toolbar** or the **Format** menu to make changes.

### Selecting Rows

- Click once in the white area *to the left of the row* you want to select.
  The cursor becomes an arrow pointing towards the row.  **Click** to select the row.

- *Alternatively*, click in any cell of the row and select **Select Row** in the **Table** menu.

### Selecting Columns

- Click once in the white space *immediately above the column* you want to select.
  The cursor becomes a black downward-pointing arrow.  **Click** to select the column.

- *Alternatively*, click in any cell of the column and select **Select Column** in the **Table** menu.

### Selecting a Single Cell or Text

- To select an individual cell, position the cursor in the left of the cell until it changes to a white arrow, then click.

- To select text in a cell, use the usual text selection methods.

### Selecting the entire table

Do *not* highlight all the rows and columns.  You must use the following procedure.

- Click in any cell in the table.

- Select **Select Table** in the Table menu.

### Deleting Rows and Columns

- Select the row or column as above.

- Select **Delete Rows** or **Delete Columns** in the **Table** menu.

## Deleting the Contents of a Row or Column

To remove the contents of a row or column without removing the row or column itself (i.e. 'clear' it):

- Select the row or column and then press the **Delete** key.

## Adding Rows and Columns

You can insert extra rows and columns after you have created the table, if it becomes necessary.

- To add an extra row, select the row *below* the position where you want to add a new row.
  Then select **Insert Rows** in the **Table** menu.

- To add an extra column, select the column to the *right* of the position where you want to add the new column.
  Then select **Insert Columns** in the **Table** menu.

## Changing the Height of a Row

- Move the cursor over the border until it becomes a bar with arrows pointing up and down.
  Hold down the mouse button and drag to the required height.

- To set an exact height, select **Cell Height and Width** in the **Table** menu.
  Cick the **Row** tab in the window that opens and enter the required height in the box.
  Click **OK**.

- To make all the rows the same height, select the whole Table and click on **Distribute Rows Evenly** in the **Table** menu.

## Changing the Width of a Column

- Move the cursor over the column border until it becomes a bar with arrows pointing left and right.
  Hold the left mouse button down and drag to the required width.

- To set an exact width, select **Cell Height and Width** in the **Table** menu.
  Click the **Column** tab in the window that opens and enter the required width in the box.  Click **OK**.

- To make all the columns the same width, select the whole Table and click on **Distribute Columns Evenly** in the **Table** menu.

## Changing the Space between Columns

To change the space between the contents of the cells and the side of the columns, do the following.

- Select **Cell Height and Width** in the **Table** menu.
  Click the **Column** tab and enter the measurement in the **Space between columns** box.
  Click **OK**.

 ## Resizing a Table

Move the pointer over the table to display the **Move** and **Resize** handles.  Drag the Resize handle to change the **size** of the table.  Drag the Move handle to **reposition** the table on the page.

Move Handle

Resize Handle

## Exercise 8B

**1** Open the **Table 1** document you created earlier.

**2** Make changes to it by deleting or inserting information as in the illustration.

**3** Format the cells as below. The final table should appear as shown below.

**4** Save the changes to the document.

| *Student Name* | *September Test* | *October Test* |
|---|---|---|
| Jean Martin | 78 | 56 |
| John Hoyt | 34 | 75 |
| Ted Wells | 48 | 69 |

## 8.5    Table Borders and Shading

Word inserts a simple line border around the table and the individual cells. You can change the border and add shading or you can choose not to have any, so that the table appears on the page with a neat, unlined appearance. To add borders and shading, proceed as follows.

- Select the table, row, column or cell that you want to put the border around.

- Select **Borders and Shading** in the **Format** menu. The Borders and Shading window opens.

- Click the **Borders** tab if it is not already clicked.

- In the **Setting** section on the left, select the kind of border you require.

- Click the **Custom** button if you want to make your own border.

- In the **Style** section, select the style, colour and width of the lines for the border.

- Look in the **Preview** box on the right to see the effect of the changes you've made.

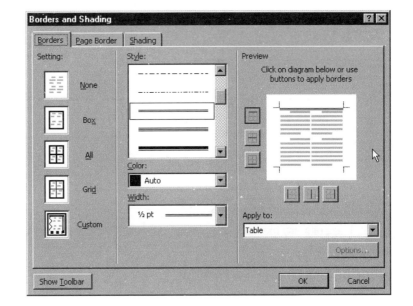

- Click the **buttons** at the left of and below the **Preview** to use partial borders, or one type of border for the top and another type for the sides and bottom, for example. Click a button again to remove the border.

- Click the **Shading** tab to choose a colour and pattern for the cells.

- Click **OK** when you have made your choices or **Cancel** if you do not want any borders.

- Check the result in the document itself or in **Print Preview**. (See Section 5.1, page 143.)

## Exercise 8C

1  Open the **Table 1** document.
2  Make a copy of the table so that you have two copies of the table in your document.
3  Add borders to the first table so that it appears as shown below.

| Student Name | September Test | October Test |
|---|---|---|
| Jean Martin | 78 | 56 |
| John Hoyt | 34 | 75 |
| Ted Wells | 48 | 69 |

4  Using the second table, add different borders yourself and also add shading.
5  Copy one of your tables and format it so that there are no borders or shading at all.
6  Preview the document.
7  Don't forget to save your work.

## 8.6    Inserting a Heading in a Table

You can join cells together to contain text that spans 2 or more columns in a row.  This is called **merging cells.**  It is useful for putting a heading in the top row of your table and centering the text across all the columns, as in the example below.

| *This is an example of a Table Heading* | | | |
|---|---|---|---|
| Ordinary | cells | in the | table |

To merge cells, do the following.

- Select the cells you want to merge.
  You may have to add an extra row for the heading.

- Select **Merge Cells in** the **Table** menu.
  The cells are merged.   Any text you type will now spread across the columns.

### Splitting Cells to undo a Heading

Merged cells can be 'unmerged' or split as follows.

- Select the cell that you want to split.

- Select **Split Cells in** the **Table** menu.
  The Split Cells window opens.

- Enter the number of Columns and/or Rows you want and click **OK**.
  The cells are split as you specified.

Note that splitting cells may cause problems with the data that they contain, especially if you've made other changes since you merged the cells.

## 8.7     Centering a Table on a Page

If a table is less than the width of the page, you can centre it on the page, as follows.

- Select the table.   (**NB:** Use the correct method as described in Section 8.4 on page 155.)
- Click the **Center** alignment button on the toolbar.

*Alternatively*:

- Select **Cell Height and Width** in the **Table** menu.
  The Cell Height and Width window opens.
- Make sure the **Row** tab is clicked.
- Select **Center** in the **Alignment** section.

 Moving the pointer over the table displays the **Move** and **Resize** handles.

Drag a handle to reposition or resize the table as required.

Move Handle

Resize Handle

## Exercise 8D

**1**  Open the **Table 1** document.

**2**  Center the Tables.

**3**  Add a heading **Test Results** to the first table, as shown below.

**4**  (This is quite an advanced task, so you can omit this question if you wish.)

Split the column with the student names into 2 columns, one to hold first names and the other to hold the surnames, as shown below.

You may have to adjust the width of the columns.  You will also have to move the surnames to the appropriate cells after you've split the cells.

**5**  Preview and print the document.

**6**  Save and close the document.

| Test Results | | | |
|---|---|---|---|
| *Student Name* | | *September Test* | *October Test* |
| Jean | Martin | 78 | 56 |
| John | Hoyt | 34 | 75 |
| Ted | Wells | 48 | 69 |

## 8.8    Creating Tables Automatically

You can use the wizards in Word to simplify many complex tasks.

The wizard for creating a table is not a full wizard, but it works in a similar way.  It formats the table for you using the **AutoFormat** tool.

- If you're creating a new Table, select **Insert Table** in the **Table** menu.

  Enter the number of rows and columns required and click the **AutoFormat** button.

- If you have already created a table, first select the Table.  Then click **Table AutoFormat** in the **Table** menu.

  The AutoFormat window opens.

- In the **Formats** section, scroll to see the styles available.

  Click on the name of a style to display a preview in the **Preview** section of the window.

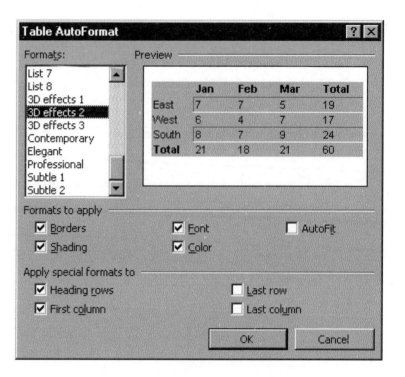

- It is possible to use part of a particular style, but to omit some effects.

  In the **Formats to Apply** section, click the box beside the effect you don't want.   (Remove the check mark.)

  Try out the different options.  The Preview panel shows the result of your choices.

- When you are satisfied with your table, click **OK**.  The new table appears in your document.

## Exercise 8E

1   Create a new document and call it **Timetable**.

2   Create a new table in the document that is big enough to hold your timetable.

   If you don't use a timetable, make one up or choose another topic for which you could use a table.

3   Use AutoFormat to add formatting to the table.  Try different styles.

4   Using Landscape orientation for the page setup may be more appropriate here than Portrait.

5   Preview and print your timetable.

6   Save and close the document.

# Section 9        Graphics

## 9.1    Using Graphics

**Graphics** are images, pictures, diagrams, charts, photographs etc. which may be **imported** or **inserted** into a Word or other document. The graphic may be on the hard disk, a floppy disk, CD-ROM or other media, or it may be scanned directly into the computer.

Word is supplied with a collection of graphics, usually referred to as **Clip Art.** Collections of Clip Art and photographs for computer use can be bought, acquired as shareware or freeware, or you can use a scanner to make your own.

Software packages such as Paintbrush (supplied with Windows) can be used to draw or edit pictures that can then be inserted into a document.

## 9.2    Inserting Clip Art

A small **Clip Art** collection is usually installed on your computer with Word. The complete Clip Art collection on the Microsoft Office CD may not have been installed in order to save hard disk space. If you find Clip Art useful, you should consider installing the complete collection.

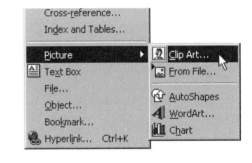

To insert Clip Art, proceed as follows.

- Select **Picture** in the **Insert** menu.

- Select **Clip Art** in the sub-menu that appears.

  The Microsoft Clip Gallery window appears.

  Make sure that the **Clip Art** tab is clicked.

- Click a category name on the left to see the graphics for that category.

  They are displayed in the large panel on the right.

- Double-click the graphic you require to select it.

- Click the **Insert** button to insert the graphic in the document.

- The graphic may have to be **resized** (see Section 9.5, page 164).

- Click the **Close** button to cancel if you change your mind.

Note that pictures, sounds and videos may also be inserted, if available. Click the tabs at the top of the window.

See Module 6, Section 8.9, page 318, for information on changing colours in Clip Art.

To insert ClipArt in Office 2000, proceed as follows.

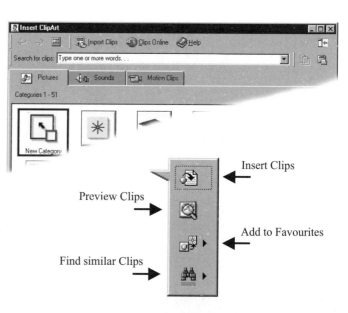

- Select **Picture** in the **Insert** menu.

- Select **Clip Art** in the sub-menu that appears.
  The **Insert ClipArt** window appears.

- Make sure the **Picture** tab is clicked.
  Icons in the main part of the window represent the different picture categories.

- Click on a category icon to display a selection of available ClipArt pictures.

- Click the picture you wish to insert.

- A vertical button menu appears with buttons for four choices.

- Click the **Insert Clips** button to place the picture in the document.
  It is inserted as an inline graphic. See Section 9.4, page 163, for information on graphics and text.

- Close the **Insert ClipArt** window.

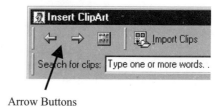

The arrow buttons in the button bar allow you to move backwards and forwards through your selections. You can also search for clips by typing key words in the **Search for clips** box.

## 9.3    Inserting a Graphic from File

Apart from the supplied Clip Art, you may have other graphics stored on the computer, images from a digital camera or a scanner, for example. There may also be Clip Art or other graphics available on CD-ROM or other media. To insert a graphic:

- Select **Picture** in the **Insert** menu and **From File** in the sub-menu.
  The **Insert Picture** window appears. (In Office 2000, there is a panel with large buttons on the left.)

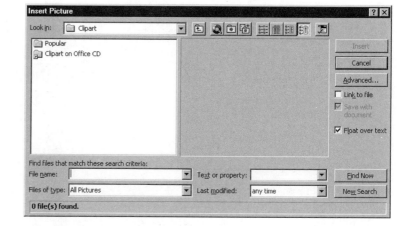

- In the **Look in** box, find the graphic file you want to insert.
  The procedure is similar to the one used to open or save a file.

- The **Files of Type** box should normally contain **All Pictures**.
  (You can specify a particular file type if you know how the graphic is stored – bitmap, jpeg, gif etc.)

- Click on the name of the graphic you want to insert. A preview of the graphic may be displayed in the panel on the right.

- Click **OK**. The graphic is inserted in the document.

## 9.4    Text Wrapping

When a graphic appears on the page, the text is set to flow or **wrap** around it.  This causes the text to move, to accommodate the drawing, which may upset your layout.  You can select a different wrapping to suit your layout or you may decide not to have any wrapping at all so that you can adjust the text yourself.

Set the text wrapping as follows.

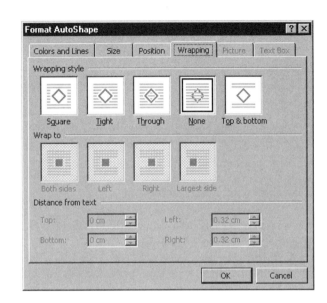

- Click on the graphic to select it.

- In the **Format** menu, click on the description of the graphic (**AutoShape**, **Object**, **Picture** etc.) at the bottom of the menu.

  The Format window opens.

- Click the **Wrapping** tab.

  The **Wrapping Style** icons and the titles underneath illustrate their respective effects.

- Select the type of wrapping you require.

  Click **None** to remove wrapping completely.

- With **None** selected, you can separate text and object more conveniently.

  The document margins (indents) on the ruler can be adjusted to give the required separation (see Section 11, page 171).

  The ruler settings for the bulleted text and illustration above are shown below (slightly reduced).

Reduced text area ◄──────────►◄────── Wider margin for graphics ──────►

Text wrapping in Office 2000 is essentially the same as described above.  The **Format** window, however, is different.

- Click the **Layout** tab in the **Format** window.

  **In line with text** is selected as the default but this may not always be convenient.

- Select one of the other options to make the graphic an *independent* graphic that can be placed anywhere on the page.

- Select **Behind text** or **In front of text** (instead of **None** in earlier versions of Office) to separate text and object on the page as described above.

## 9.5    Resizing a Graphic

When a graphic is not the right size for your purpose, you can resize it to make it bigger or smaller, wider or longer, as follows.

- Click anywhere on the graphic to select it.

  Small white squares, called **Handles**, appear at intervals around the graphic.

- Drag a **centre** handle at the sides or at the top or bottom of the graphic to **stretch** it horizontally or vertically.

  Stretching a graphic distorts the proportions.  This is not always desirable.

- Drag a **corner** handle **diagonally** to change the size of the graphic without stretching or distorting it.

  If the graphic is distorted when you drag a corner handle, hold down the **Shift** key while you drag to keep the proportions correct.

Selected Graphic
showing Handles

A graphic can also be resized using the **Format** window described in Section 9.4, page 163.

- Click the **Size** tab and enter the size you require.

- Click the tabs at the top of the window for other options.

## 9.6    Moving a Graphic

Graphics can be moved around your document using the usual techniques for moving text.

- To move the graphic to a different part of the page, drag it to the new position.

- To move to a different part of the document, use **Cut and Paste** as for text.

- Graphics can also be copied using **Copy and Paste** as for text.

## 9.7    Drawing and AutoShapes

Word has a number of drawing tools called **AutoShapes** that you can use to add drawings – lines, arrows, boxes etc. – to your documents.

Click the **Drawing** button on the toolbar to display the **Drawing** Toolbar.  It appears at the bottom of the screen. (To remove the toolbar, click the button again.)

Drawing

You can also display the Drawing Toolbar by selecting it in the **View** menu under **Toolbars**.

Buttons for commonly used AutoShapes – lines, boxes etc. – appear on the toolbar.

The Drawing Toolbar

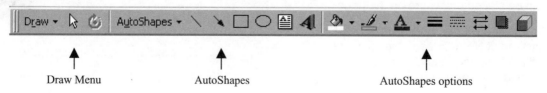

Draw Menu                    AutoShapes                    AutoShapes options

Note the **Text Box** button. Text can be placed in a separate box
of its own on the page, as in the captions under the illustrations
in this manual. See Module 6, Section 5, page 305, for more
information on text boxes.

- Click **AutoShapes** on the Taskbar to display a pop-up menu of
  other AutoShapes, each with a sub-menu of its own.

The AutoShapes Menu

## 9.8    Using AutoShapes

Using AutoShapes is similar to using other simple drawing programs.

- Click the button for the shape that you want to draw.

- Click on the document in the position where you
  want the drawing to appear.

  The cursor changes to a **crosshair**.

Crosshair

- Hold down the mouse button and drag until the
  shape is the size you require.

- Use the AutoShape **Options** menus and
  buttons on the **AutoShapes** Toolbar to adjust
  the appearance of the drawing.

  **Line** and **Fill** options, which provide for colour
  and texture, are shown here.

  The **Shadow** button at the right of the toolbar
  places a shadow behind a selected object.

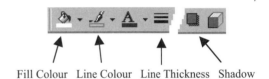

Fill Colour   Line Colour   Line Thickness   Shadow

## 9.9    Freehand Drawing

As well as using simple lines and shapes, freehand drawing is also possible.

- Select **Lines** in the **AutoShapes** menu to display the Lines sub-menu.

  The three buttons at the top are for drawing plain or arrowed lines.

  The three buttons underneath – **Curve**, **Freeform** and **Scribble** – are
  for freehand drawing.

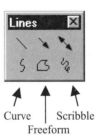

Curve | Scribble
Freeform

**To use the Curve and Freeform tools:**

- Click the appropriate button to select it.

- Click on the page where you want the line to begin.

- Move the mouse and click again. Continue to move and click to draw the required shape.

- Double-click to finish or return to the starting point and click once to draw an enclosed object.

**To use the Scribble tool:**

- Click the **Scribble** button to select it.

- The pointer becomes a crosshair and assumes the shape of a pencil when you press and hold
  down the mouse button.

- Draw the line or shape.

- Release the mouse button to finish.

## 9.10    Rotating an Object

Drawing objects can be flipped horizontally or vertically, rotated in 90° steps left or right, or rotated freely to any angle.

- Click on the object to select it.

- Click the **Draw** button on the **Drawing Toolbar** to display the Draw menu.

- Select **Rotate or Flip** and click the option in the sub-menu that you require.

- To rotate an object to any angle, select **Free Rotate** and drag one of the round handles that appear at the corners.

Note that the **Free Rotate** icon also appears on the toolbar and can be selected without using the Draw menu.

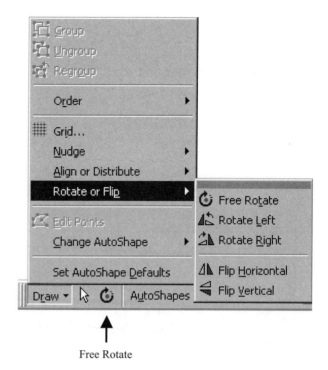

Free Rotate

## Exercise 9A

**1** Open the **My Word 1** file.

**2** Insert a Clip Art graphic from the Word collection into the document.

**3** Practise resizing the graphic and placing it in different places.

**4** If you have any Clip Art on a separate disk or file, insert some of it into your document.

**5** Preview and print the document.

**6** Save your work.

# Section 10    Tabs

## 10.1    Tabs

Using the **Space Bar** to make a list like the one below gives unpredictable results and will cause problems if you reformat the text later.  The proper way to make lists like this is to use **Tabs**.

| London | March: | Monday, Wednesday | £99.00 |
| Paris | April: | Tuesday, Thursday, Friday | £179.99 |

**Tabs** are used to create column-like lists across a page, as shown above.

Pressing the **Tab** key moves the cursor to the tabbed position on the page.  The text that you type then appears at that position.

The Tab key

Word has default tab settings, with tabs set at 1/2-inch intervals (even when the ruler is set to centimetres!) from the left margin.  You would normally set your own tabs, however, when you are making tabbed lists.

There are four different tabs that align text in different ways.

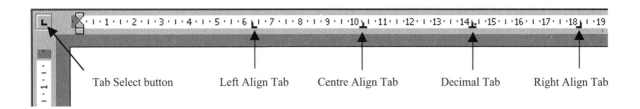

| Tab Select button | Left Align Tab | Centre Align Tab | Decimal Tab | Right Align Tab |

The positions of the tabs are shown on the ruler by small markers.  Word tabs are shown as small light gray dots along the bottom of the ruler.  Tabs that you insert yourself are shown in heavy black shapes, as in the illustration.

## 10.2    Setting Tabs on the Ruler

You can set tabs before you begin to type, or set or change tabs in text that has already been typed.

When you set a new tab, Word removes any of its own tabs to the left of the one set by you.

- If you are setting tabs in existing text, select the text first.
- Click the **Tab Select** button at the left of the ruler.
  Each time you click the button, a different tab appears.
  Click until it shows the tab that you require.
- Use the **Decimal** tab for numbers with decimal points, such as prices.
- Click on the ruler at the position where you want to set the tab.
  The tab appears on the ruler at that point.
  Drag the tab along the ruler to reposition it, if necessary.
- Press the **tab** key on the keyboard to move the cursor to the tab.  Press the key again to move to the next tab, and so on.
- Press the **Backspace** key to go back.

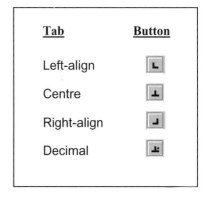

| Tab | Button |
| --- | --- |
| Left-align | L |
| Centre | ⊥ |
| Right-align | ⅃ |
| Decimal | ⅃. |

## 10.3   Setting Tabs in the Tabs Window

You can set tabs at precise positions on the ruler by selecting **Tabs** in the **Format** menu.

- Select **Tabs** in the **Format** menu.
  The Tabs window opens.

- Type the position of your first tab, e.g. 3cm, in the **Tab stop position** box.
  You do not have to type 'cm'. It will be added automatically later.
  The tab position appears in the panel underneath.

- In the **Alignment** section, click the option you want, e.g. Left.

- Click the **Set** button at the bottom of the window to place the tab on the ruler.

- Type the position of the next tab you want and so on until you have put in all the tab positions.

- Click **OK** when you are finished.

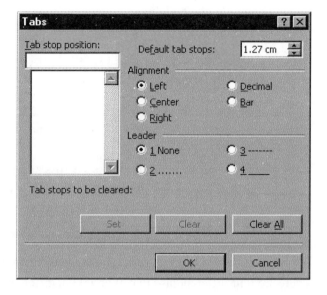

## 10.4   Tab Leaders

A **tab leader** is a line that is inserted automatically, leading from the left to the tabbed item. It leads the eye across the page to connect two items, as in the following example.

(There can also be a leader between two tabs.)

Tea...................................................................................£1.50

Coffee..............................................................................£1.60

Muffins ...........................................................................£1.35

To add a leader when you are setting a tab on the ruler, proceed as follows.

Tab leaders are set in the **Tabs** window. When you are setting tabs as described above, click the button in the **Leader** area for the kind of leader you require – dotted, dashed or continuous – before you click the **Set** button. (Click **None** to remove an existing tab leader.)

To add a leader to an existing tab on the ruler, do the following.

- Double-click the **Tab** on the ruler to open the Tabs window.

- *Alternatively*, select **Tabs** in the **Format** menu to open the Tabs window.

- Click on the required tab position in the list.

- Click the button to select the leader you require.
  Note that the leader appears to the *left* of the selected tab.
  If you want a leader *between* two tabs, apply the leader to the tab on the right.

- Click the **Set** button.

- Click **OK** when you are finished.

## 10.5   Changing the Default Tab Settings

As already mentioned, Word has **Default** (pre-set) tab settings, 1/2 inch apart.  You can change these defaults using the **Tabs** dialogue box.  If you use a centimetre ruler, for example, you will prefer the default tabs to be set in centimetres.  It is better to do this at the beginning of a document, before you enter any text.  Proceed as follows.

- Select **Tabs** in the **Format** menu to open the **Tabs** window.

- In the **Default tab stops** section, enter the new default measurement.

- Click **OK** to set the new default tab settings.

## 10.6   Moving Tabs

Tabs can be moved using the **Ruler** or the **Tabs** window.

**Using the Ruler:**

- Select the text to be affected by the changes.

- Drag the tab to the new position on the ruler.

**Using the Tabs window:**

- Select the text to be affected by the changes.

- Select **Tabs** in the **Format** menu to open the Tabs window.

- Select the tab position to be changed and type in the new position.

## 10.7   Removing Tabs

Tabs can be removed using the **Ruler** or the **Tabs** window.

**Using the Ruler:**

- Select the text in which you want to remove a tab or tabs.

- Drag the tab marker down off the ruler and release the mouse button.

**Using the Tabs window:**

- Select the text in which you want to remove a tab or tabs.

- Select **Tabs** in the **Format** menu to open the Tabs window.

- Select the tab position to be removed and click the **Clear** button.

- Click the **Clear All** button if you want to remove all the tabs from the selected text.

# Exercise 10A

1  Create a new document and save it as **Tabs 1**.

2  Set tabs at 5cm, 8cm and 14cm.  There is no tab at the left border.

3  Type the text below using tabs on the ruler.  Use Times New Roman, 10 pt.
   (The box is to frame the example only and is not part of the exercise.)

4  Save your work.

| Destination | Month | Days | Fare |
|---|---|---|---|
| London | March | Monday, Wednesday | £99.00 |
| Paris | April | Tuesday, Thursday, Friday | £179.99 |
| Amsterdam | January | Monday, Friday, Sunday | £174.50 |

# Exercise 10B

1  Make a copy of the tabbed text in Exercise 10A.

2  Working on the copy, use the **Tabs** window to change the tabs as follows.

   - Centre tab at 5cm, right tab at 10cm and decimal tab at 14cm.

   - Add leaders to the appropriate tabs so that the text appears as below.

3  Save your work.

| Destination | Month | Days | Fare |
|---|---|---|---|
| London ..............................March | | Monday, Wednesday ........................ £99.00 |
| Paris....................................April | | Tuesday, Thursday, Friday ...................... £179.99 |
| Amsterdam.......................January | | Monday, Friday, Sunday ...................... £174.50 |

**Tab Hints**    Did everything work out for you?

   - In Exercise 10A, the following tabs are used: right tab first, then a left tab and finally a decimal tab.  (There is no tab at the left margin.)

   - In Exercise 10B, first select all the text.

     - Remove the right tab at 5cm and replace it with a centre tab.

     - Don't worry about the text 'collapsing' when you remove the right tab.  It will reform when you put in the centre tab.

     - Remove the left tab at 8cm and add a right tab at 11cm.

     - Double-click any tab to open the tabs window.  Select the 5cm and 14cm tabs in the list and click the appropriate button to add dotted leaders.

     - Select the first line of the text and use the tabs window to remove the leaders from the 5cm and 14cm tabs.

# Section 11    Indents and Margins

## 11.1    Indents

     This line is indented.  It begins a little further in than the rest of the paragraph.  **Indentation** means altering the margins for some parts of the text.  It makes a line or paragraph stand out from the rest of the text.  You can apply different kinds of indentation to a paragraph.

- A **First-line indent** causes the first line of a paragraph to start further to the right than the following lines.  The paragraph above begins with a first-line indent.  The first line has a wider left margin than the other lines.

- A **Left indent** moves the entire paragraph to the right.  The left margin of the whole paragraph is wider than for rest of the text.  A left indent can be applied to more than one paragraph.  This paragraph, and the ones before and after it, has a left indent.

- A **Hanging indent** causes the first line of a paragraph to start further to the left than the following lines.  It has a narrower left margin than the other lines.  The bullet points marking these three paragraphs are examples of the use of hanging indents.

You can create indents using the **Format** menu, the **markers** on the ruler or the **Tab** key.

## 11.2    Indent Markers

There are two indent markers, one at each end of the ruler.  The marker at the left end of the ruler is divided into three parts, one above the other.  There is a single marker at the right end of the ruler.

In a new document, the markers show the positions of the margins of the document as set in **Page Setup**.  In the illustration, those margins were set to 3cm on the left and 2cm on the right.  The ruler counts back from the left margin to the edge of the page.  The margin areas appear in dark gray.

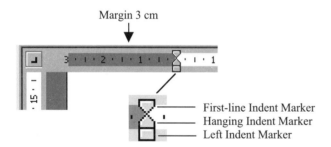

Margin 3 cm

First-line Indent Marker
Hanging Indent Marker
Left Indent Marker

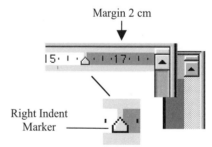

Margin 2 cm

Right Indent Marker

The markers are very small.  It takes skill and care to drag them along the ruler, especially the separate parts of the left marker.  Remember to place the **tip** of the pointer **inside** the part to be dragged.

## 11.3    Selecting Text to Indent

You can indent one or more paragraphs that you have already typed, or the whole document.

- If you only want to indent one paragraph, click anywhere in it.

- To indent more than one paragraph, select those paragraphs.

You can also set the indents before you start typing, as explained below.

## 11.4   Setting Indents on the Ruler

You can set indents before you begin to type or you can indent text that is already typed.  To set indents in existing text, first select the text.

If the ruler is not visible, select **Ruler** in the **View** menu.

- To make a **Left indent**, drag the Left indent marker – the bottom one at the left end of the ruler – to the right, towards the centre of the page.

Left Indent

- To make a **First-line indent**, drag the First-line indent marker (the top one at the left end of the ruler) to the right.

First-line Indent

- To create a **Hanging indent**, drag the Hanging indent marker (the middle one at the left end of the ruler) to the right.

Hanging Indent

- To make a **Right indent**, drag the Right indent marker – the one at the right end of the ruler – to the left, towards the centre of the page.

Right Indent

To **remove an indent**, select the text and drag the Indent marker back to its original position.

As you continue typing and press the **Return** key to make new paragraphs, the indents you have set are retained in the new paragraphs.

Note that as you move the Left indent marker – the bottom one – any First-line or Hanging indents you may have set will move with it.

## 11.5   Indent Examples

More than one indent can be applied to a paragraph.  Three indents were used in the four bulleted paragraphs in Section 11.4 above.

- A **Left** indent moved the paragraphs to the right, making them stand out from the other text on the page.

- The bullets were positioned to the left of each paragraph using a **Hanging** indent.

- A **Right** indent moved the right-hand margin to the left to make room for the graphics.

Think of the Left and Right indent markers as setting the **Page Margins** on **individual pages**, in addition to the margins set in **Page Setup** which apply to the **whole document**.  When you want a larger margin on the left, for example, move the **Left indent** marker to the right along the ruler.  Any other indents that have been set, such as a first-line indent, will be preserved – as mentioned above.

## 11.6    Setting Indents in the Paragraph Window

You can set precise measurements for indents in the **Paragraph** window.  First, select the text that you want to indent.  Indents can also be set before you type.

- Select **Paragraph** in the **Format** menu.

  The Paragraph window opens.

- Make sure that the **Indents and Spacing** tab is clicked.

- In the **Indentation** section, enter the size of the indents you require in the boxes or use the arrow keys.

- For **First-line** or **Hanging indents**, use the menu in the **Special** box to choose the indent and then type in the size.

- Click **OK** when you are finished.

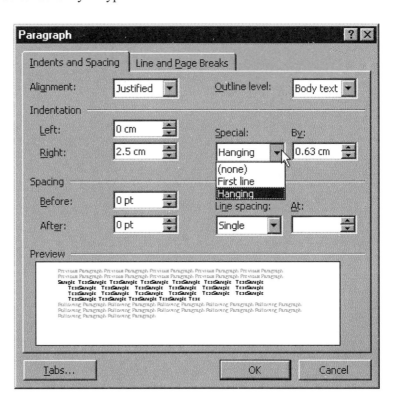

## 11.7    Setting an Indent with the Toolbar Buttons

Buttons on the toolbar allow you to make and adjust a Left indent in pre-set steps.

- Select the text to be indented.

- Click the **Increase Indent** button to make a Left indent or to increase an indent that is already in place.

- Click the **Decrease Indent** button to reduce an indent that is already in place.

- Pressing a button again increases or decreases the indent by another step.

Decrease
Indent

Increase
Indent

# Exercise 11A

1   Create a new file and call it **Indent 1**.

2   Type the following text into your document.  Use Times New Roman, 10pt.
    (The box is not part of the exercise.)

### Oscar Wilde

Oscar Wilde is remembered for many reasons nowadays: his wit, his plays and the circumstances of his personal life.  Indeed his personal life has been the subject of several films, books and plays since his death.

Those same circumstances were the inspiration for one of his most enduring works, the epic *Ballad of Reading Gaol*.  This powerful poem tells of life inside a prison and, in particular, the atmosphere when there's an impending execution.

The following lines evoke that atmosphere:

I never saw a man who looked

With such a wistful eye

Upon that little tent of blue

Which prisoners call the sky

And at every drifting cloud that went

With sails of silver by.

3   Indent the first line of the first two paragraphs by 1.5cm.

4   Make a left indent of 4cm for the lines of poetry.

5   Save your work.

# Exercise 11B

1   Prepare a new document as in the panel below, using a hanging indent for the names of the characters in the dialogue section.  Save your work as **Indent 2**.

The wit of Oscar Wilde can be seen in the following excerpt from his play *The Importance of Being Earnest*.  In this section of the play, Jack has asked Lady Bracknell for her daughter's hand in marriage.   However, Lady Bracknell is not too impressed by the story he has told her of being found in a handbag in a cloakroom when he was a baby.

Lady Bracknell:     I would strongly advise you, Mr. Worthing, to try and acquire some relations as soon as possible, and to make a definite effort to produce at any rate one parent, of either sex, before the season is quite over.

Jack:     Well, I don't see how I could possibly manage to do that.  I can produce the hand-bag at any moment.  It is in my dressing-room at home.  I really think that should satisfy you, Lady Bracknell.

Lady Bracknell:     Me, Sir!  What has it to do with me?  You can hardly imagine that I and Lord Bracknell would dream of allowing our only daughter – a girl brought up with the utmost care – to marry into a cloak-room, and form an alliance with a parcel. Good-morning, Mr. Worthing!

*Lady Bracknell sweeps out in majestic indignation.*

# Section 12    Bullets and Numbering

## 12.1    Bullets and Numbers

A list of items can be presented with each one preceded by a **bullet** or **number** for increased effect. Buttons on the toolbar allow you to make bulleted or numbered lists easily and conveniently. You can decide to type a bulleted or numbered list before you begin or you can add bullets or numbers to a list that you have already typed.

**To type a Bulleted or Numbered list:**

- Place the cursor where you want the list to begin.

- Click the **Bullet** or the **Numbering** button on the toolbar.
  The first bullet or number appears on the page.

- Type the items in the list and press **Return** after each.

- When the list is finished, press the **Return** key twice.

- If a bullet or number appears where you don't want one, click the **Bullet** or **Numbering** button again to turn off the bulleting or numbering.

Bullet

Numbering

**To Bullet or Number an existing list:**

- Make sure that the **Return** key has been pressed after each item in the list so that each one begins as a new paragraph.

- Select the text.

- Click the **Bullet** or **Numbering** button.

The Bullet and Numbering buttons apply hanging indents to achieve their effect. To alter the space between the bullet or number and the items in the list, select the list and move the **Hanging Indent** marker on the ruler.

Bulleted or numbered lists are more effective if they are indented from the left margin, as on this page. To indent a list, select the list and move the **Left indent** marker on the ruler.

## 12.2    Bullet and Numbering Formats

Word supplies a range of Bullet and Number formats that are suitable for most purposes but you can change them to suit your own requirements. You may wish not to have full stops after numbers or to have a bracket instead, for example.

You can select or change the format before you begin to type, or you can select or change the format on an existing list by selecting it first.

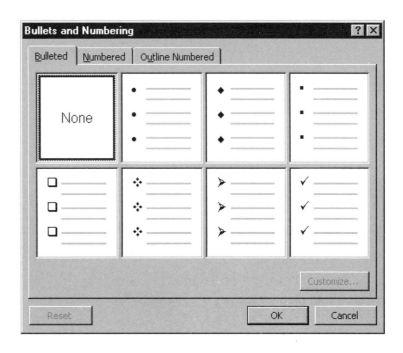

Proceed as follows.

- Select **Bullets and Numbering** in the **Format** menu.
  The Bullets and Numbering window opens (see above).

- Click the **Bulleted** or **Numbered** tab as required.

- Click the box displaying the format you require.

- Click **OK**.

The **Numbered** panel has options for how the numbering appears.

Make sure that **Restart Numbering** is selected if you want the numbers to start at 1.

To continue the numbering used in a previous list, select **Continue Previous List**. This is useful if you began a list earlier on the page and then added a few words of explanation before continuing the list again.

If none of the available options is suitable, you can set your own formats for bullets or numbering by clicking the **Customize** button and making your own choices in the window that appears.

## Exercise 12A

1 Open a new document and call it **Bullets 1**.

2 Type the following text and make a bulleted list of the names as shown below.
(The box is not part of the exercise.)

> The following are all writers:
>
> - W. B. Yeats
> - Charles Dickens
> - Mark Twain
> - Jane Austen

3 Indent the list of names by 1.5cm (not shown above.)

4 Save the document.

## Exercise 12B

1 Use **Save As** to save a copy of **Bullets 1** with the title **Bullets 2**.

2 Practise using different styles of bullets and numbering.

3 Finish by making the list a numbered list.

4 Save your work and close the document.

# Section 13    Hyphenation

## 13.1    Dividing Words

If the last word on a line of text is too long to fit, Word puts it on the next line.  When the text is fully justified – to make both left and right margins line up evenly –  this often results in a lot of white space between the words as the text is padded out with extra space to fill each line evenly.

**Hyphenation** is a means of improving the appearance of text in a document.  It divides words to fill the lines more evenly.  It reduces excess white space and gives a neater appearance to the text, especially when it is justified.

Hyphenation divides long words at the end of a line into two parts.  It inserts a hyphen (-) after the first part, and places the second part on the following line.  Words can only be divided in certain places, however, and some words cannot be divided at all.

In the following example, notice the difference a single hyphen can make.

**No Hyphenation**

> You can ask Word to hyphenate your text for you or you can choose to hyphenate it yourself.  You can also choose not to have any hyphenation at all.  Using hyphenation reduces excessive white space between words and makes text easier to read.

**Hyphenated**

> You can ask Word to hyphenate your text for you or you can choose to hyphenate it yourself.  You can also choose not to have any hyphenation at all.  Using hyphen-ation reduces excessive white space between words and makes text easier to read.

Text can be hyphenated **automatically** or **manually**. Usually, it's better to hyphenate your document **after** you have finished writing and editing it.  You can also choose to hyphenate the whole text or only certain paragraphs.

## 13.2    Automatic Hyphenation

Automatic hyphenation means that Word decides where to divide the words and place the hyphens.  This is quick and convenient.  However, you should still check the document after automatic hyphenation to ensure that there aren't any hyphens in places where you don't want them.

- If you want to hyphenate only certain paragraphs, select them first.
- Select **Language** in the **Tools** menu.
- Click **Hyphenation** in the sub-menu that appears.  The Hyphenation window opens.

Module 3

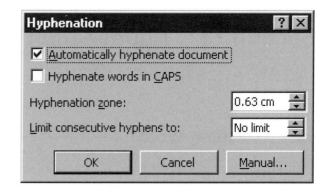

- Click the **Automatically hyphenate document** box to place a tick in it.

- Click **OK**.

  Word hyphenates the document automatically as you type.

## 13.3   Hyphenation Options

Other options in the Hyphenation window allow you to control how the hyphenation is applied.

- Click the **Hyphenate words in CAPS** box if you want to hyphenate words that are all in CAPITALS (upper case) in the document.

- The **Hyphenation zone** is the amount of space between the end of the last word in a line and the right margin.

  You can either leave this as it is in the box or change it.

  If your document is justified, it's better to leave the Hyphenation zone box setting as it is.

  If your document is **Left Aligned**, increasing the size may reduce the number of hyphens in the document but can also result in a more ragged right margin.

- When hyphens appear on several consecutive lines, they make the text awkward to read.

  You can set the maximum number of consecutive lines that can be hyphenated in the **Limit consecutive hyphens to** box.  If this is set at **No limit**, potentially every line in a paragraph could be hyphenated.  This would give the text a peculiar appearance as well as making it difficult to read.

## 13.4   Manual Hyphenation

If you hyphenate manually, Word searches the document for words to hyphenate.  It then asks you whether or not to include a hyphen, and where to position it.  This is slower than automatic hyphenation but gives you more control over the positioning of the hyphens.

If you want to hyphenate only certain paragraphs, select them first.  The procedure is as follows.

- Select **Language** in the **Tools** menu and then **Hyphenation** in the sub-menu.

  The Hyphenation window opens.

- Click the **Manual** button.

  If Word finds a potential word to hyphenate, the **Manual Hyphenation** window opens.

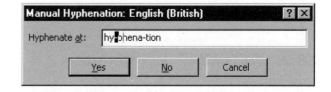

  The word is displayed with the cursor flashing in the proposed position for the hyphen.

- Click **Yes** to insert a hyphen in the suggested position.

- To insert the hyphen in a different part of the word, use the arrow keys on the keyboard to move the flashing cursor to the new position before clicking **Yes**.

- Click **No** if you don't want the word to be hyphenated.

- The procedure continues until the whole document or selection has been checked.

## 13.5   Removing a Hyphen

If automatic hyphenation inserts a hyphen in a bad position, you can change or remove it, as follows.

- Select the word containing the hyphen that you want to change or remove.

- The **Hyphenation** window opens.

- Click the **Manual** button to display the **Manual Hyphenation** window.
  The selected word is displayed with the hyphen highlighted.

- Change the hyphen as before or click **No** to remove it altogether.

## Exercise 13A

**1**  Open some of the documents you have created before and practise hyphenating them.

**2**  Use manual hyphenation on some of the documents and automatic hyphenation on others.

**3**  Read through the documents to see the effects of the hyphenation.

# Section 14        Mail Merge

## 14.1   What is Mail Merge?

**Mail Merge** is used to join or **merge** two sources of information into a single document. Its most common uses are for producing **form letters** and **mailing labels**.

A form letter is a letter with standard information to be sent to many people but where each one must have some individual information, such as a name and address.

A list of names and addresses can be used in conjunction with a form letter to prepare personalised letters for everyone in the list. The list of names and addresses can also be used to produce mailing labels for the envelopes. It can also be used to produce other similar label-based items such as identity badges for conferences.

Form letters for different purposes and occasions can be stored on the computer and can then be merged with the name and address list as required. This saves having to type the same information over and over again every time you need to send out letters.

To perform a mail merge, you need two separate files – the **form letter** and a **data source**. The list of names and addresses is a data source.

## 14.2   The Mail Merge Helper

A Word **Helper** assists you in preparing a mail merge. There are three steps involved.

- Creating or opening the Main Document, a form letter, for example.
- Creating or opening the Data Source, such as a list of names and addresses.
- Performing the **Mail Merge**, adding the names and addresses to the main document.

You can use a previously prepared main document and data source or prepare them as you go along. In this exercise, we shall be sending letters to parents of school children. Here, we shall prepare the form letter in advance and make up the data source when we need it.

## 14.3   Creating a Form Letter

Open Word and prepare the letter as show below. Note that **Dear** is the only word of the salutation and that there is no comma after it. Save the letter with the title **Thornton**.

---

**The James Thornton Trust School**
Station Road        Abbeyvale        Beaconville


Dear

We would like to invite you to attend the next meeting of the School Management Committee which will be discussing the arrangements for... etc.

---

## 14.4    Using the Helper

The **Mail Merge Helper** will take you through
the steps involved in performing a mail merge.
They are clearly numbered 1, 2 and 3.

Make sure that the **Thornton** letter is still open
on the screen before you begin.

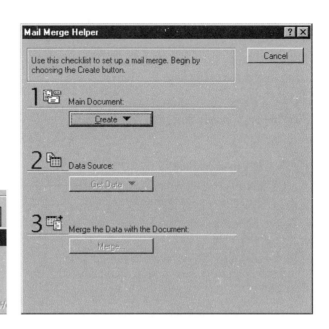

* Select **Mail Merge** in the **Tools** menu.
  The **Mail Merge Helper** window opens.

* Click the **Create** button
  to display a menu of
  options.

  Select the type of
  document you want to
  use, in this case **Form
  Letters**.

  A new window asks if
  you want to use the
  Active window (the **Thornton** letter) or create a new
  document.

* Click **Active Window** to select the **Thornton** letter
  that is open on the Desktop.

  (You would click **New Main Document** if you wanted
  to prepare a new document to use as the form letter.)

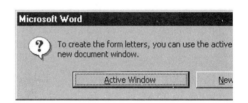

* The **Mail Merge Helper** window reappears, now with
  an **Edit** button beside the **Create** button.

  The type of main document used, e.g. form letters, and the name of the document being used now
  appear in the **Step 1** part of the window.

To edit a form letter and to change details since the last time you used it for a mail merge, click the
**Edit** button before you proceed.  (Do not do this now.  No changes are needed.)

When you have made the changes, select **Mail Merge** in the **Tools** menu to display the Mail Merge
Helper window again.  (As we did not click the **Edit** button, it is still on the screen.)

## 14.5    Creating a Data Source

You can use an existing Data Source or create a new one.  As we have no names and addresses to use
with our form letter, we shall create a new Data Source.

* Click the  **Get Data** button in the **Step 2** part of the **Mail
  Merge Helper** window to display a menu of options.

* Click **Create Data Source**.

  The Create Data Source window opens.  (See next page.)

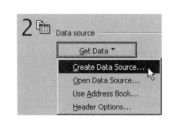

* The **Field Names in Header Row** box contains a list of
  prepared fields – storage areas – for Title, First Name etc.

The prepared fields will suffice for now but you can add new
fields or delete unwanted fields if you wish.  To add a new
field, type the new field name in the **Field Name** box and click **Add Field Name**.
(We shall not add any fields now.)

To delete a field, select the field name in the **Field Names in Header Row** box, and then click **Remove Field Name**. (We shall not delete any fields now.)

You can change the order of the fields by using the **Move** buttons on the right.

Click the **Field** you want to move and then click the appropriate button. (We shall not move any Fields now.)

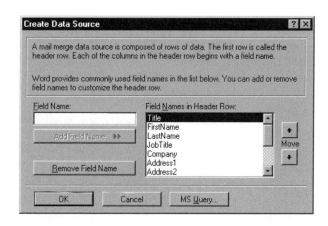

- Click **OK** to continue.
  The **Save As** window appears so that you can save the Data Source.

- Type the name **Addresses** and click **Save** to save the file.
  A message (right) appears to remind you that the Data Source you have just saved is empty.

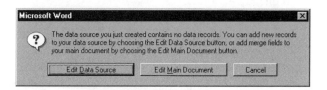

- Click the **Edit Data Source** button to begin entering information.
  The **Data Form** window opens.

- For this exercise, enter information in the **Title**, **First Name**, **Last Name**, **Address** and **City** boxes
  Press the **Tab** or **Return** key after each entry to move to the next box.
  Press **Tab** or **Return** again to skip a box if you do not want to enter anything in it.

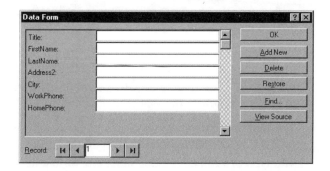

The information you enter for a single person is called a **Record**.

- To create a new record, i.e. to add information about the next person, click the **Add New** button.
  You will need at least two or three records to see the mail merge in operation.

- Click the arrows beside the **Record** box at the bottom of the window to move from record to record.
  This allows you to check the entries and to make any corrections that may be necessary.

- Click **OK** when you have finished entering all the records.

If you made changes or corrections, select **Yes** when asked if you want to save them.

You are returned to the **Main Document**, in this case the **Thornton** letter.

- You can view all the records in the form of a Table if you wish.
  - Click the **View Source** button before clicking **OK** in the previous step.
    You can glance through the records, scrolling if necessary.
  - Click the **Close** button to return to the Main Document.

The two items needed for the mail merge, the letter and the data source (names and addresses), are now ready for the final step in the process – the actual mail merge itself.

To use the Data Source you have just created (or to select a previously prepared Data Source), select **Open Data Source** instead of **Create Data Source** in the **Step 2** part of the **Mail Merge Helper** window.

For now, we shall perform the merge with the documents we have created.

## 14.6   Performing the Mail Merge

When you selected **Mail Merge** in the **Tools** menu at the beginning of the process, a new toolbar, the **Mail Merge Toolbar**, appeared with the other toolbars on the Desktop.

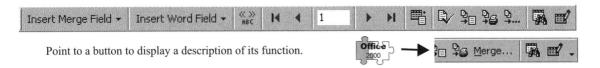

Point to a button to display a description of its function.

To complete the mail merge, we have to mark on the letter where the different items of data – the individual names and addresses – are to appear when the separate letters are printed.

First we shall insert the person's full name and address above the salutation.

Then we shall add the person's title and last name after the part of the salutation – **Dear** – that we have already typed.

Proceed as follows.

- Place the cursor where you want to start putting in the full name and address.
  In the **Thornton** letter, this is above the salutation.

- Click **Insert Merge Field** on the **Mail Merge** toolbar.
  A list of the items in the data source is displayed.

- Click on the name of the item you want to insert, in this case **Title**.
  The name of the item is inserted in the document with double-pointed brackets at each end thus: **«Title»**.

- Press the **Space Bar** on the keyboard to insert a space after the Title.

- Click **Insert Merge Field** again and click on **First Name** to insert it.

- Insert a space after **First Name** and then insert **Last Name**.

- Press the **Return** key to move to the next line.

- Insert **Address 1** and press **Return** to move to the next line.

- Insert **City**.

- Place the cursor after **Dear** and insert a space.

- Insert **Title** and **Last Name** as before, with a space between them and with a comma after **Last Name**.

The name and address markers should now appear in the letter as shown below.

---

### The James Thornton Trust School
Station Road      Abbeyvale      Beaconville

«Title» «First Name» «Last Name»
«Address 1»
«City»

Dear «Title»  «Last Name»,

We would like to invite you to attend the next meeting of the School Management Committee which will be discussing the arrangements for…  etc.

---

- Click the **View Merged Data** button on the Mail Merge Toolbar to see the actual names and addresses appear.

  The Form letter is displayed with the markers (e.g. **«Title»**) replaced by the actual information (e.g. **Mr**).

View Merged Data

- To view the different letters, use the arrow buttons on the Mail Merge Toolbar to scroll through them.

  The names and addresses are inserted and displayed in the Form letter in turn.

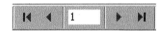

Merge Scroll Buttons

## 14.7   Completing the Mail Merge

To merge the documents for printing, do one of the following to open the Mail Merge Helper window.

Mail Merge Helper

- Click the **Mail Merge Helper** button on the Mail Merge Toolbar.

- Select **Mail Merge** in the **Tools** menu.

When the window appears, proceed as follows.

- Click the **Merge** button in Step 3 in the **Mail Merge Helper** window.

  The **Merge** window appears.

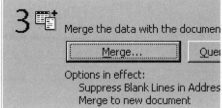

- In the **Merge to** box, **New document** is already selected.

  (If you want to print the form letters immediately, click in the **Merge to** box and select **Printer**.)

- Note that **Don't print blank lines when data fields are empty** at the bottom of the window is selected.

  This prevents unecessary blank lines – in an

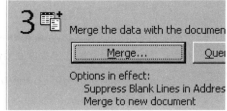

  address in the Data Source, for example – from appearing in the letter.

- Click the **Merge** button at the top right of the window.

A new document – the **Merge document** – with the name **Form Letters 1** is created.  It consists of individual letters with the names and addresses inserted.

Each letter appears on a separate page, one after the other.  Use the scroll arrows or bars, or the **Page Down** button on the keyboard, to move from letter to letter to see the result of the merge.

Save the **Merge Document** in the usual way, giving it a name of your choice.  After you have closed the document, it can be reopened later and the letters printed once more, without having to go through the Mail Merge process again.

- To print the letters, click the **Print** button on the toolbar or select **Print** in the **File** menu.

  The letters are printed out, one to a page, with the different personal details on each one.

# Section 15    Mailing Labels

## 15.1    Labels

Self-adhesive labels are supplied in sheets the same size as normal paper for use in the printer. The number of labels on the sheet varies according to the size of the labels. Labels are available in different sizes for different purposes. They are commonly used for addressing envelopes. They can also be used for identity badges, labelling floppy disks, video cassettes, filing cabinet drawers etc.

The procedure for preparing Mailing Labels is similar to preparing a mail merge. The Mail Merge Helper is used as before and the appropriate options are chosen during the 3 steps as you go through them. The main difference is in Step 2.

## 15.2    Preparing Labels

The **Mail Merge Helper** will take you through the steps involved in preparing Mailing Labels. They are clearly numbered 1, 2 and 3.

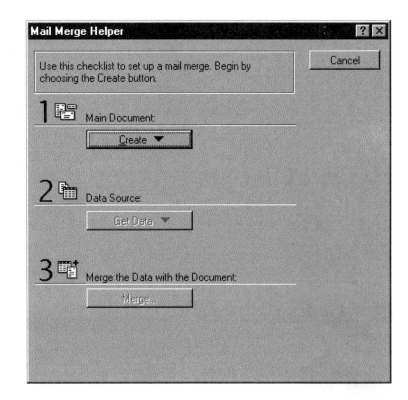

- Create a new blank Word document with nothing on it.

- Select **Mail Merge** in the **Tools** menu. The Mail Merge Helper window opens.

- Click the **Create** button to display a menu of options.

- Select the type of document you want to use, in this case **Mailing Labels**.

  A new window asks if you want to use the active window (the blank document) or create a new document.

- Click **Active Window** to select the **blank document** that is open on the Desktop.

  (You would click **New Main Document** if you wanted to prepare a new document to use for the labels.)

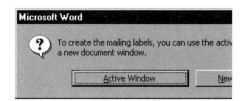

- The **Mail Merge Helper** window reappears.

  The type of main document used – e.g. Mailing Labels – and the name of the document appear in the **Step 1** part of the window.

## 15.3    Opening a Data Source

You would normally select the Data Source you prepared for the Form Letters as it has the names and addresses that you need.

(If you want to make a new Data Source, follow the steps as described for Mail Merge in Section 14.5, page 181.)

- Click the **Get Data** button in  Step 2 of the Mail Merge Helper window.

- Click **Open Data Source** in the menu.

- In the window that appears, find and open the **Addresses** Data Source prepared for the Form Letters.

   The procedure is similar to finding and opening any other saved document or file.

The next step is as follows.

- If the window on the right appears after opening or creating the Data Source, click the **Set Up Main Document** button.

- If the window does not appear, look at the **Mail Merge Helper** window.

   (Select **Mail Merge** in the **Tools** menu if the Mail Merge window is not open.)

   Click the **Setup** button beside the **Create** button in Step 1.

Whichever method you use above, the **Label Options** window appears.  It includes details of a range of proprietary **Avery** labels.  Avery is a well-known brand and has become a standard in many offices. Avery label details are used by many word processors, including Word.

## 15.4    Selecting Labels

There are different sizes of Avery labels for different purposes.  Number **L7161** is a general-purpose size that can be used for address labels, identification badges, floppy disk labels, and so on.   There are 18 labels per A4 sheet, 3 across and 6 down.

- Click in the **Label Products** box and select **Avery A4 and A5** sizes in the menu.

- Click in the **Product number** box in the bottom left of the window to select the type of label you want to use.

   Information about the selected label is displayed in the **Label Information** panel.

- Click the **Details** button to display further information on the exact size of the  labels, the number of labels per page etc.

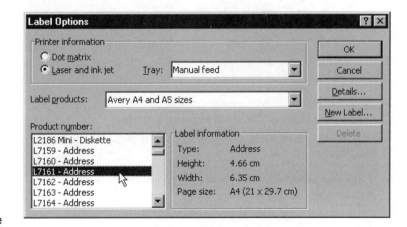

   (If you are using non-standard labels, click the **New Label** button to enter the details.)

- It is usually sufficient to select a label from the Avery list and to click **OK**.

   The **Create Labels** window appears.

## 15.5    Performing the Label Merge

The process is similar to performing the Form Letter merge.

- Click the **Insert Merge Field** button to insert the items you want to appear on the label.

  The process is similar to inserting the items on a form letter as described in Section 14.6, page 183.

  As you insert the items, they appear in  the **Sample label** box.

- Don't forget to put in spaces where needed, e.g. between Title, First Name and Surname.

- Press the **Return** key to move to a new line, as required.

- Click **OK** when the label layout is finished.

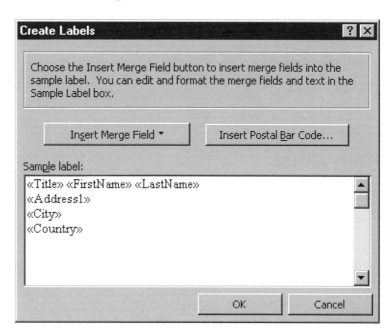

The main document now consists of a number of labels laid out in rows and columns, according to the size and type of label you have selected.

## 15.6    Viewing and Printing Labels

The Mailing Labels are displayed on the blank document, with the actual names and addresses shown instead of the place markers seen in the Form Letter.

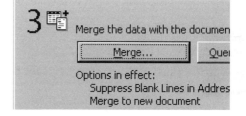

- Click the **Merge** button in Step 3 in the **Mail Merge Helper** window.  A new **Merge** window appears.

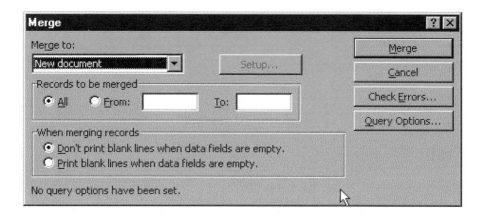

- In the **Merge to** box, **New document** is already selected.

  (If you want to print the labels immediately, click in the **Merge to** box and select **Printer**.)

- Click **Don't print blank lines when data fields are empty.**

  Remember, this will prevent blank lines – in an address, for example – from adding empty space to the labels.

- Click the **Merge** button at the top right of the window.
  The blank document you prepared earlier now has the labels arranged on it in rows and columns.

- Save the documents in the usual way.

- Print the labels by clicking the **Print** button on the toolbar or by selecting **Print** in the **File** menu.
  Remember to put **Label** stationery in the printer before you print.
  Some printers have a second paper cassette or tray that can be used for labels.

## Exercise 15A

1  Open a new document and follow the instructions for the Mail Merge process to create a form letter similar to this one.

---

**The James Thornton Trust School**
Station Road          Abbeyvale          Beaconville


Dear

We would like to invite you to attend the next meeting of the School Management Committee which will be discussing the arrangements for...  etc.

---

2  When you are preparing the Data Source, choose appropriate fields such as First name, Surname etc.

3  Enter at least three records in the Data Source.

4  When you have finished the mail merge, view the letters.
   You should see the letters with the individual details inserted from the Data Source.

5  Preview and print the letters.

6  Close all the documents, saving any unsaved ones.

## Exercise 15B

1  Use the Mail Merge process to make mailing labels.

2  Use the same data source as before so that you don't have to type in new details.

   (Select the **Open Data Source** option in the **Select Data** stage of Step 2 in the Mail Merge Helper window.  Choose the Data Source that you created in Exercise 15B above.)

3  Preview and print the labels.

4  Close all the documents, saving any unsaved ones.

# Section 16    Templates

## 16.1    Saving Time

A **template** is a document with preset styles for page layout, text, paragraphs and so on.  It is useful to have a template for a document that you use often.  It saves the time you would otherwise expend on setting up all the options.

Word has a number of built-in templates for different purposes such as CVs and faxes.  You can also make your own templates, if a suitable one is not available.

## 16.2    Using a Template

When you open a new blank document in Word, the **Normal** template is used.  This is a page layout with margins, font and font size pre-set.  To use a different template, proceed as follows.

- Select **New** in the **File** menu. (Do not use the **New** button on the **Toolbar** as this automatically opens the **Normal** template.)

  The **New** window appears.

- Click a tab at the top to display templates by subject.

- Click the **Other Documents** tab if you can't find a suitable template under one of the subject headings.

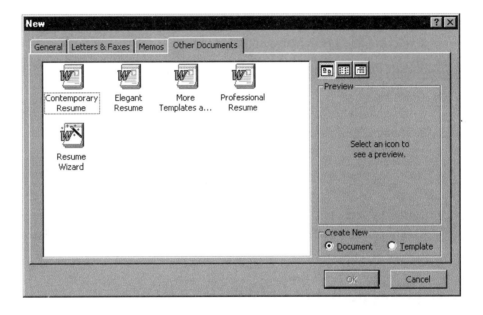

 Office 2000 Template tabs

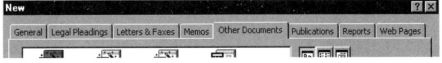

- Click once on a template to select it.

  The **Preview** box on the right in the window shows you what the selected template looks like.

- Double-click a template to open it.

  *Alternatively*, click it once to select it and then click **OK**.

  The template appears as a Word document with some text already in place.

- To use the template, select the existing text and type your own text to replace it.

  The templates usually have instructions on how to use them.

- When you save an amended template, it is saved as a normal Word document – not as a template. This ensures that the original template is unchanged and can be used over and over again.

## 16.3   Creating a Template

If none of the existing templates suits your purpose, you can create you own.  It is only necessary to open or create a document that contains the text, formatting and layout you require.  When you save the document, you save it as a **template** instead of as a normal **Word document**.  You can then use it as you would use any other template, as described above.

 To create a template, do the following.

- Open or prepare the document you want to save as a template.

- Select **Save As** in the **File** menu.  The **Save As** window opens.

- Click in the **Save as type** box to display the menu and select **Document Template**.
  You  may see the extension **.dot** appear.
  This is because all template files end in **.dot** while Word documents end in **.doc**.

- Word normally saves your template in a special folder called **Templates**.
  When you next click the **New** button in the **File** menu, your template will appear under the **General** tab along with the **Normal** and any other templates there.

To save your template so that it will appear under one of the other subject tabs (e.g. **Letters and Faxes**), do the following.

- Select the relevant subfolder in the **Templates** folder in the **Save in** box.

- Type a name for the new template in the **File name** box.

- Click **Save**.
  Your template remains open so you can still make any changes that might occur to you.
  Remember to set the margins, page size and orientation, styles and any other formats that may be necessary.

- Save any changes to the template in the usual way by clicking the **Save** button on the toolbar or by selecting **Save** in the **File** menu.

- Close the document.
  The template will now appear with the other templates under the selected subject heading when you select **New** in the **Format** menu.

## Exercise 16A

1   Try out some of the templates supplied with Word and create new documents based on them.

2   Create your own template.
   Keep the template simple to begin with.
   Just use some text, styles, headers, footers, page setup and margins.

3   Use the template you have created to produce a new document.

# Section 17    Exercises

Module 3

# Self Check Exercises

**1** A template is best described as…

- ☐ A blank page with a predetermined layout
- ☐ A blank page without a predetermined layout
- ☐ A blank page with headers and footers
- ☐ A blank page with a blank table

**2** The Standard Toolbar contains…

- ☐ Menus
- ☐ Shortcuts to infrequent functions
- ☐ Shortcuts to frequent functions
- ☐ Scroll bars

**3** To display additional toolbars, where will you find the Toolbar menu?

- ☐ In the View menu
- ☐ In the Format menu
- ☐ In the Tools menu
- ☐ In the Edit menu

**4** Which of these allows you to name a document before saving it?

- ☐ Save
- ☐ Save in
- ☐ Save as
- ☐ Save as type

**5** Tick any of the items below which may not be a proper indent.

- ☐ First-line indent
- ☐ Left indent
- ☐ Right indent
- ☐ Hanging indent

**6** Which button on the Standard Toolbar would you most likely use to undo a typing error?

- ☐ ↶
- ☐ ABC✓
- ☐ ✂
- ☐ 🖌

**7** When you open the Toolbar Menu, what do the ticks indicate?

- ☐ The option has not been selected.
- ☐ The option is not available.
- ☐ The option may be chosen.
- ☐ The option is already available.

**8** What unit of measurement is used for letter (font) size?

- ☐ Millimetres (mm)
- ☐ Points (pt)
- ☐ Inches (ins)
- ☐ Other

**9** How many ways can you align text margins using the Formatting Toolbar?

- ☐ 1
- ☐ 2
- ☐ 3
- ☐ 4

**10** How many of the following describe the functioning of the Clipboard?

- ☐ A temporary store of information
- ☐ A permanent store of information
- ☐ A temporary store of graphics
- ☐ A permanent store of graphics
- ☐ A temporary store of text
- ☐ A permanent store of text

**11** What function may this key have?

| Enter |
|-------|
| ↵ |

- ☐ It moves text around.
- ☐ It gives an upper character.
- ☐ It gives the upper case letter.
- ☐ It enters a blank line.

# Practical Exercises

## Exercise 1

The office door has been replaced for some reason. Produce the temporary notice below for the new door.

### James Mac Mahon

Assistant Head of Department

## Exercise 2

An ECDL course will be available shortly. Reproduce the advertisement below which will be placed on the company notice board.

### ECDL Course
European Computer Driving Licence

In-house computer
training for staff

20 places available

Sept. 1st to Nov. 11th

**Applications to the
In-career
Development Unit**

## Exercise 3

Prepare the page below to demonstrate text indents to ECDL students.

### Indents

To indent means to increase or decrease the margin for part of the text in a document, as in the following examples.

A **first-line indent** gives a wider margin to the first line than to the other lines in a paragraph.

A **paragraph indent** means that the margin for an entire paragraph is wider than for the rest of the text in the document.

A **hanging indent** reduces the margin for the first line of a paragraph so that it 'overhangs' to the left of the rest of the paragraph.

1  It can be used to draw attention to the beginning of a paragraph, as in the paragraph above.

2  It can be used to number a list, as in these two paragraphs.

## Exercise 4

You are in charge of staff morale. Reproduce the page below.

| Date | Event | Eligible Staff |
|------|-------|----------------|
| 21st Sept. | Tennis Tournament | Non-smokers |
| 16th Oct. | Halloween Party | Non-drinkers |
| 23rd Dec. | Christmas Party | All welcome |
| 31st Dec. | New Year Party | Available |
| 3rd Jan. | Keep Fit Classes | Volunteers |

Module 3

## Exercise 5

Reproduce the sign below.
Note: Use *AutoShapes* for the graphics.

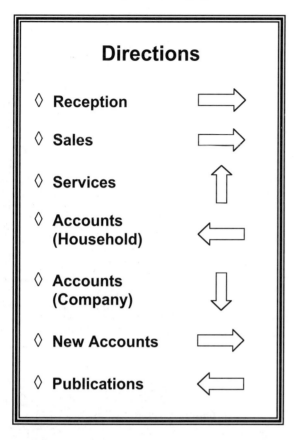

## Exercise 6

This sign warns visitors to keep out of a certain area. Reproduce it using Word.

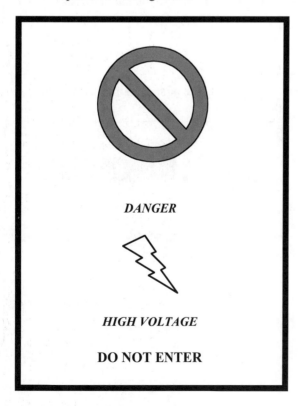

## Exercise 7

Reproduce the first two items below as separate documents, then merge them into one document and format it as shown in the lower box.

Data Protection
It is essential that any data relating to individuals, to which you have access or which you store on a computer, be adequately protected. Note the following: Under the Data Protection Act there are certain legal obligations. Guidelines for Data Controllers have been issued by the Data Protection Commissioner.

Protecting Data: 'Appropriate security measures shall be taken against unauthorised access to, or alteration, disclosure or destruction of, the data and against their accidental loss or destruction…'
Data Protection Act
'Access to your computer should be restricted to authorised staff. Systems should be password protected; information on your screen should be hidden from callers to your office; access to information should be restricted on a 'need-to-know' basis in accordance with a defined policy; all waste paper, printouts etc., should be carefully disposed of.' Guidlines to Data Controllers

### Data Protection

It is essential that any data relating to individuals, to which you have access or which you store on a computer, be adequately protected. Note the following:

Under the Data Protection Act there are certain legal obligations.

Guidelines for Data Controllers have been issued by the Data Protection Commissioner.

**Protecting Data:** 'Appropriate security measures shall be taken against unauthorised access to, or alteration, disclosure or destruction of, the data and against their accidental loss or destruction…'

*Data Protection Act*

'**Access** to your computer should be restricted to authorised staff. Systems should be password protected; information on your screen should be hidden from callers to your office; access to information should be restricted on a 'need-to-know' basis in accordance with a defined policy; all waste paper, printouts etc., should be carefully disposed of.'

*Guidlines to Data Controllers*

**Note:** *This exercise is not intended to represent a true or accurate wording of any Act as it may apply in any situation.*

# Module 4

## Spreadsheets

4

# Module 4

# Spreadsheets

Module 4

# Introduction

---

### Syllabus Goals for Module 4

**Spreadsheets** requires the candidate to understand the basic concepts of spreadsheets and to demonstrate the ability to use a spreadsheet application on a personal computer. He or she shall understand and be able to accomplish basic operations associated with developing, formatting and using a spreadsheet. The candidate shall be able to accomplish standard mathematical and logical operations using basic formulas and functions. The candidate shall demonstrate competence in using some of the more advanced features of a spreadsheet application such as importing objects, and creating graphs and charts.

---

## What is a Spreadsheet?

A spreadsheet is composed of a large number of 'boxes' or **cells**, laid out in orderly rows and columns.

A new spreadsheet is like a large sheet of paper covered with empty cells. You can put text or numbers into the cells. A completed spreadsheet displays the information you have entered in orderly rows and columns. The cell **grid** – the lines that help you identify each cell when you enter the data – is normally omitted when you print out the spreadsheet.

Each cell is an independent item. You could think of cells as being a collection of small pages, all displayed together.

The principal advantage of the spreadsheet is that it can perform actions on the data in the cells. A list of names can be easily sorted, for example. New names can be added or old ones deleted and the list is adjusted automatically.

## Calculations

You can put a **formula** in a cell that will perform a calculation on information contained in other cells and display a result. You can use a formula to add up numbers, find averages and so on. It is this ability to perform calculations that makes spreadsheets so useful. Spreadsheets are widely used where lots of numbers are related to one another, as in financial accounts.

A company budget can be prepared on a spreadsheet, with all the different items of income and expenditure laid out. A change in one item will be reflected in all the other related items, with allocations, totals, balances and so on adjusted automatically by the program.

## Graphs

The data on a spreadsheet can be displayed in **graphical** form. This is particularly useful when displaying all kinds of numerical information. Many different kinds of graphs and diagrams can be generated by the spreadsheet.

Spreadsheet information and graphs can be incorporated in other documents, such as those produced with a word processor, making the information easy to understand as well as adding interest and variety to the presentation.

---

# Reference Table

Should you begin your studies with this module, it is important to note that related material is dealt with in other sections of the manual. This reference list will assist you to locate the material conveniently.

| **Skill** | **Task** | **Module** | **Page** |
|---|---|---|---|
| **First Steps** | | | |
| | Save a new document | Module 2 | 84 |
| | Save changes to an existing document | Module 2 | 87 |
| | Close a document | Before You Begin | 24 |
| | Help | Before You Begin | 16 |
| **Adjusting Settings** | | | |
| | Change page display modes | Before You Begin | 21 |
| | Page magnification | Before You Begin | 22 |
| | Page orientation | Module 3 | 149 |
| | Toolbars | Before You Begin | 11 |
| **Document Exchange** | | | |
| | Save a file in a different format | Module 2 | 87 |
| | Save for Web posting | Module 2 | 88 |
| **Basic Functions** | | | |
| | Alignment and justification of text | Module 3 | 133 |
| | Copy, Cut, and Paste | Before You Begin | 10 |
| | Deleting | Module 3 | 127 |
| | Formatting text | Module 3 | 131 |
| | Images, graphics and objects | Module 3 | 161 |
| | Line spacing | Module 3 | 134 |
| | Preview a document | Module 3 | 143 |
| | Printers, choosing | Module 3 | 145 |
| | Print to file | Module 3 | 145 |
| | Selecting | Before You Begin | 9 |
| | Spell Check | Before You begin | 23 |
| | Templates | Module 3 | 189 |
| | Undo | Module 3 | 135 |

# Section 1      Introducing Excel

## 1.1    Opening Excel

Open Microsoft Excel by clicking the **Excel** button on the
Microsoft Office **Shortcut Bar** on the desktop.

*Alternatively*, click the **Start** button and select **Microsoft
Excel** in the **Programs** menu or sub-menu.

## 1.2    A New Spreadsheet

When you open Excel, it usually creates a new spreadsheet called **Book 1**.  It appears on the screen as
if it were a sheet of blank paper ruled with horizontal and vertical lines in the form of a grid.

If there is no spreadsheet open, blank or otherwise, the main part of the screen where the document
would normally appear will be gray.

If Excel doesn't create a new spreadsheet, you can create one yourself.

New

- Click the **New** button at the left of the **Toolbar**.
  A new spreadsheet opens, ready for you to begin.
  *Alternatively*, select **New** in the **File** menu.
  The **New** window opens, as in the illustration below, with the **Workbook** icon already selected.

- Click **OK** and a new spreadsheet appears on the screen.

The blank spreadsheet
that appears is called
a **Workbook** (see the
illustration on the
next page).

It is a good idea to
save your new
Spreadsheet **now**,
even before you
begin to work on it.
Then as your work
proceeds, you can
click the **Save**
button from time to
time and be sure that
your work will not
be completely lost in
the event of a serious
problem occurring.

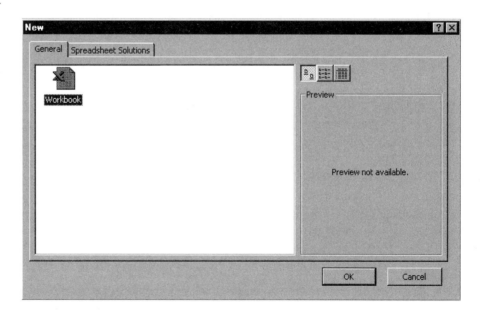

- Click the **Save** button or select **Save** in the **File** menu.
  The **Save As** window appears.

- Type a name for the spreadsheet in the **File Name** box.

- Save the spreadsheet in a folder of your choice on the **hard disk**.

## 1.3    The Excel Window

The window that appears when an Excel document is opened is similar to the windows used in other Microsoft applications.  The main features of the Excel window are shown here.

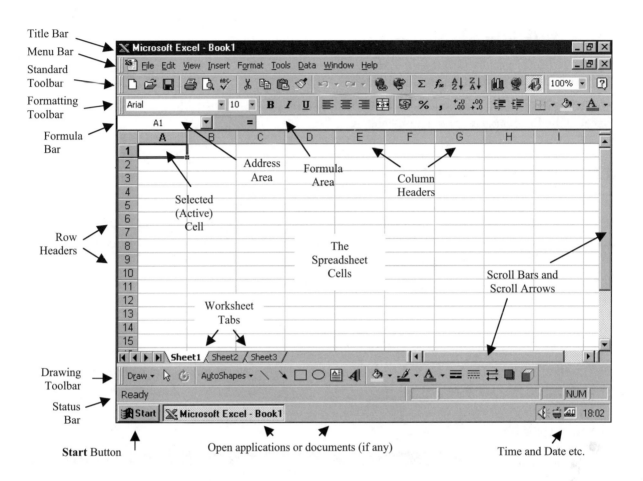

## 1.4    Excel Window Features

The new spreadsheet that appears on the screen contains a grid of columns and rows like a ledger.  The columns are labeled from left to right with letters of the alphabet, A, B, C... (called Column Headers) and so on.  The rows are labeled from top to bottom with the numbers, 1, 2, 3... (called Row Headers) and so on.  The lines between the cells are known as the cell **grid**.

The columns and rows divide the spreadsheet into thousands of boxes.  Each box is called a **cell** and it is uniquely identified by its **address** – the letter and number of the column and row that specify its position – e.g. **A1**, the address of the cell at the top left of the spreadsheet.

- The **Title Bar** displays the name of the document that you are using.

- The **Menu Bar** contains menus of actions that can be performed by the computer.
  Click on a menu to display a list of options.  As you point to a menu item, it is coloured or *highlighted*.
  Some items have a sub-menu that appears beside the first menu.

- **Scroll Bars and Arrows** are used to move left and right or up and down over a document in the in the window when it is too large to see all at once.

- **The Toolbars** contain buttons that you click to perform an action.

  Common actions are grouped together on separate toolbars, such as the Standard and Formatting toolbars described below. The user can select the buttons to be displayed to suit individual requirements.

  - **The Standard Toolbar** has buttons for the most commonly used actions, e.g. Opening, Saving and Printing.

    To see a description of a button, hold the pointer over it *without clicking*.
    You will learn how to use the buttons as you progress through the course.

  - **The Formatting Toolbar** has buttons that are used to change the appearance of text, e.g. bold, italics, font and font size, and so on.

  - **The Formula Bar** displays the address of the current cell at the left and has an area on the right where formula information is displayed.

- **The Spreadsheet Cells** are the actual spreadsheet or workbook area in which you will enter numbers and text for your work.

- **The Status Bar** displays the page number and other information, such as the line number on which the cursor is currently placed.

**Other items** may be displayed on occasion in separate windows.

## 1.5    Entering Data

A cell must be selected, or be **active**, in order to enter information in it. To make a cell active, click in it. Notice the special **cross** shape of the spreadsheet cursor. An active cell has a dark border around it and its **address** is displayed in the name box at the left of the **Formula** bar.

The Spreadsheet cursor

Text, numbers or a formula may be typed in a cell on a spreadsheet.

When a cell is active, you can type into it, just as you would on a word processing document. As you type, the text appears in both the active cell and in the Formula bar.

A **cancel** mark (**x**) and an **enter** mark (✔) appear between the text and the name box. Click the enter mark to complete an entry or the cancel mark if you change your mind.

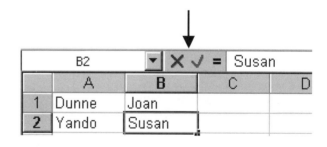

When you enter data in a cell, you must tell Excel when you have finished. Entries can be completed in a number of ways, such as by moving to another cell. Here are some of the things you can do.

- Press the **Enter Key**.
- Press the **Tab** key.
- Press the **Down Arrow Key** to move down a cell.
- Use the **Shift** and **Enter Keys** or the **Up Arrow Key** to move up a cell.
- Use the **Tab Key** or the **Right Arrow Key** to move to the cell on the right.
- Use the **Shift** and **Tab Key** or the **Left Arrow Key** to move to the cell on the left.
- Use the **Enter** mark on the **Formula Bar** to enter data and stay in the same cell.
- Use the **Mouse** to click in another cell.

## 1.6    Making Lists

Spreadsheets are commonly used for working with numbers and calculations but they can also be very useful for making, editing and sorting lists.

In the following set of exercises, we shall start with text alone and then add numbers later.

To make a list of the pupils in a class:

|    | A | B |
|----|-----------|---------|
| 1  | Dunne     | Joan    |
| 2  | Yando     | Susan   |
| 3  | Saxe      | Carmen  |
| 4  | Zealzo    | Michel  |
| 5  | Eisenberg | Wilhelm |
| 6  | Ayers     | Freda   |
| 7  | Dunne     | Ciara   |
| 8  | Montuga   | Charles |
| 9  | Divorkin  | Slava   |
| 10 | Brennan   | Michael |

- Click in cell **A1** to make it active, if it is not already selected.

- Type the surname **Dunne** in the cell.

- Press the **Tab** key or click in cell **B1** to move to the next cell across.

- Type the first name **Joan** in the new cell.

- Click in cell **A2** and type **Yando**.

- Click in cell **B2** or press the **Tab** key and type **Susan**.

- Continue in this manner until you have completed the list of names in the illustration.

- **Save** the file with the title **Class List**.

## 1.7    Toolbars

The Excel **toolbars** contain features common to other Office applications as well as some that are specific to spreadsheets and not included on Word or other toolbars.

- ▶ The **Menu** bar has the usual menus and an additional item – **Data**.

- ▶ The **Standard** Toolbar includes buttons for finding totals, calculating other mathematical functions, sorting data and inserting graphs.

- ▶ The **Formatting** Toolbar includes buttons for formatting numbers (currency, percentages, increasing or decreasing the number of digits after a decimal point) and colours.

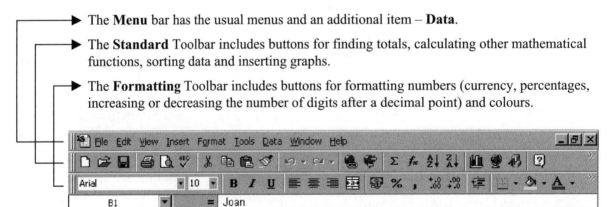

## 1.8    Simple Sorting

Lists are usually more useful when they are sorted in alphabetical order. Lists of names are usually sorted by surname. Excel can do this automatically. There are two **Sort** buttons on the toolbar for **ascending** and **descending** sorts.

An **ascending** sort – the most common – begins with the lowest letter of the alphabet or the lowest number.

A **descending** sort begins with the highest letter of the alphabet or the highest number. Descending sorts are useful for sorting numbers when you want the highest numbers to be at the top of the list.

To sort the list in alphabetical order by Surname:

- Click on any one of the Surnames.

- Click the **Sort Ascending** button.

  The list, Surnames and First Names, is sorted in order.
  Note, however, that the two **Dunnes** are not sorted in
  order according to their First Names.

All the Surnames and their associated First Names are sorted
together because they are in adjacent columns.  (If the First
Names were separated from the Surnames by a blank column,
then only the Surnames would be sorted and the list would be
incorrect.)

|    | A | B |
|----|---|---|
| 1  | Ayers | Freda |
| 2  | Brennan | Michael |
| 3  | Divorkin | Slava |
| 4  | Dunne | Joan |
| 5  | Dunne | Ciara |
| 6  | Eisenberg | Wilhelm |
| 7  | Montuga | Charles |
| 8  | Saxe | Carmen |
| 9  | Yando | Susan |
| 10 | Zealzo | Michel |

The list sorted by Surname.

When there is a lot of data on a spreadsheet, you may want to
sort only some of it and leave the other data as it is.  To sort
selected data in a particular part of a spreadsheet, first select the
**range of cells** that contain the items to be sorted.

A range of cells may be selected by pointing to the top left-hand cell and dragging to the bottom right-
hand cell.  An entire column or row of cells can be selected by clicking the **Column Header** (the letter
at the top of the column) or the **Row Header** (the number at the left of the row).

## 1.9    More Sorting

To sort the names with the first names also in order:

- Click on any one of the Surnames.

- Select **Sort** in the **Data** menu.

  The **Sort** window appears.

  Notice also that the range of cells
  containing the names is now selected.

- In the **Sort by** box in the window,
  **Column A** has already been entered.

  As Column A is the surnames column,
  the list will be sorted by surname first.

- In the **Then by** box immediately
  underneath, select **Column B** from the
  menu. (Click the menu arrow.)

  As Column B is the First Name column,
  the list will also be sorted by first name.

- Click **OK** to perform the sort.

  Notice that people with the same surname
  are now in alphabetical order by first name.

| 3 | Divorkin | Slava |
| 4 | Dunne | Ciara |
| 5 | Dunne | Joan |
| 6 | Eisenberg | Wilhelm |

A second **Then by** box allows for further sorting if required and if data is available.

- Click Header row (under My list has) if you have headers such as Surname and First Name at the
  top of the columns.  This will prevent them being included as names when the list is sorted.

## 1.10    Adding Rows and Columns

Sometimes it may be necessary to insert additional rows or columns *between* cells that already contain information.

You may wish to give each name on the list an identification number, for example, and to place it before the names you have already typed in.  Proceed as follows.

- Select column **A** by clicking the column header (the letter **A** at the top of the column).

- Select **Cells** in the **Insert** menu.

  A blank column is inserted *to the left* of the selected column.

  ID numbers can now be placed in the cell *before* each name on the list.

Note: The **Insert** menu may contain **Cells**, **Rows** or **Columns**, depending on the actual cells that have been selected.

If you wish to have headings at the top of the list, it is necessary to insert a new row *above* the present first row.  Proceed as follows.

- Select **Row 1** by clicking the Row header (the number **1** at the left of the row).
- Select **Rows** in the **Insert** menu.

  A blank row is inserted *above* the selected row.
- Type **ID Number** into the first cell in the new row, **Surname** in the second cell and **First Name** in the third cell.
- **Save** your work.

## 1.11    Deleting Rows and Columns

Selecting cells by dragging and then pressing the **Delete** key only deletes the contents of the cells, not the cells themselves.

To delete a row or column:

- Select the row or column you want to delete.
- Select **Delete** in the **Edit** menu.

## 1.12    Adjusting Cell Size

The size of the cells is set to the default size when you open a new Excel spreadsheet.  You will very quickly want to change the size of a particular cell or cells to suit your own requirements, however.

There are two ways to do this, by **dragging** to adjust the size on the spreadsheet itself or by using the **Format** menu.

**To change the size by dragging:**

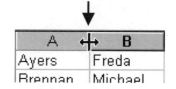

- Move the cursor slowly over the dividing line between the cells in the column or row header until it changes to a bar with an arrow at each side.

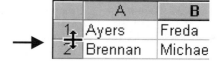

- Hold down the mouse button and drag until the cell width or height is the required size.

Changing cell size by dragging is convenient for occasional use. More often, you will want to change the cell size of a selection of cells, or of a complete row or column. Changing them individually would be tedious as well as giving uneven results.

To change the row height using the **Format** menu, proceed as follows.

- Select the cells, rows or columns whose size you want to change.

- Select **Row** in the **Format** menu and then **Height** in the sub-menu.
  The **Row Height** window opens.

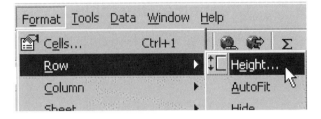

- Type the height you require (in points) in the **Row Height** box.

- Click **OK**.

To change the column width using the **Format** menu, proceed as before but select **Column** and **Width** instead of Row and Height.

Using the Format menu gives precise control over cell height and width. It allows for spacing between rows and columns and can be used to give your spreadsheet a neat and ordered appearance.

# Section 2     A Spreadsheet Timetable

## 2.1     Creating a Timetable

Spreadsheets are used mainly for their ability to analyse and calculate numbers.  They can also be used to create everyday documents such as lists and school timetables.  Refer to the illustration below as you follow these instructions.

- Open a **New Workbook** in Excel.

- Save the new workbook in an appropriate location as **Class Timetable**.

- Start entering data in the *second* row of calls.  This leaves the first row free for headings.

- Click in cell **B2** and type **Monday** in it.

- Move to cell **C2** and so on.  Continue entering the other days of the week across. *Alternatively*, use the **Fill Handle** as described in Section 2.2 below.

- Click on cell **A3** to start entering the times.  (The complete number is not displayed in the cell, but ignore this for the present.)

- Assume that some subjects are given the same time slot each day.  Only type the first one for the time being, as shown here.

|    | A    | B        | C       | D         | E        | F         | G |
|----|------|----------|---------|-----------|----------|-----------|---|
| 1  |      |          |         |           |          |           |   |
| 2  |      | Monday   | Tuesday | Wednesda  | Thursday | Friday    |   |
| 3  | 9    | Spanish  |         |           |          |           |   |
| 4  | 9.3  | Math     |         |           |          |           |   |
| 5  | 10   |          |         |           |          |           |   |
| 6  | 10.3 | Swimming | History | Computers | Swimming | Science   |   |
| 7  | 11   | Break    |         |           |          |           |   |
| 8  | 11.3 | English  |         |           |          |           |   |
| 9  | 12   |          |         |           |          |           |   |
| 10 | 12.3 | Lunch    |         |           |          |           |   |
| 11 | 1    | Singing  | Art     |           |          | Geography |   |
| 12 |      |          |         |           |          |           |   |

## 2.2     Using Fills

Excel will automatically enter of the other days into cells C2, D2, E2 and F2 after you have typed **Monday** if you use the **Fill Handle**.  The Fill Handle is the small black square at the bottom right-hand corner of the selected (or Active) cell.

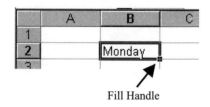

Fill Handle

- Move the cursor slowly over the **Fill Handle** until it turns into a cross.

- Drag over the cells to the right and you will see the names of the other days appear.

- Release the mouse button when you reach **Friday** to automatically insert the names in the cells.

- Select cells **B11** and **C11** and drag the **Fill Handle** through to cells **D11** and **E11** to repeat **Singing** and **Art** in those cells.

Another method of repeating data in a cell is to use the **Fill** command in the **Edit** menu.

- Select cells **B4** and **B5**.
- Select **Fill** in the **Edit** menu and then **Down** in the sub-menu.  **Math** automatically appears in cell **B5**.
- Select cells **B3 to F3**.  Select **Fill** in the **Edit** menu and then **Right** in the sub-menu.  **Spanish** automatically appears in the selected cells.

Excel will also try to help by trying to anticipate your entries.

- Click in cell **B9** and type the letter **E**.  Excel will automatically assume you wish to repeat the word **English**.  If you do not, continue to type and the word you actually type will be entered.

Fill in the remaining parts of the timetable with your own subject choices.

## 2.3    Formatting Cells

Cells can be formatted to display text and numbers in different ways.  The lesson times you typed in already are not displayed as you might have expected.  Excel recognises them as numbers rather than as times and it discards unwanted zeros and decimal points.   To display the times correctly, we shall format the cells so that the times will always display two decimal places.

Proceed as follows.

- Select cells **A3** to **A11**, which contain the lesson times.
- Select **Cells** in the **Format** menu.  The **Format Cells** window opens.
- Click the **Number** tab, if it is not already clicked.
- Click **Number** in the **Category** list on the left to select it.
- Type **2** in the **Decimal places** box.  Notice the sample displayed in the area above.
- Click **OK**. The times should now be displayed correctly.

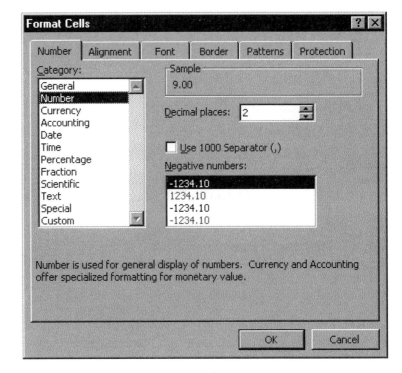

Numbers can also be displayed in other formats, such as **Currency, Date** and **Percentage**.  See Section 5.3, page 224.

To insert commas to separate largenumbers into thousands, click the **Use 1000 Separator (,)** box.

The number of digits after the decimal point can also be set by first selecting the appropriate cells.  Then use the **Increase** or **Decrease Decimal** buttons on the toolbar.

Click the tabs at the top of the window to see further ways in which cells can be formatted to display their contents.

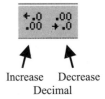

Increase    Decrease
Decimal

---

## 2.4    Text Alignment and Formatting

In spreadsheets, **numbers** are automatically aligned to the *right* of a cell.  **Text**  is aligned to the *left*. This alignment may not always be the most suitable and it can be easily changed.  To **centre** the times at the left and the days along the top, proceed as follows.

- Select the cells showing the days of the week.

- Click the **Centre Align** button on the toolbar.

   The days are aligned in the centre of the cells.

- Select the cells showing the lesson times.

- Click the **Centre Align** button on the toolbar.

   The times are centre aligned.

- To emphasise the times and days, select the appropriate cells and click the **Bold** button on the toolbar.

|    | A | B | C | D | E | F |
|----|---|---|---|---|---|---|
| 1  |   |   |   |   |   |   |
| 2  |   | **Monday** | **Tuesday** | **Wednesday** | **Thursday** | **Friday** |
| 3  | **9.00** | Spanish | Spanish | Spanish | Spanish | Spanish |
| 4  | **9.30** | Math | Drama | Math | History | Math |
| 5  | **10.00** | Math | English | English | Science | English |
| 6  | **10.30** | Swimming | History | Computers | Swimming | Science |
| 7  | **11.00** | Break | Break | Break | Break | Break |
| 8  | **11.30** | English | Geography | History | Science | Computers |
| 9  | **12.00** | English | Science | Geography | English | Art |
| 10 | **12.30** | Lunch | Lunch | Lunch | Lunch | Lunch |
| 11 | **1.00** | Singing | Art | Singing | Art | Geography |
| 12 |   |   |   |   |   |   |

- To change the font of the main part of the timetable, select the cells and choose **Times New Roman** and **11pt** in the menus on the toolbar.

- Use the **Format** menu to set columns B to F **12pt** wide and rows 1 to 11 to **20pt** high.

## 2.5    Adding a Heading

We shall enter a heading in cell A1 at the top of the sheet.

- Select **Times New Roman**, **18 point**, on the toolbar.

- Type the heading **Class Timetable** in cell **A1** and click the **Enter** button.

If the heading appears on 2 or more lines in cell A1, select **Cells** in the **Format** menu.  Click the **Alignment** tab in the **Format Cells** window and unclick the **Wrap text** box.

## 2.6    Angled Text

Text in cells can be **angled** *up* or *down* – useful for headings when too many wide columns might not fit across the page.

- Select the cells with the text you want to angle.

- Select **Cells** in the **Format** menu.  The **Format Cells** window opens.

- Click the **Alignment** tab to display the alignment options.

- **To angle the text**, drag the 'hand' around the 'clock face' in the **Orientation** panel or set the number of **degrees** in the small box below.  Then click **OK**.  (For **vertical** text, click in the vertical **Text** box.)

- Select **Row** in the **Format** menu and click **AutoFit** in the sub-menu to adjust the cell height.

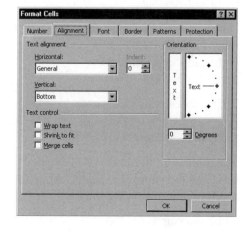

See the effect on the days of the week headings in Section 2.11 of this Module on page 211.

## 2.7    Adding a Border

A border can be added to the entire spreadsheet or around selected cells only.

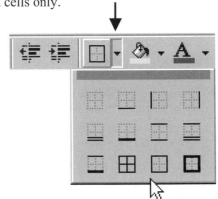

- Select the cells around which you want a border.

- Click the **Borders** button on the toolbar to apply a border.

- *Alternatively*, click the arrow beside the **Borders** button to display a menu of different border **styles**.

- Click the style that you require.

- Note that using the **Borders** button alone may apply the last border style chosen in this menu.

## 2.8    Using Find and Replace

From time to time, it may be necessary to alter the subjects on your timetable.  Rather than changing each cell by hand, you can use Excel's **Find and Replace** facility to do it automatically.

There are two options in the **Edit** menu, **Find** and **Replace**.  Click **Find** if you are looking for a specific item.  You will then be able to change or replace it if you wish.  *Alternatively*, click **Replace** if you know that you want to replace one item with another.  You may begin with either.

To replace **Singing** with **Music** in the timetable, do the following.

- Click **Find** in the **Edit** menu.
  The Find window opens.

- Type **Singing** in the **Find what** box.

- Click **Find Next** to see the cell on the spreadsheet. (Move the Find window, if necessary.)

- Click **Find Next** again to go to the next cell with the word **Singing** in it.

- Click **Replace** if you want to replace 'Singing' with another word at any point.
  The **Replace** window opens.

- In the Replace window, type **Music** in the **Replace with** box.

- Click **Replace** to replace **Singing** with **Music** in the selected cell.

- Click **Replace All** to replace **Singing** with **Music** in all the cells that contained **Singing**.

- Click **Close** when you are finished.

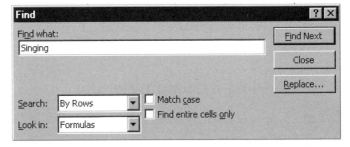

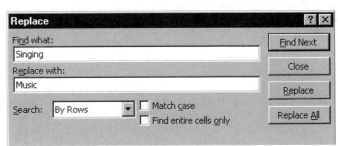

### Other Options:

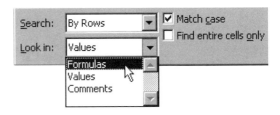

To search rows or columns, select **By Rows** or **By Columns** from the menu in the **Search** box.

The menu in the **Look in** box allows you to search in Formulas as well as in Values or Text.

Unclick **Match case** to find both upper and lower case.

Click **Find entire cells only** to find an exact match.  Leaving it unchecked will find, for example, the number 8 in cells that contain 8, 182, 2845, and so on.

## 2.9    Adding a Header

The procedure for creating a header or footer in an Excel Spreadsheet is somewhat different from creating one in a Word document.

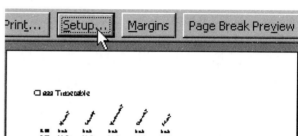

Print Preview

In Excel, headers and footers are added using the **Print Preview** button on the toolbar.

- Click the **Print Preview** button or select **Print Preview** in the **File** menu.

  A preview of the Timetable appears, with a row of buttons across the top.

- Click the **Setup** button to display the **Page Setup** window.

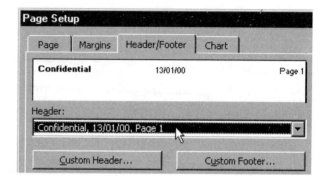

- Click the **Header/Footer** tab.

- Click in the **Header** or **Footer** boxes to display lists of preset headers and footers.

- Select the header or footer you want to use. It is displayed in the large box.

- Click **OK** to add the selected header and/or footer to your document.

## 2.10    Adding a Custom Header

To add a personal header, proceed as follows. (A personal footer can be added in the same way.)

- Click the **Custom Header** (or Footer) button. The **Header** or **Footer** window opens.
  Read the information about formatting text, and so on, at the top of the window.

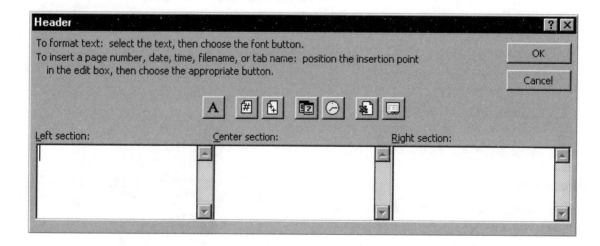

- Click in the **Left section** box and type (for this exercise) **Blackrock Junior School**.

- Select the text you have typed and click the **Font** button to open the **Font** window.

- Select **Times New Roman**, **18 pt**. **Bold**.

- Click **OK** and then **OK** in the succeeding windows to return to the spreadsheet.

## 2.11  Printing a Spreadsheet

You are now ready to print the timetable.  First, save your work by clicking the **Save** button on the toolbar, by selecting **Save** in the **File** menu, or by using the keyboard shortcut.

The spreadsheet is normally printed without the row and column headers, and without the gridlines between the cells.

Before printing, check that everything is in order:

- Click the **Print Preview** button.

- Click **Zoom** to see the timetable full size, if you wish.

- If you are satisfied, click **Print** to print the timetable or **Close** to return to the spreadsheet.

| Blackrock Junior School Class Timetable | Monday | Tuesday | Wednesday | Thursday | Friday |
|---|---|---|---|---|---|
| 9.00 | Spanish | Spanish | Spanish | Spanish | Spanish |
| 9.30 | Math | Drama | Math | History | Math |
| 10.00 | Math | English | English | Science | English |
| 10.30 | Swimming | History | Computers | Swimming | Science |
| 11.00 | Break | Break | Break | Break | Break |
| 11.30 | English | Geography | History | Science | Computers |
| 12.00 | English | Science | Geography | English | Art |
| 12.30 | Lunch | Lunch | Lunch | Lunch | Lunch |
| 1.00 | Music | Art | Music | Art | Geography |

The printed Timetable

## 2.12  Printing Part of a Spreadsheet

To print part of a spreadsheet, do the following.

- Select the cells you want to print.

- Select **Print Area** in the **File** menu and **Set Print Area** in the sub-menu.
  (Select **Clear Print Area** to print the whole spreadsheet later.)

- Print the spreadsheet as usual.  Only the selected cells will be printed.

## 2.13   Print Options

Before printing a spreadsheet, various options and settings can be selected.

- Select **Page Setup** in the **File** menu.

  The Page Setup window appears.

- Click the **Page** tab, if it is not already clicked.

- Click **Landscape** to print a spreadsheet that will not fit on an upright (Portrait) page.

- In the **Scaling** area of the window, click the **Adjust to** button to reduce or enlarge to a percentage of its normal size.

  Enter the required percentage in the box to the right.

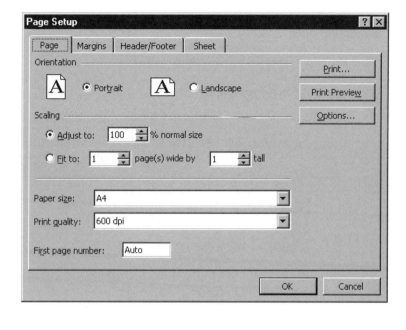

- To set the number of pages a spread-sheet is printed on, click the **Fit to** button.

  Select the number of pages in the boxes to the right.  The spreadsheet will be scaled automatically to fit on the pages, or even on a single page, if required.

- Select **A4** in the **Paper size** box to use the standard paper size.

Click the **Margins** tab to set the page margins.  At the bottom of the Margins panel, click the appropriate box to centre the spreadsheet on the page.

Click the **Sheet** tab to display further options.

- The area to be printed is shown in the **Print area** box.

- In the **Print** area, click the **Gridlines** box if you want the grid to be printed.

- In the **Page order** area, select how you want a large spreadsheet printed over several pages.

- When you have made your choices, click the **Print** button to print the spreadsheet.

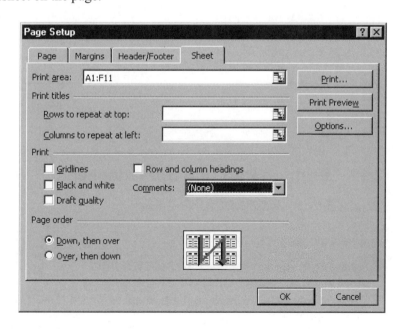

# Section 3      Working with Numbers

## 3.1     Using a Formula

Many powerful functions in Excel can be used for various mathematical, statistical and financial calculations. A **formula** can be used to automate certain calculations, such as adding numbers. The formula is *entered* in a cell and the **result** of the formula is then *displayed* in the cell, not the actual formula that produced it.

In this exercise, we shall number the children in the Class List prepared earlier (Section 1.6, page 196). Numbers will be added in the ID Number column beside each name. Rather than enter each number individually, a formula will be used and the numbers inserted automatically by Excel.

- Open the **Class List** spreadsheet used in Section 1.

- Click on cell **A3** and type **1** in the cell.

- Click on cell **A4** and type the formula **=A3+1**. This tells Excel to add **1** to whatever is in cell **A3**.

- Click the **Enter** mark. The **result** of the formula, the number **2**, now appears in cell **A4**.

    (Notice that the actual formula appears in the **Formula Bar** while the *result* of the Formula appears in the cell.)

- Click on cell **A4**. Drag to the bottom of the list to select the cells down to **A12**.

- Select **Fill** and then **Down** in the **Edit** menu

    The other ID numbers appear automatically in the selected cells.

    *Alternatively*, click in cell **A4** and drag the **Fill Handle** down to insert the numbers.

| | A | B | C |
|---|---|---|---|
| 1 | | | |
| 2 | ID Number | Surname | First Name |
| 3 | | Ayers | Freda |
| 4 | | Brennan | Michael |
| 5 | | Divorkin | Slava |
| 6 | | Dunne | Ciara |
| 7 | | Dunne | Joan |
| 8 | | Eisenberg | Wilhelm |
| 9 | | Montuga | Charles |
| 10 | | Saxe | Carmen |
| **11** | | Yando | Susan |
| 12 | | Zealzo | Michel |
| 13 | | | |

- Select the ID number cells and click the **Centre Align** button on the toolbar for a neat appearance.

Click on the numbers in turn and look at the formula that appears in the Formula Bar. Notice that in each case from cell **A4** on, Excel adds **1** to what is in the previous cell to calculate the new number.

## 3.2     Adding New Data

When a list such as the Class List has been entered on a spreadsheet, it can be useful in various ways. Test results may be entered as they become available. The total and average marks can then be calculated by Excel.

In this exercise, test results for the four weeks in September will be used as an example.

- Type **September** in cell **A1**. Use the font **Times New Roman**, **18pt** (for this cell only).

- Type **Week 1** in cell **D2**. Use the **Fill Handle** to drag through cells **E2, F2, G2** to add **Weeks 2, 3 and 4** automatically.

- Insert a blank row above the first name in the list.

- Type the maximum scores for each week – **20**, **25**, **28** and **30** – in cells **D3**, **E3**, **F3**, and **G3**.

To improve legibility and appearance, insert a blank column between the names and the test results.

- Select column **D**.

- Select **Column** in the **Insert** menu.  A blank column is inserted.

Enter marks for each pupil for each week, keeping in mind the maximum marks above.
Format the text, numbers, alignment, column widths etc. as necessary to approximate the illustration.

| | A | B | C | D | E | F | G | H |
|---|---|---|---|---|---|---|---|---|
| 1 | September | | | | | | | |
| 2 | | | | | Week 1 | Week 2 | Week 3 | Week 4 |
| 3 | ID Number | Surname | First Name | | 20 | 25 | 28 | 30 |
| 4 | 1 | Ayers | Freda | | 14 | 20 | 24 | 24 |
| 5 | 2 | Brennan | Michael | | 15 | 19 | 21 | 26 |
| 6 | 3 | Divorkin | Slava | | 14 | 17 | 20 | 21 |
| 7 | 4 | Dunne | Ciara | | 18 | 20 | 26 | 24 |
| 8 | 5 | Dunne | Joan | | 20 | 22 | 28 | 30 |
| 9 | 6 | Eisenberg | Wilhelm | | 20 | 25 | 28 | 30 |
| 10 | 7 | Montuga | Charles | | 19 | 25 | 26 | 28 |
| 11 | 8 | Saxe | Carmen | | 12 | 12 | 10 | 9 |
| 12 | 9 | Yando | Susan | | 18 | 20 | 17 | 19 |
| 13 | 10 | Zealzo | Michel | | 19 | 23 | 18 | 27 |
| 14 | | | | | | | | |

## 3.3    Sorting Data Numerically

If the list is sorted numerically, it is sorted according to the marks (numbers), not alphabetically.  When **Descending Order** is chosen for the sort, the children with the highest marks appear at the top of the list and those with lower marks below.  To sort by the **Week 1** marks in descending order, do the following.

- Drag to select all the cells from **B4** to **H13**.

- Select **Sort** in the **Data** menu. The **Sort** window appears.

- Select **Column E** (the **Week 1** column) in the menu in the **Sort by** box.

- Click **Descending**.

- Click **OK** to perform the sort.
  (The ID numbers now serve as ranking numbers.)

In Office 2000, Excel warns you of data in cells adjacent to those that you have selected for sorting.  You may or may not wish to include this data.

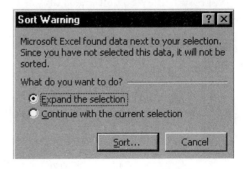

To sort the cells you have selected, click **Continue with the current selection**.

To include the adjacent data, click **Expand the selection**.

Click the **Sort** button when you have made your selection.

## 3.4    Adding Numbers

To find the total of the marks each pupil received for the four weeks, you can use a formula and make Excel do the calculations.

Calculations can be made automatically using the **AutoSum** button.

- Click in cell **J2** and type the heading **Total**.

- Click in cell **J3** to select it.

- Click the **AutoSum** button on the toolbar.

$\Sigma$

AutoSum

Excel makes an 'intelligent guess' at the numbers that you want to add. It surrounds them with a broken line and inserts a formula to add them up in cell **J3** (and also in the Formula Bar).

| | Week 1 | Week 2 | Week 3 | Week 4 | | Total |
|---|---|---|---|---|---|---|
| Max. | 20 | 25 | 28 | 30 | | =SUM(E3:I3) |

- Click the **Enter** mark to accept Excel's suggestion.
  The total is entered in cell **J3**.

In the example above, the formula **=SUM(E3:I3)** is displayed. This tells Excel to add all the numbers from cell E3 to cell I3. The colon between the two cell addresses means **from... to**. (Cell I3 is currently empty and does not affect the calculation.)

The formula can now be copied to add the actual marks obtained by the children.

- Click in cell **J3** to select it, if it is not already selected.

- Drag the **Fill Handle** down to cell **J13** and release the mouse button.
  The total marks for each child are calculated and displayed.

*Alternatively*, use the **Edit** menu.

- Select the cells from **J3** to **J13**.

- Select **Fill** and then **Down** in the **Edit** menu.
  The total marks for each child are calculated and displayed.

| G | H | I | J |
|---|---|---|---|
| ek 3 | Week 4 | | Total |
| 28 | 30 | | 103 |
| 24 | 24 | | 82 |
| 21 | 26 | | 81 |
| 20 | 21 | | 72 |
| 26 | 24 | | 88 |
| 28 | 30 | | 100 |
| 28 | 30 | | 103 |
| 26 | 28 | | 98 |
| 10 | 9 | | 43 |
| 17 | 19 | | 74 |
| 18 | 27 | | 87 |

## 3.5    Functions

A **Function** is a special formula, like the **SUM** function used to add up the marks above. Excel has a large number of functions for various purposes.

**Functions** can be accessed through the **Paste Function** button on the toolbar or by using **Function** in the **Insert** menu.

Paste Function

In the next part of the exercise, we shall use the **AVERAGE** function to find each pupil's average mark for the four weeks.

- Type the heading **Average** in cell **K2**.

- Click in cell **K4** to select it.

- Click the **Paste Function** button on the toolbar.

  The **Paste Function** window appears.

- Select **Average** in the **Function name** list on the right.

- Click **OK**.

  The Average window appears

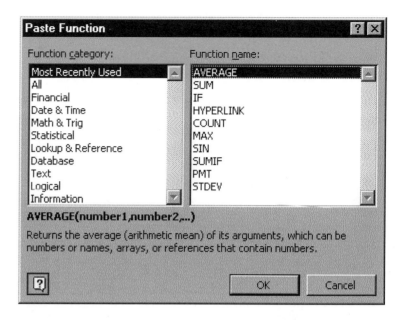

An explanation of the **Average** function appears in the bottom of the window. It is in mathematical terms, however, and may not be very useful.

Excel assumes that you want to find the average of the cells from **E3** to **J3** and has entered those in the **Number 1** box.

The numbers in those cells are displayed to the right of the box. You will notice that they include the empty blank cell (**0**) and the actual total (**103**) of the four numbers whose average we want to find.

To accept this Excel suggestion would not give the correct average, so we need to change the range of cells in the **Number 1** box.

If the Average window hides the cells in the spreadsheet, the window can be **reduced** by clicking the button at the right-hand end of the **Number 1** box. Click the button again to restore the box.

- Enter the range of cells for which you want to find the average – **E3:H3** – in the Number 1 box.

  *Alternatively*, you can drag across the cells on the Spreadsheet to enter the range of cells in the Number 1 box.

- Click **OK**. The average of the four numbers is inserted in cell **K3** and the formula appears in the **Formula Bar**.

- **Fill Down** as before to calculate and display the averages for all the children.

- Centre the numbers in the cells and format them to display one place of decimals.

| Total | Average |
|-------|---------|
| 103   | 25.8    |
| 82    | 20.5    |
| 81    | 20.3    |
| 72    | 18.0    |
| 88    | 22.0    |
| 100   | 25.0    |
| 103   | 25.8    |
| 98    | 24.5    |
| 43    | 10.8    |
| 74    | 18.5    |
| 87    | 21.8    |

# 3.6    Cell References

When calculating the **total** (sum) and the **average** marks, it was possible to use a formula entered in the top cell for all the pupils on the list.  This is because Excel automatically changes the references to the cells as it goes down the list when you tell it to **Fill Down**.  This is called using **Relative References** in its formulas.

Thus, when a formula was entered into cell **J3** and **Fill Down** was used, Excel changed the reference from cell **J3** to cell **J4**, then to cell **J5** and so on as it moved down the column.  This meant that it used each child's data in turn to calculate the results for each individual child.

However, to calculate each child's total marks as a percentage of the *maximum* marks, Excel must always refer back to the maximum marks in cell **J3** and it must **not** change this reference as it goes down the list.  This kind of fixed reference is called an **Absolute Reference**.

To enter an absolute reference in a formula, a **dollar sign** (**$**) is added before each letter or number, so that **J3** becomes **$J$3**.  Then, as Excel moves down the list, it always refers to cell **J3** when calculating that part of the formula.

To demonstrate this, we shall calculate each pupil's total marks for September as a percentage of the month's maximum mark.  We shall use both Relative and Absolute references to demonstrate the difference between them.

# 3.7    Absolute References

To calculate the percentages correctly, it is necessary to mark the reference to cell **J3** with dollar signs so that Excel will always use that cell it as it moves down the list.

The dollar signs can be added automatically by using the **F4** key at the top of the keyboard, or you can type them in manually.  In the following example, each child's total marks will be calculated as a percentage of the total marks possible (**103**).

**Add a new heading:**

- Type the heading **%** in cell **L2**.

- Add a new blank row above the names to separate the headings from the rest of the list for greater readability.

**Type the formula:**

Use the following steps to enter the formula, **=J3/$J$3*100** in cell L3.

- Click in cell **L3**.

- Type **=J3/J3** (only).

- Press the **F4** key on the keyboard.
  Dollar signs are added to the last cell reference you typed (J3) and the formula is now displayed as **=J3/$J$3**.

- Type *****100** to complete the formula.

- Click the **Enter** mark to display the resulting percentage (100) in cell **L3**.

- Note that the formula now appears only in the Formula Bar.

|    | J | K | L |
|----|-----|--------|-------|
| 1  |     |        |       |
| 2  | Total | Average | % |
| 3  | 103 | 25.8 | 100.0 |
| 4  |     |        |       |
| 5  | 82  | 20.5 | 79.6 |
| 6  | 81  | 20.3 | 78.6 |
| 7  | 72  | 18.0 | 69.9 |
| 8  | 88  | 22.0 | 85.4 |
| 9  | 100 | 25.0 | 97.1 |
| 10 | 103 | 25.8 | 100.0 |
| 11 | 98  | 24.5 | 95.1 |
| 12 | 43  | 10.8 | 41.7 |
| 13 | 74  | 18.5 | 71.8 |
| 14 | 87  | 21.8 | 84.5 |

## Calculate the Percentages:

- Use the **Fill Handle** or **Fill Down** as before to calculate and display the percentages for the individual children.

- Centre the percentages and format them to one place of decimals.

- Delete the **0.0** in cell **L4**.

  (When you used **Fill Down**, 0.0 appeared in cell L4 in the blank row.  Deleting 0.0 is for the sake of neatness only in this case.)

See also **Percentages** on page 225 for another method, using the **Percent Style** button on the toolbar.

### How the Formula works

The Formula is  **=J3/$J$3*100**.  Cell **J3** contains the total marks possible.

The formula for cell **L3** is thus **=(103/103)*100**.  If a child achieves the maximum marks (103/103) they have attained 100%.  Multiplying by **100** makes the answer a percentage in this case.

As Excel moves down to the first name, **J3** becomes **J5** in the formula but **$J$3** does not change.

The formula for cell **L5** is thus **=(82/103)*100**, which gives 79.61%.

**J3, J4, J5** and so on are **Relative** references.  They represent each child's individual totals and they change as Excel moves down the list.

**$J$3** is an **Absolute** reference.  It does **not** change as Excel goes down the list and so all the totals are calculated as percentages of **J3**, the total marks possible (103).

## 3.8  Special Symbols and Characters

The majority of special characters you may require for formulae are available on the keyboard.  Some keys have two characters, upper and lower.  For the upper character, hold down the **shift** key while pressing the character key (just as you would to obtain a capital letter).

Type an equals sign (=) before you enter a formula or function in a cell.

### Mathematical symbols

*      The asterisk is used for multiplication.  Use it to multiply two numbers, such as in **100*17**. You can also use it to multiply the contents of two cells by typing the cell addresses, such as in A3*B1.

/      The forward slash is used for division.  For example, C6/8 divides the value of cell C6 by 8.

-      The minus sign, or hyphen, is used to subtract one value from another, as in 8-4.

+      The plus sign is used for addition of two or more values, as in 8+4.

^      The caret is used to raise the power of one number to another.  For example, 3^2 (3 to the power of 2) gives a value of 9.

You can combine mathematical operations in Excel as you would in any normal mathematical exercise.  The rules regarding multiplication, division, addition and subtraction and the use of parentheses are the same, as in an expression such as (A5+(B6-F3))/D7.

## Other symbols

:  The colon is used to designate a range of cells, as in A5:A12. It can also designate a range of cells over more than one row or column, as in A5:C7.

,  The comma may be used as a thousands separator in large numbers, as in 1,000,000.

.  The full stop is used to denote decimal values, as in 24.68.

#  The hash character is used in two ways.

   In the first, a number of hash characters appear in a cell to indicate that the cell is not wide enough to display all the characters required.

   In the second, it indicates that an error has occurred (see Section 3.9 below).

5E+08  This is scientific notation, a way of writing large numbers. It is used by Excel when a cell is not wide enough to display a number in the usual way. If you increase the width of the cell sufficiently, the number will be displayed normally. (5E+08 is five hundred million.)

~  The tilde character may be used when searching for an asterisk in a worksheet. In the **Find what** box, the asterisk would be preceded by the tilde as follows. ~*34. It behaves like a wildcard (see Section 5.4, page 90).

## 3.9   Error Messages

From time to time an **error message** may appear. Some common ones are described here. Use Excel **Help** to find more information on error messages.

- **####**       The column is not wide enough to display the number.

- **#DIV/0!**    The formula is trying to divide by zero, which is not possible.

- **#Value!**    Text has been entered when the formula expects a number.

- **#Name!**     Text has been entered in a formula, which is not allowed.

- **#N/A**       The value is not available.

## 3.10   The Completed Spreadsheet

At the end of the exercise, the completed spreadsheet should appear as below.

| | A | B | C | D | E | F | G | H | I | J | K | L |
|---|---|---|---|---|---|---|---|---|---|---|---|---|
| 1 | September | | | | | | | | | | | |
| 2 | | | | | Week 1 | Week 2 | Week 3 | Week 4 | | Total | Average | % |
| 3 | ID Number | Surname | First Name | Max. | 20 | 25 | 28 | 30 | | 103 | 25.8 | 100.0 |
| 4 | | | | | | | | | | | | |
| 5 | 1 | Ayers | Freda | | 14 | 20 | 24 | 24 | | 82 | 20.5 | 79.6 |
| 6 | 2 | Brennan | Michael | | 15 | 19 | 21 | 26 | | 81 | 20.3 | 78.6 |
| 7 | 3 | Divorkin | Slava | | 14 | 17 | 20 | 21 | | 72 | 18.0 | 69.9 |
| 8 | 4 | Dunne | Ciara | | 18 | 20 | 26 | 24 | | 88 | 22.0 | 85.4 |
| 9 | 5 | Dunne | Joan | | 20 | 22 | 28 | 30 | | 100 | 25.0 | 97.1 |
| 10 | 6 | Eisenberg | Wilhelm | | 20 | 25 | 28 | 30 | | 103 | 25.8 | 100.0 |
| 11 | 7 | Montuga | Charles | | 19 | 25 | 26 | 28 | | 98 | 24.5 | 95.1 |
| 12 | 8 | Saxe | Carmen | | 12 | 12 | 10 | 9 | | 43 | 10.8 | 41.7 |
| 13 | 9 | Yando | Susan | | 18 | 20 | 17 | 19 | | 74 | 18.5 | 71.8 |
| 14 | 10 | Zealzo | Michel | | 19 | 23 | 18 | 27 | | 87 | 21.8 | 84.5 |
| 15 | | | | | | | | | | | | |

# Section 4    Multiple Spreadsheets

## 4.1    More than one Worksheet

When a **Workbook** (a Spreadsheet) is opened in Excel, it automatically contains *three* **Worksheets**, although we only used one for the Class List.

A **Tab** for each Sheet is displayed at the bottom of the screen. The tabs are used to move from one Sheet to another.

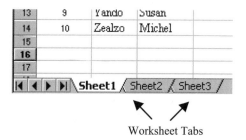

Worksheet Tabs

## 4.2    Adding Worksheets

The three worksheets contained in one Workbook provide a convenient way of recording the results of class tests given at the end of each of three school terms, Term 1, Term 2 and Term 3.

A **summary** of results could then be calculated at the end of the year. Since one sheet has already been used, another sheet could be inserted.

- Select **Worksheet** in the **Insert** menu.
  A fourth sheet is added and the **Sheet4** tab appears at the bottom of the screen.
  Note that the new worksheet is added before the current one.

- Add additional worksheets in a similar way.
  Each additional worksheet is numbered with a tab at the bottom of the screen.

- To rename a worksheet, double-click the tab and type the new name. (See also Section 4.4, at the bottom of page 221)

## 4.3    Copying Between Worksheets

The **Copy** and **Paste** buttons on the toolbar, or the commands in the **Edit** menu, can be used to copy data from one part of the same worksheet to another.

It can also be convenient to copy some data from an existing spreadsheet to a new one to save having to type it again.

To copy the **Class List** names to another worksheet, proceed as follows.

- Open the **Class List** Spreadsheet.

- Select the cells containing the **Names** of the pupils.

- Click the **Copy** button or select **Copy** in the **Edit** menu.

- Click the **Sheet 2** tab at the bottom of the worksheet.

- Select cell **A1** and click the **Paste** button or select **Paste** in the **Edit** menu.

  The list of names is now displayed on both Sheet 1 and Sheet 2.

| ID Number | Surname | First Name |
|-----------|-----------|------------|
| 1 | Ayers | Freda |
| 2 | Brennan | Michael |
| 3 | Divorkin | Slava |
| 4 | Dunne | Ciara |
| 5 | Dunne | Joan |
| 6 | Eisenberg | Wilhelm |
| 7 | Montuga | Charles |
| 8 | Saxe | Carmen |
| 9 | Yando | Susan |
| 10 | Zealzo | Michel |

## 4.4    Using Multiple Worksheets

Test results for three school terms may be recorded on three different worksheets.

Results may be entered on each worksheet as the term progresses.  At the end of the year, Excel can total the marks on the different worksheets to produce a summary for the year.

(For this exercise, as an alternative to entering similar data on the three different worksheets as described below, enter the data on one worksheet and then **Copy** and **Paste** it into the others, changing **Term 1** to **Term 2** and **Term 3** on the second and third worksheets.)  Proceed as follows.

- Open the **Class List** spreadsheet.
- Select the cells containing the names of the pupils and copy them.
- Paste the names into three new worksheets.
- Insert two blank rows at the top of each sheet and type **Test Results** in cell **A1**.
- Type **Term 1**, **Term 2** and **Term 3** respectively in cell **E1** of each sheet.
- Type the subjects, **Spanish**, **English**, **Maths**, **History** and **Geography** on each sheet, beginning with cell **E2**.
- Type **Max.** in cell **D3** and align it to the right.
- Enter the maximum marks, **100**, **80**, **100**, **75** and **75** for each subject.
- Enter marks for each child under each subject.

  (They are not needed for the rest of this exercise if you haven't the time!)

- Format the text and adjust column widths as necessary.

|   | A | B | C | D | E | F | G | H | I |
|---|---|---|---|---|---|---|---|---|---|
| 1 | Test Results | | | | Term 1 | | | | |
| 2 | | | | | Spanish | English | Maths | History | Geography |
| 3 | ID Number | Surname | First Name | Max. | 100 | 80 | 100 | 75 | 75 |
| 4 | | | | | | | | | |

Term 1 Worksheet

|   | A | B | C | D | E | F | G | H | I |
|---|---|---|---|---|---|---|---|---|---|
| 1 | Test Results | | | | Term 2 | | | | |
| 2 | | | | | Spanish | English | Maths | History | Geography |
| 3 | ID Number | Surname | First Name | Max. | 100 | 80 | 100 | 75 | 75 |
| 4 | | | | | | | | | |

Term 2 Worksheet

|   | A | B | C | D | E | F | G | H | I |
|---|---|---|---|---|---|---|---|---|---|
| 1 | Test Results | | | | Term 3 | | | | |
| 2 | | | | | Spanish | English | Maths | History | Geography |
| 3 | ID Number | Surname | First Name | Max. | 100 | 80 | 100 | 75 | 75 |
| 4 | | | | | | | | | |

Term 3 Worksheet

Worksheet tabs can be renamed to be more meaningful.

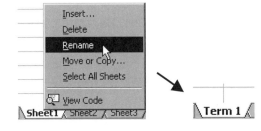

- Right-click on the tab you want to rename and select **Rename** in the menu that appears.
- Type the new name and press **Return** or click on the spreadsheet when you are finished.

---

## 4.5    Finding Totals on Multiple Worksheets

Excel can total the marks across the several worksheets.  It can find the total marks each pupil received in each school term, entered on separate spreadsheets, for example.

For this exercise, we shall insert a new worksheet and start by finding the maximum total marks for each subject.

- Insert a new worksheet (**Sheet 5**).
- **Copy** and **Paste** the headings, subject headings and names into it.  (The children's names are not shown in the illustration below to save space on the page.)

|   | A | B | C | D | E | F | G | H | I |
|---|---|---|---|---|---|---|---|---|---|
| 1 | Test Results | | | | Year Totals | | | | |
| 2 | | | | | Spanish | English | Math | History | Geography |
| 3 | ID Numbe | Surname | First Nam | Max. | | | | | |
| 4 | | | | | | | | | |

- Type **Year Totals** in cell **E1**.
- Click in cell **E3** to select it.  The formula to add the total of the maximum marks on the three Term Sheets will be entered here.

The following instructions assume that the three Term Sheets are **Sheet 2**, **Sheet 3** and **Sheet 4**. You can type the formula for the totals yourself or let Excel help you.

### Type the Formula.

- In the **Formula Bar**, type =SUM(Sheet2!E3, Sheet3!E3, Sheet4!E3).

  Notice that there are no spaces in the names of the Sheets.  An **exclamation mark** (!) is used before the cell address (E3) in each case.  A comma separates the sheets.  (The space after the comma is optional.)
- Click the **Enter** mark on the **Formula Bar**.

  The sum of the marks on the three sheets, **300**, appears in cell **E3** on **Sheet 5**.

### Let Excel help you.

- In the **Formula Bar**, type the beginning of the formula only:  =SUM(
- Click the tab for **Sheet 2** at the bottom left of the spreadsheet.

  **Sheet 2!** is automatically added to the formula.  It now appears as  =SUM(Sheet2!
- Click cell **E3** in Sheet 2.  It is automatically added to the formula, now =SUM(Sheet2!E3
- Type a comma in the Formula Bar.  The formula is now  =SUM(Sheet2!E3,
- Click the **Sheet 3** tab at the bottom left of the spreadsheet.  Then click cell **E3**.  The Sheet 3 details are added to the formula.
- Type a comma and repeat the previous step for **Sheet 4**.
- Click the **Enter** mark on the toolbar.  Excel adds the final bracket to the formula, now **=SUM(Sheet2!E3,Sheet3!E3,Sheet4!E3)**, and displays Sheet 5.
- The sum of the marks, 300, appears as before in cell **E3** on **Sheet 5**.

Use the **Fill Handle,** or **Fill Right** in the **Edit** menu, to complete the totals for the other subjects.

If you have entered marks for the children for each term, you can use the **Fill Handle,** or **Fill Down** in the **Edit** menu, to calculate and display the individual totals for each child for the whole year.

# Section 5      Other Options

## 5.1    Using Spreadsheets in Word Documents

Inserting a spreadsheet in Word is similar to inserting a table. There is an **Excel** button on the toolbar, similar to the **Table** button.

Excel Button

- Open a Word document or create a new one.

- Click the **Excel** button. A grid appears.

- Drag across and down the boxes to select the number of rows and columns you require.

  As you drag, the original grid will expand, if necessary. (7 across and 3 down will produce a spreadsheet with seven columns and three rows.)

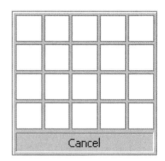

When you release the mouse button, a spreadsheet with the selected number of columns and rows appears on the page, surrounded by a frame.

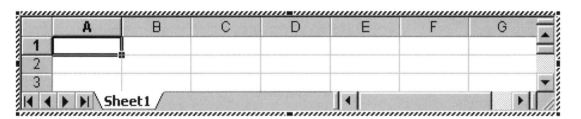

- The Menu Bar and Toolbars at the top of the screen change to Worksheet bars, and data can be entered as in a normal Excel workbook.

The spreadsheet on the Word page is a fully functioning spreadsheet and can be used in the same way as a normal full-sized spreadsheet.

- Type the data shown in the illustration below.

- Use the usual spreadsheet methods to format and centre the text and numbers.

- Use the **Sum** button on the toolbar to find the total expenditure for the months of January, February and March.

- Use a formula to calculate the balance.

- Select all the cells with numbers and click the **Currency** button on the toolbar to format the numbers as currency.

Currency Button

- When all entries have been completed, click outside the spreadsheet.

  Notice that the spreadsheet is presented on the page as a **table** and that the Menu Bar and toolbars revert to their Word formats.

| Income | | Expenses | | | | |
|---|---|---|---|---|---|---|
| | | Jan | Feb | March | Total | Balance |
| £ 1,240.00 | | £ 128.20 | £ 135.69 | £ 144.25 | £ 408.14 | £ 831.86 |

To make alterations or to continue working on the spreadsheet, double-click in the table.

## 5.2    Importing Objects

Objects, text files, graphics and so on can be added to a spreadsheet column by selecting the appropriate item in the **Insert** menu.  The process is similar to importing an object in a Word Processing document.

To add a picture to your spreadsheet:

- Select **Picture** in the **Insert** menu.

- Select the picture you want from **Clip Art** or from a **File**.

- Click **Insert**.

The picture can be moved, resized and so on, as in a Word document.

## 5.3    More Cell Formatting

You will have already formatted cells, making the text bold and displaying numbers with two decimal places, for example.  Some other formatting options are described here.

- First, select the cells that you want to format.

- Select **Cells** in the **Format** menu.

  The **Format Cells** window appears.

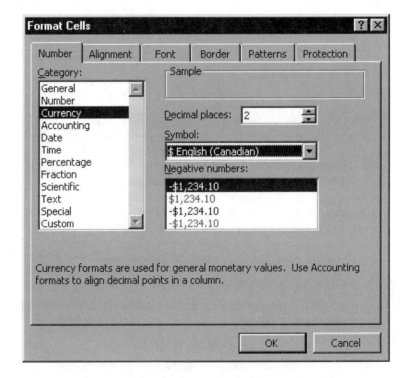

### Currency Symbols

Symbols for all major currencies are available.

- Click the **Number** tag, if it is not already clicked.

- Click **Currency** in the **Category** panel on the left.

- Click in the **Symbol** box to display a menu of available currency symbols.

- Select the symbol you wish to use.

- Click **OK**.

### Date Formats

You can set the date format that you prefer.

- Click **Date** in the **Category** panel on the left.

- Select the date format you want in the **Type** box.

- Click **OK**.

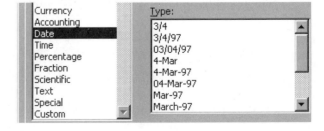

## Percentages

The Percentage option assists you in calculating percentages and displays the percent symbol (**%**) in the individual cells.

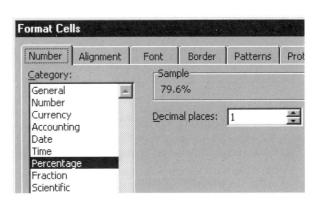

- Select the number of decimal places you want in the **Decimal places** box.

- Click **OK**.

### To display a percentage using the Percent Style button:

- Enter the fraction as a formula in the cell where you want to display a percentage, cell **L5** in the illustration below.

   In this example, the formula is **=J5/$J$3**.

Percent Style

- Click the **Percent Style** button on the toolbar.

   The cell is formatted as a percentage with the percent symbol displayed, as in the illustration.

- Apply the formula to any other cells you want to include (**Fill Down** in the example).

- Centre the data in the cells.

See Section 3.7 on page 217 for details of calculating percentages manually.

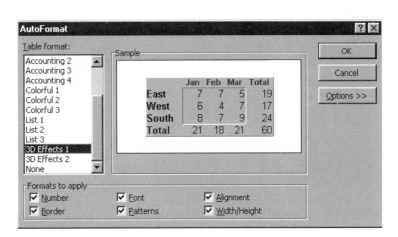

| | I | J | K | L |
|---|---|---|---|---|
| 1 | | | | |
| 2 | | Total | | % |
| 3 | | **103** | | **100** |
| 4 | | | | |
| 5 | | 82 | | 79.6% |
| 6 | | 81 | | 78.6% |
| 7 | | 72 | | 69.9% |
| 8 | | 88 | | 85.4% |
| 9 | | 100 | | 97.1% |

## 5.4   Using AutoFormat

As well as formatting cells and applying styles as described above, a number of pre-set formats and styles can be applied automatically using **AutoFormat**.

The process is similar to formatting tables in Word, as described in Module 3, Section 8.8, page 160.

Proceed as follows.

- Select the range of cells to be formatted.

- Select **AutoFormat** in the **Format** menu.

   The AutoFormat window appears.

- Click a format in the list in the **Table Format** panel.

   A sample appears in the Sample panel.

- Select the format of your choice.

- Click **OK**.

   The format is applied to the selected cells.

- Click the **Options** button to display more choices.

   You can de-select an element from the formatting, if required.  Click the appropriate box in the **Formats to apply** area of the window to remove the tick.

# Section 6      Charts

## 6.1      Creating Charts

Excel can create charts and graphs in three different ways:

Chart Wizard
Button

- On the **worksheet** currently being used.

- In a **separate sheet** in the workbook being used.

- In a **separate workbook**.

We shall use Freda Ayer's test marks to create
a simple graph on the worksheet we have
prepared previously.

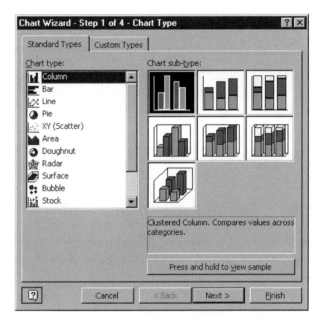

- Open the **Class List** file.

- Select cells **B5** to **H5** by dragging across
  them (Freda's name and her weekly marks
  for September).

- Hold down the **Ctrl** key while selecting cells
  **E2** to **H2** (Week1 to Week4).

- With the two sets of cells selected, click the
  **Chart Wizard** button on the toolbar.

- The Chart Wizard displays the first of four
  dialogue boxes that will lead you through the
  process of creating the graph.

- Select **Column** as the **Chart type** if it is not
  already selected.

- Click **Next** to go on to the next step.

The **Step 2** window shows how the final
graph would be displayed at this stage.

- Click **Next** to go on to **Step 3**.

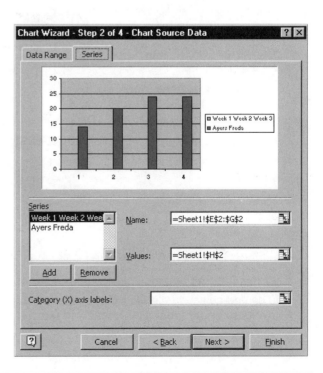

---

**Chart Types**

In the **Step 1** window above, **Column** is
selected in the **Chart type** panel on the
left.  Different kinds of Column charts
are displayed in the panel on the right.
Click on a Column type to see a
description underneath.

Click on other chart types in the **Chart
type** panel to see them illustrated.
Popular chart types are **Bar** charts, **Pie**
charts and **Line** charts.  These are
illustrated in the exercises on page 230.

See also Section 6.3, page 227.

---

In the **Step 3** window, we add a **title** and **labels** for the **axes**. We also remove the **legend** – the box to the right of the chart in the illustration in the window.

- Type **Test Results** in the **Chart title** box.

- Type **Weeks** in the **Category (X) axis** box.

- Type **Marks** in the **Value (Y) axis** box.

- Click on the **Legend** tab and click in the **Show Legend** box to remove the check mark (and the Legend from the graph).

- Click **Next** to go to the final step, **Chart Location**.

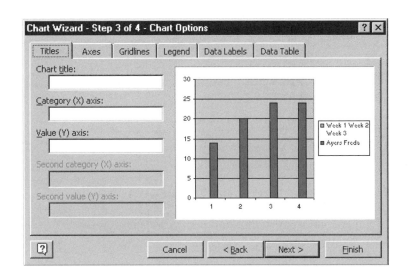

The location, **As an object in: Sheet 1**, where the chart will appear, is already selected.

- Click **Finish**.
  The chart appears on the worksheet.

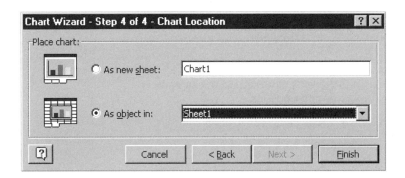

# 6.2    Moving, Sizing and Deleting Charts

If the graph is not in the desired location on the spreadsheet, or if it is not the correct size, it can be moved and resized.

- Move the chart by clicking anywhere inside it and dragging.

- To resize the chart, first click on it to select it.  **Handles** appear around it.

- Hold down the **Shift** key and drag one of the corner handles to change the size.
  (Holding down the Shift key keeps the proportions correct.)

- To delete a chart, first select it and then press the **Delete** key.

# 6.3    Other Chart Types

Excel can produce many types of graphs. Create a chart to compare the results of two pupils, as follows.

- Select the range of cells for each pupil. Drag to select the first pupil's range and hold down the **Ctrl** key while selecting the second pupil's details.

- Hold down the **Ctrl** key as before and select **Week 1** to **Week 4**.

- Click the **Chart** button and proceed through the steps.

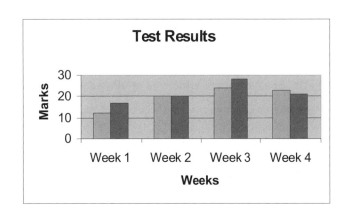

To change the **Bar** chart to a **Line** graph.

- Select the chart by clicking inside it.

- Select **Chart Type** in the **Chart** menu to display the Chart window as before.

- Select **Line** in the list on the left.

- Click **OK**.

## 6.4     Changing Chart Colours

If you are not happy with the colours in a chart, you can change them.

- Right-click the section you wish to change.

- Click **Format Data Series** in the pop-up menu that appears.

- The Format Data Series window opens.

- Click the colour you want to apply.

- Click the tabs at the top of the window to explore other options.

- Click **OK**.

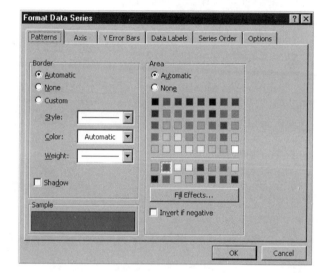

## 6.5     Printing Charts

Printing charts (or graphs) is much like printing worksheets. The worksheet data and chart may be printed together. The chart may also be printed on its own.

To preview and then print your work:

- Click outside the chart to deselect it if you want to print both spreadsheet and chart.

- Click the chart to select it if you only want to print the chart.

- Click the **Print Preview** button on the toolbar.

- If you wish to change the way your work is presented – to reposition the chart, for example – click the **Close** button to return to your work. Then click the **Print Preview** button again.

- Click the **Setup** button on the **Print Preview** Toolbar to display the Page Setup window.

- Select **Portrait** or **Landscape**, according to the size and shape of the spreadsheet.

- Click **OK** or click the **Print** button to print the spreadsheet.

## 6.6     Saving Charts

Charts are saved in the same way as other documents are saved.

If you have a chart on a worksheet you have already saved, click the **Save** button on the toolbar and Excel automatically saves all the work on the sheet.

If you wish to save your work in a new file, select **Save As** in the **File** menu. Give the file a name and choose an appropriate location.

# 6.7    Formatting  Charts

Charts can be changed and edited, both in worksheets and in documents into which they have been pasted.  The pattern of lines, scales, font, numbers and alignment can all be changed if required.

To format the **scale** of a chart, for example, proceed as follows.

- Click on any numeric value alongside an axis to select the axis.

- Click **Selected Axis** in the **Format** menu. The **Format Axis** window appears.

- Click the **Scale** tab in the window.

- Enter appropriate values in the boxes. On some charts, for example, it might not be appropriate to start the scale at zero.

- Click **OK** to apply the new scale.

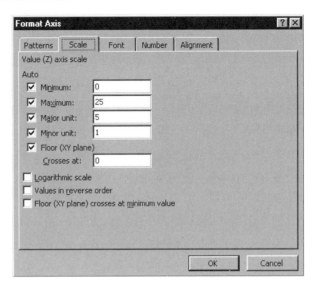

You can see the effect of the values in the boxes on the right in the chart below.

To change a **Chart Title**, do the following.

- Click the current title to select it. The title text is highlighted (see right).

- Type the new title in the **Formula Bar**.

- Click the **Enter** check mark (✔) on the Formula Bar when you have finished. The new title appears on the chart.

To format text – such as the title or axes labels – in a chart on the worksheet:

- Double-click on the text.

- A **Format** window appears with the **Font** tab clicked, as in the illustration below.

- Select the font, style, size and so on as appropriate.

- Click **OK** to apply the formatting.

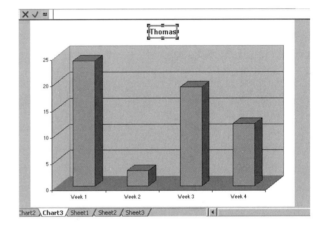

To change the chart **type**, right-click on the chart and select **Chart Type** from the pop-up menu that appears.  Select the type of chart you require.  It will replace the old chart while keeping its properties, i.e. labels and scaling, intact.  In a pasted chart, right-click the chart.  Select **Worksheet Object** in the menu that appears and **Edit** in the sub-menu.  Then continue as before.

For other options, click on the chart to select it.  Then select **Chart Options** in the **Chart** menu.  Click the appropriate tab in the Chart Options window that appears.

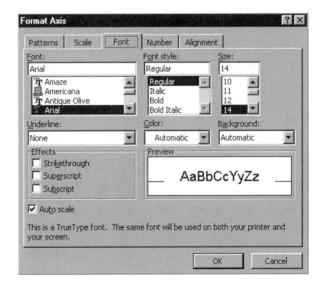

## Exercise 6A

These **Pie** charts illustrate a pupil's performance.

The first chart labels the performance by the week.

The second chart displays the scores attained each week as a percentage of the pupil's total score.

Reproduce the graphs based on the details below.

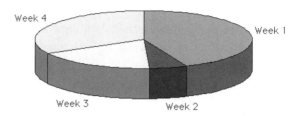

Pupil's Performance (Synge)

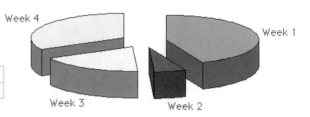

Pupil's Performance (Synge)

|        | Week 1 | Week 2 | Week 3 | Week 4 |
|--------|--------|--------|--------|--------|
| Syng   | 24     | 3      | 10     | 18     |

## Exercise 6B

The difference between the performances of two pupils demonstrates the range of attainment scores within a class.

Using the data below, reproduce the **Bar** chart.

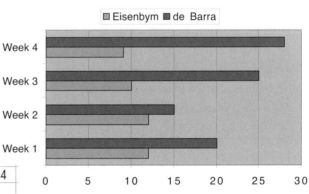

Pupil Performance

|          | Week 1 | Week 2 | Week 3 | Week 4 |
|----------|--------|--------|--------|--------|
| Eisenbym | 12     | 12     | 10     | 9      |
| de Barra | 20     | 15     | 25     | 28     |

## Exercise 6C

Reproduce the **Line** chart on the right to illustrate the performance of the three pupils in the table below.

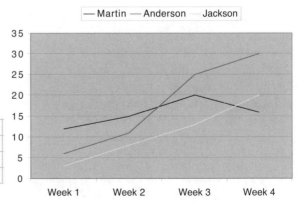

Pupil Performance

|          | Week 1 | Week 2 | Week 3 | Week 4 |
|----------|--------|--------|--------|--------|
| Martin   | 12     | 15     | 20     | 16     |
| Anderson | 6      | 11     | 25     | 30     |
| Jackson  | 3      | 8      | 13     | 20     |

# Section 7    Exercises

# Self Check Exercises

1  What kind of information is commonly put into a spreadsheet cell? (*Tick all possible answers.*)

☑ Text
☑ Numbers
☑ Mathematical Formulae
☐ Cell Addresses

2  How would you identify the active cell on your spreadsheet?

☑ Darkened border
☐ Flashing border
☐ The contents of the cell are darkened.
☐ The contents of the cell flash.

3  Which best describes a range of cells?

☐ A single column of cells
☐ A single row of cells
☑ A rectangular block of cells

4  Which of these represents a correct cell reference?

☐ A
☐ 5
☑ B6
☐ D:7

5  Which of these represents a correct range reference?

☐ A1
☑ A1:B6
☐ 6:B
☐ C:7/D:8

6  What is a row header?

☐ A reference number to the left of the row
☑ A reference letter to the left of the row

7  What appears in a selected cell immediately after clicking the **Paste Function** button?

☐ A formula
☐ An equal sign
☐ A cell reference
☐ A range reference

8  Which of the following would best apply to a cell containing the formula =(A3+1)?

☑ The contents of this cell equals that in cell A3 plus 1.
☐ The contents of cell A equals 3 plus 1.
☐ The contents of cell A3 must start with +1.
☐ None of the above.

9  If, having typed 'Monday' in A1, you drag the *fill handle* across to the right, what will happen?

☐ Monday will be copied into each of the other cells as well.
☐ The other days of the week will appear in the cells.

10  What icons from the Standard Toolbar are not matched to a correct label explaining their function?

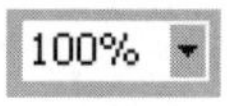

☑ [100% ▼]  Perform a percentage calculation.

☐ [A↓Z]  Perform an Ascending alphabetical sort.

☐ [Σ]  Perform an Addition operation.

11  Having selected a **Paste Function**, what appears next in the selected cell?

☐ A numeric value
☐ A formula
☐ The name of the function
☐ Nothing

# Practical Exercises

### Exercise 1

You are required to make a report on the unit sales of electronic office equipment you have distributed to the company's Munster regional retail centre. The results for the first quarter are available. Reproduce the first quarter's spreadsheet below.

**N.B.** *It is important that you reproduce the spreadsheet exactly. Make sure your columns and rows match the chart below.*

| | A | B | C | D | E |
|---|---|---|---|---|---|
| 1 | Munster Office First Quarterly Report | | | | |
| 2 | | | | | |
| 3 | | | | | |
| 4 | | | September | October | November |
| 5 | | | | | |
| 6 | | | | | |
| 7 | | Telephones | 116 | 79 | 56 |
| 8 | | Answer Mach. | 47 | 50 | 35 |
| 9 | | Calculators | 9 | 38 | 17 |
| 10 | | Shredders | 297 | 225 | 120 |
| 11 | | Laminators | 79 | 56 | 34 |
| 12 | | Binding Mach. | 83 | 88 | 38 |
| 13 | | Mini recorders | 57 | 69 | 7 |
| 14 | | Transcribers | 57 | 69 | 36 |
| 15 | | | 745 | 674 | 343 |

### Exercise 2

In the next column, include the unit monthly average achieved for each piece of equipment.

### Exercise 3

In the next two columns, show the figures for the following:

| Target |
|---|
| 350 |
| 150 |
| 300 |
| 200 |
| 220 |
| 250 |
| 100 |
| 100 |
| 1670 |

- The total unit sales for each item.

- The unit target sales you had set.

### Exercise 4

If you have not already tidied up your numbers, return to each column and format the numbers to two decimal places.

### Exercise 5

Insert another column showing the sales achieved for each unit as a percentage of the target sales for the unit.

### Exercise 6

Add one more column to show what percentage of the total sales is represented by each piece of equipment

### Exercise 7

How would you quickly check that the results are correct?

### Exercise 8

Explain why you should **not** choose the percentage option when formatting the percentage numbers to reduce them to two decimal places.

### Exercise 9

Using formulae, calculate the following in the indicated cells:

The total number of units sold (in cell G18)

The total number of target units (in cell G19)

The percentage of the target total represented by the sold unit total (in cell G20)

### Exercise 10

Make the chart below.

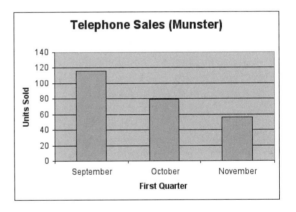

### Exercise 11

Make the following chart representing the total unit sales per month.

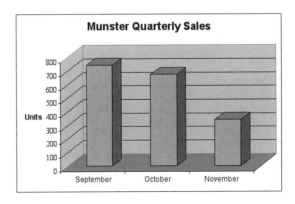

Module 4

# Module 5

## Database

5

# Module 5

# Database

Module 5

# Introduction

## Syllabus Goals for Module 5

**Database** requires the candidate to understand the basic concepts of databases and demonstrate the ability to use a database on a personal computer. The module is divided in two sections; the first section tests the candidate's ability to design and plan a simple database using a standard database package; the second section requires the candidate to demonstrate that he or she can retrieve information from an existing database by using the query, select and sort tools available in the database. The candidate shall also be able to create and modify reports.

## What is a Database?

Data is **information**. A database **stores** information and **makes it available** for later use.

A traditional office filing cabinet is a simple database. The data is stored like this. The filing cabinet usually has a number of drawers. Inside each drawer are files. Inside the files are sheets of paper. On the sheets of paper are items of information.

Another type of database is the traditional card-index used in a library. Items of information about each book are written on cards. The cards are stored in different drawers. The drawers are arranged in the catalogue cabinet.

## Finding Information

An office filing cabinet database is just a storage facility. Any work in making use of it has to be done manually. To retrieve data, the database has to be searched. Very often, only some of the data is required: the other data is temporarily ignored. For example, your business might want to retrieve an order for equipment sent in May last year… or was it June? The librarian may be asked for a book on gardening by McNulty… or was it McNiely? Finding the relevant information, or data, can be very laborious and time-consuming.

## A Computer Database

A **computerised database** such as **Access** is essentially the same as the filing cabinet or card-index, but the data is stored *electronically* rather than on pieces of paper. This has major advantages over a manual system.

The information still has to be gathered and entered into the computer, but even here, the entry of some items can be automated. The main advantage arises from the machine's ability to search for, sort and present the information in any way the user requires, and with great speed.

A user can find all the orders sent in May or June, or both, at the touch of a key. They are listed instantly and can then be printed out, if necessary. The librarian can find all the gardening books written by authors beginning with 'McN' and print out a list, if required.

Module 5

Compared with a card-index system, an electronic database takes up no physical space. Records which would require 100,000 catalogue cards will easily fit on a computer's hard disk.

The computer can use and display the information in the database in other documents such as letters, lists and reports. The office can send out letters to customers who may be interested in a new product. The librarian can send out reminders about overdue books. The computer does the work. Only one document needs to be prepared. Individual information for each customer or borrower is inserted from the database and printed out automatically.

## Database Terms

It will help to be familiar with some commonly-used terms.

**Field**    In a computer database, an area where a single item of information, such as a book title, is stored.

**Record**    One or more fields (e.g. Author, Title, Publisher etc.) are stored in a record, corresponding to one card or one sheet of paper.

**File**    All the records for a particular database are stored in a file, corresponding to a manila document file.

**Folder**    On a computer, different files are stored in separate folders, corresponding to different drawers in the filing cabinet.

## Setting up a Database

The database program you will use in this course is **Microsoft Access**. You will start with a blank database, give it a name and save it in a folder on the hard disk.

Before you can start entering information, you will need to set up a field for each item.

Access can sort the information in the database in many different ways. To help it do this, it must know what kind of information is stored in each field – whether it is text or numbers, for example. This is done with the click of a button when you are setting up the database.

## Names and Addresses

When you are storing people's names in the database, each name may need three fields (Title, First Name, Last Name). This makes it more convenient to extract and use the information. The fields can be joined together later if needed, as for address labels.

With separate fields, the computer can make a list of people, such as John Murphy, Margaret Adams, and so on for use in the office. It can prepare letters to them beginning with 'Dear Mr Murphy', and then address the envelope to 'Mr John Murphy'.

It is also a good idea to divide addresses into different fields, such as Street Address, Town, and County (and perhaps Country). You might need to search for information by Town or County, for example, or use the town name in the body of a letter or document.

When you have decided what fields you need and have set them up, you will have to design layouts or reports to make the database easy to use, both for entering data and displaying, and using it later.

## Using the Database

Once the database has been set up and information entered, it can be put to work. Access can perform calculations such as adding numbers, calculating averages and much more. The data can be sorted in a variety of ways to interpret the information in many different ways. Access can use the information in the database to prepare address labels, lists, reports or other documents for whatever purpose the user wishes. It can then present it in an appealing and attractive way.

# Reference Table

Should you begin your studies with this module, it is important to note that related material is dealt with in other sections of the manual. This reference list will assist you to locate the material conveniently.

| Skill | Task | Module | Page |
|-------|------|--------|------|
| **First Steps** | | | |
| | Save a new document | Module 2 | 84 |
| | Save changes to an existing document | Module 2 | 87 |
| | Close a document | Before You Begin | 24 |
| | Help | Before You Begin | 16 |
| **Adjusting Settings** | | | |
| | Change page display modes | Before You Begin | 21 |
| | Page magnification | Before You Begin | 22 |
| | Page orientation | Module 3 | 149 |
| | Toolbars | Before You Begin | 11 |
| **Document Exchange** | | | |
| | Save a file in a different format | Module 2 | 87 |
| | Save for Web posting | Module 2 | 88 |
| **Basic Functions** | | | |
| | Alignment and justification of text | Module 3 | 133 |
| | Copy, Cut, and Paste | Before You Begin | 10 |
| | Deleting | Module 3 | 127 |
| | Formatting text | Module 3 | 131 |
| | Images, graphics and objects | Module 3 | 161 |
| | Printing | Module 3 | 143 |
| | Preview a document | Module 3 | 143 |
| | Printers, choosing | Module 3 | 145 |
| | Print to file | Module 3 | 145 |
| | Selecting | Before You Begin | 9 |
| | Spell Check | Before You begin | 23 |
| | Symbols and special characters | Module 3 | 124 |
| | Templates | Module 3 | 189 |
| | Undo | Module 3 | 135 |

Module 5

# Section 1     Getting Started

## 1.1     An Access Database

The basic structure of an Access database is a **table** containing columns and rows, somewhat similar to a Spreadsheet.

Each column heading contains a **field name**, such as 'First Name', 'Last Name', 'Telephone Number' and so on.   The cells under the headings represent the **fields**, which contain the individual items of information.

Each row in the table is a **record**, a collection of fields laid out across the page.

A **table** shows all the records (rows) together, but you may have to scroll up and down to see all the records and across to view all the fields (columns).

| ID Number | Title | First Name | Last Name | Gender | Date of Birth |
|---|---|---|---|---|---|
| 1 | Mr. | Don | Lipman | Male | 15/04/64 |
| 2 | Mr. | James | Conway | Male | 22/03/74 |
| 3 | Ms. | Janet | Verano | Female | 23/05/75 |
| 4 | Ms. | Niamh | Jones | Female | 30/04/71 |
| 5 | Ms. | Diane | Ferelle | Female | 04/07/68 |
| 6 | Mr. | Niall | Hegarty | Male | 25/05/70 |

A Table

The records contained in the table can be presented in a different way by creating a **form**.

A form shows all the fields together but only displays one record at a time.

A form takes its information from a table.  You cannot create a form before you create a table. Information edited or added in the form will also be recorded in the table.

A Form

## 1.2     Multiple Tables

Access is a very powerful database application that allows you to create many tables.

This is very useful as it means you don't need separate database files for employees, clients, products, suppliers, and so on.  Details of each can be stored in separate tables within a single company database.

Separate tables can be linked together – or *related* – to create a single **relational** database.

## 1.3    Basic Concepts

There are four main components of an Access database that you should be familiar with,
i.e. **Tables**, **Forms**, **Queries** and **Reports**.

**Tables**    are the basic storage structures where all data is stored in columns and rows.

**Forms**    are created from tables.  They display all or selected fields on a single page.
Each record is viewed in isolation.

**Queries**    are used to search for specific data contained in a table.  The found data fields
and records are presented in table format.

**Reports**    are used to present data from a table or a query on a page for printing.

The following pages will take you through the process of developing a simple company database.
It will contain a single table for employee information, a related form, queries and a report.

## 1.4    The Access Window

Unlike other Office applications, Access does not display a single document such as the sheet of paper
in **Word** or the spreadsheet grid in **Excel**.  Instead, the appearance of the window varies according to
the component of Access – table, form etc. – that is in use at any particular time.  You will become
familiar with the different windows as you progress through the module.

## 1.5    Menus and Toolbars

The Menu Bar contains many of the menus common to other Office applications as well as menus
specific to Access.

The toolbars are similar in appearance to the toolbars in other Office applications but contain buttons
specific to Access and to the component in use at a particular time.  You will learn to recognise and
use them as you proceed through the Module.

## 1.6    A Company Database

A fictitious software company called **Financial Systems International** with offices in Dublin,
London, New York and Sydney is used for the exercise.

The company operates three departments – Sales, Technical Support and Administration.

We shall concentrate on recording information relating to the employees of the company in the course
of the module.

# Section 2    A New Database

## 2.1    Opening Access

Open Access by clicking the **Access** button on the Office **Shortcut Bar** on the desktop.

*Alternatively*, click the **Start** button and select **Microsoft Access** in the **Programs** menu or sub-menu.

## 2.2    Opening Choices

When you open Access, three options are presented in the window that appears:

- Create new **Blank Database**.

- The **Database Wizard** helps you make a new database using a default layout (template).

  Click **OK**, select a template and follow the instructions on the screen.

- Open an **Existing Database**.

  Click on a database – listed in the lower part of the window – to select it and then click **OK**, or click **More Files** to search for other databases on the hard disk.

For the purpose of this exercise, we shall create a new blank database.

- Click **Blank Database**.

- Click **OK**.  The **File New Database** window opens.

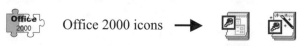 Office 2000 icons

You must now give the new database a name and save it before proceeding.

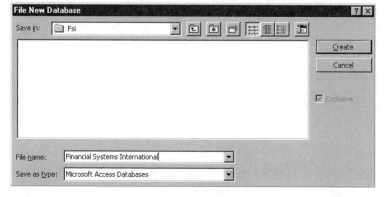

- Type **Financial Services International** in the **File Name** box.

 In Office 2000, the window has a panel of buttons on the left.

- Select a suitable location in which to save the database.

  If necessary, make a new folder on the hard disk.

- Click **Create**.

  A new blank database is saved and a window opens, showing the database name in the Title Bar.

  There are tabs for Tables, Queries, Forms and so on.

 In Office 2000, the tabs along the top are replaced by a series of buttons in a panel at the left of the window.

- The basic structural element of an Access database is a **Table**.

  You must begin by creating a new table.

## 2.3    Creating a New Table

Follow these steps.

- Click the **Tables** tab in the **Database** window, if it is not already clicked.

- Click the **New** button.
  The **New Table** window opens.

- Click on **Design View** to select it.

- Click **OK**.  The **Table** window opens.

Before you begin to make a database, you will have decided what **fields** you will need in the database and what names to give them.

- Double-click **Create table in Design view** in the main part of the window.

*Alternatively:*

- Click the **Tables** button in the panel at the left of the window if it is not already clicked.

- Click the **New** button in the toolbar at the top of the window.

- Click the **Design** button in the toolbar.

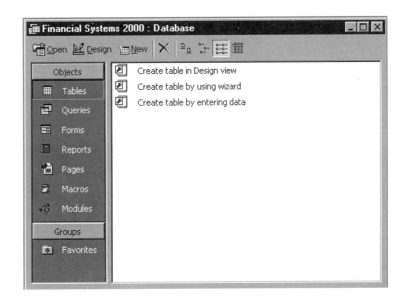

For each field you want in the table, you will enter a title in the **Field Name** column.

Then you will click in the **Data Type** box and select a data type from the pop-up menu.

You may add a description in the **Description** box but this is not essential.

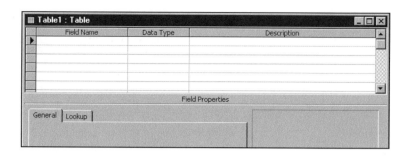

One of the fields in the table must be a **Primary Key** field, generally a number field.

> **Primary Key**
>
> A primary key field is one that uniquely identifies each record in a table. Access does not allow duplicate primary key fields, so each one is unique. They are used with related tables (see Section 1.2, page 240) – not an ECDL requirement.
>
> Most tables have a single primary key field. In an employee table, each person would have a unique ID number – a good choice for the primary key field.

Primary Key

## 2.4    Creating Fields in the Table

Press the **Tab** key to move from box to box as you enter the field names. In this example, a variety of field types are used. Enter the fields as follows.

- Type **ID Number** in the first **Field Name** box.

- Press the **Tab** key to move to the next box.

- Select **AutoNumber** from the **Data Type** menu.

| Field Name | Data Type |
|---|---|
| ID Number | AutoNumber |
| Title | Text |
| First Name | Text |
| Last Name | Text |
| Gender | Text |

- Click the **Primary Key** button on the toolbar.
  This makes the ID Number field the primary key for the table.
  (A key symbol appears to the left of the Field Name.)

- Press the **Return** key to go to the next line.

- Type **Title** in the next **Field Name** box. Select **Text** as the Data Type.

- Type **First Name** in the next Field Name box. Select **Text** as the Data Type.

- Type **Last  Name** in the next Field Name box. Select **Text** as the Data Type.

- Type **Gender** in the next Field Name box. This time, select **Lookup Wizard** as the Data Type.

Primary Key

## 2.5    The Lookup Wizard

The **Lookup Wizard** window appears when you select it in the **Data Type** menu.

The Lookup Wizard is used where the same text or data is to be entered in many fields. It saves having to type it in every time.

The text or data is stored in a list and you can enter the information when you create the field. The Lookup Wizard can also find the information in an existing table.

- Click **I will type in the values that I want**.

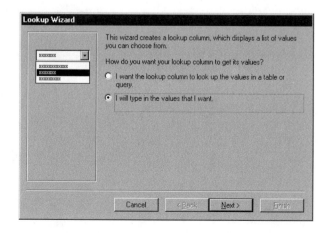

- Click **Next**.

  A new window appears with a column for you to type the values you will want in the fields.

- Type **Female** and press the **Tab** key to move to the next box.

- Type **Male** in the next box.

- Click **Finish**.

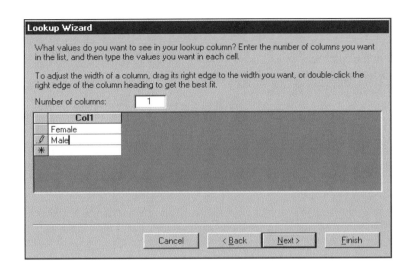

> **Warning**
>
> Do not use the **Enter** key instead of clicking **Next**: it will close the wizard.

## 2.6    Creating More Fields

When you have used the Lookup Wizard for the **Gender** field, the Data Type will appear as **Text**. Continue to enter fields as follows.

- Type **Date of Birth** in the next Field Name box and select **Date/Time** as the Data Type.

- Type **Address** and select **Text** as the Data Type.

- Type **City** and select **Lookup Wizard** as the Data Type.   Use the **Lookup Wizard** as before and enter **Dublin**, **London**, **New York** and **Sydney**.

- Type **Post Code** in the next box and select **Text** as the Data Type.

- Type **Country** in the next box and use the **Lookup Wizard** again.  This time, enter **Ireland**, **United Kingdom**, **United States** and **Australia**.

- Type **Telephone** in the next box and select **Text** as the Data Type.

  Do not use **Number** as the Data Type if you want to allow spaces or other characters in the telephone number, such as between the area code and the number.

- Type **Department** in the next box and use the **Lookup Wizard** to enter the department names, i.e. **Sales**, **Technical Support** and **Administration**.

- Type **Position** in the next box and select **Text** as the Data Type.

- When all fields have been entered, click the **View** button on the toolbar.

- You are prompted to save the table first.  Name the table **Employees**.

View

The table has now been set up and it is ready for actual data to be entered.

The Employees Table

You may close the table at this stage and enter the data later, if you prefer.

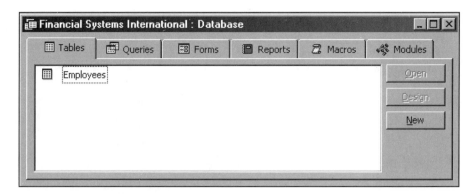

Notice the table **Employees** is now listed in the Database window.

The Financial Services International Database window.

The Office 2000 window looks like this.

## 2.7 Opening an Existing Database

If you have closed the database at the end of the previous Section, you can reopen it, or open any existing database, by opening **Access** and doing *one* of the following.

- Select **Open an Existing Database** in the opening screen (see Section 2.2, page 242).

- Click the **Open** button on the toolbar.

- Select **Open** in the **File** menu.

Find the database you want to open in the usual way.

Click the **Table**, **Form** or other tab in the database window, as required.

If you have modified records, added new ones or made any other changes, click the **Save** button on the toolbar to save your changes before closing Access.

# Section 3    Entering Data

## 3.1    Entering Data in a Table

If the **Employees** table is not open, select **Employees** in the Database window and click **Open**.

The fields are in rows across the table.  You will have to scroll over and back to view them all.

In the first box, **AutoNumber** is highlighted.  Access will automatically enter a number here for you. Use the Tab key or mouse to move to the next box.  (You do not need to type anything.)

- Type **Mr** in the **Title** field.
  As soon as you start typing, Access enters **1** in the **ID Number** box.
  Each time you enter data in a new row, a new consecutive **ID Number** is entered.
  If at a later stage you delete one of the records, its particular **ID Number** will **not** be re-used.

- Enter the information about each employee as shown on page 248.

> **Lookup Wizard fields**
>
> When entering information into a Lookup Wizard field, click in the box.
> Then click the list button and choose from the list.
>
> *Alternatively*, type the first letter of the word and the rest of the word is inserted automatically.  In the **Country** field, typing **A** would insert **Australia**.
>
> However, where entries are similar (United Kingdom or United States) you must continue typing until Access identifies which country is required.

- To correct or change any of the data in the table, click in the appropriate box and make the required adjustment.
  You will not be able to alter the **ID Number**.

| ID Number | Title | First Name | Last Name | Gender | Date of Birth | Address |
|---|---|---|---|---|---|---|
| 1 | Mr. | Don | Lipman | Male | 15/04/64 | 1245 Bennett Avenue |
| 2 | Mr. | James | Conway | Male | 22/03/74 | 145 Dunmore Road |
| 3 | Ms. | Janet | Verano | Female | 23/05/75 | 1568 Vermont Street |
| 4 | Ms. | Niamh | Jones | Female | 30/04/71 | 184 Leinster Avenue |
| 5 | Ms. | Diane | Ferelle | Female | 04/07/68 | 2129 Monroe Street |
| 6 | Mr. | Niall | Hegarty | Male | 25/05/70 | 225 Brandon Road |
| 7 | Ms. | Margaret | O'Brien | Female | 01/08/68 | 25 Granitefield Park |
| 8 | Mr. | John | Pollard | Male | 30/12/63 | 251 Dalton Road |
| 9 | Ms. | Marie | Jones | Female | 11/06/66 | 254 Collingbourne Road |

- To delete an entire record, click in the left margin to highlight the row and press the **Delete** key.

- To save the table, or any modifications you make to it, click the **Save** button.

## 3.2    Adding Fields

Design
View

Extra fields can be added to the table at any time.

- Open the table and click the **Design View** button.

- Click in the next available **Field Name** box and enter the title of the field and select an appropriate **Data Type**.

View

Click the **View** button to return to the normal view of the table.
You will be prompted to save the table.

| ID | Title | First | Last | Gender | Birth | Address | City | Post | Country | Telephone | Department | Position |
|----|-------|-------|------|--------|-------|---------|------|------|---------|-----------|------------|----------|
| 1 | Mr. | Don | Lipman | Male | 15/04/64 | 1245 Bennett Avenue | New York | 10033 | United States | + 1 212 636 5855 | Technical Support | Technical Director |
| 2 | Mr. | James | Conway | Male | 22/03/74 | 145 Dunmore Road | Dublin | D5 | Ireland | + 353 1 235 2457 | Sales | Sales Director |
| 3 | Ms. | Janet | Verano | Female | 23/05/75 | 1568 Vermont Street | New York | 10025 | United States | + 1 212 625 2365 | Administration | Office Manager |
| 4 | Ms. | Niamh | Jones | Female | 30/04/71 | 184 Leinster Avenue | Dublin | D8 | Ireland | + 353 1 458 4578 | Technical Support | Technical Director |
| 5 | Ms. | Diane | Ferelle | Female | 04/07/68 | 2129 Monroe Street | New York | 10002 | United States | + 1 212 658 6595 | Sales | Sales Representative |
| 6 | Mr. | Niall | Hegarty | Male | 25/05/70 | 225 Brandon Road | Dublin | D3 | Ireland | + 353 1 287 4658 | Administration | Office Manager |
| 7 | Ms. | Margaret | O'Brien | Female | 01/08/68 | 25 Granitefield Park | Dublin | D12 | Ireland | + 353 1 487 6589 | Administration | Financial Controller |
| 8 | Mr. | John | Pollard | Male | 30/12/63 | 251 Dalton Road | Sydney | 2475 | Australia | + 61 2 9458 6325 | Administration | Office Manager |
| 9 | Ms. | Marie | Jones | Female | 11/06/66 | 254 Collingbourne Road | London | W12 | United Kingdom | + 44 181 8248 4575 | Sales | Sales Representative |
| 10 | Mr. | John | Mason | Male | 25/01/70 | 256 Willow Vale | London | SE18 | United Kingdom | + 44 181 8855 8245 | Technical Support | Technical Director |
| 11 | Ms. | Clare | O'Brien | Female | 25/08/75 | 30 Ardmore Grove | Dublin | D5 | Ireland | + 353 1 235 1245 | Technical Support | Technician |
| 12 | Mr. | Barry | Bollinger | Male | 06/11/75 | 32 Denison Street | Sydney | 2256 | Australia | + 61 2 9685 6587 | Technical Support | Technician |
| 13 | Mr. | James | Edwards | Male | 25/06/62 | 358 Sherman Avenue | New York | 10034 | United States | + 1 212 658 4578 | Sales | Sales Director |
| 14 | Mr. | Sean | Flynn | Male | 25/04/74 | 362 Casement Road | Dublin | D6w | Ireland | + 353 1 258 2568 | Sales | Sales Representative |
| 15 | Mr. | Trevor | Harvey | Male | 09/05/56 | 39 Meadowland Road | Sydney | 2548 | Australia | + 61 2 9581 4578 | Sales | Sales Director |
| 16 | Mr. | Brian | Harvey | Male | 02/08/59 | 40 Carrig Avenue | Dublin | D3 | Ireland | + 353 1 287 3532 | Administration | Managing Director |
| 17 | Mr. | Luis | Martinez | Male | 21/05/73 | 414 Carmine Street | New York | 10014 | United States | + 1 212 547 5689 | Technical Support | Technician |
| 18 | Ms. | Sarah | Nestor | Female | 05/08/65 | 427 Rosemeath Avenue | Sydney | 2548 | Australia | + 61 2 9457 2545 | Technical Support | Technical Director |
| 19 | Ms. | Helen | Martin | Female | 02/05/70 | 54 Admaston Road | London | SE 18 | United Kingdom | + 44 181 8475 6589 | Administration | Office Manager |
| 20 | Mr. | Larry | Power | Male | 06/09/69 | 548 Selbie Road | London | NW 10 | United Kingdom | + 44 171 8459 4517 | Technical Support | Technician |
| 21 | Ms. | Maria | Lopez | Female | 14/07/76 | 587 Dudley Street | Sydney | 2447 | Australia | + 61 2 9658 5874 | Sales | Sales Representative |
| 22 | Ms. | Janet | Went | Female | 15/03/62 | 877 Lancaster Drive | London | W11 | United Kingdom | + 44 171 7794 4568 | Sales | Sales Director |

## 3.3   Viewing Records

The **Employees** table now contains more than a dozen pieces of information about each employee. As the database expands to suit the needs of the company, more fields can be added.

Viewing the information on an individual employee in a table layout means that you have to scroll back and over across the table to see all the available field columns.

A more useful method of viewing individual records is to create a **Form** that contains only the fields you wish to view.

# Section 4      Creating a Form

## 4.1     Forms

The table contains **all** the information about each employee.  In many cases, however, you do not need to see all the data in a record at the same time.

For example, you may need a list of names and addresses only, or you may need a list of employees in a particular department.  A **form** uses some or all of the data contained in an existing table and presents it in a **new layout**.

While you are working with a form, any changes made to the data in the form will also be updated in the table.

## 4.2     Creating a New Form

A **Wizard** is available to help you create a new form using fields and data from an existing table.

- Click the **Forms** tab In the **Database** window.

  As no forms have been prepared yet, the window is empty.

- Click the **New** button.

  The **New Form** window opens.

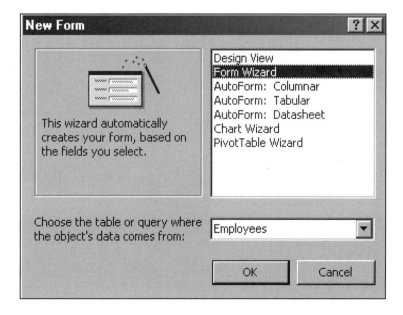

- Select **Form Wizard** in the list in the right of the window.

- Select the **Employees** table in the menu in the **Choose the table or query**... box.

  (As the Employees table is the only one available so far, it is already selected.)

- Click **OK**.

  The Form Wizard window opens.

To create a new **Form** in Office 2000:

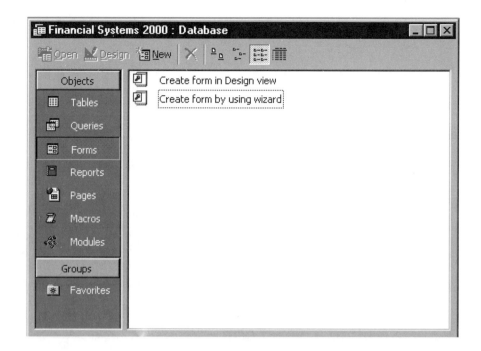

- Click the **Forms** button in the panel at the left of the window.

- Double-click **Create form by using wizard** in the main part of the window.

  The Form Wizard window opens.

## 4.3   The Form Wizard

The **Form Wizard** lets you select those fields you want to display in the form. (The appearance of the Form Wizard window may vary in different versions of Office.)

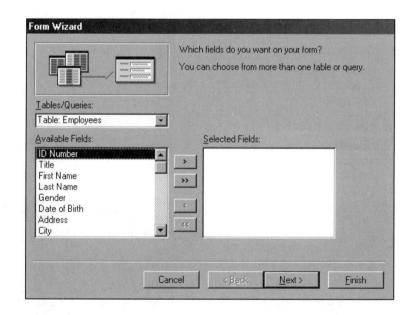

The **Table/Queries** box already shows the **Employees** table. (If other tables are listed, select the Employees table.)

The **Available Fields** panel lists all the fields available in the table selected above.

The **Selected Fields** panel on the right will list the fields you select for inclusion on the form.

To include a field, click the field in the list to select it. Then click the **single arrow** button at the top between the two panels. The field is moved across to the Selected Fields panel.

Click the **double arrow** button to move all the fields across.

The two lower buttons enable you to move one or all of the fields back, should you change your mind.

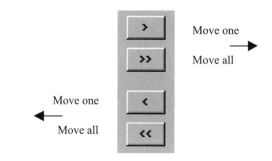

- For the purpose of this exercise, move **all the fields** across to the Selected Fields panel.

- Click **Next** when you have moved all the fields.

- A new window gives a choice of layout. Click the different options to see examples.
  Select **Columnar** and click **Next**.

- Another window gives a choice of style.
  Click the different options to see examples. (The styles available may vary between different versions of Office.)
  Select **Colorful 2** (or **International** in Office 2000) and click **Next**.

- The last window asks for a **Title** for the form.
  The name **Employees** is already suggested, as the information is taken from a table called **Employees**. Keep this title.

  You are also given an option to view or enter information or to modify the design. At this stage, it is better to view the information first, so keep that option and click **Finish**.

  The form is created, as shown below.

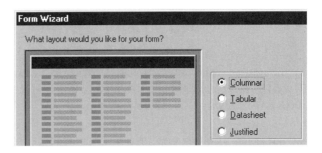

Layout Options

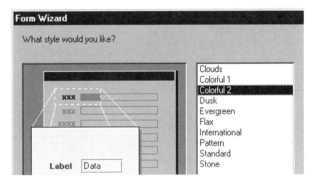

Style Options

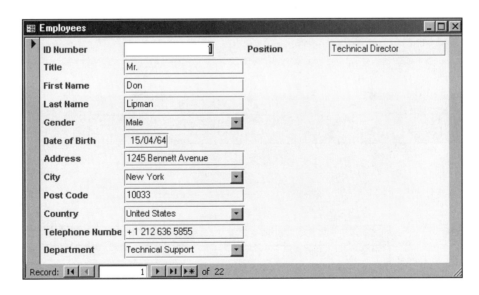

The completed Form

# 4.4   Changing a Form Layout

Open the form, **Employees**, if it is not already open.  Click the **Design View** button on the toolbar.  This shows the different components of the form with a toolbox. The **field label boxes** are on the left and immediately to their right are the **field data boxes** in which the actual data will appear, as in the illustration on page 251.

Design
View

- Close the **Toolbox** window if it is in the way.

- The font, style etc. of the labels and field boxes can be changed.

  For example, click the **ID Number** label box. Change the **font size** to **10 pt** and make it **italics**.

- Click the **View** button on the toolbar to view the effect on the form.

- Click the **Design View** button to return.  Click the **Italics** button again to remove the italics.

- To change the position of a field box on the form, you must select it first.

  The **ID Number** label box should still be selected.  If not, click it and move the cursor slowly over the edge of the box.  The cursor becomes a hand.  You can now drag the box to a different location.

View

- If you make a mistake, click the **Undo** button on the toolbar.

- To highlight **all** the field boxes, hold down the **Shift** key on the keyboard and click *on the Ruler* above each column of boxes.

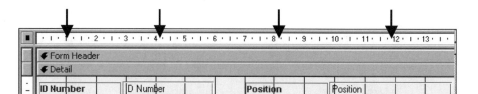

Design
View

Undo

- When all the boxes are highlighted, change the **Font size** to **12 pt**.

- Click the **View** button on the toolbar to see the effect.

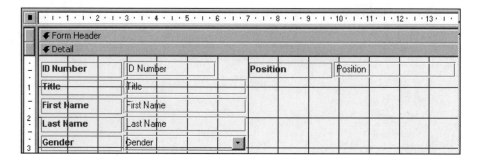

- Notice that some of the boxes are not wide enough or tall enough to display the information because we increased the font size to 12 pt.

  Click the **Design View** button to continue working.

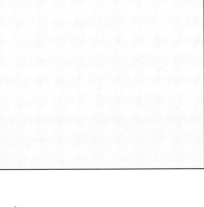

- Ensure that all boxes are highlighted as before.

  Select **Size** in the **Format** menu and **To Fit** in the sub-menu.

  The boxes are now tall enough but they are still very close together.

  We need to increase the vertical spacing between them.

- With all the boxes highlighted, select **Vertical Spacing** in the **Format** menu and click **Increase**. Repeat this to increase the spacing again.

- Click the **View** button to see the effect.

- Notice the **Telephone Number** label is too wide and some of the field boxes are still not wide enough. Also, the **Position** field is isolated and needs to be moved.

Design
View

- Click the **Design View** button to continue.

## 4.5    Repositioning Fields

The **Position** field needs to be placed under the **Department** field at the bottom of the list. First it is necessary to make more space for it.

If necessary, scroll down to the bottom of the list.

- Move the cursor slowly over the edge of the **Form Footer** until it changes to a **bar with arrows** pointing up and down.

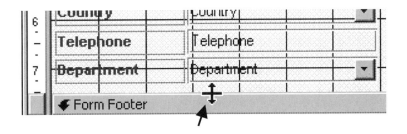

- Drag downwards to move the **Form Footer** and make more space under the Department field.

- Now click on the **Position** data box.

  Move the cursor slowly over the edge of the box until it changes to a **hand**.

- Drag the box with the hand and position it under the **Department** field.

  Both data and label boxes move together.

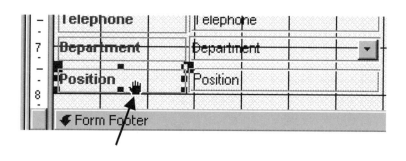

It may be difficult to judge if the spacing between the boxes is equal. You can adjust the vertical spacing automatically, however.

- Click on the ruler above the boxes to highlight them. Make sure to click at the left end of the ruler so that short boxes, such as **City,** are included in the selection.

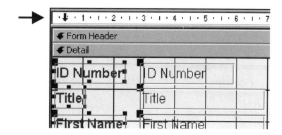

- Select **Vertical Spacing** in the **Format** menu, and click **Make Equal** in the sub-menu.

  The fields and field labels are spaced apart evenly.

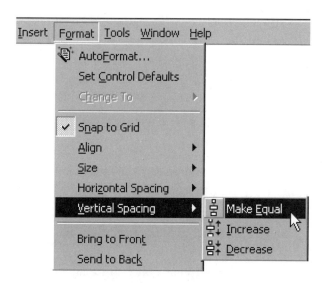

The next task is to allow enough space for the **Telephone Number** label. All the field data boxes must be moved to the right, leaving the label boxes in their current positions on the left.

To highlight all the data boxes, you normally click on the ruler. However, because the Telephone Number label extends into the data box area on the right, the label box would be included in the selection. Instead, select them individually.

- Hold down the **Shift** key and click on each field data box in turn.

  Be sure to select the Telephone Number data box (on the right) and not the label box on the left.

- To make all the data boxes the same width, select **Size** in the **Format** menu, and **To Widest** in the sub-menu.

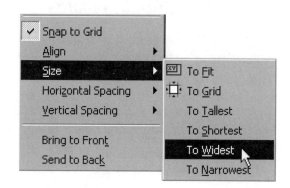

## 4.6    Moving Fields

To move a field, you usually point to the edge of the box and drag. However, this moves both the field label and field data box.

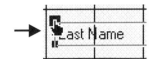

To move either the label or the data box independently, drag the black handle in the top left corner of the box – the cursor changes to a hand pointing upward.

Unfortunately, this method does not work with multiple boxes – you can only move one at a time.  But you can accomplish the task in another way.

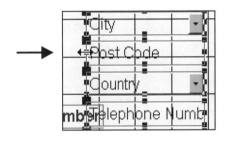

- With **all** the field data boxes still highlighted, move the cursor slowly across the **middle handle** on the left side of any one of the boxes.

    The cursor changes to two black arrows pointing left and right.

- Drag the handle to the right until the boxes are clear of the **Telephone Number** label.  (All the boxes move together.)

    This does not actually move the field data boxes, however.  It just shortens them.  They will have to be stretched to the right to make them the correct width again.

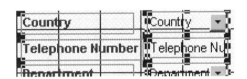

- Move the cursor slowly across the **middle** resize handle on the **right** side of one of the data boxes and drag to the right to restore the width of the boxes.

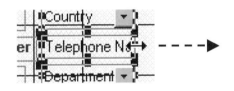

- To align all the text inside the boxes so that the information is presented starting at the left side of the box, highlight all the columns.  Then click the **Left Align** button on the toolbar.

- Click the **View** button to see the effect of these changes.

    The form should now appear as in the illustration below.

Left Align          View

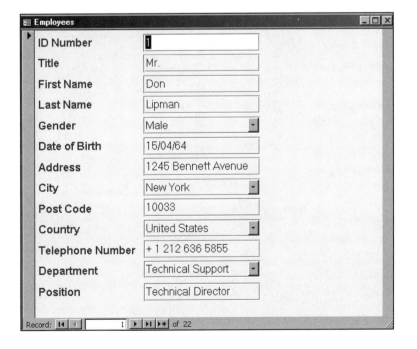

The Employees Form

## 4.7    Changing Colours

The colour of field boxes and field labels can be changed.  You can also change the colour of the
background to suit your own design requirements.

To change **text colour** in a field label or data box:

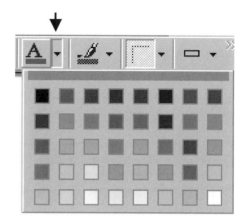

- Click on the box to highlight it.

- Hold down the **Shift** key to highlight more than one
  box as you click on them in turn.

- Click the small list button to the right of the **Font Color**
  button on the toolbar to display a palette of colours.

- Click on the colour you want.

To change the **background** colour of a label or text box, first
select the box or boxes.

- Click on the **Fill/Back Color** button on the toolbar to
  display a colour palette

- Click on the colour you want.

To change the colour of the **form background**, click on any
blank area of the grid.  Use the **Fill/Back Color** button to select
a colour as before.

**Note:** Not all style options may allow colours to be changed.  To experiment with changing colour, the
**Standard** choice is the most flexible.

## 4.8    Importing Graphics

Graphics can be imported to the background of a form.  The process is similar to importing graphics in
other Office applications.

- Click on a blank
  area of the form.

- Select **Picture** in
  the **Insert** menu.

- The **Insert Picture**
  window opens.

- Locate the graphic
  file you want to use
  in the usual way.
  (The buttons at the
  left of the Office
  2000 window may
  be helpful.)

- Click **OK**. The
  graphic is inserted
  on the form.

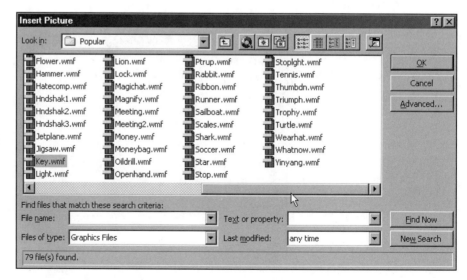

To practise, you can
use a graphic or a Clip Art image from the MS Office folder:

C:\Program Files\MS Office\Clipart\Popular.

# 4.9    Using Graphics on a Form

Graphics can be inserted on a form (or report) in different ways.

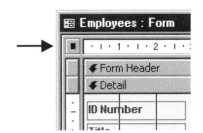

You can set how the graphic will be inserted before importing it.  If the graphic has already been inserted, you can still change the way in which it can be used on the form.

Proceed as follows.

- Open the form in **Design View**.

- Double-click the **Form Selector** button.
  (The black square in the centre of the button will appear when you click on it.)
  The **Form** window opens.

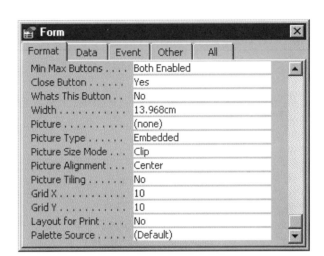

- Click the **Format** tab, if it is not already clicked.

- Scroll down to display the **Picture** options.

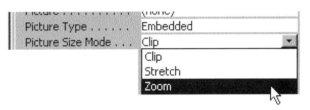

- Click in the **Picture Size Mode** box to display a menu giving three choices.

    **Clip**    displays the picture at actual size but crops it if it is larger than the form.

    **Stretch**    adjusts the picture to fit in the form but it may distort it.

    **Zoom**    automatically adjusts the picture to fill either the height or width of the form but does not distort it.

- Click on your choice to select it.

- Close the **Form** window.

An inserted graphic can be dragged to position it on the form.  (The cursor changes to a hand when it moves over the graphic.)

Dragging the handles resizes the graphic according to the option you selected in the **Picture Size Mode** menu.  To resize a graphic in the usual way, select **Zoom** in the menu.

To change the attributes of a graphic that has already been inserted on a form:

- Double-click on the graphic.
  The **Form** window opens.

- Select Clip, Stretch or Zoom in the **Picture Size Mode** box as described above.

- Close the **Form** window.

Module 5

## 4.10   Headers and Footers

Two kinds of header and footer are used in Access.  The procedure for adding either one is the same.  The only difference is in the way they appear on the screen or on printed pages.

A **Form Header** displays information for every form.  It appears at the top of the form and also at the top of the first page if the form is printed out.  Similarly, a **Form Footer** appears at the bottom of a form and also at the bottom of the last page if the form is printed out.

A **Page Header** or **Page Footer** appears only when the form is printed out.  They are not visible on the screen.

Headers and footers can only be added in pairs but if you only want one, the other can be hidden.

To add a **Form Header**, proceed as follows.

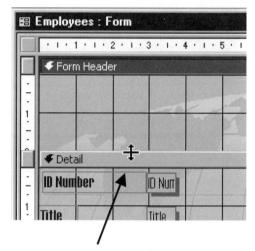

- Open the **Employees** form, if it is not already open.

- Click the **Design View** button on the toolbar.

- Select **Form Header/Footer** in the **View** menu.
  A Form Header appears on the form.  Adjust the size of the header area, if required, by dragging the lower border.

To add text in the header, you have to first draw a 'label' box.

- Click the **Label** button in the **Toolbox**.  (If the Toolbox is not displayed, select it in the **View** menu.)
  When you move back to the header area, the cursor becomes a capital '**A**' with a crosshair.

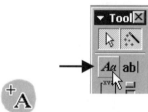

- Click and drag to draw a label box in the header area.

- Type the text, for this exercise **Financial Services International**.  It appears in the same style as other text in the form.

- Click outside the label box when you have finished.

- To change the text style, click inside the label box again to select it.  The **Formatting toolbar**, previously hidden, is now displayed.

- Format the text as required, e.g. Times New Roman, 24 pt., centred.  (You do not have to select the text first.)  See the illustration above.

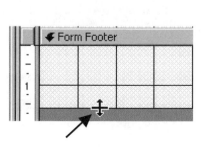

- Reposition the label box, if required, using the 'hand' as described earlier in this Section.  You can resize the box, if necessary, by dragging the handles.

- Click the **View** button to see the header in place on the form. (You may have to resize the Form window to see all the form.)

Hide an unwanted empty header or footer by dragging the lower border.

# Section 5    Working with Records

## 5.1    Records in a Form

To view each individual record, use the **Record Navigation** buttons at the bottom of the screen.

Record Navigation Buttons

The number of the record currently displayed is shown in the box.

The inner left and right arrows on each side of the box move through the records, one record at a time.

The second set of buttons moves to the first and the last records.

The last button on the right opens a new blank record to allow for new data to be entered.

- Open a blank record and enter the following details of a new employee.
    Ms. – Paula – Magee – Female – 4/8/74 – 5 Hillview Road – Dublin – D5 – Ireland – + 353 1 235 2487 – Sales – Sales Representative

- Find the following records and change some of the details as indicated.
    Larry Power – Change **Telephone No.** to + 44 181 8855 4517 and **Post Code** to SE18.
    Marie Jones – Change **Department** to Technical Support and **Position** to Technician.

- Close the Form.  You are returned to the **Database** window.

- Open the table **Employees** and check to see whether the additions and changes you made have been updated in the table.

- To save the changes and modifications made to the records, click the **Save** button.

## 5.2    Sorting Records in a Table

The records in the table are listed in order of the **ID Numbers**.
It is usually more convenient to sort them by **Last Name**.

- Open the **Employees** table in the **Financial Systems International** database.  Maximise the table window.

- Click anywhere in the **Last Name** field column to select it.

- Click the **Sort Ascending** button on the toolbar.
    This sorts and lists the employees in alphabetical order from A to Z, according to last name.

Sort Ascending

- Click **Sort Descending** to see the list sorted in reverse, from Z to A.

- To return to the original order, click in the **ID Number** field and click **Sort Ascending**.

Sort Descending

- Practise sorting the records according to Gender, Date of Birth, Department, and so on.
    Click in the particular field and click **Sort Ascending** or **Sort Descending**.

**Note**: Sorting works by comparing the first character in each record, then the second, then the third, and so on.  In the case of the **Address** field, the mixture of numbers and letters cannot be sorted properly.  Using a separate City or Town field enables sorting by location.

These **Sort Ascending/Sort Descending** buttons are quick and easy to use, but they only allow you to sort the records according to one criterion or one field.

An **Advanced Filter/Sort** uses more than one field to group the records and gives more options.

## 5.3    Indexed Fields

An **index** helps to find and sort records faster in large databases.  Like the index in a book that directs you to particular pages, indexed fields make it easier for the database to find the information.

An index can be set up on fields that you search or sort frequently.  To set up an index, you mark a field (or fields) as indexed.  Indexes operate in the background when you use sorts, queries or grouping, as described in this section. **To create an index**, do the following.

Open the **Employees** table in Design view, if it is not already open.

- In the upper part of the window, click the field you want to index, **Last Name**, for example.

- In the lower part of the window, click in the **Indexed** box.

  A button appears at the right of the box.

- Click the button to display a menu

  Click **Yes (Duplicates OK)** if you are happy that more than one record can have the same data in this field.  (There may be several employees with the same last name.)

  Click **No (No Duplicates)** if you want to ensure that no two records are the same. (You may want every stock item to have a unique name.)

- Close the table.

- Click **Yes** when asked if you want to save the changes.  The index is saved with the table.

If you frequently search or sort using more than one field at a time, such as **Last Name** and **First Name**, you can create a multiple index for those fields.  This is done in the **Indexes** window.

Proceed as follows.

- Open the **Employees** table in Design view, if it is not already open.

- Select **Indexes** in the **View** menu.

- The Indexes window opens.

  (Notice that the Primary Key field is automatically indexed.)

- Type **Full Name** in the **Index Name** box.

- Click in the **Field Name** box

  to display a button at the right.  Click the button to display a list of fields.

- Enter **Last Name** in the **Field Name** box.

- Enter **First Name** in the **Field Name** box *on the next line*, as in the illustration.

- Close the Indexes window.

- When you close the table, click **Yes** when asked if you want to save the changes.

**Note:** Knowledge of the use of indexed fields is not an ECDL test requirement but it is mentioned in some ECDL documents.

# 5.4    Advanced Filter/Sorts in a Table

When you sort the employee records according to Gender, all the Females and Males are grouped separately together.  If you want the Employees sorted according to Gender, it would also be convenient to have both the women and men listed in alphabetical order.

For this kind of sorting, you need an **Advanced Filter/Sort**.

- Select **Filter** in the **Records** menu, and then **Advanced Filter/Sort** in the sub-menu.

  The **Filter** window opens.

- Click in the first **field** box in the lower part of the window.

  A button appears at the right of the box.

- Click the **button** and select **Gender** from the menu.

- Click in the **Sort** box below the field box. A button appears as before.

- Select **Ascending** from the menu.

- Repeat these steps in the next field boxes (to the right) to select **Last Name** and **Ascending**.

  These steps tell Access to sort the records first according to **Gender** in ascending order and then, within that grouping, to sort them according to **Last Name**, also in ascending order.

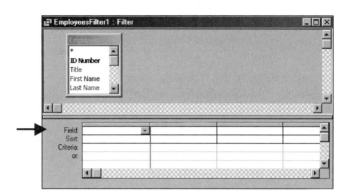

- Click on the **Apply Filter** button on the toolbar.  This returns you to the table, which is now sorted as in the illustration.

Apply
Filter

Notice that all the Females and Males are now grouped together.  Within that grouping, all the **Jones** and **Harvey**s are together.  However, we did not include **First Name** in the **Filter** so **Marie Jones** is not listed before **Niamh Jones** and **Brian Harvey** is not listed before **Trevor Harvey**.

- To include **First Name**, in the sort, open the **Advanced Filter/Sort** window again.

- Add **First Name** and **Ascending** to the third field box along.

  Then click the **Apply Filter** button.

| ID Number | Title | First Name | Last Name | Gender | Date of Birth |
|---|---|---|---|---|---|
| 5 | Ms. | Diane | Ferelle | Female | 04/07/68 |
| 4 | Ms. | Niamh | Jones | Female | 30/04/71 |
| 9 | Ms. | Marie | Jones | Female | 11/06/66 |
| 21 | Ms. | Maria | Lopez | Female | 14/07/76 |
| 23 | Ms. | Paula | Magee | Female | 04/08/74 |
| 19 | Ms. | Helen | Martin | Female | 02/05/70 |
| 18 | Ms. | Sarah | Nestor | Female | 05/08/65 |
| 11 | Ms. | Clare | O'Brien | Female | 25/08/75 |
| 7 | Ms. | Margaret | O'Brien | Female | 01/08/68 |
| 3 | Ms. | Janet | Verano | Female | 23/05/75 |
| 22 | Ms. | Janet | Went | Female | 15/03/62 |
| 12 | Mr. | Barry | Bollinger | Male | 06/11/75 |
| 2 | Mr. | James | Conway | Male | 22/03/74 |
| 13 | Mr. | James | Edwards | Male | 25/06/62 |
| 14 | Mr. | Sean | Flynn | Male | 25/04/74 |
| 15 | Mr. | Trevor | Harvey | Male· | 09/05/56 |
| 16 | Mr. | Brian | Harvey | Male | 02/08/59 |

- If you want the men at the top of the list, select **Descending** for the **Gender** sort.

- Practise sorting according to **Country** and **Department**.

- Finally, sort the records again according to the **ID Number**.

Module 5

## 5.5    Saving an Advanced Filter/Sort

Having gone to the bother of setting up an Advanced Filter/Sort, it is useful to save it.  This means you can use it again without having to set it up from the beginning every time.  By saving several different sorts, you can quickly view the records in many different arrangements, as you require them.

To save a query to sort the employees by country, proceed as follows.

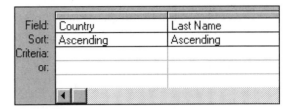

- Open the **Employees** table, if it is not already open.

- Select **Filter** in the **Records** menu. Then select **Advanced Filter/Sort** in the sub-menu.

- Enter the **Country** and **Last Name** fields as shown.

- Click the **Save As Query** button. The Save As Query window opens.

Save as
Query

- Give the **query** a name, such as *Employees by Country*.

- Click **OK**.

- Click the **Apply Filter** button. The records are sorted.

Apply
Filter

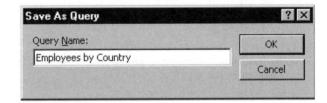

## 5.6    Another Filter/Sort

Now set up another sort for the **Department** and **Date of Birth.**

Open the **Advanced Filter/Sort** window again and enter the **Department** and **Date of Birth** fields as in the illustration.

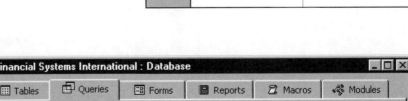

- Save this query as *Employees by Dept and DoB.*

- Click **Apply Filter**.

- **Close** the Table.

In the **Database** window, click the **Queries** tab to see the queries listed.

You can select and open a query at any time to sort the records appropriately.

In the Office 2000 **Database** window, click the **Queries** button in the panel at the left to see the **queries** listed in the main part of the window.

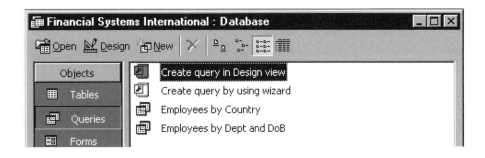

## 5.7    Sorting Records in a Form

Open the **Employees** form from the database window.

The records are presented one by one, in order of the **ID Number**.  You can change the order in which the records are displayed to suit your own requirements.

- To sort according to a different field, click in the field box, **City** for example. (New York in the illustration.)

- Click the **Sort Ascending** or **Sort Descending** button on the toolbar.

  Scan through the records using the **Record Navigation Buttons** at the bottom of the screen.

  Notice that the presentation order is now according to **City**.

- To display the records in **Last Name** order, click the **Last Name** field box.

- Click the **Sort Ascending** or **Sort Descending** button on the toolbar to sort and display the records by **Last Name**.

You can also use an **Advanced Filter/Sort** in a form by following the same procedures as outlined above.  This will allow you to sort the records using more than one field. The results will be displayed in the form.

Record Navigation Buttons

However, if you save the **Advanced Filter/Sort** as a **Query**, as outlined in the previous section, the results are displayed in **Table** format when re-opened.

## 5.8    Using Find and Replace

Using **Find and Replace** is
similar to using Find and Replace
in Excel (see Module 4, Section
2.8, page 209).

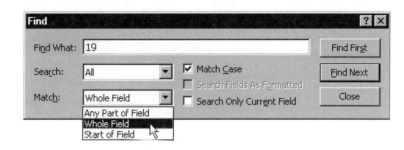

First click in the field in which
you want to search.

In Access, however, the **Match**
box enables you to search whole
fields or parts of fields.
For example, to search for the number **19**:

- **Whole Field** finds fields containing **19** only.

- **Any Part of Field** finds fields with 19 in any number, e.g. 18**19**34.

- **Start of Field** finds only fields with numbers beginning with 19, e.g. **19**/10/99, **19**834 and so on.

To search for an item with the upper/lower case text (capital and small letters) *exactly* as you typed it
in the **Find What** box, click the **Match Case** box.

To use **Search Field As Formatted**, you must first select **Whole Field** in the **Match** box.

When **Search Fields As Formatted** is *not* clicked, it allows searches for data in different formats.
Searching for the date **5/06/00**, for example, will recognise any date format – such as **June 5, 2000**.
When the box *is* clicked, only the format as entered in the **Find What** box is found.

In Office 2000, select the column
in which you want to search from
the menu in the **Look in** box.
Then type what you are looking
for in the **Find What** box.

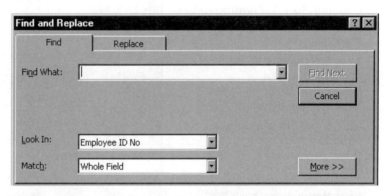

Click the **More** button to display
a further **Search** box. Select
from the Search box menu
according to how you want to
search through the selected
column (in the **Look in** box).

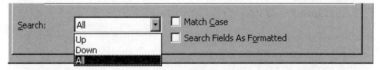

To find and replace data, click
the **Replace** tab.

- Select the column in which
  you want to search from the
  menu in the **Look in** box.

- Enter the data you want to
  find in the **Find What** box.

- Enter the data you want to
  replace it with in the
  **Replace With** box.

- Click the **Find Next** button.

- Click **Replace**.

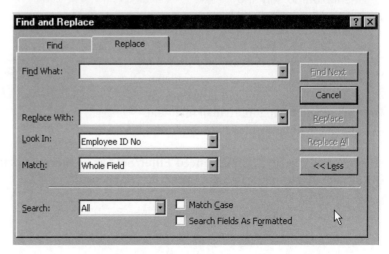

# Section 6     Filter by Selection

## 6.1     Using Filter by Selection in a Table

**Filter by Selection** is a simple method of querying a table to view only those records that contain the information you want to see.

Open the **Employees** table in the **Financial Systems International** database.

Filter by
Selection

- Click in any box in the **Gender** column that contains **Female**.

- Click the **Filter by Selection** button on the toolbar.

- Now only those records containing **Female** in the **Gender** field are displayed (see illustration below).

- To view all the records again, click the **Remove Filter** button to switch off the filter.

  (The **Apply Filter** button is now **Remove Filter**.)

Remove
Filter

| ID Number | Title | First Name | Last Name | Gender | Date of Birth | Address |
|---|---|---|---|---|---|---|
| 1 | Mr. | Don | Lipman | Male | 15/04/64 | 1245 Bennett Avenue |
| 2 | Mr. | James | Conway | Male | 22/03/74 | 145 Dunmore Road |
| 3 | Ms. | Janet | Verano | Female | 23/05/75 | 1568 Vermont Street |
| 4 | Ms. | Niamh | Jones | Female | 30/04/71 | 184 Leinster Avenue |
| 5 | Ms. | Diane | Ferelle | Female | 04/07/68 | 2129 Monroe Street |
| 6 | Mr. | Niall | Hegarty | Male | 25/05/70 | 225 Brandon Road |
| 7 | Ms. | Margaret | O'Brien | Female | 01/08/68 | 25 Granitefield Park |
| 8 | Mr. | John | Pollard | Male | 30/12/63 | 251 Dalton Road |
| 9 | Ms. | Marie | Jones | Female | 11/06/66 | 254 Collingbourne Road |
| 10 | Mr. | John | Mason | Male | 25/01/70 | 256 Willow Vale |
| 11 | Ms. | Clare | O'Brien | Female | 25/08/75 | 30 Ardmore Grove |
| 12 | Mr. | Barry | Bollinger | Male | 06/11/75 | 32 Denison Street |
| 13 | Mr. | James | Edwards | Male | 25/06/62 | 358 Sherman Avenue |
| 14 | Mr. | Sean | Flynn | Male | 25/04/74 | 362 Casement Road |

All Employees

When using **Filter by Selection,** it is often sufficient to just click in a box containing the value you are looking for.

Therefore searching for **Female** requires only that the insertion point be in the **Gender** box.

If the field contains variations on the value, however, you must highlight exactly what you are looking for.

| ID Number | Title | First Name | Last Name | Gender | Date of Birth | Address |
|---|---|---|---|---|---|---|
| 3 | Ms. | Janet | Verano | Female | 23/05/75 | 1568 Vermont Street |
| 4 | Ms. | Niamh | Jones | Female | 30/04/71 | 184 Leinster Avenue |
| 5 | Ms. | Diane | Ferelle | Female | 04/07/68 | 2129 Monroe Street |
| 7 | Ms. | Margaret | O'Brien | Female | 01/08/68 | 25 Granitefield Park |
| 9 | Ms. | Marie | Jones | Female | 11/06/66 | 254 Collingbourne Road |
| 11 | Ms. | Clare | O'Brien | Female | 25/08/75 | 30 Ardmore Grove |
| 18 | Ms. | Sarah | Nestor | Female | 05/08/65 | 427 Rosemeath Avenue |
| 19 | Ms. | Helen | Martin | Female | 02/05/70 | 54 Admaston Road |
| 21 | Ms. | Maria | Lopez | Female | 14/07/76 | 587 Dudley Street |
| 22 | Ms. | Janet | Went | Female | 15/03/62 | 877 Lancaster Drive |
| 23 | Ms. | Paula | Magee | Female | 04/08/74 | 5 Hillview Road |
| (AutoNumber) | | | | | | |

Female Employees only

The **Country** field contains entries for both the United Kingdom and the United States. If you click in a box containing **United Kingdom** and then click the **Filter by Selection** button, Access will find records for the United Kingdom only.

| Date of Birth | Address | City | Post Code | Country |
|---|---|---|---|---|
| 15/04/64 | 1245 Bennett Avenue | New York | 10033 | United States |
| 22/03/74 | 145 Dunmore Road | Dublin | D5 | Ireland |
| 23/05/75 | 1568 Vermont Street | New York | 10025 | United States |
| 30/04/71 | 184 Leinster Avenue | Dublin | D8 | Ireland |
| 04/07/68 | 2129 Monroe Street | New York | 10002 | United States |
| 25/05/70 | 225 Brandon Road | Dublin | D3 | Ireland |
| 01/08/68 | 25 Granitefield Park | Dublin | D12 | Ireland |
| 30/12/63 | 251 Dalton Road | Sydney | 2475 | Australia |
| 11/06/66 | 254 Collingbourne Road | London | W 12 | United Kingdom |

To find a person living in any **United** country, then you must highlight the word **United,** in any row.

- Highlight **United**, in any row.

- Click the **Filter by Selection** button and only those records containing **United** are displayed.

Before continuing with the next example, you must remove the previous filter so that all the records are listed.  In this example, we want to find anyone who is a director in any department.

Remove
Filter

- Double-click the word **Director** in any row in the **Position** column to highlight just that one word.

- Click the **Filter by Selection** button to display a list of all the Directors.

- To see all the records again, click the **Remove Filter** button.

| Country | Telephone Number | Department | Position |
|---|---|---|---|
| United States | + 1 212 636 5855 | Technical Support | Technical Director |
| Ireland | + 353 1 235 2457 | Sales | Sales Director |
| Ireland | + 353 1 458 4578 | Technical Support | Technical Director |
| United Kingdom | + 44 181 8855 8245 | Technical Support | Technical Director |
| United States | + 1 212 658 4578 | Sales | Sales Director |
| Australia | + 61 2 9581 4578 | Sales | Sales Director |
| Ireland | ı 353 1 287 3532 | Administration | Managing Director |
| Australia | + 61 2 9457 2545 | Technical Support | Technical Director |
| United Kingdom | + 44 171 7794 4568 | Sales | Sales Director |
|  |  |  |  |

With **Filter by Selection,** you can only make a query using one field at a time.  However, you can narrow your search for information by using **Filter by Selection** twice in succession.

For example, out of all the records in the table, we may want to isolate anyone living in **Ireland** who is working in the **Administration** department.

- Select any box with **Ireland** in it.

- Click the **Filter by Selection** button.
  This gives us a list of eight people from various departments.

- Now click in any box containing **Administration**.

- Click the **Filter by Selection** button again.
  This gives a final list of just three records which satisfy our criteria.
  Access can do this just as effectively with hundreds or even thousands or more records!

Filter by
Selection

## 6.2    Using Filter by Selection in a Form

You can also use **Filter by Selection** when working with a **form** by following the same procedures.

- Open the **Employees** form.  **Record 1** should be **Don Lipman**.
  If not, click in the **ID Number** box and click **Sort Ascending**.

- Don Lipman's **Department** is **Technical Support**.
  Click in the **Technical Support** box and then click the **Filter by Selection** button.

- Now, only records containing Technical Support are displayed.
  Scan through them using the **Record Navigation Buttons** as before.

- Notice that the **Record Selector** indicates that only 9 records match the filter.

- Click the **Remove Filter** button to display all the records again.

## 6.3    Using Filter by Form in a Table

**Filter by Form** allows you to query a table using more than one field.

Filter by
Form

- In the **Employees** table, click the **Filter by Form** button on the toolbar.

- This table may contain entries from previous filters, such as the **Female** one shown below.
  To remove them, click the **Clear Grid** button.

Clear
Grid

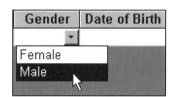

- Click in the **Gender** box.
  (Scroll left and right, if necessary, to find it.)

- Click the button at the right of the box and select **Male** from the list.

- Click in the **Department** box and select **Technical Support** from the list.

  This tells Access to find any records containing **Male** in the **Gender** field and **Technical Support** in the **Department** field.

- Before you click the **Apply Filter** button to view the results, you have the option of clicking the **Save as Query** button to save the results for future use.

Save as          Apply
Query            Filter

# Section 7     Sorts, Filters and Queries

## 7.1     Introduction

When working with a database application like Access, the difference between sorting, filtering and querying can be confusing.

Each can be a very useful feature and all are worth understanding properly.

## 7.2     Sorts

**Sorting** is used in a **table** or a **form** to change the **order** in which records are displayed.

For example, instead of seeing the employees listed in order of their ID Number, you might prefer them listed in alphabetical order or in order of the Department that they are in.  **Sort Ascending** or **Sort Descending** change the order in which records are displayed but shows <u>all</u> the records.

## 7.3     Filters

**Filters** are used to **narrow the list** of records displayed.

A filter looks for specific information in each record and then lists only those records that contain that specific information.

Whether you use **Filter by Selection** or **Filter by Form**, the action is the same.  The only difference is the manner in which you tell Access what you are looking for.  The filter displays all the fields in a table.

## 7.4     Queries

**Queries** are essentially more powerful filters.

The advantage of a query is that you can decide which fields will be shown and then what information will be sought.  A query is based on a table. It uses the fields and records contained in the table which are then displayed as required.

The most useful aspect of a query is that the information you seek can be quite complicated.
For example, you might want to see all the employees who were born after a particular date and who work in either Sales or Administration.

---

For **ECDL** database **tests**, you may be asked to find specific information and save it.

This requires you to create a **Filter** and then use the **Save as Query** function, or else design a query from scratch.

While using the filter is sufficient, it is advisable that you understand how Queries work as explained in Section 8 on page 269.   Remember that the table contains the raw information.  A form or a query merely presents that information in a different layout.

---

# Section 8      Queries

## 8.1      Creating a Query

Designing a query from scratch allows more flexibility than using Filters or Sorting.

It allows you to choose which fields to display and search only for particular information.

- Click the **Queries** tab In the **Database Window**.

- Notice the two **queries** listed in the window.

  They are the filters we created earlier and saved as queries.

- Click the **New** button.

  The **New Query** window opens.

- Select **Simple Query Wizard** and click **OK**.

  The Simple Query Wizard window opens.

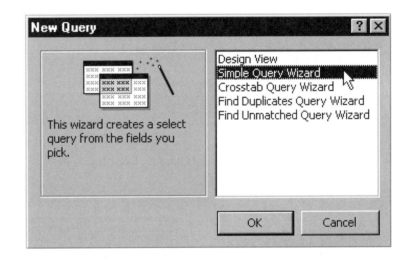

To create a new query in Office 2000:

- Click the **Queries** button in the panel at the left.

- Double-click **Create query by using wizard**.

In the Simple Query Wizard window, you choose which table or existing query on which to base your new query.

You also choose the fields you want to use in the query.

- Select **Table: Employees** in the Table/Queries box.

- Click **ID Number** and then click the single arrow button to move it across to the **Selected Fields** box.

- Repeat for **First Name, Last Name, Gender, Country** and **Department**.

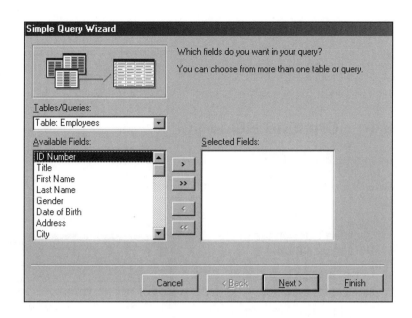

The fields you have selected should now be listed in the **Selected Fields** box.

- Click the **Next** button to continue.

  A new window opens and you are asked to give the query a name.

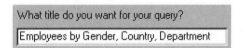

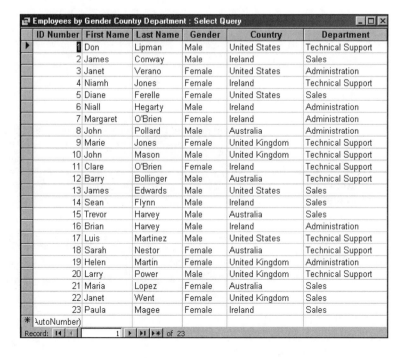

- Name the query **Employees by Gender, Country, Department**.

In a large database, you may have many different tables and many queries.

Giving each query a meaningful name that reflects its contents will make it easier to manage.

- Click **Finish**.

  The query is completed and the data is displayed in table format with only the selected fields shown.

  At this stage, all records are listed.

This is a simple but very useful use of queries.

| ID Number | First Name | Last Name | Gender | Country | Department |
|---|---|---|---|---|---|
| 1 | Don | Lipman | Male | United States | Technical Support |
| 2 | James | Conway | Male | Ireland | Sales |
| 3 | Janet | Verano | Female | United States | Administration |
| 4 | Niamh | Jones | Female | Ireland | Technical Support |
| 5 | Diane | Ferelle | Female | United States | Sales |
| 6 | Niall | Hegarty | Male | Ireland | Administration |
| 7 | Margaret | O'Brien | Female | Ireland | Administration |
| 8 | John | Pollard | Male | Australia | Administration |
| 9 | Marie | Jones | Female | United Kingdom | Technical Support |
| 10 | John | Mason | Male | United Kingdom | Technical Support |
| 11 | Clare | O'Brien | Female | Ireland | Technical Support |
| 12 | Barry | Bollinger | Male | Australia | Technical Support |
| 13 | James | Edwards | Male | United States | Sales |
| 14 | Sean | Flynn | Male | Ireland | Sales |
| 15 | Trevor | Harvey | Male | Australia | Sales |
| 16 | Brian | Harvey | Male | Ireland | Administration |
| 17 | Luis | Martinez | Male | United States | Technical Support |
| 18 | Sarah | Nestor | Female | Australia | Technical Support |
| 19 | Helen | Martin | Female | United Kingdom | Administration |
| 20 | Larry | Power | Male | United Kingdom | Technical Support |
| 21 | Maria | Lopez | Female | Australia | Sales |
| 22 | Janet | Went | Female | United Kingdom | Sales |
| 23 | Paula | Magee | Female | Ireland | Sales |

As we have seen, tables can contain many fields which are difficult to view properly when you have to scroll over and back repeatedly. At any time, you are probably only interested in viewing a small number of fields. These can be isolated in a query.

You could have one query that shows employees and their addresses and another one that shows employees and their departments and positions etc.

The next step is to apply **criteria** to the fields to narrow the selection and provide more detailed information.

## 8.2    Using Criteria in Queries

Design
View

Ensure the **Employees by Gender, Country, Department** query is open. Maximise the window and click the **Design View** button.

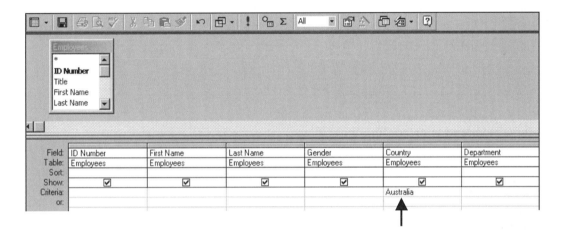

The grid in the lower part of the window shows the fields we are using in the query and the tables they come from.

The **Field** row shows the fields and the **Table** row shows the tables the fields are in.

To apply a criterion to a field, click in the appropriate **criteria** box and enter the value you want.

In this example, we shall first look for employees in Australia.

- Type **Australia** in the **Country** field box (arrowed above).

- Click the **Run** button on the toolbar.

- The employees in Australia are listed and displayed.

Run

- Click the **Design View** button to return to the query window.

- Type **Ireland** in the box under **Australia**.

- Access now looks in the **Country** field for records containing **either** Australia **or** Ireland.
  (Notice the quote marks Access adds to the text.)

- Click the **Run** button on the toolbar.

- The matching records are listed and displayed.

Click the **Design View** button again to return to the query window. This time we shall remove the **Ireland** criterion and add a criterion – **Sales** – to the **Department** field:

| ID Number | First Name | Last Name | Gender | Country | Department |
|---|---|---|---|---|---|
| 2 | James | Conway | Male | Ireland | Sales |
| 4 | Niamh | Jones | Female | Ireland | Technical Support |
| 6 | Niall | Hegarty | Male | Ireland | Administration |
| 7 | Margaret | O'Brien | Female | Ireland | Administration |
| 8 | John | Pollard | Male | Australia | Administration |
| 11 | Clare | O'Brien | Female | Ireland | Technical Support |
| 12 | Barry | Bollinger | Male | Australia | Technical Support |
| 14 | Sean | Flynn | Male | Ireland | Sales |
| 15 | Trevor | Harvey | Male | Australia | Sales |
| 16 | Brian | Harvey | Male | Ireland | Administration |
| 18 | Sarah | Nestor | Female | Australia | Technical Support |
| 21 | Maria | Lopez | Female | Australia | Sales |
| 23 | Paula | Magee | Female | Ireland | Sales |
| * | (AutoNumber) | | | | |

| Field: | ID Number | First Name | Last Name | Gender | Country | Department |
|---|---|---|---|---|---|---|
| Table: | Employees | Employees | Employees | Employees | Employees | Employees |
| Sort: | | | | | | |
| Show: | ☑ | ☑ | ☑ | ☑ | ☑ | ☑ |
| Criteria: | | | | | "Australia" | "Sales" |
| or: | | | | | | |

- Remove **Ireland** from the **Country** box.

- Enter **Sales** in the **Department** box.

- Click the **Run** button on the toolbar.
  The employees in **Australia** working in **Sales** are listed and displayed.

- **Close** the query.

## 8.3    Another Query Example

In this example, we shall find all the employees listed by **Date of Birth** and **Department**.

- Click the **Queries** tab in the **Database window**.
  The three previously saved queries are listed.

- Click the **New** button.

- Choose **Simple Query Wizard** in the next window.

- Click **OK**.

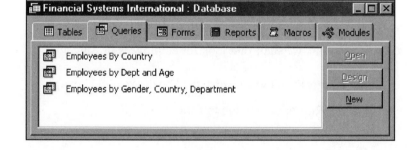

In the Office 2000 **Database** window, click the **Queries** button in the panel at the left to see the **queries** listed in the main part of the window.

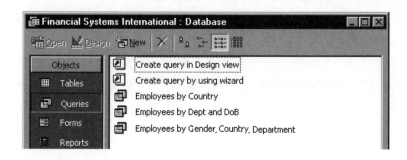

In the Simple Query Wizard window, choose the **Employees** table and move the **fields** to the **Selected Fields** box as shown in the illustration.

- Click the **Next** button to move to the next window.

- Save the query as **Employees by Date of Birth and Department**.

- Click **Finish**.

**Simple Query Wizard**

Which fields do you want in your query?
You can choose from more than one table or query.

Tables/Queries:
Table: Employees

Available Fields:
ID Number
Title
Gender
Address
City
Post Code
Country
Telephone Number

Selected Fields:
First Name
Last Name
Date of Birth
Department
Position

Cancel    < Back    Next >    Finish

All the records are displayed.

| First Name | Last Name | Date of Birth | Department | Position |
|---|---|---|---|---|
| Don | Lipman | 15/04/64 | Technical Support | Technical Director |
| James | Conway | 22/03/74 | Sales | Sales Director |
| Janet | Verano | 23/05/75 | Administration | Office Manager |
| Niamh | Jones | 30/04/71 | Technical Support | Technical Director |
| Diane | Ferelle | 04/07/68 | Sales | Sales Representative |
| Niall | Hegarty | 25/05/70 | Administration | Office Manager |

## 8.4    A Further Query Example

In this example, we shall find all the employees from *either* **Administration** *or* **Sales** who were born on or after 1/1/70.

Design
View

- Click the **Design View** button to return to the Query window.

- Type **>=1/1/70** in the **Date of Birth** Criteria box.

  This tells Access to search for dates that are **greater than** or **equal to** 1/1/70.

| Field: | First Name | Last Name | Date of Birth | Department | Position |
|---|---|---|---|---|---|
| Table: | Employees | Employees | Employees | Employees | Employees |
| Sort: | | | | | |
| Show: | ☑ | ☑ | ☑ | ☑ | ☑ |
| Criteria: | | | | | |
| or: | | | | | |

- Click the **Run** button on the toolbar to check.

  12 records should be listed.

  Then return to **Design View**.

Run

- Now enter **Administration** in the first **Department** criteria box.

- Click the **Run** button on the toolbar to check.

  Only 3 records that satisfy both criteria should be listed, i.e. born on or after 1/1/70 and in Administration.

  Return to **Design View**.

| Date of Birth | Department | Positi |
|---|---|---|
| Employees | Employees | Empl |
| | | |
| ☑ | ☑ | |
| >=#01/01/70# | "Administration" | |
| | "Sales" | |

Notice the extra characters that
Access adds to the text you enter.

- We now want employees from Administration or Sales, so we need to add **Sales** under **Administration**.

- Run this to check.  It should list 11 records.  Look closely, however, and notice that 4 of the Sales employees were born before 1970, which is outside our range.  **Why?**

Look at the criteria rows again.  Each complete row is interpreted separately by Access.  The first row asks Access to find employees who are born on or after 1/1/70 and who are also in Administration.

We then have a second **Or** row.  This asks Access to include employees who also satisfy the criteria on that line, i.e. employees in Sales. But there is no mention of **Dates of Birth**.

The result thus includes employees from Administration with the *specified* Dates of Birth criteria and employees from Sales with **no** Date of Birth specified.  To rectify this, we need to include the Date of Birth criteria in **both** rows.

- Go back again to **Design View**.

- This time, include the same date criteria in both rows, i.e. **>=1/1/70**

- **Run** this to check.

- There should now be only 7 records.

- **Close** and **Save** the query.

## 8.5    Wildcard Queries

When creating a query, you can use a **wildcard** character that will find variations of text and numbers.

A character commonly used for wildcard searches is the asterisk (*) but other characters are also used.

The wildcard character acts as a kind of abbreviation for any other 'unknown' characters, enabling you to search for several different possibilities.  For example, to find all employees whose surname begins with 'M', you would enter M* in the criteria box.

Some of the characters that are used to find different combinations are listed here.

| | |
|---|---|
| * | This will find any number of characters.<br>e.g.    **B*** would find Byrne, Batty, Battersby etc.<br>**\*an** would find Callaghan, Monaghan, Horan etc. |
| ? | This will find a single character.<br>e.g.    **Sm?th** would find Smith, Smyth etc. |
| [ ] | This will find any character listed in the brackets.<br>e.g.    **B[ae]ll** would find Ball and Bell *but not* Bill or Bull etc. |
| ! | This will find any character <u>not</u> in the brackets.<br>e.g.    **B[!ae]ll** would find Bill and Bull but not Ball or Bell. |
| - | This will find any one of a range of characters listed in alphabetical order.<br>e.g.    **b[a-c]d** finds bad, bbd, and bcd. |
| # | This will find any single numeric character.<br>e.g.    **1#3** finds 103, 113, 123. |

# Section 9    Reports

## 9.1    Designing a Report

Reports are used to present information from a table or query in a format suitable for printing out. You can, of course, print directly from a table or query but the data is printed as it appears in the table. That method is not very flexible.

- Click the **Reports** tab in the **Database window** and then click the **New** button.

  The **New Report** window opens.

- Select **Report Wizard** in the panel on the right.

- Click in the **Choose the table or query...** box in the lower part of the window and select in the menu the table or query that contains the data you want to use.

  In this case, select the **Employees** table.

- Click **OK**.

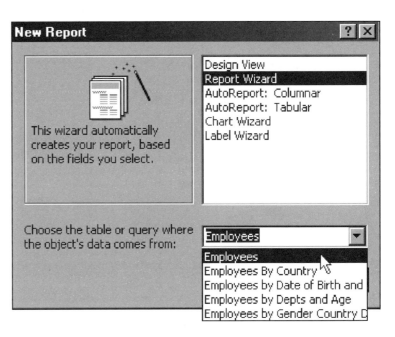

- In the following window, select the fields that you want to display in the report.

- Click the **single arrow** button to add the selected fields to the right-hand box.

  *Alternatively*, double-click a field to move it across.

  Add the following fields: **First Name, Last Name, Country, Department** and **Position**.

- Click the **Next** button to continue.

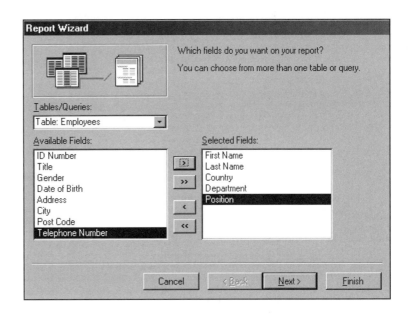

The next window lets you group the data, so that instead of a single list of all employees, you can list them in groups.

Employees from the same country can be listed, for example. Within each group, the employees can then be listed in alphabetical order.

Click **Country** in the grouping panel and click the arrow button to move it across.

- Click the **Next** button to continue.

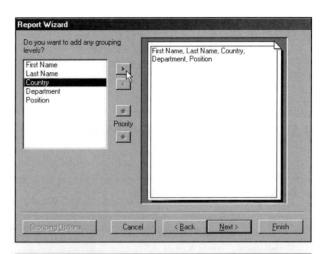

- In the new window, you can sort the records using one of the chosen fields.
  Select **Last Name** from the menu in the first box.

- Select **First Name** from the menu in the second box.

- Click the **Next** button to continue.

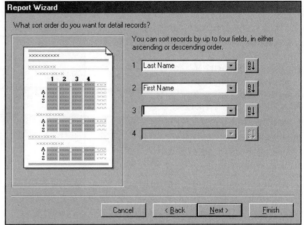

- This window gives a choice of layouts.
  Click the different options to see a sample displayed in the panel.
  Choose **Align Left 1** for now.

- Click **Next** to continue.

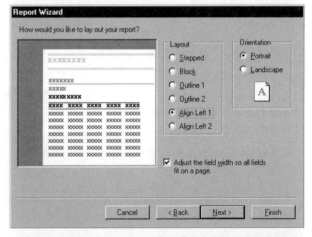

- Choose a **Style** in the following window.
  **Corporate** is a good choice for now.

- Click **Next** to continue.
  You are asked to give the report a title in the window that appears.

- Type **Employees by Country** as the title.

- Click **Finish** to display the completed report.

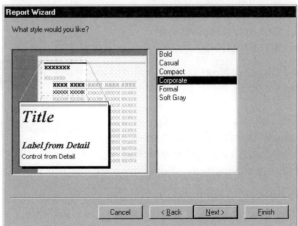

## 9.2    Previewing a Report

The report is displayed in **Preview** mode, which shows how it will appear on the printed page.

To change any aspect of the report before you print it, click the **Design View** button, which shows how the report is constructed.

Compare the **Design View** (right) and the **Preview** (next page) to see the different components of the report as they are assembled by Access and as they are printed on the printer.

The format of the report can be altered in Design view, as outlined below, to suit personal preferences.

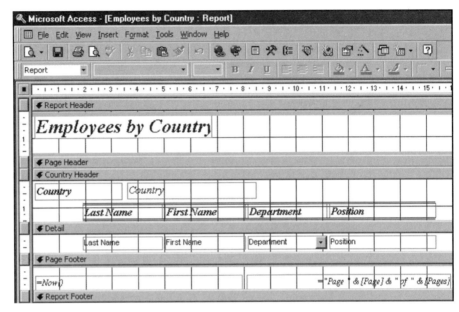

Design View

- The **Report Header** is where the title of the report appears.
- The **Page Header** would show a separate page header.
  (There is none in our example.)
- The **Country Header** displays the name of each country and also the labels of the fields that appear in the next section below.
- The **Detail** section displays the data for each record that will be listed.
- The **Page Footer** displays the usual footer information such as the data and page numbers.
- The **Report Footer** would show a separate report footer.
  (There is none in our example.)

Text formatting can be changed for any part of the report in the same way as you would change the formatting in a Word Processor.  First select the item or items you want to change.

- To select a single item, click on it.
- To select a number of items, hold down the **Shift** key and click on each box in turn.
- Click in the left ruler to select all the items on that row.
- Click on the top ruler to select all the items underneath.

For example, select all the items in the **Detail** section by clicking on the left ruler beside the section.  Change the **font** to **Times New Roman** and the **font size** to **10 pt**.   To centre the title on the page, click to select it and drag it to the centre.

- Click the **Preview** button to preview the report (see next page).
- To print out the report, click the **Print** button.

Preview

Report Preview

## Employees by Country

| Country | Australia | | Total | 5 |
| --- | --- | --- | --- | --- |
| **Last Name** | **First Name** | **Department** | **Position** | |
| Bollinger | Barry | Technical Support | Technician | |
| Harvey | Trevor | Sales | Sales Director | |
| Lopez | Maria | Sales | Sales Representative | |
| Nestor | Sarah | Technical Support | Technical Director | |
| Pollard | John | Administration | Office Manager | |

| Country | Ireland | | Total | 7 |
| --- | --- | --- | --- | --- |
| **Last Name** | **First Name** | **Department** | **Position** | |
| Conway | James | Sales | Sales Director | |
| Flynn | Sean | Sales | Sales Representative | |
| Harvey | Brian | Administration | Managing Director | |
| Hegarty | Niall | Administration | Office Manager | |
| Jones | Niamh | Technical Support | Technical Director | |
| O'Brien | Clare | Technical Support | Technician | |
| O'Brien | Margaret | Administration | Financial Controller | |

| Country | United Kingdom | | Total | 5 |
| --- | --- | --- | --- | --- |
| **Last Name** | **First Name** | **Department** | **Position** | |
| Jones | Marie | Sales | Sales Representative | |
| Martin | Helen | Administration | Office Manager | |
| Mason | John | Technical Support | Technical Director | |
| Power | Larry | Technical Support | Technician | |
| Went | Janet | Sales | Sales Director | |

| Country | United States | | Total | 5 |
| --- | --- | --- | --- | --- |
| **Last Name** | **First Name** | **Department** | **Position** | |
| Edwards | James | Sales | Sales Director | |
| Ferelle | Diane | Sales | Sales Representative | |
| Lipman | Don | Technical Support | Technical Director | |
| Martinez | Luis | Technical Support | Technician | |
| Verano | Janet | Administration | Office Manager | |

*22 May 2000*                                                    *Page 1 of 1*

## 9.3    Reprinting a Report

When a report is saved, it can be printed at any time.

- Click the **Reports** tab in the **Database window**.

- Select the report you want to print by clicking it once.

- Click the **Preview** button.
  A preview of the report is displayed.

- Click the **Print** button.

To print a saved report in Office 2000:

- Click the **Reports** button in the panel at the left of the window.

- Select the report you want to print by clicking it once.

- Click the **Preview** button on the toolbar at the top of the window.
  A preview of the report is displayed.

- Click the **Print** button.

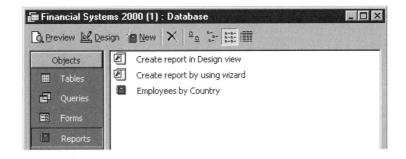

Module 5

# Section 10   Working with Numbers

## 10.1   Using Numbers

An Access report will show each record from the table or query on which the report is based. How the records are displayed depends on how they were grouped and sorted when the report was designed.

When records are grouped as shown in the previous section, you can also calculate totals and subtotals of numeric data fields (numbers) in the report. This section shows how to include such totals.

First, it will be useful to add another field to the **Employees** table

- Open the Employees table in **Design View**.

- Create a new field called **Salary**.

- Set the data type to **Number** or **Currency**.

- Enter values in the table as shown here.

| First Name | Last Name | Salary |
|------------|-----------|--------|
| Don | Lipman | 50000 |
| James | Conway | 50000 |
| Janet | Verano | 30000 |
| Niamh | Jones | 50000 |
| Diane | Ferelle | 35000 |
| Niall | Hegarty | 30000 |
| Margaret | O'Brien | 65000 |
| John | Pollard | 30000 |
| Marie | Jones | 35000 |
| John | Mason | 50000 |
| Clare | O'Brien | 25000 |
| Barry | Bollinger | 25000 |
| James | Edwards | 50000 |
| Sean | Flynn | 35000 |
| Trevor | Harvey | 50000 |
| Brian | Harvey | 75000 |
| Luis | Martinez | 25000 |
| Sarah | Nestor | 50000 |
| Helen | Martin | 30000 |
| Larry | Power | 25000 |
| Maria | Lopez | 35000 |
| Janet | Went | 50000 |

## 10.2   A New Report

The process is the same as that described in Section 9.1, page 275.

- Click the **Reports** tab in the **Database window** and then click the **New** button.
  The **New Report** window opens.

- Select **Report Wizard** in the panel on the right.
  Click in the **Choose the table or query...** box in the lower part of the window and select the **Employees** table.

- Click **OK**.

A list of available fields is displayed on the left with a panel for the selected fields on the right.

- From the **Employees** table select the following fields for inclusion in the Report:
  **First Name**, **Last Name**, **Salary**, **City**.

- Click the **Next** button.

- In the **Grouping Level** section, select **City**.

- Click **Next** to proceed to the next window.

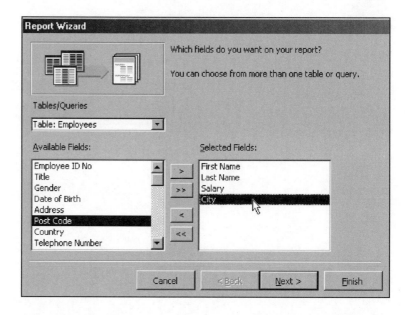

- Select **Last Name** in the first sorting field box.

- Click the **Summary Options** button to display the Summary Options window (see below).

  The Summary Options window lists the available fields on which calculations can be performed. In this case only **Salary** is listed.

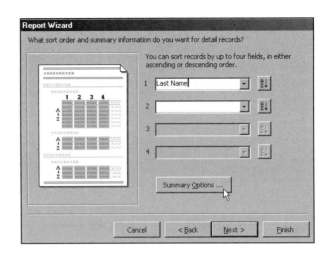

## 10.3   Summary Options

In the Summary Options window, you can select one or more of four values for each field to perform calculations as follows.

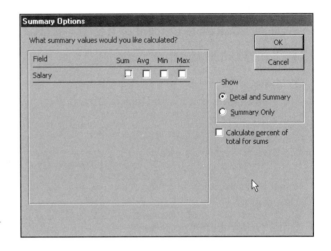

**Sum**   Adds the salaries for each record in the group and the entire report.

**Avg**   Finds the average salary of the records in the group.

**Min**   Shows the lowest value from the Salary field in the group.

**Max**   Shows the highest value from the Salary field in the group.

There is also a tick box at the right of the window (**Calculate percent...**) that allows you to calculate what percentage of the total is represented in each group.

(In this example it would indicate that the sum of the salaries for Sydney is 190,000 and that this value is 21.11% of the total salaries in the report.)

The final option in this window relates to how the information is displayed, either **Detail and Summary** or **Summary only**.

**Detail and Summary**

This shows details of each record in the group with a summary of the calculations for the group underneath.

| City | Dublin | | |
|---|---|---|---|
| **Last Name** | **First Name** | | **Salary** |
| Conway | James | | 50000 |
| Flynn | Sean | | 35000 |
| Harvey | Brian | | 75000 |
| Hegarty | Niall | | 30000 |
| Jones | Niamh | | 50000 |
| O'Brien | Clare | | 25000 |
| O'Brien | Margaret | | 65000 |
| *Summary for 'City' = Dublin (7 detail records)* | | | |
| **Sum** | | | *330000* |
| **Avg** | | | *47142.8571* |
| **Min** | | | *25000* |
| **Max** | | | *75000* |
| **Standard** | | | *36.67%* |

Module 5

## Summary Only

This shows a summary of the calculations for the group but does not show any individual record details

| City | Dublin | | |
|------|--------|---|------|
| | Last Name | First Name | Salary |
| Summary for 'City' = Dublin (7 detail records) | | | |
| Sum | | | 330000 |
| Avg | | | 47142.8571 |
| Min | | | 25000 |
| Max | | | 75000 |
| Standard | | | 36.67% |

# 10.4 Finishing the Report

For the purpose of this example, do the following.

- In the **Summary Options** window above, select all the calculation options, **Sum**, **Avg**, **Min**, **Max**.

- Select **Calculate percent of total for sums**.

- Select **Detail and Summary.**

- Click **OK**.
  This returns you to the Report Wizard window.

In the Report wizard window:

- Click **Next** to proceed to the next window.

- Select **Align Left 1** and click **Next** to proceed to the next window.

- Select the **Corporate** style and click **Next** to proceed to the next window.

- In the final window, name the report **Salary by City**.

- Click **Finish**.
  The Report is displayed, as shown here.

### Salary by City

| City | Dublin | | |
|------|--------|---|------|
| | Last Name | First Name | Salary |
| | Conway | James | 50000 |
| | Flynn | Sean | 35000 |
| | Harvey | Brian | 75000 |
| | Hegarty | Niall | 30000 |
| | Jones | Niamh | 50000 |
| | O'Brien | Clare | 25000 |
| | O'Brien | Margaret | 65000 |
| Summary for 'City' = Dublin (7 detail records) | | | |
| Sum | | | 330000 |
| Avg | | | 47142.8571 |
| Min | | | 25000 |
| Max | | | 75000 |
| Standard | | | 36.67% |
| City | London | | |
| | Last Name | First Name | Salary |
| | Jones | Marie | 35000 |
| | Martin | Helen | 30000 |
| | Mason | John | 50000 |
| | Power | Larry | 25000 |
| | Went | Janet | 50000 |

# Section 11 Exercises

Module 5

# Self Check Exercises

**1** Which of these would you click to include a field in a query?

☐ Yes
☐ Include
☑ ✓
☐ >

**2** What is the name of the database application you are using for this exercise?

☑ Microsoft Access
☐ Microsoft Excel
☐ Microsoft PowerPoint

**3** Which of these items do you need to create in your database if you wish to include an additional new category of information?

☑ A field
☐ A record
☐ A file
☐ A folder

**4** In a database, what is shown in a table?

☐ All records in a particular database
☐ All fields related to a particular record

**5** Which of the following does a single form in a database display?

☐ Fields from a particular table or query
☐ The records in a database

**6** Tick the statement(s) that is/are true of a query?

☐ A query may present a set of complete records.
☐ A query may present a set of modified records.

**7** Columns in a database table correspond to which of the following?

☑ Fields
☐ Records

**8** In any given database, at least one field is usually assigned as which of the following?

☐ A field name
☐ A wild card
☑ A primary key

**9** If you can see all the records and fields on your computer screen, which of these are you most likely to be viewing?

☐ The query
☐ The form
☑ The table

**10** You wish to search a database for all dates after 15th Nov. 1987. Which formula would you use?

☑ >=15/11/87
☐ >15/11/87
☐ <=15/11/87
☐ <15/11/87

**11** Tick which data items will be matched with the formulae: **=B\* and =Sm?th**.

☐ Smith
☐ Brennan
☐ O'Brien
☐ Smyth

**12** Match the wildcard characters to their functions.

**o\***      Finds the words with letters o to w inside.

**t[!ow]n**      Finds words beginning with o.

**b[o-w]t**      Excludes the words with the letters o to w inside.

**13** Tick the *inaccurate* statements.

The form wizard allows you to...

☐ select any number of fields for display.
☐ select all fields for display.
☐ display not more than a limited number of fields.

**14** Which is the correct statement?

☐ You may save a query as a filter.
☐ You may save a filter as a query.

# Practical Exercises

Edge of screen ——→

Table extends off the screen. ——→

*With a large table, you will have to use the scroll arrows to see the parts of the table that extend beyond the edges of the screen.*

**Microsoft Access - [Staff Location]**
File Edit View Insert Format Records Tools Window Help

**Staff Location : Table**

| Reg Number | Surname | First Name | Department | Home District | Location | City | Country | Sex | Date Assigned |
|---|---|---|---|---|---|---|---|---|---|
| 19893251 | Kelly | Sam | Customer Servi | Dublin | 16 Harbour Road | Wexford | Ireland | F | 08/01/98 |
| 19892405 | Berry | Ger | Operations | West | 1756 Applead Trail | Orlando | USA | M | 27/06/95 |
| 19782323 | Murphy | Sandy | Sales | West | 19 Corbhaile Avenue | Limerick | Ireland | F | 01/04/83 |
| 19845678 | Smyth | Pat | Engineering | South West | 19 Valentia Road | Cork | Ireland | M | 16/02/99 |
| 19671212 | White | Phil | Software | Dublin | 25 Rue de Bordeaux | Renne | France | M | 22/05/99 |
| 19781234 | Smith | Bob | Engineering | South | 25 Rue de Paris | Bordeaux | France | F | 25/09/98 |
| 19857172 | Power | Fran | Sales | Norht West | 5 Castle Court | Kilkenny | Ireland | M | 19/09/99 |
| 19964321 | Barry | Alex | Research | South East | 7 High Street | Manchester | England | F | 15/11/97 |
| 19891523 | Reddington | Joe | Customer Servi | Midlands | 97A Wilhelm Strasse | Berlin | Germany | F | 17/09/99 |

## Exercise 1

Your company has assigned personnel to various locations in Europe. Create a database table with the information above and save it under 'Personnel Assigned'.

## Exercise 2

Create a simple form showing all the data using the international background supplied.

## Exercise 3

Present a table view of the data in ascending alphabetical order. Print out the table.

## Exercise 4

You will notice that the first four digits of the personnel registration number show the year each person started to work for the company. Using the fact that years of service determine seniority, sort the personnel according to seniority and print out the table.

## Exercise 5

If you had to present a seniority list of the female employees, how would you sort the table?

## Exercise 6

In an effort to monitor gender issues, what would you do to isolate only the essential information which would show the male/female personnel distribution in seniority?

## Exercise 7

On the same theme, how would you present all the information and show the distribution of M/F personnel on assignment in Ireland? Would a filter by selection be suitable?

## Exercise 8

Find the personnel who

1. came to the firm in 1978.
2. are assigned in France.
3. are based in Ireland.

Save each answer under a suitable name.

## Exercise 9

Construct a query or a form that presents only the following information:

- Surname
- First name
- Registration Number
- Location
- Home District

## Exercise 10

Find all the female personnel who were assigned after 24/06/99.

Module 5

# Module 6

## Presentation

# Module 6

# Presentation

Module 6

# Introduction

---

## Syllabus Goals for Module 6

**Presentation** requires the candidate to demonstrate competence in using presentation tools on a personal computer. The candidate shall be able to accomplish basic tasks such as creating, formatting and preparing presentations for distribution and display. The candidate shall demonstrate the ability to create a variety of presentations for different target audiences or situations. The candidate shall demonstrate the ability to accomplish basic operations with graphics and charts and to use various slide show effects.

---

## Presentations

The professional presentation of information is an integral part of modern communication. A clear and effective presentation of important points facilitates the understanding of new projects and ideas. Information presented in a lively and colourful manner stimulates an audience. People's attention is caught and retained more easily. In the past, the range of techniques to do this was limited.

Traditional blackboard and chalk gave way to the flipchart which made it possible to prepare material in advance. The overhead projector extended the possibilities of the flipchart. Now it is the turn of the computer.

## Computers

A computer presentation offers several advantages over traditional methods. Presentations can be prepared on-screen, edited, sorted and transported with ease (on a floppy disk, for example). Instead of the old static displays, animation can be added. Sound and video clips can be used. Audience reaction can be anticipated and suitable material can be displayed in response to it, or kept hidden if not needed.

## Displays

Computer presentations are intended to be displayed on a big screen. While it is possible to use an ordinary computer monitor, this is only suitable for a very small group. Large monitors are very expensive and even the largest monitors are not big enough for a very large audience.

Making a presentation to a large audience requires the use of a screen and a special projector that can be plugged into the computer. The operator can then view the presentation on the computer monitor while behind him or her, it is projected onto a large screen for the audience.

## Projection

Two means of projection are commonly used for computer presentations. The first uses a projection panel in conjunction with an overhead projector. This is a very inefficient method, however. The area of the panel is far smaller than the area of the light tray on the overhead projector, so a lot of light is wasted. In addition, a standard overhead projector is not bright enough and a special OHP with high-power light output has to be purchased in addition to the projector.

The best solution is a data projector. This is a special projector with its own light source, designed so that no light is wasted. Modern projectors are compact and can be easily transported and set up.

In either case, it is advisable to use a strong projector stand and a good-quality screen.

---

# Reference Table

Should you begin your studies with this module, it is important to note that related material is dealt with in other sections of the manual. This reference list will assist you to conveniently locate the material.

| <u>Skill</u> | <u>Task</u> | <u>Module</u> | <u>Page</u> |
|---|---|---|---|
| **First Steps** | | | |
| | Save a new document | Module 2 | 84 |
| | Save changes to an existing document | Module 2 | 87 |
| | Close a document | Before You Begin | 24 |
| | Help | Before You Begin | 16 |
| **Adjusting Settings** | | | |
| | Change page display modes | Before You Begin | 21 |
| | Page magnification | Before You Begin | 22 |
| | Page orientation | Module 3 | 149 |
| | Toolbars | Before You Begin | 11 |
| **Document Exchange** | | | |
| | Save a file in a different format | Module 2 | 87 |
| | Save for Web posting | Module 2 | 88 |
| **Basic Functions** | | | |
| | Alignment and justification of text | Module 3 | 133 |
| | Cut, Copy and Paste | Before You Begin | 10 |
| | Deleting | Module 3 | 127 |
| | Formatting text | Module 3 | 131 |
| | Images, graphics and objects | Module 3 | 161 |
| | Line spacing | Module 3 | 134 |
| | Printing | Module 3 | 143 |
| | Preview a document | Module 3 | 143 |
| | Printers, choosing | Module 3 | 145 |
| | Print to file | Module 3 | 145 |
| | Selecting | Before You Begin | 9 |
| | Spell Check | Before You begin | 23 |
| | Symbols and special characters | Module 3 | 124 |
| | Templates | Module 3 | 189 |
| | Undo | Module 3 | 135 |

# Section 1      Getting Started

## 1.1     What is PowerPoint?

**PowerPoint** is a presentation tool increasingly used by lecturers, teachers, conference speakers and business people.  It improves the quality of their presentations by using high-quality text, graphics and pictures.  Presentations are usually structured by displaying only relevant points during the talk, with the speaker outlining these points in greater detail.

The completed presentation can be shown in many ways.  It can be presented on a computer screen, or projected on a large conference screen using a computer data projector.  It can also be printed out on paper for distribution as handouts or on transparent acetate sheets for use on conventional overhead projectors.  35mm slides of the presentation can be prepared for use with a standard 35mm photographic slide projector.

There are also many educational applications for PowerPoint, apart from its use as a presentation tool.  Many teachers have used the simple multimedia elements of the package to create short projects with their students.  These, and other applications of the package, will become apparent as you become more familiar with the program.

## 1.2     Slides

A PowerPoint presentation is made up of a number of **slides**.  Each slide typically has a title with supporting text in bulleted list format and/or graphics.  The drawings can be created with PowerPoint or imported as standard Clip Art from the supplied library or from other sources.

Presentations can be made more attractive with the use of **transitions** – special effects to switch from one slide to another – and **builds** which use animation effects to reveal bullet points one at a time rather than displaying them all at the beginning.

## 1.3     Opening PowerPoint

Open Microsoft PowerPoint by clicking the **PowerPoint** button on the Microsoft Office **Shortcut Bar** on the desktop.

Alternatively, click the **Start** button and select **Microsoft PowerPoint** in the **Programs** menu or sub-menu.

## 1.4     The PowerPoint Window

The **PowerPoint** window is similar in appearance to that used in other Office Applications, with menus and toolbars at the top, a workspace in the main part of the screen and other bars at the bottom.

The appearance of the window varies according to the component of PowerPoint that is in use at any particular time.  You will become familiar with the different windows as you progress through the module.

Module 6

## 1.5    Menus and Toolbars

The Menu Bar contains many of the menus common to other Office Applications as well as menus specific to PowerPoint.

The Toolbars are similar in appearance to the toolbars in other Office applications but contain buttons specific to PowerPoint and to the component in use at a particular time.  You will learn to recognise and use them as you proceed through the module.

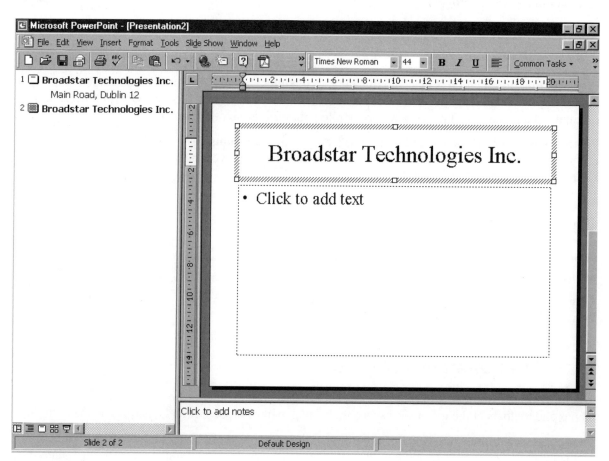

The Office 2000 toolbars differ slightly from those in earlier versions of Office.

The illustration shows the full PowerPoint window with a slide being prepared in the main part of the window on the right.  As slides are added to the presentation, they are listed in the panel on the left.

# Section 2    Creating a Presentation

## 2.1    A New Presentation

For this exercise, we shall create a short two-slide presentation, giving a brief overview of an imaginary school.

When PowerPoint opens, a number of choices are presented in the opening window.

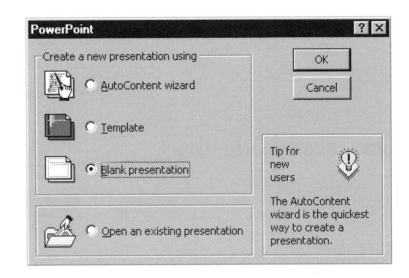

- Select **Blank Presentation**, if it is not already selected, and click **OK**.

- If PowerPoint is already open, click the **New** button on the Toolbar.

New

  The **New Slide** window appears.

- A number of different types of slides are presented for you to chose from.

  Click the samples in turn to see a description in the panel at the bottom right of the window.

  The first slide on the top row – a **Title Slide** – is already selected.

- Click **OK**.

  The first slide appears on the screen.

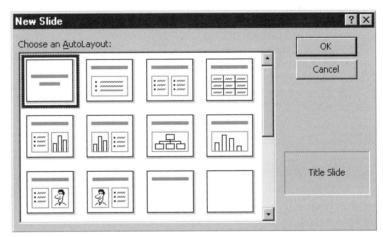

## 2.2    Adding Text

- Click once in the **Click to add title** box.

  The **Click to add...** text is removed and you can now enter your own information.

- Type **Broadstar Technologies Inc.**

  Do not press the **Return** key or a blank line will be added.

- Click once in the **Click to add sub-title** box.

- Type **Main Road, Dublin 12**.

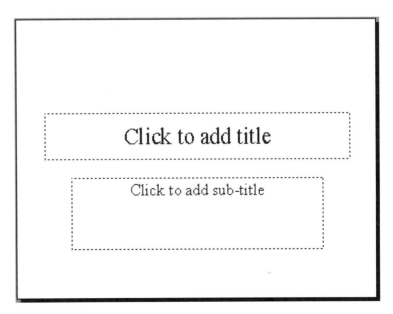

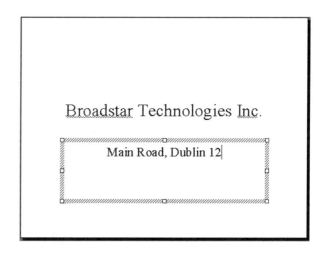

The first slide has been created.
It should appear as in the illustration.
At the moment it only contains a title
and a sub-title on a blank background.

In Office 2000, the slides are listed in
a panel at the left of the PowerPoint
window (see illustration on page 292).

The next step is to add a new slide.

## 2.3    Adding a New Slide

You can add a new slide in a
number of ways.

- Click the **New Slide** icon on
  the toolbar.

- Select **New Slide** in the
  **Insert** menu.

- Select **New Slide** on the
  **Common Tasks** toolbar, if it
  is displayed.

- Use the keyboard shortcut,
  **Ctrl + M.**

The New Slide window opens.

As you have already used a **Title** slide, a
new slide layout called **Bulleted List** has
already been selected for you in the **Choose
an AutoLayout** panel.

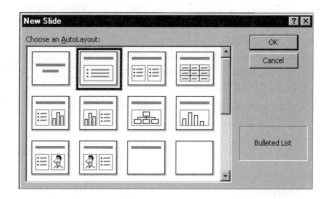

(You can choose a different layout later, if
you wish, when you are making up your
own presentations by clicking the
AutoLayout you want.)

- Click **OK** to add the new **Bulleted List**
  slide.

- The new slide appears with spaces for a
  title and text.

- Type the same title as before in the title
  space, **Broadstar Technologies Inc.**

The next step is to add some text in the form
of a **bulleted list**.

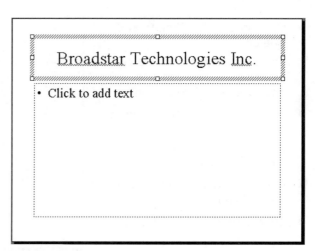

## 2.4   Bullets and Numbering

A **bullet point** is a short piece of text with a bullet – a black spot (•) – in front of it to catch the eye, as used in this manual.  PowerPoint adds the bullets automatically.

Note that automatic numbering is only available in Office 2000.  To make a numbered list in Office 97 or earlier versions, you must type the numbers manually.

For now, you will enter a set of simple bullet points.  Under the title you have just entered, there is a space where the bullet points will be added.

- Click in the **Click to add text** box.
  As before, the text is cleared and you can type your own.
  Notice that the first bullet is already in place.

  • Click to add text

- Type the items on the right and press the **Return** key after each line, *except the last*.
  Pressing the **Return** key moves to a new line and adds a bullet for the text that is to follow.

  **Operations**
  **Sales**
  **Customer**
  **Support**
  **Training**
  **Research**

The second slide has now been completed.

You can select numbering instead of bullets in Office 2000 in two ways.

**Start with a bulleted list:**

- When the first bullet appears on the slide, press the **Backspace** key to delete it.

- Type the number one (1) followed by a full stop or a bracket.

- Type the text you want and press **Return**.
  The numbering continues automatically.

**Use the buttons on the toolbar:**

- Click the **Numbering** button on the toolbar.

- To use bullets or to change back to bullets from Numbering, click the **Bullets** button.

If the Bullets and Numbering buttons do not appear on the toolbar, display them as follows.

- Click the chevrons beside the **Common Tasks** button at the right of the toolbar (arrowed in the illustration).
  A selection of extra buttons is displayed.

- Click on the **Numbering** or **Bullets** button as required.
  The buttons will then appear on the toolbar.

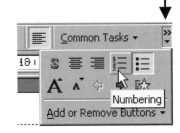

Bullets can be of different shapes, sizes and styles for different effects.
Select **Bullet** (or **Bullets and Numbering**) in the **Format** menu to make your own choices.

Formatting Bullets and Numbering is described in detail in Module 3, Section 12, page 175.

## 2.5    Master Slides

The fonts and formatting that you want to appear on all the slides can be set on a **Slide Master**. These will then be reproduced automatically on the other slides.  You can also set the background and add text, graphics or images.

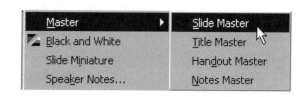

- Select **Master** in the **View** menu and then **Slide Master** in the sub-menu.
  A blank master slide is displayed.

Click in the text in the **Autolayout** areas and set the font, size, colour and so on in the usual way, or right-click in the Autolayout area to display a menu of options.

Text that you want to appear on every slide must be placed in a text box on the slide.

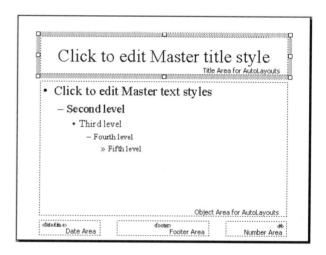

Graphics, images and autoshapes may be placed on the slide using **Insert**, **Copy** and **Paste**, and the **Drawing** toolbar functions. Be careful to leave space for the content of the other slides.

Header and footer information may be entered by selecting **Header and Footer** in the **View** menu.

Click the Master **Close** button or the **Slide View** button to return to the normal window.

- Look also at the other Master options for **Titles**, **Handouts** and **Notes**.

## 2.6    Inserts

Many different items can be inserted on individual or master slides.  You can add text, spreadsheets, tables, charts and other graphics.

Very often you can use **Cut** or **Copy and Paste** for text, graphics and other objects in the same way as you would in other applications.

For a wider choice of options, you can use the **Insert** menu.

Click **Insert** on the **Menu** bar to display the options available.  Many have sub-menus listing further options. Some of them are illustrated here.

**Insert Picture** allows you to import **Clip Art** from the Microsoft Office collection or other graphics you have saved on disk (Use **From File**), among others.

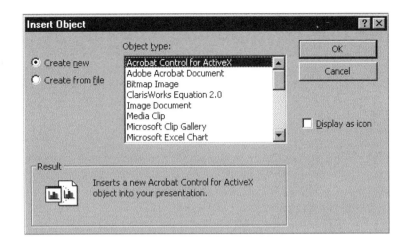

The **Insert Object** option gives yet further choices.

With this range of choices, there should be no difficulty in making your PowerPoint presentations interesting and attractive.

## 2.7    Deleting Text and Images

Text can be deleted from a slide in the usual ways as used in Word Processing.  Generally, select the text you want to delete and press the **Delete** key.

To delete an image, graphic or other object, first click on it to select it.  Then press the **Delete** key.

## 2.8    Deleting Slides

To delete a single slide, first select the slide you want to delete.

- Select **Delete Slide** in the **Edit** menu.

To delete several slides, select **Slide Sorter** or **Outline View** (See Section 4.1, page 302).

- Hold down the **Shift** key while you click the slides in turn.
- Click **Delete Slide** in the **Edit** menu.

Module 6

# Section 3    Saving, Closing and Opening

## 3.1    Saving a Presentation

When you start to create a presentation, it is good practice to **save** it from the beginning and at regular intervals as you proceed. If a problem occurs, any unsaved work may be lost and you will have to start all over again. If you save after preparing each slide, you will only lose one slide in the event of a major problem occurring.

To save a presentation for the first time, do one of the following.

- Select **Save** from the **File** menu.

- Click the **Save** button on the toolbar.

- Press **Ctrl + S** on the keyboard.

Whichever you choose, the **Save** window appears. (The Office 2000 **Save As** window is illustrated in Module 2, Section 3.8, page 81.)

- Type a name for the presentation in the **File Name** box.

  PowerPoint automatically assigns the extension **.ppt** to the file name.

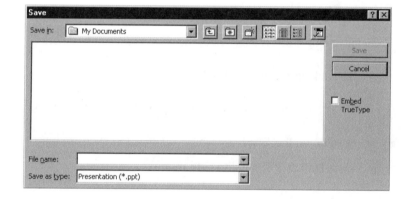

- Click in the **Save in** box to select a suitable location for the presentation.

- If necessary, click the **New Folder** button to save the presentation in a new folder.

- Click the **OK** button.

The **Save** procedure is described in more detail in Module 2, Section 4, page 84.

## 3.2    Saving in Other Formats

A PowerPoint presentation is normally saved as a presentation but it can be saved in several other different formats, if required. You can, for example, save the presentation as a **template** that you can use later to prepare similar presentations without having to set up everything from the beginning.

Current versions of PowerPoint allow presentations to be saved in **HTML**, a format for use on the World Wide Web. See Module 2, Section 4.9, page 88 for information on saving for the World Wide Web.

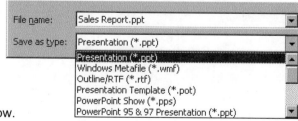

- Click in the **Save as type** box in the **Save** window.

- Select the format you require from the menu.

## 3.3    Saving Again

When you have named the file and saved it on disk, you can save any further additions or changes without having to go through the whole Save procedure again.  Use one of the following methods.

- Click the **Save** button on the Toolbar.

- Select **Save** in the **File** menu.

- Press **Ctrl** + **S** on the keyboard.

Save

## 3.4    Closing a Presentation

A presentation can be closed at any time.  You can close the presentation only and leave PowerPoint open, or you can close both.  To close a presentation, follow these steps.

- Click anywhere on the presentation you want to close.

- Select **Close** in the **File** menu or press **Ctrl** + **F4** on the keyboard.

- If you have made any changes since you last saved, a window appears asking you if you want to save the changes.

- Click **Yes** or **No** as you require.  If you click **Cancel**, no action is taken and you are returned to the presentation.

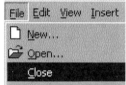

   When you close a presentation in Office 2000, the Office Assistant may ask you whether or not you want to save the changes.

## 3.5    Opening a Presentation

To open an existing presentation:

- Select **Open** in the **File** menu.
- Click the **Open** button on the toolbar.
- Press **Ctrl** + **O** on the keyboard.

Whichever you choose, the **Open** window appears (see Module 2, Section 4.12, page 90, for the Office 2000 **Open** window.)

- Click in the **Look in** box and select from the menu the location in which the file is stored.

- Select the folder in which the file was saved.
  A list of the presentations in the folder is displayed.

- Click once on the file you want to open.  The first slide appears in the preview area on the right.

- Double-click on the file or click it once and then click the **Open** button.

## 3.6    Finding a Presentation

If you forget where you saved a file, PowerPoint can help you find it.

- Click the **Open** button on the toolbar or use one of the other methods, as before.
  (Only the lower part of the Open window is displayed in the illustration above.)

- In the **Look in** box at the top of the window, find the location in which you want to search, the **My Documents** folder or the hard disk (**C:**), for example.

- Type the file name or other information in the box or boxes at the bottom of the **Open** window.

- Click **Find Now**.

In Office 2000, the process is similar, but more options are available.

- Click the **Open** button on the toolbar or use one of the other methods, as before.
  The Open window appears.

- Click the **Tools** button at the top right of the window and select **Find** in the sub-menu that appears.

- The **Find** window opens (only the lower part is shown below).

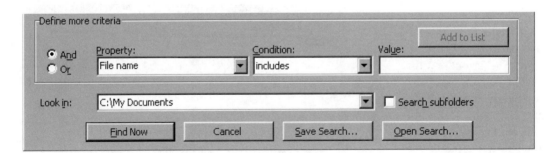

The **Look in** box is at the bottom of the **Find** window.  Find the location in which you want to search.  The **My Documents** folder is shown here.

The **Define more criteria** panel allows for detailed searching.  To find a presentation with AGM in the name, type AGM in the **Value** box.  The three boxes then read, from left to right, 'File name includes AGM'.

For other searches, select from the menus in the **Property** and **Condition** boxes and type a suitable value in the **Value** box.

Click the **Find Now** button when you have made your choices.

## 3.7    File Information

Information on PowerPoint presentations can be obtained in the same way as for any other files.

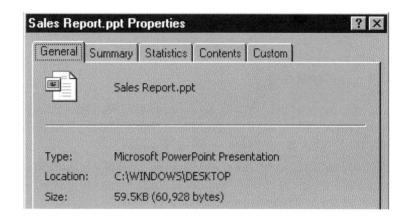

- Open the PowerPoint presentation.

- Select **Properties** in the **File** menu.

  The Properties window opens.

- Click the tabs at the top of the window to display further information.

## Exercise  3A

Your task is to make a 3-slide presentation on the company, International Computing.

1    Use **International Computing** as the title on all three slides.

2    Type the following address on the first slide:

> **15 Long Street**, **Sydney**.
> **Tel: 2677777 Fax: 2677778**
> **info@ic.au**
> **www.ic.com**

3    Use different fonts to give an attractive appearance.

4    Type the following on slide two:

> **IC offers:**
>
> 1  **Professional Networks**
> 2  **Internet Access**
> 3  **E-mail Accounts**

5    Type the following on slide three:

> **Make the most of our facilities.**
> **Call us for further information.**

6    Save the presentation, using your own name, e.g. **Paul**

7    Close the presentation (do not close PowerPoint).

8    Open the presentation again.

9    Modify the text in any way you wish to improve its appearance.

10    Save the presentation again.

Module 6

# Section 4     Slide Shows

## 4.1     Controls

You can run your slide show at any time to see your presentation taking shape.  There are five small control buttons at the lower left-hand corner of the screen.

Control Buttons

The buttons are used to alter the view of the slide and allow editing of individual slides.   At present you are in **Slide View**: the button on the left is selected.  The views available are:

- **Slide View**     displays individual slides.  You can prepare or edit the slide in this view.

Slide View

- **Outline**     makes it easier for you to see the overall organisation of your presentation.

Outline

- **Slide Sorter**     displays 'thumbnail' versions of the slides which you can rearrange easily.

Slide Sorter

- **Notes View**     displays each slide on a page with space for Speaker's notes to be added underneath.

    The notes pages can be printed out as an aid for the presenter.  (See Section 10.1, page 320.)

Notes View

(Normal View in Office 2000)

- **Slide Show**     hides the PowerPoint window and starts the presentation, displaying the slides on the full screen.

Slide Show

## 4.2     Viewing a Presentation

You can view a slide show at any time to see how the presentation looks.

To view a slide show, do the following.

- Open the presentation you want to view.
- Click the **Slide Show** button at the bottom of the screen.

    The first slide in the presentation appears, full screen, as it would in a slide show.

Slide Show

- To display the next slide, click the left mouse button.

    *Alternatively*, press the right **arrow** key or the **Page Down** key.

- Use the left **arrow** key or the **Page Up** key to display the previous slide.
- To quit the slide show, press the **Escape** key.

You can start a slide presentation with any slide, not just the first one.

- Click the **Slide Sorter** button to display the slides.
- Select the slide you want to start with by clicking on it.
- Click the **Slide Show** button to begin the presentation with the selected slide.

Slide Sorter

## 4.3   On-Screen Assistance

An **on-screen menu** is available to assist the presenter during a slide presentation.  Click the **semi-transparent button** at the bottom left-hand corner of the screen to reveal the menu.

The semi-transparent button

If the button is not visible, move the cursor down to the corner first. Alternatively, right-click anywhere on the slide.

The menu items are generally self-explanatory but note the following.

- **Meeting Minder** allows the presenter to insert notes that are saved with the slide.  (Click Meeting Minder again to display them.)

- **Speaker Notes** allows similar notes to be inserted, which then appear on the **Notes** pages.

  The Speaker's Notes can be displayed and/or amended at any time during the presentation.

- The **Pen** allows you to draw on the slides.

- The **Slide Meter** displays information on the timing of the presentation.

## 4.4   Slide Transitions

PowerPoint can add **slide transitions** to vary the way in which one slide follows another.

You can specify two settings for a transition, the **effect** and the **timing.**

The **effect** will apply when changing from the previous slide to the current slide.

The **timing** will apply from the current slide to the next slide.

To apply a slide transition, follow these steps.

- Display the slide to which you want to add a transition.

- Select **Slide Transition** in the **Slide Show** menu.

  The Slide Transition window appears.

- Click in the box in the **Effect** panel – showing **No Transition** in the illustration – to display a list of effects.

- Click on an effect in the list to see it demonstrated in the panel above.

- Click the **Slow**, **Medium** or **Fast** button underneath to set the desired speed for the transition.

- **On mouse click** is already selected in the **Advance** panel.  This means that the transition will not take place until you click the mouse button.

- Click **Automatically after** to cause the transition to occur after a certain time.  Type the required number of seconds in the **seconds** box.

- To select a sound to accompany the transition, select a sound from the **Sound** list.

- Click the **Apply** button for this slide only or **Apply to All** for all the slides.

- Click the **Slide Show** button to see the transition in practice.

Slide Show

# 4.5    Animation

PowerPoint has many features that can add simple animation to the text and graphics of your slides. This is what to do.

- Display the slide to which you want to add the animation.
  In this case, we will use a text slide with a bulleted list of four items.

- Select the bullet point to which you want to add the animated feature.
  (Click, hold down the button on the mouse, and drag over the text.)

Animation

- Click the **Animation** button on the toolbar.
  **The Animation Effects** Toolbar appears.
  Move the cursor over a button to display a description of the effect.

- Click on one of the **Animation** buttons on the toolbar.
  The effect will apply to whatever bullet point is highlighted.

- Close the Animation Effects Toolbar if you do not want to apply any other animations.

- Now, when you run your slide show, the bullet point will only appear – with the animation you have chosen – when you click the mouse button.

# 4.6    Custom Animation

Further effects are available when you click the **Custom Animation** button on the Animation Effects Toolbar.  The Custom Animation window opens.

Click the tabs in the centre of the window to display options for **Timing**, **Effects**, **Chart Effects** and **Play Settings**.  (In Office 2000, **Timing** is changed to **Order and Timing**.)

Custom Animation

Experiment to find out how you might use these to make your slides more effective.

Click the **Timing** (or **Order and Timing**) tab, for example, and set a piece of text or a graphic to appear on the slide after a certain time has elapsed.

Be aware, however, that over-use of transitions and animations has an irritating effect on the viewer. An effective presentation uses the many facilities that are available sparingly and tellingly.

In Office 2000, slides with animations are displayed in Slide Sorter view with an animation icon underneath.

# Section 5    Text and Text Boxes

## 5.1    Text Boxes

Text is not typed directly onto a slide but into a **text box** on the slide.  When you click on text on a slide, a 'sloping line' border appears around the text box in which the text appears.  It indicates the position and size of the text box.

Inserting Text

A text box is like a graphic in that it can be moved, resized and positioned anywhere on the slide.

When you click on the *border* of a text box, or on one of the handles, the border becomes a 'dotted' border, indicating that it can now be moved or resized.

Drag the **border** of the text box (between the handles) to move the box.  Drag a **handle** to resize it.  When a text box is resized, the size of the text in the box does not change. PowerPoint wraps text automatically, as needed, to fit in the text box, but the text box may have to be resized to display it all.

Drag to resize.

Drag to move box.

To delete a text box, select it (so handles appear around it), and then press the **Delete** key.

## 5.2    Formatting Text Boxes

The text boxes that appear on slides usually have no border or shading.  This means that the text appears to have been typed directly on the slide with nothing to indicate that it is actually in a box.  If you wish, you can add borders and shading to text boxes.

- Select the text box to which you want to add a border or shading by clicking on its border.  (Click on the text first to display the border.)

- Select **AutoShape (Placeholder** in Office 2000) at the bottom of the **Format** menu.
  The **Format AutoShape** window appears.
  Notice that **No Fill** and **No Line** are specified.

- To fill the text box with colour, click in the **Colour** box and select a colour from the palette that appears.

- To add a line border to the text box, first select a colour for the line and then select from the other options in the **Line** panel.

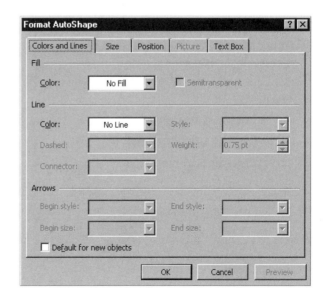

A text box that you insert on a slide *yourself* will appear as **Text Box** (rather than AutoShape or Placeholder) in the **Format** menu and the window will appear as the **Format Text Box** window.

## 5.3    Formatting Text in a Text Box

Text in a text box can be edited or changed in the same way as you would edit or change it in a Word Processing Application.  You can change the font, size, style and so on by using the menus and buttons on the toolbars.

Further font options are available in the **Format** menu.  First click anywhere in the text to select the text box.

- Select  **Font** in the **Format** menu.

- The Font window opens.

  Here you can set the font, size and style, effects such as **Shadow** and **Emboss**, as well as **Superscript** and **Subscript**.

  The text **Colour** can also be set.

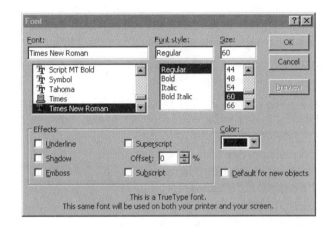

- When you drag over text to select it, PowerPoint selects whole words.

  To select individual characters, select **Options** in the **Tools** menu.  Then select **Automatic Word Selection** to turn it off.

  Then click **OK**.

- **Insert**, **Delete**, **Cut**, **Copy** and **Paste** text as you would in a Word Processing Application.

## 5.4    Text Alignment and Case

When you first type text, it is set against the left edge of the text and is single-line spaced.  To change the paragraph alignment, do the following.

Alignment buttons

- Select the paragraph you want to align by clicking anywhere in it.

- Click the appropriate **Alignment** button on the toolbar.

  *Alternatively*, select **Alignment** in the **Format** menu.  The Alignment sub-menu appears.

  Click **Left, Center, Right** or **Justify** to align the paragraph as desired.

  Note the keyboard shortcuts in the Alignment sub-menu:

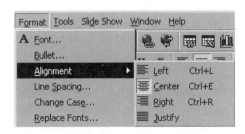

     **Ctrl + L** for left alignment

     **Ctrl + R** for right alignment

     **Ctrl + E** for centred text

To change the case of text without having to type it all out again, do the following.

- Select the text you want to change.

- Select **Change Case** in the **Format** menu.

- Click to select the format you require.

- Click **OK**.

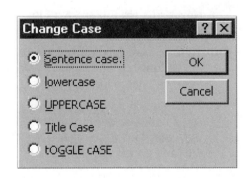

## 5.5    Line Spacing

To change the line spacing in a paragraph, first click in the paragraph in question.  Alternatively, select all the paragraphs if there are more than one.

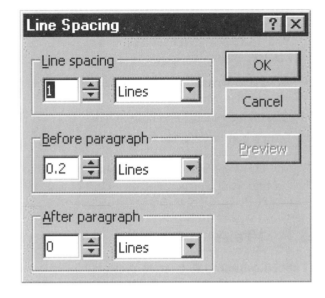

- Select **Line Spacing** in the **Format** menu.

  The Line Spacing window appears.

- **Line spacing** controls the space between the lines in a paragraph.

  - Click in the right-hand box to select either **Lines** or **Points** as the unit of measurement.  Points allow finer control over the spacing.

  - Set the number of Lines or Points in the left-hand box.

- **Before paragraph** controls the space *between* a paragraph and the paragraph that comes *before* it.

  Set your preferences as for line spacing.

- **After paragraph** controls the space *between* a paragraph and the paragraph that *follows* it.

  Set your preferences as for Line spacing.

- Click **OK**.  Your line and paragraph spacing choices are applied.

---

**Lines** or **Points**?

The menus that appear let you set the line spacing in either lines or points.  A **line** is the current line height, based on the text size in use.  Spacing can be set in full lines or half lines.  **Points** are the preferred unit used by designers and printers to measure text.  There are 72 points to an inch so much finer spacing is possible.

---

## 5.6    Using WordArt

**WordArt** is a program for manipulating text as graphic objects.  Text can be angled, stretched, coloured, and so on to give various effects.

To insert a WordArt object into a slide, perform the following steps.

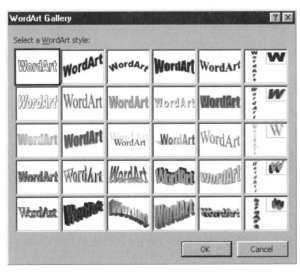

- Display the slide on which you want the WordArt object placed.

- Click on the **WordArt** button on the **Drawing** Toolbar.

  *Alternatively*, select **Picture** in the **Insert** menu and **WordArt** in the sub-menu.

  The WordArt Gallery window appears.

- Click on a style to select it.

- Click **OK**.

  The **Edit WordArt Text** window appears.

- Click in the box containing **Your Text Here**. **Your Text Here** is removed and you can then type your own text.

  Notice the font menus and buttons at the top of the window. Use them to select a different **font**, **size** or **style**.

- Click **OK**.

  Your text appears on the slide in the selected style.

- Move or resize the WordArt graphic as you would any other graphic.

  Click in the graphic and drag to move it.

  Drag a handle to resize it.

To edit the WordArt object at any time, double-click it to display the WordArt Toolbar and text entry box. Make your changes, and then click outside the WordArt object.

## 5.7   Tabs

**Tabbed columns** can be used to display information in a presentation. For example, you may use tabs to create a list as shown in the illustration.

To set the tabs for such a list, perform the following steps.

- Click anywhere in the text box for which you want to set the tabs.

- If you have already typed text in the text box, select the text.

- Select **Ruler** in the **View** menu to display the ruler at the top of the window.

- Click on the **Tab** button in the upper left corner of the window until you see the tab you require.

Broadstar Technologies Inc.

| Distribution of Employees | | | |
|---|---|---|---|
| Operations | 94 | 57 Male | 37 Female |
| Support | 78 | 25 Male | 53 female |
| Training | 62 | 30 Male | 32 Female |
| Research | 57 | 25 Male | 27 Female |

| | |
|---|---|
| **L** | Aligns the left of the text against the tab. |
| **⊥** | Centres the text on the tab. |
| **⌐** | Aligns the right of the text against the tab. |
| **⊥·** | Aligns the tab on a decimal point, as in numbers and prices. |

- Click on each place on the ruler where you want to set the selected tab.

  You can set different types of tabs at different positions.

- To change the position of an existing tab, **drag** it along the ruler to its new position.

  If you have first selected the text governed by the tab, the text will automatically follow the tab to the new position.

- To **delete** a tab, drag it off the ruler.

- To remove the ruler, select **Ruler** in the **View** menu again.

## 5.8    Checking Spelling

Spelling can be checked in a
similar way to checking
spelling in other applications.

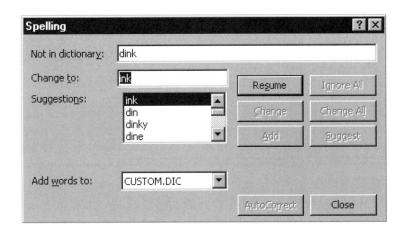

- Click the **Spelling** button on
  the toolbar.

  *Alternatively*, select
  **Spelling** in the **Tools** menu.
  The Spelling window opens.

- Make any corrections or
  changes in the usual way.

## Exercise  5A

Your task is to make a three-slide presentation on the Millennium Museum.

**1**    Use **Arial** font on all three slides.

**2**    Use the same title **The History Museum** on all three slides.

**3**    Use WordArt to style the appearance of the title.

**4**    Type the following text on the first slide. Use tabs or a table to create the text.

| | | |
|---|---|---|
| **Permanent Collections** | **Tues – Sun** | **13.00 – 16.00** |
| **Special Exhibitions** | **Tues – Sat** | **10.00 – 16.00** |
| **Library** | **Tues – Fri** | **10.00 – 16.00** |

**5**    Type the following text on the second slide.

**Entry:**

| | |
|---|---|
| **Adults** | **£3.50** |
| **Children up to 16** | **Free** |
| **Senior Citizens** | **£2.00** |
| **Students** | **£2.00** |

**6**    Use animation effects as you wish to display the entry fees.

**7**    Type the following text on slide three.

**Exhibitions**

| | |
|---|---|
| **Vikings** | **12 Jan – 30 Mar** |
| **Medieval Crafts** | **16 Feb – 14 Apr** |
| **Ancient Egypt** | **13 Jun – 15 Nov** |

**8**    Arrange the list of exhibitions to fit neatly on the page.

**9**    Add transitions between the slides.

**10**    Save the presentation.

**11**    Use the Slide Show function to display the presentation.

# Section 6    Colours and Backgrounds

## 6.1    Colour Schemes and Backgrounds

PowerPoint simplifies the use of colour by providing a set of pre-set **Color Schemes**. These are sets of professionally selected colours designed to be used as the principal colours in a presentation. Each colour scheme controls the colour of the background, lines, text, shadows, fills and other items on a slide. Using one of these colour schemes ensures that your presentation will look appealing and professional.

**Backgrounds** can be simple colours or special designs that control the way the colour is used on a slide. For example, you can select a background design that spreads the colour out from the upper left corner to the rest of the slide.

You can select a colour scheme and background for the master slide (which controls all the slides in the presentation), for the current slide or for all slides in the presentation (thus overriding the master slide). The following sections explain how to select and manipulate colour schemes and backgrounds.

## 6.2    Selecting a Colour Scheme

You can select a colour scheme for one slide or for all the slides in your presentation. Be careful when selecting a colour scheme for a single slide in the presentation. You don't want one slide to clash with the rest.

As you will see later, you can apply the new colour scheme to one or all of the slides.

Perform the following steps.

- Display or select the slide whose colour scheme you want to change.

- Select **Slide Color Scheme** in the **Format** menu.
  The Color Scheme window appears.

- Click the Colour Scheme you want, to select it.

- Click the **Apply** button to apply the scheme to the selected slide.

- Click the **Apply to All** button to apply the scheme to all the slides.

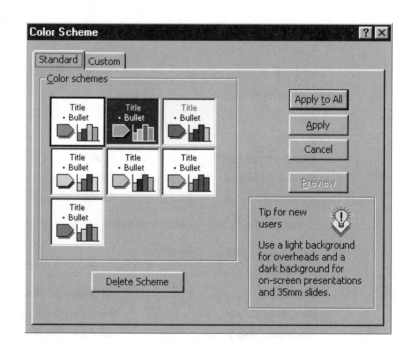

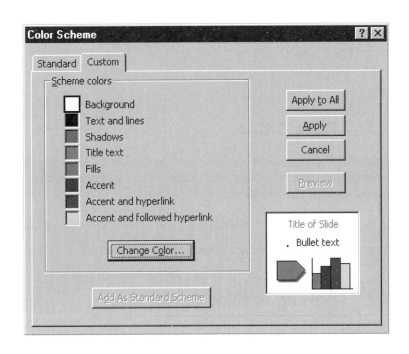

To make your own colour scheme, click the **Custom** tab and select from the options displayed.

You can apply your selection to one slide or to them all, as before.

For further choices, click the **Change Color** button. This allows you to select from a much wider range of colours.

## 6.3    Background Designs

An effective background design can add a professional look to your presentation.  To change the background or to modify an existing background, perform the following steps.

- Display or select the slide whose background you want to change.

- Select **Apply Design** in the **Format** menu.  (**Apply Design Template** in Office 2000)
  The Apply Design window appears.

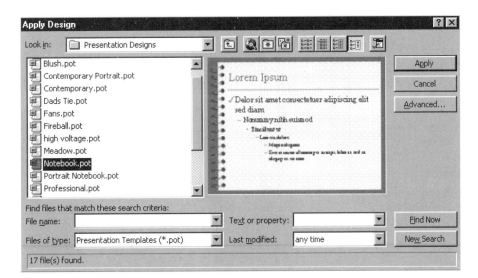

- Click on one of the designs in the list on the left, to select it.  (The designs available may vary between different versions of Office.)
  A preview appears in the panel on the right.

- When you have selected a suitable design, click the **Apply** button.
  The design is applied to all the slides.

# Section 7      Rearranging Slides

## 7.1     Slide Order

There may be times when you will need to change the sequence of slides in a presentation.  In PowerPoint, you can re-order the slides in either **Slide Sorter** view or **Outline** view.

Slide Sorter

- In **Slide Sorter** view, drag a slide to place it in a different place in the order.

- In **Outline** view, drag the slide to its new position.

Outline

## 7.2     Sorting in Slide Sorter View

**Slide Sorter View** shows miniature versions of the slides in the presentation.  This allows you to view many of your slides at one time.

To rearrange the slides in Slide Sorter View, proceed as follows.

- Click the **Slide Sorter** view button.
  *Alternatively*, select **Slide Sorter** in the **View** menu.

- Click on the slide that you want to move.

- Hold down the mouse button and drag the slide to its new position between two other slides.

  As you drag the slide, a vertical line appears between the slides to show its present position.

- Release the mouse button in the new location.

- The other slides are moved and the selected slide appears in its new position.
  The slides are automatically renumbered.

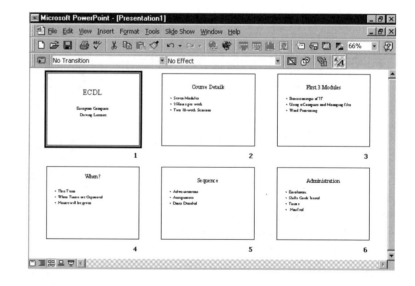

- The **Slide Sorter Toolbar** allows you to apply transitions and effects to the slides.

## 7.3     Copying Slides

You can copy a slide in **Slide Sorter View** as easily as you can move a slide.

- Click on the slide you want to copy.

- Hold down the **Ctrl** key and drag the slide to where you want the copy to appear.

- When you release the mouse button, a *copy* of the slide appears in the new position.

- **Cut**, **Copy** and **Paste** can also be used to copy slides.

## 7.4    Sorting in Outline View

In **Outline View**, a small icon represents each slide in list form, with the title and text beside it.  This gives you a clear picture of the content and organisation of your presentation.  Because of this, you may prefer to rearrange your slides in Outline View.

Proceed as follows.

- Click the **Slide Outline** view button.
  Alternatively, select **Slide Sorter** in the **View** menu.

- Click on the **numbered slide icon** – *not* on the text – that you want to move.
  The icon and the slide contents are highlighted.

- Hold down the mouse button and drag the slide up or down over the other slides.
  As you drag the slide, a line appears showing its present position.

- Release the mouse button in the new location.

- The other slides are moved and the selected slide appears in its new position.
  The slides are automatically renumbered.

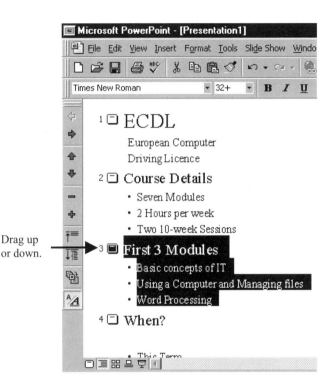

Drag up or down.

## 7.5    Moving Information

When you only want to move information from one slide to another, you don't have to move an entire slide.  You can move the contents – text or graphics – of one slide to another by selecting only what you want to move and dragging it to its new location.

- Click the **Slide Outline** view button.
  Alternatively, select **Outline** in the **View** menu.

- Select the item you want to move.

- Click the **Move Up** or **Move Down** buttons in the Outlining Toolbar as in the illustration.
  The selected item is moved within its own slide or, if you continue, to the next slide.

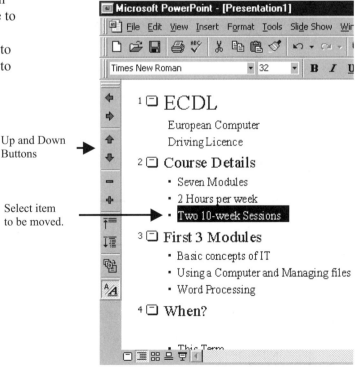

Up and Down Buttons

Select item to be moved.

## 7.6    Hidden Slides

Before you give a presentation, you should try to anticipate questions from your audience and be prepared to answer them. It is possible to create slides to support your answers and then keep them hidden until you need them. You can hide slides in **Slide**, **Outline**, or **Slide Sorter** view.

To hide one or more slides, do the following.

- Display or select the slide you want to hide.

- Select **Hide Slide** in the **Slide Show** menu.

- In **Slide sorter** view, the number of the hidden slide appears, with a line through it, in a box beneath the slide.

Hidden slide number

To display a hidden slide during a presentation, do the following.

- Click the **semi-transparent** button at the bottom left on the slide *before* the hidden slide.

  Alternatively, right-click the slide *before* the hidden slide.

- Select **Go** in the menu that appears and then **Hidden Slide** in the sub-menu.

  The hidden slide is displayed.

The semi-transparent button

**Slide Navigator** allows you to display any hidden slide at any point during a presentation. You can also use it if **Hidden Slide** is not available in your version of Office. Proceed as follows.

- Right-click any slide in the presentation, or click the semi-transparent button at the bottom left of the current slide.

- Select **Slide Navigator** in the menu that appears.

  A list of slide numbers is displayed, with the numbers of hidden slides in brackets.

- Double-click the number of the hidden slide you want to display.

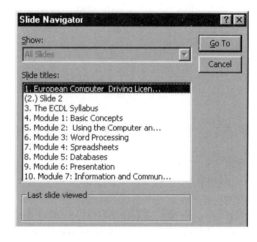

## 7.7    Numbering Slides

Slides can be numbered consecutively on the screen. This helps the presenter keep track of the progress of the presentation.

- Select **Headers and Footers** in the **View** menu to open the Header and Footer window.

- Click the **Slide number** box to place a tick in it.

  Notice the small **Preview** panel in which you can see where the number will appear on the slide. (Unclick **Date and Time** and **Footer** to see more clearly.)

- Click **Apply** to place a number on the selected slide or **Apply to All** to number all the slides.

- The **Date and Time** can be added, as well as a title or other text in the **Footer**.

- Click the **Notes and Handouts** tab to include information in notes and handouts.

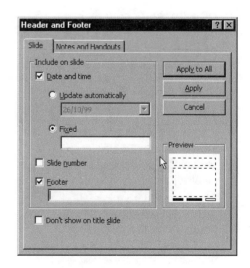

# Section 8    Graphics

## 8.1    Drawing Tools

The **Drawing Toolbar**, displayed along the bottom of the screen in **Slide View**, has a range of drawing tools which will help you to enhance your presentation graphically. Different kinds of lines, including freehand lines, and basic shapes such as boxes, circles and so on, can be drawn on slides.

The Drawing Toolbar is the same one that is available in other Office applications. The Drawing Toolbar and its functions are described in detail in Module 3, Section 9.7, page 164.

- If the Drawing Toolbar is not visible, select **Toolbars** in the **View** menu and then click **Drawing** in the list of toolbars.

## 8.2    Drawing a Line or Shape

The general procedure for drawing an object is the same, no matter which object you draw.

- Click the button on the **Drawing** toolbar for the line or shape you want to draw.

- Move the mouse pointer to where you want the line or one corner of the shape to begin.

- Hold down the mouse button and drag to draw the line or shape.

- Release the mouse button. The object appears on the page.

- To modify the line or shape, click one of the line buttons on the toolbar and choose from the menu that appears.

Line Buttons

## 8.3    Colour and Fill

The colour of a simple line or the outer line of a shape can be set or changed. You can also select a colour to fill a simple shape. Follow these steps.

- Select the line or shape.

- Click the **Menu** button beside the **Line Colour** icon on the Drawing Toolbar.

  A window showing available lines and colours appears.

- Select the colour you require.

- Notice that you can select **No Line** for a shape.

  No line is useful when you have filled the shape with a colour and you do not want to have a line around the edge.

- Line **width** and **pattern** can be set by clicking the appropriate buttons on the Drawing Toolbar.

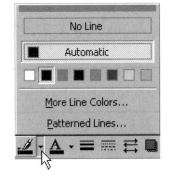

The procedure for filling a shape with colour is similar.

- Click the **Menu** button beside the **Fill Colour** icon on the Drawing Toolbar and select the colour you require.

Fill

## 8.4    Working with Objects

Working with objects in PowerPoint is the same as working with objects in other applications.
Here are some reminders.

- To **select** an object, click on it.

- To **delete** an object, select it and press the **Delete** key.

- To **move** an object, select it and drag it to its new position.

- To **resize** an object, select it and drag one of its handles.

- To **copy** an object, hold down the **Ctrl** key and drag to where you want the copy to appear.

- To **draw a uniform object** (a circle or square), hold down the **Shift** key while drawing.

- To draw an object starting from the centre rather than from a corner, hold down the **Ctrl** key while drawing.

- To **draw several objects** of the same shape, double-click on the tool.  It then remains selected while you draw the objects and saves you from having to go back to click on the tool for every new object.
  When you have drawn all the objects, click on the tool again to de-select it.

## 8.5    Text Boxes and WordArt

The Drawing Toolbar contains buttons for inserting
**Text Boxes** and **WordArt**.

Text Boxes are described in detail in Section 5, page 305.

WordArt is described in Section 5.6, page 307.

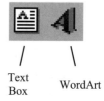

Text
Box          WordArt

## 8.6    Rotating an Object

Objects added to slides can be rotated for extra effect.

Rotate

- Select the object you want to rotate.

- Click the **Rotate** button on the **Drawing** Toolbar.
  Circular handles appear at the corners of the object.

- Drag one of the circular handles until the object is in the desired position.

- Release the mouse button.

## 8.7    Adding Text to an Object

Text can be added to objects on slides.

- Select the object in which you want the text to appear.

- Type the text.  As you type, the text appears in a single line across the object.

Various options can be applied, if required.

- Select **AutoShapes** in the **Format** menu.  Click the **Text Box** tab in the window.

- Select any required options and click **OK**.

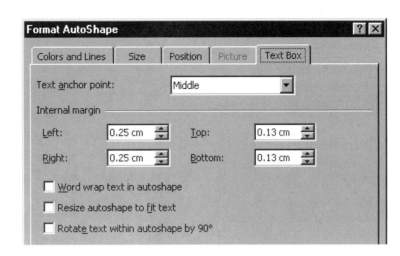

## 8.8    Adding Clip Art

There are hundreds of Clip Art images supplied with PowerPoint that you can use in your presentation.

To insert a Clip Art image on a slide, do the following.

Insert
Clip Art

- In **Slide View**, display the slide on which you want to insert the Clip Art image.

- Click the **Insert Clip Art** button on the toolbar.
  *Alternatively*, select **Picture** in the **Insert** menu and then **Clip Art** in the sub-menu.
  The Microsoft Clip Gallery window opens.

- In the **Category** list on the left, click to select a category.
  The images are displayed in the main part of the window.

- Click on the image you want to insert and then click the **Insert** button.

- Drag the image to position it on the slide and resize it, if necessary, by dragging a handle.

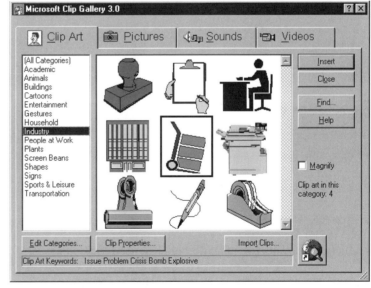

 Inserting Clip Art in Office 2000 is described in Module 3, Section 9.2, on page 162.

## 8.9    Changing Colours

If the colours on a Clip Art image clash with the colours in your presentation, you may want to change them.  Proceed as follows.

- Select the image.

- Select **Picture** in the **Format** menu.
  The Format Picture window opens.

- Click the **Picture** tab and then click the **Recolor** button.

- Click the colour in the **Original** list that you want to change.

- Click in the corresponding **New** box and select a new colour in the menu.

- Click **OK** and then **OK** in the **Format Picture** window.

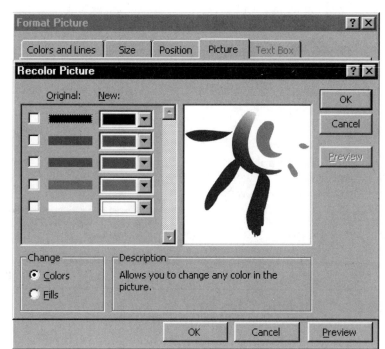

## Exercise  8A

1   Open the presentation on **The History Museum**.

2   Add appropriate Clip Art to the slides.

3   Insert a new slide.

4   Select a Design Template and apply it to all four slides.

5   Type the title on the new slide: **The History Museum**.

6   Use the drawing tools to draw a sketch of the location of the museum (it doesn't have to be based on reality) in relation to a train station, bus stop and taxi rank.  Indicate street names.

7   Save the presentation.

# Section 9     Multimedia

## 9.1     Adding Sound and Video

Multimedia elements such as sound, music and video files can be added to PowerPoint presentations.

To add a sound to a slide, do the following.

- Display the slide to which you want to apply the sound.

- Select **Movies and Sounds** in the **Insert** menu.
  A sub-menu displays a list of choices.

- Click on **Sound from Gallery** to add a sound from the Clip Art gallery (if there are any in the gallery).

- Select **Sound from File** if the file is stored elsewhere.

- To record your own sound, click **Record Sound**.

- Click **Movie from Gallery** or **Movie from File** as appropriate to add a **Video** clip.

# Section 10    Output and Printing

## 10.1    Output Options

A PowerPoint presentation can be used in a variety of ways.

**On-screen presentations** can be given on a computer screen or projected onto a large screen with the aid of a data projector.

**Notes and handouts** can be printed for distribution to the audience, either as slides alone or with space for notes.  Slides can be printed with one or more slides to the page.

**Speaker's notes** can also be printed to aid the presenter.  A reduced copy of the slide is printed at the top of the page with the speaker's notes underneath.  (Select **Notes Page** in the **View** menu.)  See Section 4.1, page 302 and Section 10.3, page 321.

**Overhead transparencies** can be printed on most printers for use on standard overhead projectors. It is important to use the correct transparency material for the type of printer you are using.  Laser printer transparency sheets will not absorb the ink from inkjet printers and inkjet material may cause damage to laser printers.  Transparency material must be inserted in the printer the right way up.

**35mm slides** for use with a 35mm slide projector can be prepared from PowerPoint presentations by service bureaux.

PowerPoint presentations can be made available for distribution on the **Internet**. (See Section 3.2, page 298.)

## 10.2    Page Setup

Before you begin the presentation or print out the slides or notes, you should check the **Page Setup** settings.

- Open the presentation you want to print from.

- Select **Page Setup** in the **File** menu.

  The Page Setup window appears.

- Select the type of printout you require in the **Slides sized for** menu.

- The **Orientation** for both the **Slides** and **Notes etc**. is already set but you can change it if necessary

- Set page numbering and sizes if you want to change the pre-selected settings.

- Click **OK**.

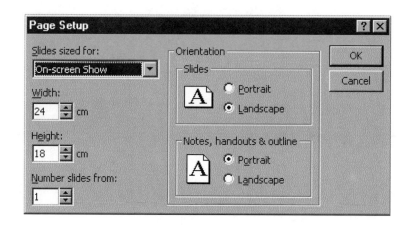

# 10.3   Printing

A presentation can be printed on paper in a variety of formats.

- Select **Print** in the **File** menu.

  The Print window appears.

- The printer currently in use appears in the Printer **Name** box.

  To select a different printer, click in the **Name** box and select the printer you want to use from the menu.

- In the **Print Range** area, you can select to print all the slides, the currently displayed slide or a selection of slides.

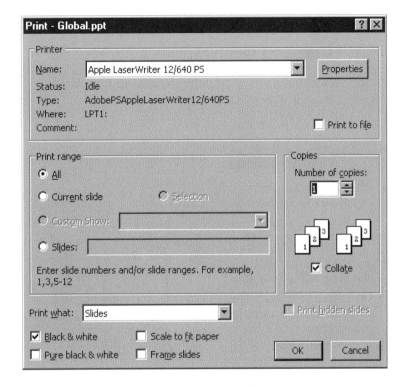

- Click in the **Print what** box to display a menu.

  Select what you want to print from the menu (slides, handouts, speaker's notes etc.)

  If you are printing handouts, select the number of slides to appear on each page.

- In the **Copies** area, specify the number of copies to be printed and other options, as necessary.

- Click the **OK** button to start printing.

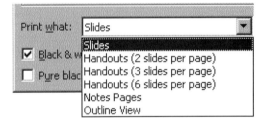

**Print what** Options

In Office 2000, the lower part of the Print window displays extra options. A **Handouts** panel allows for either horizontal or vertical order and displays how the slides will appear on the printed page.

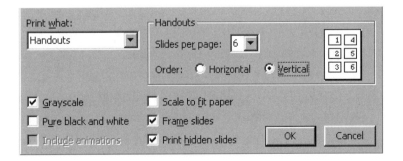

# Section 11    Adding Graphs

## 11.1    Creating Graphs

PowerPoint includes a program called **Microsoft Graph** that can help you prepare effective graphs (charts) for use in a presentation.

To create a chart, proceed as follows.

- Display the slide to which you want to add the chart.

- Click the **Insert Chart** button on the toolbar.

  *Alternatively,* select **Chart** in the **Insert** menu.

- A sample graph appears on the slide with a **Datasheet** window in front.

  The datasheet is like a small spreadsheet with rows, columns and cells.  It contains sample information.

  (You can move the datasheet from over the chart by dragging its title bar.)

Insert Chart

| School - Datasheet | | | A | B | C | D | |
|---|---|---|---|---|---|---|---|
| | | | 1st Qtr | 2nd Qtr | 3rd Qtr | 4th Qtr | |
| 1 | | East | 20.4 | 27.4 | 90 | 20.4 | |
| 2 | | West | 30.6 | 38.6 | 34.6 | 31.6 | |
| 3 | | North | 45.9 | 46.9 | 45 | 43.9 | |
| 4 | | | | | | | |

- Click on the cells in turn and enter your own information to replace what is there.

  The graph in the background adjusts automatically as you enter the information.

- When you have entered all the information, close the Datasheet window.

  The graph remains on the slide.

- **Position** and **resize** the graph on the slide, as required.

- To return to the slide, click anywhere outside the graph.

## 11.2    Editing a Graph

A graph you have inserted on a slide can be edited or changed at any time.

- Display the slide that contains the graph you want to edit.

- Double-click anywhere inside the graph.

  **Microsoft Graph** opens and displays the graph.

  *Alternatively,* Select **Chart Object** in the **Edit** men and either **Edit** or **Open** in the sub-menu.

- Replace or change the data in the **Datasheet** as required.

- When you have made the changes, close the Datasheet window and click anywhere outside the graph on the slide.

- To change the graph type, to a **Pie** or **Line** chart, for example, see the following Sections.

For more on charts, see Module 4, Section 6, page 226.

## 11.3   Working with Datasheets

To amend data on a chart, you first have to display the datasheet.

Do *one* of the following.

- Double-click on the chart to select it.

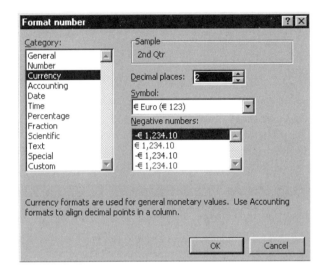

Show Datasheet

*Or*

- Click once on the chart to select it.
- Click the **Show Datasheet** button that appears on the toolbar.

*Or*

- Click once on the chart to select it.
- Select **Chart Object** in the **Edit** menu and either **Edit** or **Open** in the sub-menu.

The first row and the first column of the datasheet are reserved for titles by default. Numbers can be entered in all the other cells.

While the datasheet behaves like a spreadsheet, its functions are limited.  It is not possible to use formulas in the cells, for example.  You can, however, reformat the data if necessary.

- Select the cells that you want to reformat.

- Select **Number** in the **Format** menu. The **Format number** window appears.

In the illustration, the Euro currency format has been selected.  The font in selected cells can be formatted in a similar manner.

## 11.4   Chart Types

The chart type that appears by default when a chart is inserted on a slide is a column chart. It can display all the information in all the cells in the datasheet at the same time.

Not all charts are able to display all the information.  If you want to use a different kind of chart, be sure that the chart type you select is able to display information in the datasheet that you want it to show.

A pie chart, for example, would be unable to show all the information in the datasheet together.  It would only be able to display the information in the cells of one row only.

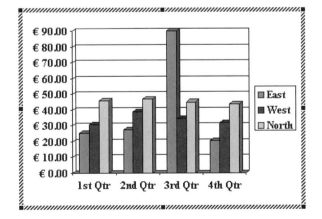

To make a graph using one column or one row in the datasheet, the other columns or rows can be deselected, leaving the rest of the data *live*.  To deselect a column or row, double-click the appropriate column or row header.   The chart is adjusted automatically to reflect the changes.

## 11.5   Modifying Datasheets

The following examples demonstrate how different graphs may be produced from selected data by modifying the datasheet.

The datasheet shows the data in column **B** as live, the other data having been de-selected by double-clicking the column headers.

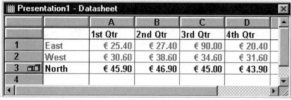

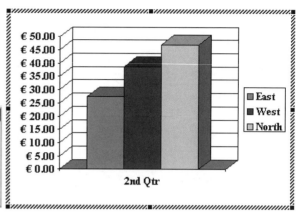

The graph displays the **2nd Qtr** data in column B.

This datasheet shows the data in row **3** as live.  The other data has been deselected by double-clicking the row headers.

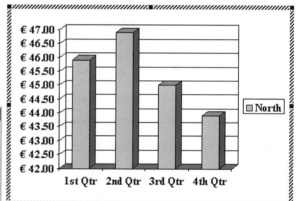

The chart displays the **North** data in row 3.

## 11.6   A Pie Chart

To change the graph type in the above example to a Pie chart, do the following.

- Select the chart and display the Datasheet.

- Select **Chart Type** in the **Chart** menu.
  The Chart Type window opens.

- Select **Pie** in the list of chart types and a sub-type in the sub type panel, if required.

- Click **OK**.
  The Pie Chart appears.

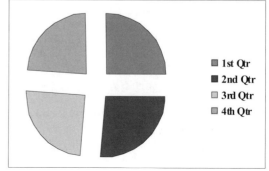

An 'exploded' Pie chart

# Section 12    Organisation Charts

## 12.1    Adding an Organisation Chart

New Slide

An **organisation chart** (**organisational chart** in Office 2000) can be used to show, for example, the management structure of an organisation.

To add a new slide with an Organisation Chart on it, do the following.

- Click the **New Slide** button on the toolbar.
  The New Slide window opens.

- Select the **Organisation Chart** slide (see illustration) and click **OK**.
  The new slide appears.

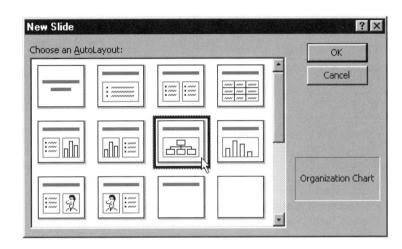

- Add a title to the slide, if required.

- Double-click in the lower box on the slide to add the chart.
  The Organisation Chart window opens (see next page).

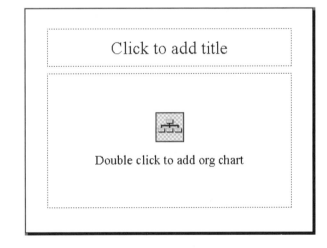

To add an Organisation Chart to an existing slide, do the following.

Display the slide on which you want to place the chart.

- Select **Object** in the **Insert** menu.
  The **Insert Object** window opens.

- Scroll through the **Object type** list and click **Microsoft Organization Chart 2.0**.

- Click **OK**.
  The Organisation Chart window opens.

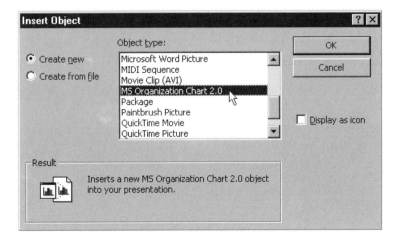

## 12.2   The Organisation Chart Window

Some boxes are displayed in the chart window containing sample text.  **Type name here** is already selected in the box at the top (which overlaps the box underneath temporarily).  We shall replace the sample text to illustrate the administrative structure of Broadstar Technologies.

- Type **Peter Johnson**.

  It replaces **Type name here** in the central box.

- Press **Return** and type **Managing Director**.

- Click in the box on the left.

  The three sub-ordinate boxes now appear under the Managing Director's box.

- Type **Maria Peters** to replace **Type name here** in the left-hand box.

- Press **Return** and type **Operations**.

- Repeat the previous two steps to enter **John Murphy**, **Support** and **Andrea Kenny**, **Training** in the other two boxes.

- Select **Chart Title** and replace it with **Broadstar Technologies Inc**.

- Click outside the boxes to see the completed chart.

- Select **Exit and Return to** in the chart window **File** menu (*not* the PowerPoint **File** menu) to return to the slide and insert the chart.

  (Click **Yes** to the **This Object has been changed** message.)

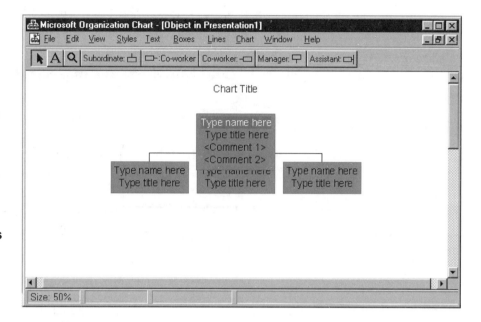

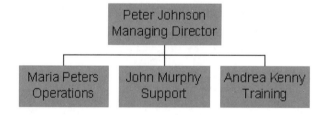

## 12.3   Editing an Organisation Chart

An Organisation Chart on a slide can be edited or changed at any time.

- Display the slide that contains the chart you want to change.

- Double-click the Organisation Chart.
  The chart window opens

- Make the changes that you require.

- Select **Exit and Return to** in the chart window **File** menu to return to the slide and insert the chart.  (Click **Yes** to the **This Object has been changed** message.)

## 12.4   Expanding the Chart

Buttons at the top of the Chart window make it easy to add extra boxes to the chart.  The icons and text on the buttons indicate the positions in which they can be added to an existing box.

The chart can be expanded before or after it is placed on the slide.  Start by adding a **Co-worker** box on the right for the **Research** manager.

- If the chart is on a slide, double-click the chart to re-open the Organisation Chart window.

- Click the right **Co-worker** button (arrowed) to select it.

  The cursor assumes the shape of the icon on the button.

  Note the small connecting line on the icon that indicates that this box can be added to an existing box on the left.

- Click in the **Andrea Kenny** box.

  A new box is added.

- Click in the new box and enter **Sarah Martin**, **Resources**.

- Click on the appropriate buttons and add other boxes as required.

- Select **Exit and Return to** in the chart window **File** menu to return to the slide and insert the revised chart.

  (Click **Yes** to the **This Object has been changed** message.)

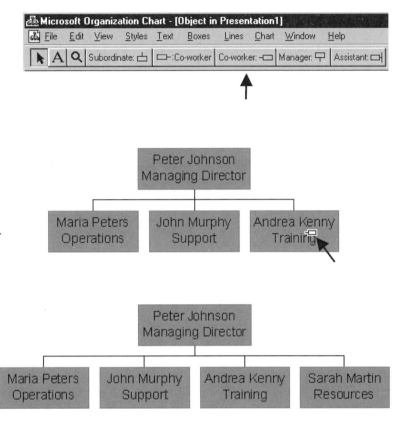

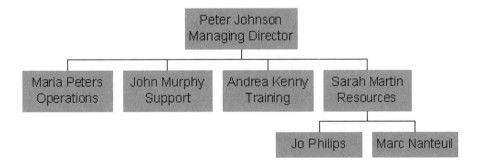

The chart expanded

# Section 13    Exercises

# Self Check Exercises

**1** What is the function of *slide transitions*?

- ☐ They enable the slide show to progress automatically.
- ☐ They facilitate the creation of animations between slides.

**2** Which of these icons would you select to use Word Art?

- ☐ 
- ☐ 
- ☐ 

**3** Which of these would you use to set uniform text formats in a set of slides?

- ☐ A Text Box
- ☐ An AutoLayout Area
- ☐ An AutoShape

**4** Which of these would you normally use to obtain a slide background?

- ☐ Insert Object
- ☐ Apply design
- ☐ Slide Sorter View
- ☐ Slide Transition

**5** Which two settings can be specified in the Transitions window?

- ☐ Effect
- ☐ Frequency
- ☐ Timing
- ☐ Size

**6** Is it possible to move text from one slide to another without using the normal copy/paste function?

- ☐ Yes
- ☐ No

**7** Having inserted a graphic from a Clip Art collection, is it possible to change the colours?

- ☐ Yes
- ☐ No

**8** Which tab icon is correctly matched to its function?

- ☐ ⌐ Aligns the left of the text to the tab.
- ☐ L Aligns the left of the text to the tab.
- ☐ ⊥ Centres the text on the page.

**9** Tick the icons that could be used to add a co-worker box to an organisation chart.

- ☐ 
- ☐ 
- ☐ 
- ☐ 
- ☐ 

**10** Is it correct to say that in a PowerPoint presentation, you may hide slides in a presentation sequence?

- ☐ Yes
- ☐ No

**11** Tick the items that can be animated.

- ☐ A slide
- ☐ A title
- ☐ Other text

**12** By pressing the keys **Ctrl** and **S** during your work, what function are you performing?

- ☐ Re-start
- ☐ Sort
- ☐ Save

Module 6

# Practical Exercises

## Exercise 1

Use the New Slide window to make the slide shown here.

## Exercise 2

Enhance the background as below, selecting the *High Voltage* design from the appropriate window.

## Exercise 3

Enhance the slide by inserting your company logo and animating the text as follows.

- Place your company logo on the slide.
- *Look good* appears on the slide first.
- *Looking good is…* appears second.

## Exercise 4

Create two more similar slides. Use the following text and insert the slide number in a footer.

Sound good.
Tell them what they want to hear.

Be good
V.F.M.
Quality
Backup
Reliability

## Exercise 5

Format all three slides as follows:

- Centre align all the titles.
- Left align the text in slides one and two.
- Bullet the text in slide three.

## Exercise 6

Create a Summary Slide as shown below.

The word IMAGE should appear five seconds after the slide has been first displayed.

## Exercise 7

Create a new slide titled, Make it good.

Insert a graph titled, *Why the Buyer Buys* and enter your own % numbers for each of the categories in the *Be good* slide.

Also, rearrange the slides so that the summary slide comes last.

## Exercise 8

Create the slide below which will be used to open a presentation on computer care and maintenance.

*Note: You should start with a blank presentation template.*

# Module 7

## Information
### and
## Communication

7

# Module 7

# Information and Communication

Module 7

Module 7

# Reference Table

Should you begin your studies with this module, it is important to note that related material is dealt with in other sections of the manual.  This reference list will assist you to locate the material conveniently.

| Skill | Task | Module | Page |
|---|---|---|---|
| **First Steps** | | | |
| | Save a new document | Module 2 | 84 |
| | Save changes to an existing document | Module 2 | 87 |
| | Close a document | Before You Begin | 24 |
| | Help | Before You Begin | 16 |
| **Adjusting Settings** | | | |
| | Change page display modes | Before You Begin | 21 |
| | Page magnification | Before You Begin | 22 |
| | Page orientation | Module 3 | 149 |
| | Toolbars | Before You Begin | 11 |
| **Document Exchange** | | | |
| | Save a file in a different format | Module 2 | 87 |
| | Save for Web posting | Module 2 | 88 |
| **Basic Functions** | | | |
| | Alignment and justification of text | Module 3 | 133 |
| | Copy, Cut, and Paste | Before You Begin | 10 |
| | Deleting | Module 3 | 127 |
| | Formatting text | Module 3 | 131 |
| | Images, graphics and objects | Module 3 | 161 |
| | Line spacing | Module 3 | 134 |
| | Printing | Module 3 | 143 |
| | Preview a document | Module 3 | 143 |
| | Printers, choosing | Module 3 | 145 |
| | Print to file | Module 3 | 145 |
| | Selecting | Before You Begin | 9 |
| | Spell Check | Before You begin | 23 |
| | Symbols and special characters | Module 3 | 124 |
| | Templates | Module 3 | 189 |
| | Undo | Module 3 | 135 |

# Introduction

---

**Syllabus Goals for Module 7**

**Information and Communication** is divided in two sections. The first section, Information, requires the candidate to accomplish basic Web search tasks using a Web browser application and available search engine tools, to bookmark search results and to print Web pages and search reports. The second section, Communication, requires the candidate to demonstrate their ability to use electronic mail software to send and receive messages, to attach documents or files to a message and to organise and manage message folders or directories within electronic mail software.

---

## E-mail

One of the most widely-used features of networks is the ability to send and receive electronic mail, or **e-mail**. Messages can be sent world-wide in a matter of seconds and at minimal cost. Other documents and files can be attached to e-mail messages and sent to addresses in virtually any part of the world. Long-distance, cheap, instant communication makes it possible to exchange messages as never before, whether between friends and family or in the world of big business.

## The Internet

The successful use of networks by universities and corporations for the exchange of information led to the network idea spreading to the private sector, giving birth to the **Internet**. The Internet is a world-wide network of separate computers, and computer networks, connected together so that information can be exchanged between them.

The Internet was completely text-based until the late 1980s. Then a group of scientists, looking for a more convenient way to share documents, conceived the idea of an easy-to-use World Wide Web of information. Clicking on a word in a document on the screen would automatically connect to related documents on other computers, a technique known as **hypertext**. These developments greatly increased the opportunities for accessing information and led to the expanded use of the Internet as we know it today.

## The World Wide Web

The expansion of the simple text systems to include the use of hypertext and the ability to incorporate sounds, images and video led to the rapid development of a new branch of the Internet known today as the **World Wide Web (WWW)**.

The World Wide Web is now an enormous library of information. The ease with which it can be used has led to the term, the **Information Superhighway**. It provides opportunities for global communication between individuals and groups. The WWW is used by universities, government agencies, libraries, commercial companies and individuals.

Module 7

# Section 1     Getting Started

## 1.1     HTTP

Because the Internet is made up of different networks and computers, the WWW needed a common method for exchanging documents.  The protocol – set of rules – that allows text with built-in links (hypertext) to be transmitted from computer to computer is called the **HyperText Transfer Protocol**, or **http**.  World Wide Web addresses typically begin with the letters **http**.

## 1.2     HTML

Documents on the Web are written in a computer language called **HyperText Markup Language (HTML)**.  This language provides for links not only to other parts of the same document but to other documents on computers in any part of the world.

## 1.3     Internet Resources

Apart from the WWW, the Internet can be used to send electronic mail (**e-mail**) and to transfer files between computers.

**File Transfer Protocol (FTP)** is a program that allows you to transfer files between computers on the Internet as distinct from transferring files for immediate viewing.  Transferring a file from a remote computer to your own computer is called **downloading** the file.  Sending a file to a remote computer is called **uploading** the file.

Other facilities available on the Internet include **News Groups** for the dissemination of information to interested groups, and **Internet Relay Chat** which allows people to communicate with each other instantly by typing text on the keyboard – rather than by talking on the telephone.

## 1.4     Connecting to the Internet

To connect a home computer to the Internet, you will need the following.

- A computer
- A modem
- A telephone line
- An account with an Internet Service Provider (ISP)
- Software: a Web browser and e-mail program

## 1.5     The Computer

Any computer that is not more than a few years old can be used to connect to the Internet.  However, as the graphics and video content on the WWW is becoming increasingly complex, requiring large amounts of memory and processing power, a more recent computer is advisable.  The relevant software for your computer is freely available and is usually supplied with modern computers.

## 1.6    The Modem

A **modem** and a **telephone line** are needed to provide Internet access to one computer.  The modem changes computer signals into telephone signals and vice versa so that they can be sent from computer to computer over standard telephone lines.  A modem can be fitted to your computer internally or externally.  A single modem and telephone line cannot normally be shared by other computers.

Most computers sold today are equipped with **internal** modems.  Modem speeds are measured in thousands of bits per second (Kbps).  At the moment, a modem speed of 56 Kbps is the standard.  Factors such as the quality of the telephone lines, however, commonly prevent modems from operating at maximum speed, so an older 33.6 Kbps or even a 28.8 Kbps modem may provide adequate service.

## 1.7    Telephone Lines

You need a telephone line to connect to the Internet.  The line can be an ordinary telephone line or an ISDN line.

An **ISDN (Integrated Services Digital Network)** line is a high-speed **digital** line.  It does not need a modem – other equipment is used instead – as it can transmit the computer signals without having to convert them into normal telephone **analogue** format (see The Telephone System, page 46).

**Internet Explorer**

With a single ISDN line, a large number of computers can have access to the Internet at the same time if they are already connected together in a network.  ISDN lines can also accommodate video conferencing.

Inetwiz

## 1.8    Internet Service Providers

To connect to the Internet, you also need an account with an **Internet Service Provider (ISP)**.  The account may be a **subscription** account or a **free** account.

A **subscription account** involves paying a monthly or yearly subscription to the company, in return for which you can expect to receive a certain level of service and support.

**Outlook Express**

**Free accounts** do not require a subscription to be paid.  However, if you have problems that you are not able to solve yourself, calls for telephone help may be charged at a premium rate.

With either a subscription or a free account, you will still have to pay the cost of using the telephone line while you are connected to the Internet.  This is the cost charged by the telephone company and it is completely separate from any costs due to the ISP.  Some ISPs have special low-cost connections but with others, you will have to pay the standard rates.

Msn

When you open an account with an ISP, it supplies you with a Username, a Password and other details which enable you to connect to and use the Internet.

Modern computers already have the necessary Internet and e-mail software installed.  You need to configure the software before it can be used, however, by entering your account details as provided by the ISP.  This requires a certain level of technical knowledge and should be undertaken by a competent person.

**Connect to the Internet**

Internet and WWW icons

Module 7

## 1.9    Web Browsers

**Microsoft Internet Explorer** and **Netscape Navigator** are computer programs known as **browsers**. They allow people to access information, view images, hear sounds and watch video on the WWW. Other Web browsers are available which work in a similar manner.

Many ISPs distribute software on CD-ROM with instructions for installing it on your computer. If the installation is successful, this will automatically configure your computer and establish an Internet connection. However, installing software over similar software that is already present on your computer may cause problems. You should seek advice before using such CDs.

Once you have successfully connected to the Internet for the first time, you should not have to bother about configurations and settings again.

The details of configuring a computer to connect to the Internet is not an ECDL requirement and is thus outside the scope of this manual.

# Section 2    The World Wide Web

## 2.1    Opening Internet Explorer

Open Internet Explorer by double-clicking the **Internet Explorer** icon
on the desktop or by clicking once on the icon on the taskbar.

*Alternatively*, click the **Start** button and select **Internet Explorer** in
the **Programs** menu or sub-menu.

Internet
Explorer

If your computer is connected to the Internet over a network, it may
make a connection immediately.  If you are using a modem, the
**Dial-up Connection** window appears.

## 2.2    The Dial-up Connection Window

The **Connect to** box displays the name of
your ISP.

Your **username** and **password** – received
from the ISP – will be entered in the
appropriate boxes.

Click the **Save password** box after you have
typed your password to avoid having to
enter the password every time you connect.

To connect without showing this window in
the future, click the **Connect automatically**
box.  (Do not click it for now.)

Clicking the **Connect** button starts the
connection process.

Click the **Settings** button to display the
various technical details required to make
the connection.  (You will not normally
have to look at these.)

Click the **Work Offline** button to start
Internet Explorer without connecting to the
Internet.  Web pages that have been saved
on your computer can then be viewed
without incurring connection charges.

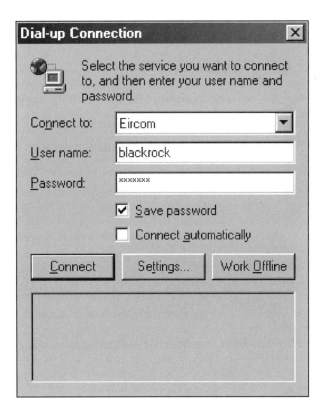

When you click the **Connect** button, the
panel at the bottom of the window keeps
you informed of progress.  Various
messages such as the following are
displayed.

> *'Dialing... Connected to remote computer....*
> *Verifying user name and password... Logging on...'*

When the connection has been made, the Dial-up Connection window closes and a Web page appears.

Module 7

## 2.3    Connecting

Connecting to the Internet or to any other
network is often referred to as **logging on**.
When the Dial-up Connection window
appears, do the following.

- Type your user name in the **User name**
  box if it is not there already.

- You may have to type your Password in
  the **Password** box (if the **Save password**
  box was not clicked).

- Click the **Connect** button.

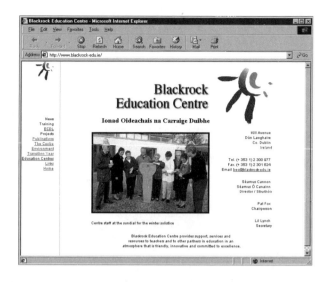

The modem dials the ISP number and makes
the connection.  When the connection is
successful, Internet Explorer opens the
preset **Home Page** (or **Start Page)**.

If a connection cannot be established, a message to that effect appears on the screen.

The Home Page that you see first is a Web page that has been chosen as a starting point for each
session on the Internet.  In many cases, the Start Page is the home page of your ISP.  You can change
the Start Page, however, to any Web page of your choice.  Changing the Home Page is dealt with in
Section 2.11, page 343.

## 2.4    Toolbars

Various toolbars are displayed at the top of the Explorer window, as in other applications.

- The **Title Bar** shows the name of the current Web site or page.
- The **Menu Bar** contains the usual menus as well as some specific to Internet Explorer.
- The **Button Bar** has a number of buttons that are used for various purposes.
- The **Address Bar** displays the address of the current Web site or page.  It also has a **Go** button
  at the right-hand side.

If the current page extends below the viewing area, scroll bars enable the user to move over the page.

## 2.5    Hyperlinks

As you move the mouse over text on the Web page, notice that the arrow
pointer changes to the text I-beam.  However, for some of the text, the
mouse pointer changes to a hand with a pointing finger.  This indicates
that this particular piece of text is a **hyperlink**.

News

Training

ECDL

Pro jects

Publications

A hyperlink is a piece of text, an object or graphic that acts like a button.
Clicking a hyperlink performs an action such as moving to a different
part of the same page or displaying a new page.

Anything that changes the mouse pointer to the hand as you move over it is a hyperlink.

## 2.6    Browser Buttons

As you click on links to go from page to page, you can use the browser buttons to assist you. Some of them are described here.

- **Back** returns to the previous page.

- **Forward** moves to the next page (but only if you have previously moved back).

- **Stop** stops the current action. Use this if the page is taking too long to appear or you change your mind about what you are doing.

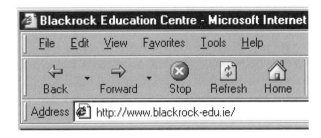

- **Refresh** reloads the current page. Use this button if the page has not appeared properly or if you know it has changed since it first appeared.

- **Home** returns to the Home Page as set in the browser.

## 2.7    Web Addresses

Every Web page has its own unique address, known as a **URL** (**Uniform Resource Locator**).

A Web address is written in lower case (small letters) and is composed of a protocol abbreviation and a number of other parts separated by dots (full stops).

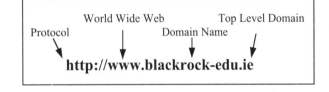

- **http** stands for hypertext transfer protocol.

- **www** shows that this is a world wide web address.

- The **domain name** is a principal part of the address. (A domain is a location or area where the pages are stored.)

- The **top level domain** often refers to a country or is one of a number of international domains such as **.com** (commercial), **.net** (network) **.org** (organization) **.gov** (government) and so on.

Domain names can be registered – by an individual, company or organisation – with the appropriate body in each country, on a 'first-come-first-served' basis. In Ireland, the administration of the **.ie** domain is handled by IE Domain Registry Limited. (http://www.domainregistry.ie)

Scoilnet Home Page

As you click on links to view other Web pages – called **following the links** – at a particular Web site, notice how the Web address changes.

When you click a link, the address of the new page appears in the Address box.

Pages on a site are usually stored in folders and sub-folders. Forward slashes separate the parts of the address, which now shows the path to the page that is displayed.

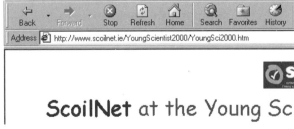
Scoilnet Young Scientists Page

## 2.8    Typing Web Addresses

To find and display a Web page by typing an address, do the following.

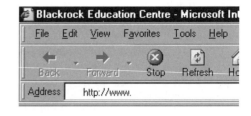

- Click in the **Address** box. The current address is highlighted.

  *Alternatively*, click again to the right of the current address in the address box.

  Use the backspace key to delete back to the dot after **www** to save typing the first part of the address again.

- Type the new address.

- Press the **Return** key or click the **Go** button at the end of the address box.

**Note:** You do not need to type **http://** when you are typing an address. Start with **www**.

## 2.9    Web Sites and Web Pages

A **Web site** is a collection of Web pages related to a particular organisation or topic. The first page of a Web site that appears is called the **Home Page**.

A Web site home page is the starting point for exploring the particular site. It usually contains links to the other parts of the site, similar to the contents page of a book. As you explore a Web site, you will often notice hyperlinks called **Home**. These links bring you back to the site home page.

A Web site home page should not be confused with the Home Page or Start Page that is set on your browser. The Start Page on your browser can be set to any Web page of your choice.

## 2.10    Some URLs to Explore

Blackrock Education Centre
**http://www.blackrock-edu.ie**          The people who produced this book.

Paris
**http://www.paris.org**          Cité magique, temple des amoureux…

Football
**http://www.fifa.com**          World Cup 2002, etc. etc.

Europe
**http://www.euroseek.net**          A multilingual Euro search and Directory

Scoilnet
**http://www.scoilnet.ie**          Educational site for Irish schools

Fashion
**http://www.fashion.net**          All the latest news, even shopping!

Deckchair
**http://www.deckchair.com**          The cheapest holiday flights, and more.

> **Information** on the Internet changes all the time. New pages are added, old pages disappear, information is constantly being updated. New materials, pages and sites are constantly appearing, often on a daily basis. Web sites, pages and addresses you saw last week – or even yesterday – may not be the same today!

## 2.11   Changing the Home Page

The first page – the **Home Page** – that is displayed when
you connect to the Internet will usually have been set by the
browser vendor or the ISP.

You can set the page with which the browser opens to any
page of your choice.  The easiest way to set a new start page
is to first find and display the page you want to use.

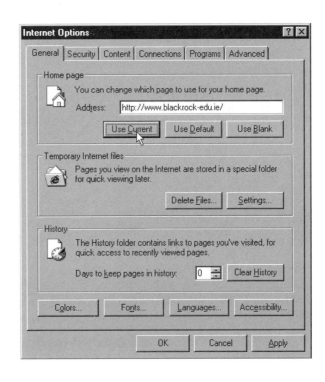

- Open **Internet Explorer** if it is not already open.

- Find the page that you want to set as the
  start page, the **Blackrock Education
  Centre** page, for example.

- Select **Internet Options** in the **Tools** menu.
  The Internet Options window appears.

- Click the **General** tab at the top of the
  window, if it is not already clicked.

  The address of the pre-set Home Page
  appears in the **Address** box in the **Home
  page** section.

- Click the **Use Current** button.

  The address of the page currently
  displayed is inserted in the **Address** box.

- Click the **Apply** button to make your
  choice effective.

- Click **OK**.

  Now, when you next open Internet
  Explorer, your own choice of Home Page
  is the one that will be displayed.

*Alternatively*, type the address of your
  choice in the **Address** box.  (The page
  does not have to be displayed first.)
  Then click **Apply** and **OK** as before.

## 2.12   Turning off Graphics

When you turn off graphics, animations and
so on, pages will download faster but then,
only the text is displayed.  This may be
preferable in some circumstances.

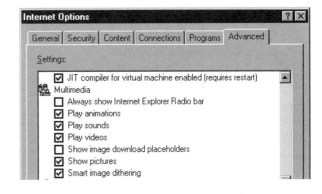

- Click the **Advanced** tab in the Internet
  Options window.

- Scroll to find the **Multimedia** section.

- Click to remove the tick from the **Play
  animations**, **Play sounds**, **Play videos**,
  **Show pictures** check boxes, as
  required.

- Click **Apply** to make your choices effective.

- Click **OK**.

Module 7

## 2.13   Toolbar Buttons

Buttons can be added to or removed from the
toolbar to suit your personal preferences.

Proceed as follows.

- Select **Toolbars** in the **View** menu and
  then **Customise** in the sub-menu.

  The **Customise Toolbar**
  window opens.

  The buttons currently on the
  toolbar are listed on the
  right.  Other available
  buttons are listed on the left.

- To add or remove a button,
  click the required button in
  the relevant list.

- Click the **Add** or **Remove**
  button in the centre, as
  required.

- Click the **Close** button when
  you are finished.

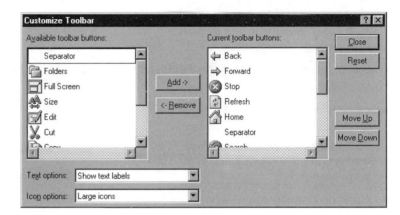

## 2.14   Display Options

The Web page is the principal item displayed in the Internet Explorer window.

Other items can also be displayed to assist you in your work.  Toolbars have already been mentioned
(Section 2.4, page 340).  Other bars that can be displayed are the **Favourites**, **Search**, **History** and
**Folder** bars.  They are described later in this Module.  The **Tip of the Day** can also be displayed.  The
bars can be displayed by clicking on buttons on the toolbar or by selecting them in the **View** menu.

When extra bars are displayed, the space available for the Web page is reduced.  When you are
familiar with Internet Explorer, you may wish to dispense with all the bars and menus and devote the
whole screen to the Web page by selecting **Full Screen** in the **View** menu.

## 2.15   Closing and Disconnecting

Closing Internet Explorer disconnects you from the Internet.  It is also possible to disconnect but to
leave the Browser window open.

It is not necessary to remain connected to see a page that is already being displayed on the screen.

- Click the **Close** button in the top
  right-hand corner of the Browser window.

- Click **Disconnect** in the window that
  appears.

To disconnect but leave the Browser
window open:

- Double click the **Connected**
  **to** icon on the **Status Bar** at
  the bottom of the screen.

Connected to

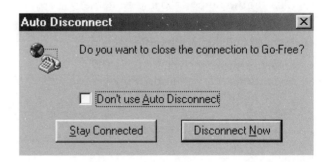

# Section 3    Working with Web Pages

## 3.1    Saving Web Addresses

When you find a site or page of particular interest, its URL can be saved as a **Favourite** (Internet Explorer) or **Bookmark** (Netscape).

When you want to return to the site at a later date, it can be easily accessed without having to be typed in or searched for. (Outlook Express uses the American spelling, 'Favorite'.)

To save a Favourite, you can use the Favourites button on the toolbar or the Favourites menu on the **Menu** bar.

### Using the Favourites button

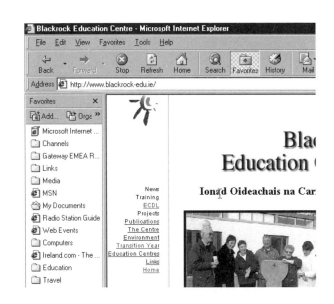

- Make sure that the page whose address you want to save is displayed.

- Click the **Favourites** button on the toolbar. The Favourites panel appears at the left of the window.

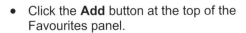

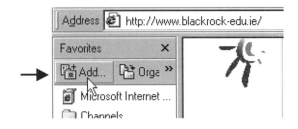

- Click the **Add** button at the top of the Favourites panel. The **Add Favourite** window opens.

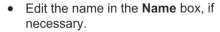

- Edit the name in the **Name** box, if necessary. You may wish to shorten it or make it more meaningful.

- Click **OK** to add the address immediately to the list of Favourites. It is better, however, to save the address in a **subject folder** as described in the following steps.

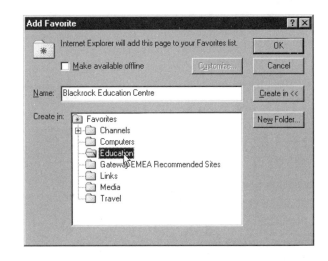

- Click the folder in the **Create in** panel in which you want to save the address. Click the **Create in** button if the folders are not displayed. Click the **New Folder** button to create a new folder, if required.

Module 7

- Click **OK**.

- Click **Close** in the next window. The Favourite is added to the folder.

- Click the **Favourites** button again on the toolbar to close the Favourites panel.

  *Alternatively*, click the **Close** button at the top of the Favourites panel.

### Using the Favourites menu

- Make sure that the page whose address you want to save is displayed.

- Select **Add to Favourites** in the **Favourites** menu.

  The **Add Favourite** window opens, as before.

- Follow the steps for the Add Favourites window as described above.

## 3.2    Using Favourites

To return to a site or page at a later time, you can use either the Favourites button on the toolbar or the Favourites menu on the **Menu** bar.

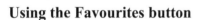

### Using the Favourites button

- Click the **Favourites** button on the toolbar.

  The Favourites panel appears at the left of the window, as before.

- Click the name of the site or page you require in the list or in the appropriate folder.

  If you wait for a moment before clicking, the full name and Web address are displayed.

  The browser finds and displays the page.

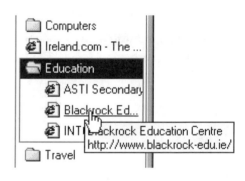

### Using the Favourites menu

- Click **Favourites** on the **Menu** bar.

  The Favourites menu appears. It may contain individual Favourites and subject Folders, depending on how the favourites were saved originally.

- Click the name of the site or page you require, if it is not in a folder.

If the URL you require is in a folder:

- Point to the folder in the menu to display its contents.

- Click the name of the site or page you require.

  The browser finds and displays the page.

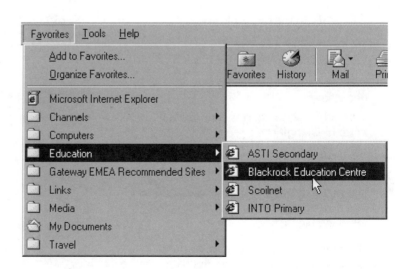

## 3.3    Organising Favourites

If you did not save your Favourites in an organised way, you can arrange or organise them later.

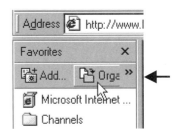

You can use either the Favourites button on the toolbar or the Favourites menu on the **Menu** bar.

### Using the Favourites button

- Click the **Favourites** button on the toolbar.

  The Favourites panel opens at the left of the window, as before.

- Click the **Organise** button at the top of the panel.

  The Organise Favourites window opens.

- Click a Favourite or Folder to select it.

  Details of the selected item appear in the panel at the bottom left of the window.

- Click the **Move to Folder** button.

  The **Browse for Folder** window opens.

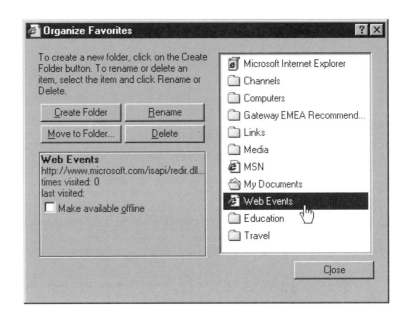

- Click the folder to which you want to move the selected item.

- Click **OK**.

  The item is moved to the folder.

- Click the **Close** button in the **Organise Favourites** window.

### Using the Favourites menu

- Select **Organise Favourites** in the **Favourites** menu.

  The Organise Favourites window opens as before.

- Follow the steps as described above when using the Favourites button.

Module 7

## 3.4    Copying and Pasting Text

Text and graphics can be copied from Web pages and used in other applications.

- First, select the text as you would in a word processor.
- Then, either…
  - Right-click on the text and select **Copy** in the menu that appears.
  - Select **Copy** in the **Edit** menu.
  - Use the keyboard shortcut, **Ctrl + C**.

  A copy of the selected text is stored on the clipboard.

To paste the text into a document in another application, such as **Microsoft Word**, do the following.

- Either…
  - Right-click where you want to insert the text and then select **Paste** in the menu that appears.
  - Select **Paste** in the **Edit** menu.
  - Use the keyboard shortcut, **Ctrl + V**.

  The selected text is pasted into the document.

## 3.5    Pasting Text into an E-mail Message

Pasting text from a Web page into an e-mail message is similar to the above.

- Select and copy the text on the Web page as described above.
- Go to the message in the e-mail application.

- Click in the main message section where you want to insert the text.
- Paste the text.  Do one of the following.
  - In Outlook Express, click the **Paste** button on the toolbar.
  - Select **Paste** in the **Edit** menu.
  - Use the keyboard shortcut, **Ctrl + V**.

E-mail is described in detail in Section 5 of this module, page 356.

## 3.6    Saving Text

Text from some Web pages can be saved as a normal file.  (If the text is in a frame, you may not be able to save it.)  First open the page containing the text you want to save and then do the following.

- Select  **Save** or **Save As** in the **File** menu.

- Type or edit the name for the text in the **File name** box.

- Select **Text File** in the **Save as type** menu.

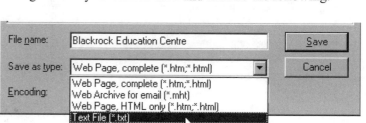

- Choose the location in the **Save in** box where you want to save the file.

- Click **Save**.

## 3.7    Copying and Pasting Graphics

Copying and pasting Web graphics is similar
to copying and pasting text.

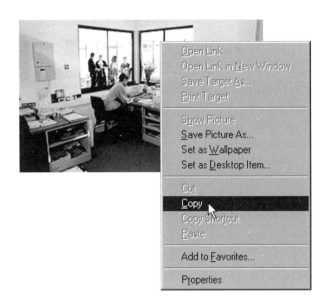

- Right-click on the Web page graphic and
  select **Copy** in the menu that appears.
  (You cannot use the **Edit** menu for this
  operation.)

To paste the graphic into a document in
another application:

- Go to the application.

- Click **Paste** in the **Edit** menu.
  The graphic is pasted into the document.

## 3.8    Pasting a Graphic into an E-mail Message

A Web page graphic can be copied and
pasted into an e-mail message as follows.

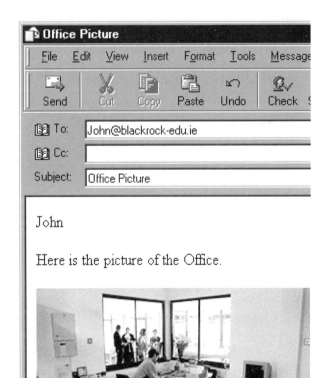

- Right-click the graphic that you want to
  copy on the Web page.

- Select **Copy** in the menu that appears,
  as before.

- Go to the e-mail message and click
  where you want to insert the graphic.

- Click the **Paste** button on the toolbar.
  *Alternatively*:
  – Select **Paste** in the **Edit** menu.
  – Use the keyboard shortcut, **Crtl + V**.
  The graphic appears in the message box.

Module 7

## 3.9   Saving a Web Graphic

Graphics on Web pages can be saved for future use.

- Right-click the graphic and select **Save Picture As** in the menu that appears.
  The Save Picture window opens.

- In the **Save Picture** window, select the location in the **Save in** box where you want to save the graphic.

- Type a name for the graphic in the **File name** box.

- Click **Save**.

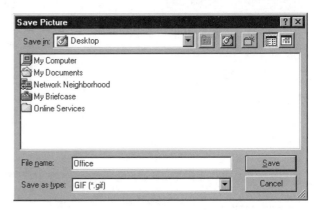

## 3.10   Saving a Web Page

To save a Web page, do the following.

- Make sure that the page you want to save is displayed on the screen.

- Select **Save As** in the **File** menu.
  The **Save Web Page** window opens.

- In the Save Web Page window, select the location in the **Save in** box where you want to save the page.

- Click in the **Save as type** box and select the format (file type) in which you want to save the page from the menu (see below).

- Click the **Save** button

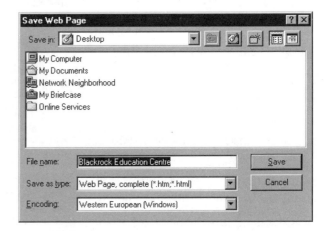

**Save as type** formats:

**Web Page, complete** saves all the files needed to display the page in their original format. The Web page is saved as a separate file and a folder is created to store the graphics etc.

**Web Archive for email** saves all the information, including graphics, as a single file which can be attached to an e-mail message (see note below).

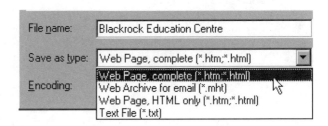

**Web Page HTML only** saves the text on the page but not the graphics or other files. If the Web page contains frames, it will not save each frame.

**Text File** saves the text as plain text without any formatting. The contents of frames (see below) are not saved.

Note: To send a Web page via e-mail, you can also use the **Send** command on the **File** menu.
It automatically inserts the page in a new message. See Section 5 of this module, page 356, for more information about e-mail.

## 3.11    Frames

Web page designers often divide pages into several **frames**. They provide more flexibility in layout and display than would be possible otherwise.

The page in the illustration is composed of two frames, with the menu in the left-hand frame and the main information in the large frame on the right.

Frames behave as if they were independent pages within the main page. When a link is clicked in the menu in the example, only the main display frame changes, leaving the menu on display for further choices.

Frames cannot be displayed by older browsers. Also, pages with frames may not always print out as the user might expect.

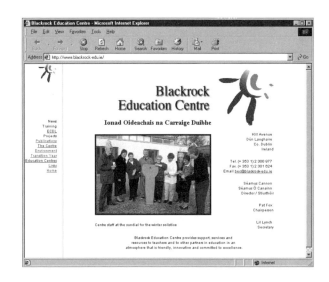

## 3.12    Printing a Page

A Web page can be printed like any other page but pages that contain frames need special attention.

To print a page directly, do the following.

- Make sure that the page you want to print is displayed on the screen.

- Click the **Print** button on the toolbar. The page is printed.

To print a page with frames:

- Select **Print** in the **File** menu. The Print window opens.

- Click the appropriate button in the **Print frames** panel in the lower part of the window.

- Click **OK**.

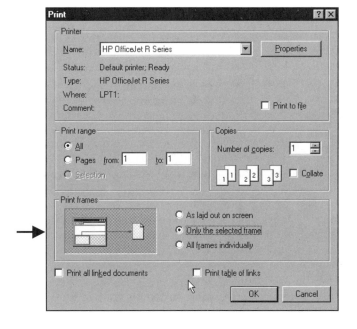

**Print frames** options:

- **As laid out on screen** prints the entire page as you see it on screen.
- **Only the selected frame** prints one frame only. (Click in the frame on the Web page to select it before clicking **OK**.)
- **All frames individually** prints each frame on a separate page.

Other Options:

- Click **Print all linked documents** to print all the documents with links on the page. (Use this with caution as there may be a lot of pages!)

- Click **Print table of links** to print a list of the links without printing the actual linked pages.

Module 7

# Section 4    Search Engines

## 4.1    Searching for Information

A **search engine** is a program that helps you to find information on the Web. It stores listings of Web sites from all over the world and makes them easily available. Different search engines search in different ways, so you may find information using one that may be overlooked by another.

Search engines compile their listings either by using **human editors** or **automated crawlers**. A third kind of search engine – a **Meta** search engine – uses other search engines to do the work. Some examples of different search engines are given here.

### Human

| | | |
|---|---|---|
| LookSmart | www.looksmart.com | These search engines use **people** to classify Web sites into categories. They are good for finding information on general topics. |
| UK Plus | www.ukplus.co.uk | |
| Yahoo! | www.yahoo.com | |

### Automated

| | | |
|---|---|---|
| AltaVista | www.altavista.com | |
| Excite | www.excite.com | **Automated crawlers** read large numbers of Web pages and store the text. They are good for finding very specific information. |
| Fast | www.alltheweb.com | |
| Google | www.google.com | |
| Lycos | www.lycos.com | |
| WebCrawler | www.webcrawler.com | |

Create your Start Page!                          Choose your favorite photo! »
New Members **Sign Up**  ▪  Excite Members **Sign In**  ▪  **Help** New!

### Meta

| | | |
|---|---|---|
| AskJeeves | www.askjeeves.com | **Meta** search engines send your query to several other search engines and then list the results in one location. |
| Go2Net | www.go2net.com | |
| SavvySearch | www.savysearch.com | |

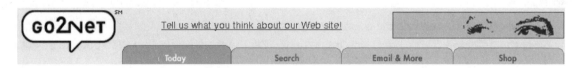

Searching for information involves entering key words in a box or boxes on the search engine page. A list of Web sites which contain those key words is then displayed. The individual sites can then be accessed as required.

Many search engines have local versions for different areas. Check the main site for details. Yahoo!, for example, has a site for the UK and Ireland. Searching can be world-wide or concentrated on sites in the UK and Ireland, as desired.

## 4.2    A Simple Search

Searching often results in a very large number of pages being found.  Do the following.

- Open **Internet Explorer**.

- Go to the **AltaVista** site – www.altavista.com

- Type university in the **Find this** box.

- Click the **Search** button.

The results page will show the number of Web pages found containing the word 'university' – in this case, many millions.

The results are listed in order, starting with those with the highest usage of the word.

The first 10 or 20 sites are listed.  At the bottom of the page, as in the example on the right, a list of **Result Pages** is displayed with the current page bold – in this case page **1**.

**1. The University of Queensland Home Page**
Access information about the University of Queensland, its departments, faculties and the courses they offer....
**URL:** www.cc.uq.edu.au/
Last modified on: 7-Aug-1999 - 20K bytes - in English
[ Translate ]

Result Pages: **1** 2 3 4 5 6 7 8 9 10 11 12 13 14 15 16 17 18 19 20   [Next >>]
word count: university: 54477079

Click **2** to see the next page.  Click any page number to go to a particular page.  Click **Next** at the end of the list to go to the next set of pages, listing further sites.

Search results can be printed in the usual way, as described in Section 3.12, page 351.

## 4.3    The Search Button

The **Search** button on the toolbar can be used in a number of ways.

- Click the **Search** button on the toolbar.

- A search engine page is displayed in a large panel at the left of the screen, **Yahoo!** in the illustration.

- Type the subject of your search into the box at the top of the panel.

- Click the **Search** button beside the box.

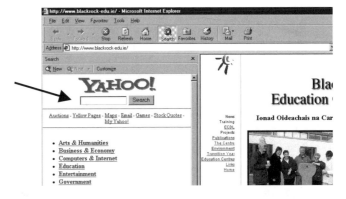

After a few moments, the results of the search that match your request are displayed.

Click the **New** button at the top of the panel to start a new search.

## 4.4    Search Button Settings

The search engine that appears when you click the **Search** button on the toolbar can be set to one of your choice.

Proceed as follows.

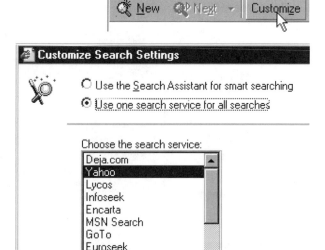

- Click the **Customise** button at the top of the Search panel.

- The **Customise Search Settings** window opens.

- Click the item in the list that you want to use (**Yahoo** in the illustration).

- Click the **OK** button at the bottom of the window.

  The search engine appears in the Search panel.

- Click the **Search** button again to close the Search panel when you are finished.

  *Alternatively*, click the **Close** button at the top of the search panel.

## 4.5    The Search Assistant

Instead of a search engine, you can use the Search Assistant when you click the **Search** button.

Proceed as follows.

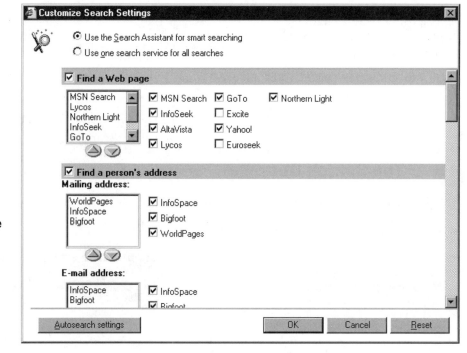

- Click the **Customize** button at the top of the Search panel.

  The **Customize Search Settings** window opens.

- Click **Use the Search Assistant for smart searching**.

  A large number of search options are displayed. Use the scroll arrows to see them all.

  For now, do not make any changes.

- Click the **OK** button at the bottom of the window.

  The Search Assistant appears in the Search panel.

- Click the **Search** button again to close the Search panel when you are finished.

  *Alternatively*, click the **Close** button at the top of the search panel.

## 4.6    Detailed Searching

Typing a word or two into a search engine usually brings up a very wide range of results that can be confusing and unhelpful.  **University** finds millions of matches which are of little use if, for example, you are only interested in universities in Dublin.

The more precise the key word or phrase you use, the more relevant the results will be.  Some ways to narrow your search in order to find more relevant information are described here.

- Go to the **AltaVisita** site again.

- Type **university + dublin** in the **Find this** box.

  Typing **+** before a word means that the word must be included in the results.

  Typing **–** before a word means that the word must be excluded.

- Click the **Search** button.  The number of pages found is now thousands instead of millions.

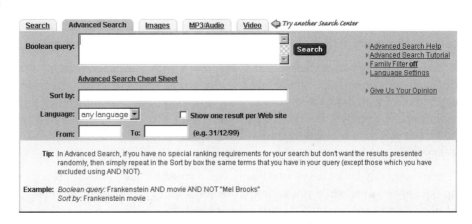

Search engines usually have an **Advanced Search** facility.  A range of options helps you find the exact information you need.

There is usually an **Advanced Search** button.  AltaVista is shown here.  Note the links on the right to help you with advanced searches.

## 4.7    Search Engine Tips

Here are some tips to help you use search engines effectively.

- Use the **+** and **–** symbols to include or exclude words, as described above.

- When you use upper case letters (capitals), the search will find only capital letters.  Lower case finds both lower and upper case.

- To search for an exact word order, use quotation marks, e.g. **"Trinity College Dublin"**.

  In Web Crawler, typing **trinity college dublin** without quotes finds over a hundred thousand pages.  With quotes, the number of pages found is reduced to hundreds.

- When you are not sure of the exact word or phrase to use, you can expand your search by using **wildcard** symbols.  For example, **program\*** finds programme, programming, programs and so on.

- The Web sites of many large organisations can be accessed by typing in just a single word, e.g., **ireland**, **yahoo**, **aerlingus**, **dogpile**.

  Type the word in the Address box and press the Return key.

- **Meta** Search Engines, such as  **dogpile** and **askjeeves,** search all the regular search engines simultaneously.

- The **askjeeves** search engine allows you to type questions in normal English.

# Section 5    Electronic Mail

## 5.1    Mail and Mail Programs

**Electronic mail**, or **e-mail** as it is commonly known, is one of the most widely used facilities available on the Internet.  Mail programs such as **Microsoft Outlook**, **Outlook Express**, **Netscape Mail**, **Eudora** and **Pegasus Mail** allow you to send and receive messages locally or internationally for the price of a local telephone call.

E-mail is fast, cheap and convenient.  You can send e-mail to an individual or to a group of people at the same time.  You can create mailing lists so that you can write a message and send it automatically to a number of people.   In addition, you can send files such as spreadsheets, pictures and sounds as **attachments** to your message.

E-mail messages can be prepared in advance before you connect to your ISP and then sent all together when you connect, thus saving on connection costs.  When you are preparing mail without being connected, you are working **offline**.  When you are connected, you are **online**.

E-mail is delivered immediately to the **recipient's ISP** to await collection.  It does not go directly to the recipient's computer.  E-mail that is addressed to you is received and stored by **your ISP**.  In each case, the recipient has to check to see if there is any e-mail.  Only then is it downloaded to the individual's computer.  It works like the post office box system, where your mail is not sent to your home but placed in a box at the post office.  You do not see your mail until you go to the post office to collect it.

E-mail is usually collected automatically when you first open the Mail program but you can also dial up later at any time while you are using the program to check again for mail.  You can also set the Mail program to check for mail at regular intervals.

## 5.2    E-mail Addresses

You need an e-mail address before you can send or receive e-mail.  A unique e-mail address is allocated to you when you sign up with an Internet Service Provider.

The address is usually written in lower case (small) letters and contains no spaces.   A distinctive feature is the **@** symbol which separates the person's name from the domain part of the address.

Each e-mail address has to be unique.  The part after the @ symbol is usually the same for a particular ISP, so the person's actual name – before the @ symbol – cannot be duplicated.  People often use a variation of their actual name to distinguish them from others with similar names.  If Ethna Boland, for example, wanted to have the name **eboland**, she may be told by her ISP that this particular name has already been taken.  She would then have to choose another.

In this example, Ethna Boland has an e-mail address with an ISP in Ireland called netlink.  She has chosen **ethnab** as her username.  Her address would be read aloud as **Ethna B at netlink dot ie** but written as shown on the right.

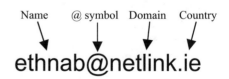

Many e-mail addresses use the domain name of a company or organization. Blackrock Education Centre has its own domain name.  The Centre's e-mail address is shown on the right.

bec@blackrock-edu.ie

## 5.3    Opening Outlook Express

There are several mail programs available. The program used in this module, Outlook Express, is found on many Windows (95, 98, ME) computers.

Outlook Express

A more elaborate program, Microsoft Outlook, is supplied with Microsoft Office.

To open Outlook Express, double-click the icon on the desktop or click once on the icon on the taskbar.

## 5.4    The Outlook Express Window

When Outlook Express opens for the first time, it appears as in the illustration on the right. Information on different functions of the program is available by clicking on the links.

When you are familiar with Outlook Express, it is more convenient to go directly to your mail when you open the program.

Click the check box at the bottom of the window – **When Outlook Express starts, go straight to my Inbox**. The next time you open the program, your mail will be displayed instead of this opening screen.

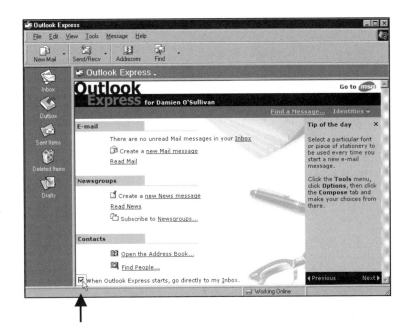

## 5.5    Layout Options

To select what appears on the screen when you open Outlook Express, do the following.

- Select **Layout** in the **View** menu.
  The **Window Layout Properties** window opens.

- In the **Basic** section at the top of the window, you can select which components you wish to view.
  For the moment, choose the settings in the illustration.

- In the **Preview** section, other choices can be made.
  For the moment, choose the settings in the illustration.

- Click **OK** to close the window.

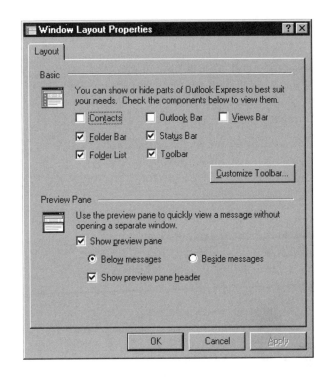

Module 7

## 5.6   Outlook Express Settings

Outlook Express can automatically connect to the ISP when it starts up, and send and receive e-mail messages (if any) immediately. While this is useful for many people, others will want to compose new e-mail messages before connecting (work offline) in order to minimise connection charges.

To set various preferences, do the following.

- Select **Options** in the **Tools** menu.

- Click the **General** tab, if it is not already clicked.

- Click the **When starting, go directly to my Inbox folder** box at the top of the window.

  The program will open with the Inbox instead of the introductory screen.

- In the **Send/Receive Messages** section, click **Send and receive messages at startup**. Outlook Express will send any unsent mail and check for new mail immediately it is opened.

  Remove the tick (click the ticked box) if you want to work offline. Messages will then not be sent or received until you click the **Send/Receive** button on the toolbar.

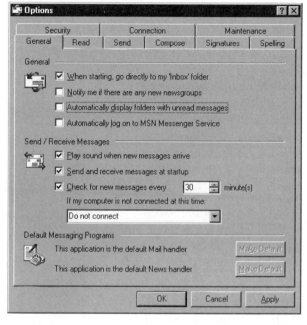

- When the **Check for new messages every** box is clicked, Outlook Express automatically checks for mail at the interval you set in the box to the right.

  To disable automatic checking, click to remove the tick.

- Click **Apply** and then **OK** when you have made your choices.

## 5.7   Send Options

Click the **Send** tab at the top of the window to display the Send options. The options are generally self-explanatory but note the following:

When the **Send messages immediately** box is ticked, messages are sent immediately when you click the **Send** button at the top of the message window.

Click to remove the tick if you want to work offline. Clicking the **Send** button then places the message in the Outbox and it is not sent until you click the **Send/Receive** button.

When **Include message in reply** is ticked, a copy of the original message appears in your reply. Click to remove the tick if you would prefer not to include the message.

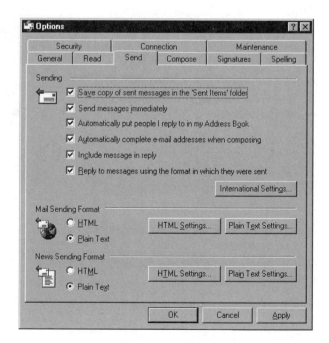

## 5.8    Message Formats

E-mail messages are usually sent in one of two formats – **Plain Text** or **HTML**.

`Plain Text format allows no formatting of text. Messages generally appear in Courier font, like this.`

The plain text format is used by older Browsers.

HTML format allows the use of different fonts, font sizes, font colours, styles, bullets, numbering, and so on as in word processing. Current versions of Browsers use this format.

The format for sending messages is set in the lower part of the **Options** window, illustrated in Section 5.7, page 358.

- Click the **Send** tab, if it is not already clicked.

- Select **HTML** or **Plain Text** in the **Mail Sending Format** section.

- Click **Apply** and then **OK**.

When Outlook Express is set to send messages in **HTML** format, the usual word processing toolbar appears in the **New Message** window.

You can then use fonts and formatting as you would in a word processing document.

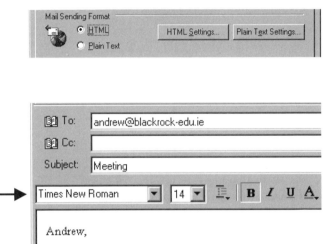

Module 7

# Section 6    Sending and Receiving Mail

## 6.1    Preparing a Message

To learn the skills required by ECDL, it is be important to practise sending and receiving e-mail. If possible, ask a friend for their e-mail address and arrange to exchange messages.  You can, however, also practise these skills by sending e-mail to yourself.

(This module does not cover how to set up an e-mail account.  It is assumed that your account has been set up and is working.)

- Open **Outlook Express**.

- Click the **New Mail** button on the toolbar or select **New Message** in the **Message** menu.
  The **New Message** window opens.

- In the **To** box, type in the recipient's e-mail address (e.g. **ethanb@netlink.ie**)

- In the **Subject** box, type a brief subject heading for the message.

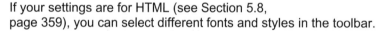

Typing a subject is important.  It allows the recipient to decide which messages to read first and/or which to leave until later, ignore or delete.

- Type the message in the main part of the window.

  If your settings are for HTML (see Section 5.8, page 359), you can select different fonts and styles in the toolbar.

- To check the spelling, click the **Spelling** button on the toolbar.
  *Alternatively*, select **Spelling** in the **Tools** menu.

## 6.2    Sending and Receiving Mail

When Outlook Express is open, you can send and receive mail at any time, using either the **Send** or the **Send/Recv** buttons.

- Click the **Send** button on the toolbar in the **New Message** window.

  The message is either sent immediately or stored in the **Outbox** to be sent later, depending on what options have been set.  (See Section 5.7, page 358.)

- Click the **Send/Recv** button on the toolbar in other windows.

  - If you are already connected, any mail that you have prepared is sent.  Any mail waiting for you at the ISP is received.

  - If you are not connected, Outlook Express will dial your ISP.  Depending on the settings, you may be presented with the same **Dial-up Connection** window used when starting Internet Explorer.

    Enter your user name and password as before and click the **Connect** button.

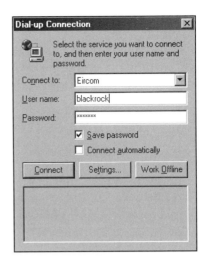

Note that when you send mail to yourself, it may not arrive
back immediately after you click the **Send/Recv** button.
This is because it may take a few seconds to be processed
by the ISP. In that case, wait a few moments and click
**Send/Recv** again.

## 6.3   Send and Receive Options

Click the menu arrow beside the **Send/Recv** button to
display Send and Receive options.

You can choose to…

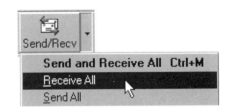

- **Send and Receive All** mail – send mail
  you have prepared and check for any
  new mail

- **Receive All** – check for new mail

- **Send All** – send mail you have prepared

## 6.4   Closing the Connection

When you are finished sending or receiving mail, there are a number of options.

- Close Outlook Express.

  If **Auto Disconnect** is set on your
  computer, you will be prompted to **Stay
  Connected** or to **Disconnect Now**.
  Click the appropriate button.

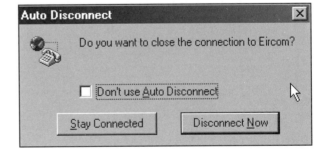

- Keep Outlook Express open but go
  offline (disconnect).

  Select **Work Offline** in the **File** menu.
  You will be prompted to hangup
  (disconnect). Click the appropriate
  button.

- Close Outlook Express, open **Internet
  Explorer** and explore the World Wide
  Web.

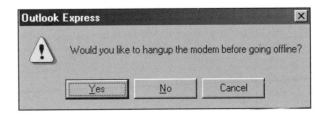

  Having made the connection to your ISP,
  you may be charged a full call unit by
  your telephone company. Why
  disconnect before the time unit is up?

If you intend continuing to work through the following examples, select **Work Offline** and close the
connection to your ISP (disconnect).

## 6.5    Viewing Messages

Outlook Express stores e-mail messages in different folders.  Incoming messages are stored in a folder call the **Inbox**.  Copies of messages waiting to be sent are stored in the **Outbox**, and so on. The folders are displayed down the left-hand side of the window.

- Click the **Inbox**, if it has not already been clicked.

  A list of messages already received, represented by envelope symbols, appears on the right.

  The sender, subject and other details are displayed for each message.

- Click on a message to display its contents in the lower part of the window.

  Use the scroll arrows if the message is a long one.

- Double-click a message to display it in a separate window.

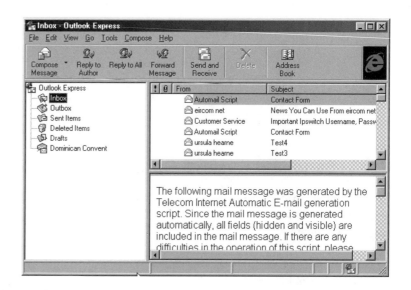

## 6.6    Sorting Messages

Messages in the **Inbox** or other folders can be sorted according to the header labels: subject, date and so on.

- Click the appropriate header bar at the top of the list to sort the messages.

Click here to sort by Subject.                    Click here to sort by Date.

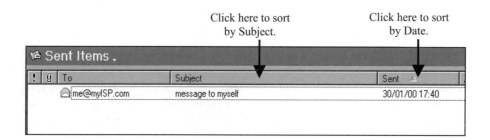

- Right-click a header bar to select either **Ascending** or **Descending** for the sort.

(If there are no messages in the **Inbox**, click the **Sent Items** folder in the left of the window.  The message you have just sent is displayed but you will not be able to see the effect of sorting with only a single message.)

## 6.7    Marking Messages

Messages displayed in the Inbox are marked as **Read** or **Unread** by the appearance of the message icon.  When a messages is received, the icon is a closed envelope.  The message details – sender etc – are in **bold**.

If you view the message in the lower part of the window or open it in a separate window, the icon changes to an open envelope after a few seconds.  Also, the message details – sender etc. – are changed to plain text.

Messages can be marked as Read or Unread for your own purposes.

- Right-click on the message and select **Mark as Read** or **Mark as Unread** in the menu that appears.
  *Alternatively*, highlight the message and select **Mark as Read** or **Mark as Unread** in the **Edit** menu.

To set the number of seconds of viewing before a message is marked as read, do the following.

- Select **Options** in the **Tools** menu.
  The Options window appears.

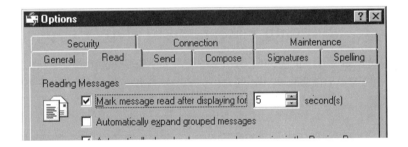

- Click the **Read** tab.

- In the **Reading Messages** section, set the time in the **Mark messsages...** box at the right.

### Other Markers

- Click to the left of a message icon to mark the message with a **Flag** – to remind you to to return to the message later, for example.
  Click again to remove the flag.

- A paper clip beside a message indicates that there is an attachment with the message (see Section 8, page 367).

Module 7

# Section 7    Message Options

## 7.1    Advanced Messaging

In the next few pages, we shall create and send a single message to more than one person.

We shall learn how to add a 'signature' to the message automatically.

We shall also learn how to attach another document to the message and how to assign a level of priority to it.

To prepare for this, do the following.

- Create a Word document and save it with the name **Report**.  A few words will do for the purpose of the exercise.
  We shall attach this file to the new message later.

- Click the **New Mail** button on the toolbar or select **New Message** in the **Message** menu.

- The New Message window opens.

## 7.2    Sending a Message to Many People

You can send the same e-mail message to more than one person.  Each person receives the message. They can also see the list of other addresses to whom the message has been sent.

There are two options.

- Type each recipient's e-mail address in the **To** box.  Use a semi-colon (;) to separate the addresses.
  For this exercise, include your own e-mail address.

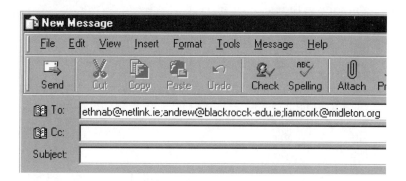

- Enter each recipient's e-mail address in the **Cc** (Carbon copy or Courtesy copy) box. Use a semi-colon (;) to separate the addresses.

There is a minor disadvantage in using the **Cc** box rather than the **To** box.

When you view messages in the **Sent Items** folder, you will not see the **Cc** recipients listed unless you open up the message fully.

## 7.3    Using Blind Carbon Copy

**Bcc** (Blind carbon copy) is similar to using Cc, with one difference. Each person receives the message as before but they cannot see the list of other addresses to whom the message has been sent

The Bcc box is not normally shown in a **New Message** window but if it is not visible, it can be displayed. To use Bcc, do the following.

- In the **New Message** window, select **All Headers** in the **View** menu.

- The **Bcc** box appears below the **Cc** box.

- Enter the addresses as before.

**Note:**  Typing one individual address in the **To** box personalises the message for that recipient while still hiding the addresses in the **Bcc** box.

## 7.4    Signatures

An e-mail signature is a piece of text that is added to a message automatically by Outlook Express. If you normally sign messages in the same way, you can save time by preparing a signature, e.g. 'Best Regards, Jim Brown'.

To add a signature, proceed as follows.

- Open **Outlook Express**, if it is not already open.

- Select **Options** in the **Tools** menu.
  The Options window appears.

- Click the **Signatures** tab.

- Click the **New** button in the **Signatures** section.
  **Signature #1** and **Default signature** appear in the Signatures panel.

- Type the text of the signature in the **Edit Signature** panel.
  (The **Insertion Cursor** is already flashing there, waiting for your text.)

- To **Add signatures to all outgoing messages**, tick the box at the top of the window. (For now, do not tick it.)

- Click **Apply** and then **OK**.

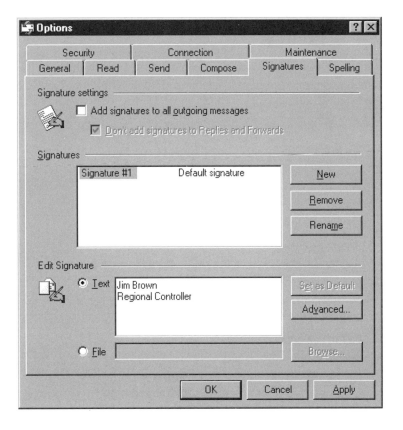

To rename **Signature #1** to be more meaningful, **Office**, for example:

- Click **Signature #1** in the Signatures panel.

- Click the **Rename** button.

- Type **Office**.

- Click **OK**.

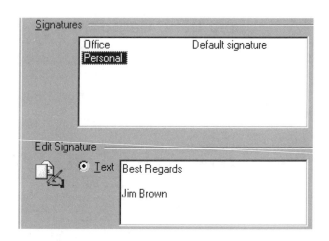

Try adding another signature, such as **Best Regards, Jim Brown** for personal e-mail.

Name the new signature **Personal**.

## 7.5    Inserting a Signature

Insert a signature in a message as follows.

- In the **New Message** window, place the Insertion Point where you want the signature to appear – for our example, at the end of the message.

- Select **Signature** in the **Insert** menu
  The signature is added at the Insertion Point.

Where there is more than one signature, select the one to use from the sub-menu.

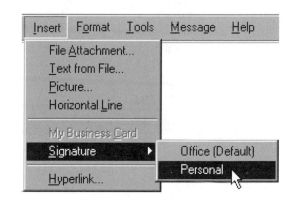

## 7.6    Priority

An e-mail message can be given a level of priority to indicate its relative importance. The speed at which the message is sent is unchanged but a symbol indicates either high or low priority to the recipient.

There are three priority levels:   **Normal** (no symbol)

                          **High** (a red exclamation mark)

                          **Low** (a blue arrow)

Messages are usually sent with normal priority.

Assign high or low priority to a message as follows.

- Click the small arrow at the right of the **Priority** button to display a menu.
  *Alternatively*, select **Set Priority** in the **Message** menu.

- Select the appropriate level. (**Normal** will have no effect.)
  For this example, select **High Priority**.
  A bar with the priority setting appears above the **To** box.

When the message is received, the recipient sees the priority mark to the left of the envelope icon.

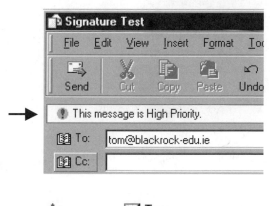

# Section 8     Attachments

## 8.1     Attaching a File

Practically any type of computer file can be added to an e-mail message as an **attachment**.  Word documents, spreadsheets, pictures, sounds etc. can all be sent to another person quickly and cheaply.

To send an attachment with a message, proceed as follows.

- Click the **Attach** button on the toolbar.
  *Alternatively*, select **File Attachment** in the **Insert** menu (of the **New Message** window).
  The **Insert Attachment** window opens.

- In the **Look in** box, find the location of the file you want to attach.
  For this example, locate the **Report** document you saved earlier.

- Click on the file to select it.

- Click the **Attach** button at the bottom right of the window.
  A new box is added under the **Subject** box in the Message window.  It displays the attached file.

- Repeat the above to attach another file or files.

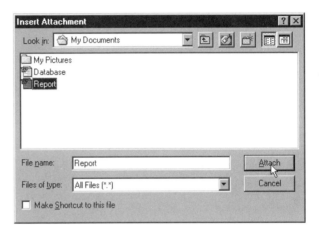

## 8.2     Deleting an Attachment

Attachments can be removed from a new message in Outlook Express before the message is sent, should you change your mind.

Attachments cannot be removed from e-mail messages you receive with Outlook Express.  The entire message must be deleted.  You can, however, remove an attachment from a received message that you are forwarding (see Section 9.2, page 369) to another person.

To remove an attachment from a message before sending (or forwarding) it:

- Right-click the file in the **Attach** box.
- Select **Remove** in the menu that appears.

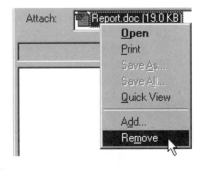

To remove an attachment from a message in the **Drafts** or **Outbox** folders, do the following.

- Double-click the message.
  It opens in a separate window.

- Right-click the file in the **Attach** box.

- Select **Remove** in the menu that appears.

Module 7

## 8.3    Opening and Saving Attachments

Attachments that you receive with e-mail messages are normally stored in a temporary folder on the hard disk.  An attachment can be opened directly or saved for future use.  It is recommended that you save attached files in a more useful location.

In this example, we shall use the **My Documents** folder.  The sample message with the attached **Report** can be used for the exercise.

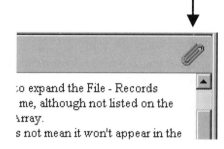

- Click the message with the attachment, to select it.

  The message is shown in the lower part of the window.

  A paper clip icon appears in the top right-hand corner of the message area.  This represents the attachment.

- Click the paper clip to display a menu.

- Click the name of the attachment, **Report**, to open it

  *Alternatiively*, click **Save Attachments** to save it.

You may see the **Open Attachment Warning** window.

### Note the virus warning!

Computer viruses can be spread through the Internet as attachments.

If you are unsure about the source of the message or were not expecting to receive an attachment, consider deleting the message.

Be particularly wary of files with the extension **.exe**.

Also note the check box at the bottom of the window, **Always ask before opening this type of file**.  If you unclick this box, the warning will not be displayed in future and the risk of virus infection is increased.

There are two options.

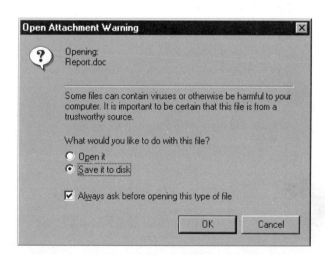

- **Open it.**  Select this option to open the file attachment.  You can then re-save the file in your preferred location by selecting **Save As** in the **File** menu.

- **Save it to disk.**  Select this option to save the file without opening it.

  The **Save Attachment As** window opens.  Select a folder in which to save the document.  You can also give the attachment a new name, if you wish.

  **Important:** If you give the attachment a new name, be sure to retain the 3-letter extension (if shown).

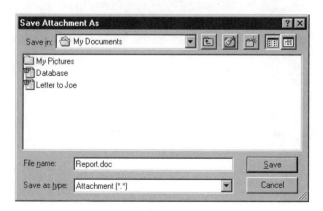

# Section 9      Managing Mail

## 9.1     Replying to Mail

It is not necessary to click the **New Mail** button when you want to reply to a message. Two buttons on the toolbar help you to reply to messages that you have received.

The **Reply** button opens a new message addressed to the original sender.

The **Reply All** button opens a new message addressed to all the recipients of the message if it was originally addressed to more than one person.

- Click the message in the **Inbox** to which you want to reply.

  For this exercise, click the message that you have sent to yourself (and received it).

- Click the **Reply** button to reply to the message. In this example, the reply goes back to yourself (again!). A new message window opens.

Notice that in the new message window…

- the e-mail address for the reply is already inserted in the **To** box.

- the **Subject** box contains **Re:** and the subject of the original message.

- the message section displays the original message with the heading:  **--- Original Message ---**

Continue:

- Click in the message area and type the reply.

  It is customary to type the reply above the original message.

- Click the **Send** button to send the message.

**Note:**   When you reply to a message, you can choose to include the original message in your reply or not. Including the message allows the recipient to relate your reply to the original. (See Section 10.1, page 371.)

You can also choose to reply to messages in the same format – plain text or HTML – as they were received. This ensures that people with older e-mail programs will be able to read your replies. (See Section 5.8, page 359.)

## 9.2     Forwarding Mail

When you forward an e-mail message, you pass it on to another person or persons. Forwarding is similar to replying insofar as the original message is quoted in the new message.

- Click the message in the **Inbox** that you want to Forward.

- Click the **Forward** button on the toolbar.

- A new message is created in a separate window.

Notice that in the new message window…

- the **To** box is empty. You must enter the address to which you want to forward the message.

- the **Subject** box contains **Fw:** and the subject of the original message.

- the message section displays the original message (with the heading  **--- Original Message ---**).

Continue:

- You may add an additional message, if you wish.

- Click the **Send** button to send the message.

## 9.3    Deleting Mail

Mail is stored in the Inbox and other folders until you decide to delete it.

To delete mail, do the following.

- Click the message in the **Inbox** (or other folder) that you want to delete.

- Click the **Delete** button on the toolbar.
  *Alternatively*, press the **Delete** key on the keyboard or select **Delete** in the **Edit** menu.
  The message is moved to the **Deleted Items** folder.  (It is not actually deleted at this stage.)

### To recover a 'deleted' message

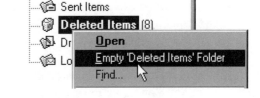

- Double-click the **Deleted Items** folder, in the panel at the left of the Outlook Express window, to open it.

- Drag the message out of the folder and drop onto the Inbox (or other folder).

*If you deleted the sample message with the attachment, you should now move it back to the **Inbox**.*

### To permanently delete mail

- Right-click the **Deleted Items** folder.

- Select **Empty 'Deleted Items' Folder** in the menu that appears.
  *Alternatively*, select **Empty 'Deleted Items' Folder** in the **Edit** menu.

- Click the message in the **Inbox** (or other folder) that you want to delete.

- Click the **Delete** button on the toolbar.

To permanently delete a single message, open the **Deleted Items** folder and click the message you want to delete, to select it.  Then click the **Delete** button on the toolbar.

## 9.4    Printing Mail

E-mail messages can be printed out, as follows.

- Click the message you want to print, to select it .

- Click the **Print** button on the toolbar.
  *Alternatively*, select **Print** in the **File** menu.
  The Print window opens.  It is similar to the Print window in other applications..

- In most circumstances, it is sufficient just to click **OK** to print the message.

# Section 10    Managing Outlook Express

## 10.1    Mail Options

As with other applications, you can set various e-mail options to suit your own way of working. Some of the most commonly used ones are shown here. The options are self-explanatory. It is only necessary to set them once. They will then stay in effect until you decide to change them.

- Select **Options** in the **Tools** menu.
  The Options window opens.

- Click the **Send** tab.

- In the lower part of the window, select or deselect the options you prefer.
  (Clicking an item with a tick in the box removes the tick.)

- Click **Apply** for your choices to take effect.

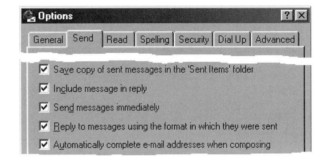

**Save copy...** keeps a copy of all messages that you send.

**Include message...** inserts the original message in your reply.

**Send messages...** sends the message when you click the **Send** button.
If unclicked, messages are sent to the Outbox until you decide to send them.

**Reply to...** uses the same format (plain text or HTML) as the received message.

**Automatically...** saves typing (and mistakes!).

## 10.2    Creating a New Message Folder

The Inbox and Sent Items folders fill up and become cluttered very quickly. You may like to organise the messages that you send and receive in a more meaningful way.

Sub-folders can be created in the main folders. They can be named to suit different kinds of mail, e.g. personal, office, club etc. As mail is viewed, you can then place it in the appropriate folder or delete it if you do not want to keep it.

To create a new folder in the Inbox, for example, do the following.

- Right-click on the **Inbox** folder in the panel at the left and select **Folder** in the menu that appears.

  *Alternatively*, select **New** in the **File** menu and click **Folder** in the menu that appears.

  The **Create Folder** window appears.

- Type  **Personal** in the **Folder Name** box.

- Click on the **Inbox** in the lower part of the window, to select it.

- Click **OK**.

  The new **Personal** folder is created as a sub-folder in the Inbox.

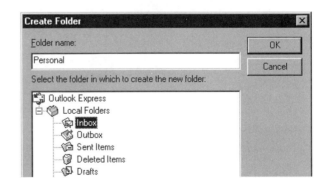

## 10.3  Moving and Copying Mail

Messages can be moved or copied from one folder to another.

To move a message into the Personal folder, for example:

- Select the message you want to move.

- Drag the message into the **Folder List**.

- Drop the message onto the **Personal** folder.
  (Do not release the mouse button until the **Personal** folder is highlighted.)
  Click the Personal folder to view the messages inside.

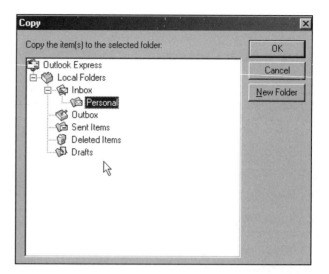

To place a copy of a message in another folder:

- Right-click the message you want to copy.

- Select **Copy to Folder** in the menu that appears.

- *Alternatively*, select **Copy to Folder** in the **Edit** menu.

- In the **Copy** window, select the folder in which to place the copy.
  Notice that you can click the **New Folder** button to create a new folder here, if required.

- Click **OK**.

## 10.4   Searching for Messages

When you have many folders and large numbers of messages, you may need help to find a particular one.  You can search for messages using a number of criteria.

- Click the **Find** button on the toolbar.
  *Alternatively*, select **Find** and **Message** in the **Edit** menu.
  The **Find Message** window opens.

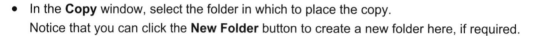

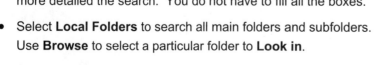

- Enter the appropriate information in the boxes.
  The more information you can enter, the more detailed the search.  You do not have to fill all the boxes.

- Select **Local Folders** to search all main folders and subfolders.
  Use **Browse** to select a particular folder to **Look in**.

- Click **Find Now**.

To begin a new search, click the **New Search** button.

# Section 11    Address Books

## 11.1    Storing Addresses

The **Outlook Express Address Book** is used to store contact information
– names and addresses, telephone numbers, and so on.

It can also be use to store and use e-mail addresses to save time and reduce
typing errors.

In addition, **Mailing Groups** can be
created when messages are sent to a
number of recipients on a regular basis.
This saves having to type all the
addresses individually.

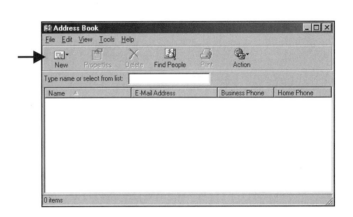

To add new contact details to the
Address Book, do the following.

- Click the **Addresses** button on the
  toolbar.
  The Address Book window opens.

- Click the **New** button on the toolbar
  and select **New Contact** in the menu
  that appears.
  The **Properties** window
  opens.

- Type the name – first,
  middle (if  any) and last
  name – and title and
  nickname, if required, in
  the boxes.

- Type the e-mail address in
  the **E-mail Addresses** box.

- Click the **Add** button.
  Th e-mail is set as the
  default address for that
  person.
  If the person has more
  than one e-mail address,
  you can enter them all
  and then select the one
  you wish to set as the
  default.

- To correct mistakes, click
  the **Edit** button and retype.

- To delete an address,
  click to select it and then
  click the **Remove** button.

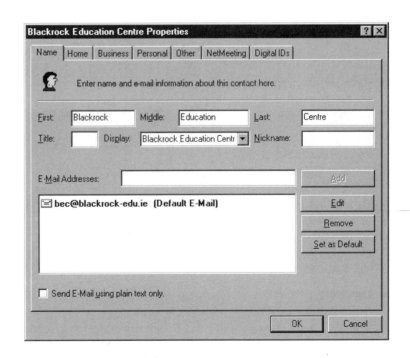

## 11.2   Adding Addresses Automatically

A sender's e-mail address can be added to the Address Book from a received e-mail message without having to type it by hand.

Do the following.

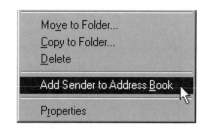

- Right-click on the message in the **Inbox** or other folder.

- Select **Add Sender to Address Book** in the menu that appears.

- Open the **Address Book** to check the new entry.

- Double-click on the address to add any additional information in the window that appears, if required.

  Click the tabs at the top of the window for more detailed entries.

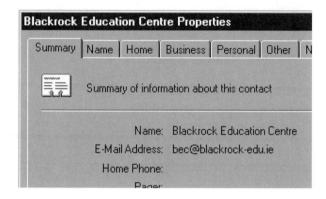

## 11.3   Using the Address Book

The Address Book can be used to insert an e-mail address automatically when you are preapring a new e-mail message.

- Click the **New Message** button on the toolbar to open the new message window.

- Click the **To** button to the left of the address box.

  The **Select Recipients** window opens.

- Click the required contact or group (see below) in the panel on the left.

- Click the **To ->** button in the centre to add the contact to the **Message recipients** box on the right.

  Repeat the process if you are sending the message to more than one person.

  (You can also enter contacts in the **Cc** and **Bcc** boxes.)

- Click **OK**.

  The selected contact is automatically entered in the address box in the **New Message** window.

  (The contact's name is displayed rather than the e-mail address.)

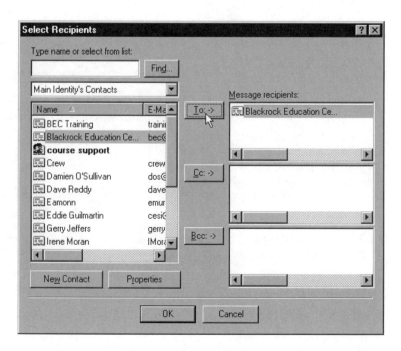

## 11.4 Deleting an Address

Unwanted contacts and their addresses can be deleted as follows.

- Open the **Address Book**.

- Right-click the contact you wish to delete.

- Select **Delete** from the menu that appears.

## 11.5 Group Addresses

If you regularly send e-mail to more than one person, you can create a **Mailing Group** or **Distribution List** in your Address Book to avoid having to enter all the addresses individually. People in the Address Book can belong to more than one group.

To create a new group, proceed as follows.

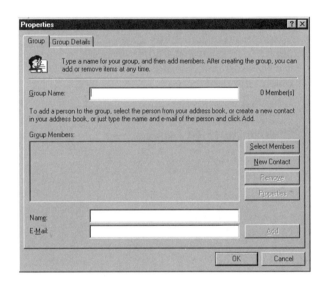

- Open the **Address Book**.

- Click **New** and select **New Group** in the menu that appears.
  The **Properties** window opens.

- Enter a name for the group in the **Group Name** box.

- Click the **Select Members** button.
  The **Select Group Members** window appears.

- In the list of Address Book entries on the left, click on a name you wish to add to the group.

- Click the **Select** button to add the selected name to the group.
  The name appears in the **Members** box on the right.

- Repeat the steps above to add further names.

- To add a name not already in the Address Book, click the **New Contact** button.
  When you add the new name, it appears in the Address Book and can then be added to the group.

- Click **OK** when the group is complete.

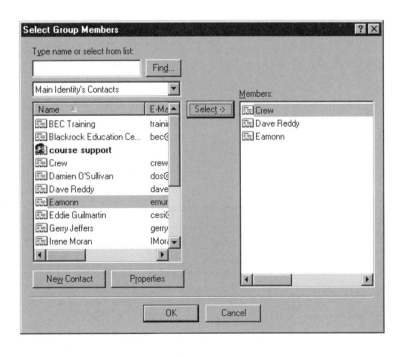

Module 7

## 11.6   Sending Group Mail

Sending an e-mail message to everyone in a group is similar to using the Address Book to send a message to an individual.  It is only necessary to select the Group name instead of an individual's.

- Click the **New Message** button on the toolbar to open the New Message window.

- Click the **To** button to the left of the Address box.

  The **Select Recipients** window opens.

- Click the name of the required group in the list of Address Book entries on the left, to select it.

- Click the **To** button in the centre to add the group to the **Message recipients** box on the right.

  Note that you can also add extra individual contacts or other groups to the **To**, **Cc** or **Bcc** boxes.

- Click **OK**.

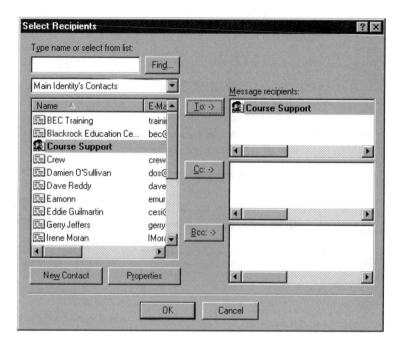

# Section 12    Exercises

Module 7

# Self Check Exercises

**1** In how many of these activities could you engage while using a browser?

☐ View images

☐ Listen to music

☐ Watch a video

☐ Use a search engine

**2** Which of the following is used for exchanging information over the Internet?

☐ DOS

☐ C

☐ HTTP

☐ Word

**3** Match these abbreviations to their functions.

| | |
|---|---|
| **FTP** | An Internet address. |
| **ISP** | Links computers across the telephone network. |
| **ISDN** | Commercial provider of Internet access. |
| **URL** | Allows file transfer between computers. |

**4** Place these components of an e-mail address in correct order, in a line, from left to right.

- ISP
- Name
- @ symbol
- Domain or country of origin

**5** What function is performed by the Outbox?

☐ It is a temporary store for composed e-mail.

☐ It provides a template for composing e-mail.

☐ It stores a record of sent e-mail.

☐ It retains a 'carbon copy' of the e-mail that has been sent.

**6** You would choose Forward on the Toolbar to perform which of these functions?

☐ To send an e-mail in the normal manner

☐ To send a carbon copy of an e-mail to someone

☐ To send a received e-mail to another address

☐ To send a copy of an e-mail to a folder

**7** Does a computer always need a modem to access the internet?

☐ Yes

☐ No

**8** Place in order in a line, left to right, these components of a Web address.
- The category or country to which the name belongs
- The abbreviation for a Web page
- A company's or individual's name

**9** Match these icons on the Browser's Standard Toolbar to their functions.

| | |
|---|---|
| Home | Allows you to search the Internet. |
| Refresh | Lists the sites you visited over a time. |
| Search | Opens Outlook Express. |
| Stop | Brings you to the Browser's start page. |
| History | Loads a new copy of the current page. |
| Mail | Lists sites whose addresses you have stored. |
| Favorites | Cancels the current search. |
| Back | Returns you sequentially through the pages you are browsing. |

# Practical Exercises

These exercises assume you have access to the Internet and that you have an e-mail address. For the e-mail exercises, you will also need the co-operation of two other people with e-mail addresses to practise with.

**Exercise 1**

- Create a folder on the desktop and name it Internet Samples.
- Open the site **www.blackrock-edu.ie**.
- Open a document in Word and save it in your folder as Internet Exercises. Then answer these questions:
  1. What kind of establishment have you contacted?
  2. What is its purpose?

**Exercise 2**

Using the same site as in Exercise 1...

- Save the Home Page in your folder.
- Search the site for a picture of the courtyard and save it also.

**Exercise 3**

Still using the same site, find details of other similar organisations throughout the country and save a copy of any accompanying graphics in your folder.

**Exercise 4**

Use the search engine, **www.yahoo.com**, and...

- Look for a site that gives you access to the newspapers of the world.
- Find the link to the Top 250 Newspaper Sites.
- Add its address to your Favourites.
- Answer these questions:
  1. What is the first paper listed for Scotland?
  2. In England, which paper is listed third?
  3. How many Irish newspapers are listed?

**Exercise 5**

Use any search engine and find the following:

1. The address of the *Los Angeles Times* and the number of editions it has.
2. The address of the Irish Government's Web site.
3. A reasonably priced hotel in Paris for a weekend trip.

**Exercise 6**

Open Outlook Express and send an e-mail with the subject **My Conquest of the WWW** to **friend1@isp.ie**

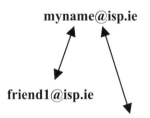

You must substitute **real** e-mail addresses for these sample ones.

**Exercise 7**

Send another e-mail to **friend2@isp.ie** but this time, while using the same subject, copy and paste the message from your first letter to your second.

*A little off-line work may be needed to encourage replies before the next exercise.*

**Exercise 8**

Add addresses to your Outlook Express Address Book as follows:

- Enter the address you used in Exercise 1.
- Enter the address from the e-mail you received in Exercise 2.

**Exercise 9**

Reply to the sender of one of your received e-mails without actually having to manually type the sender's address into the To box.

**Exercise 10**

Using your address book, send the same letter to friends 1 and 2 thanking them for their co-operation.

**Exercise 11**

Organise your Messages as follows:

- Create a new folder in Outlook Express, name it Experiments and do the following:
  1. Copy all the messages you received into the Experiments folder.
  2. Delete all the messages in your Inbox.

Module 7

# Solutions

# Solutions

**Self Check Solutions**

**Practical Exercises Solutions**

Solutions

381

# Module 1     Self Check Exercises – Solutions

**1** Which of these is not an input device?

☐ Touchscreen
☐ Scanner
☑ Monitor
☐ Touchpad

**2** Tick the terms that could apply to a computer in a network.

☑ Client
☑ Peer
☑ Server
☑ Station

**3** What is the number system used by computers?

☐ Decimal
☑ Binary
☐ Natural
☐ Primary

**4** Tick the correct statement.

☑ 8 bits make 1 byte.
☐ 8 bytes make 1 bit.

**5** Which of these refer to an area for storing data? Tick all correct answers.

☐ Data
☑ File
☑ Record
☑ Field

**6** In which of the following are the instructions to start up the computer stored? Tick.

☐ RAM
☑ ROM
☐ Cache

**7** Are the terms 'Application' and 'Program' interchangeable?

☑ Yes
☐ No

**8** One of these devices does not normally affect the performance (speed) of the computer. Which one?

☑ Monitor
☐ RAM
☐ Graphics Accelerator
☐ Hard disk

**9** Tick the peripheral device/s you would not expect to find on a multimedia computer.

☐ Microphone
☐ Loudspeakers
☐ Floppy Disk Drive
☑ VGA Monitor

**10** In a Web page, what is most likely to be used to link you directly to another page or Web site?

☑ Hypertext
☐ A Search Engine
☐ E-mail
☐ An Account

**11** Which of these terms refer to viruses your computer may 'catch'? Tick.

☑ A Trojan Horse
☐ A Drop
☐ A Maggot
☑ A Worm

**12** Tick the terms that refer to equipment.

☑ Hardware
☐ Shareware
☐ Software
☑ Peripheral

**13** Tick the terms you would associate with computer networks.

☑ WAN
☑ Dumb terminal
☑ LAN
☑ Client

# Module 2    Self Check Exercises – Solutions

1  To shut down your computer from the
  desktop, which menu would you select?
- ☐ File
- ☐ View
- ☐ Settings
- ☑ Start

2  From the list below, select the items
  that may be represented by an icon.
- ☑ File
- ☑ Folder
- ☑ Object
- ☑ Disk drive

3  What is another name for a folder?
- ☐ File
- ☑ Directory
- ☐ Menu
- ☐ Icon

4  The Return key may also be known as
  which of the following?
- ☐ Shift
- ☐ Delete
- ☐ Backspace
- ☑ Enter

5  In which of these may you store a folder?
- ☑ Hard disk (C:)
- ☑ Folder
- ☑ Floppy Disk (A:)
- ☑ My Documents

6  When searching for a file or a folder
  with the Find function, which sign may
  precede the name in some cases?
- ☐ +
- ☐ -
- ☑ *
- ☐ /

7  A file name has two components.
  The first is the actual name you give the
  file. What is the second?
- ☐ The suffix
- ☐ The address
- ☐ The location
- ☑ The extension

8  Place the following in order of size,
  starting with the smallest.
    Bit
    Byte
    Kilobyte
    Megabyte
    Gigabyte

9  Which of these is the usual representation
  of the computer's hard disk?
- ☐ A:
- ☑ C:
- ☐ D:
- ☐ E:

10  Which of these functions would be used in
  the process of replacing a corrupted file?
- ☐ Backup
- ☐ Format
- ☑ Restore
- ☐ Insert

11  What happens when you delete a file from
  a floppy disk (A:)?
- ☐ It is temporarily deleted.
- ☐ It is placed in the Recycle Bin.
- ☑ It is permanently deleted.
- ☐ It is placed in My Documents.

12  What happens when you format the
  computer's hard disk (C:)?
- ☑ Files essential to operating the
    computer are erased.
- ☐ Only temporary files are erased.

# Module 3    Self Check Exercises – Solutions

**1** A template is best described as…

- ☑ A blank page with a predetermined layout
- ☐ A blank page without a predetermined layout
- ☐ A blank page with headers and footers
- ☐ A blank page with a blank table

**2** The Standard Toolbar contains…

- ☐ Menus
- ☐ Shortcuts to infrequent functions
- ☑ Shortcuts to frequent functions
- ☐ Scroll bars

**3** To display additional toolbars, where will you find the Toolbar menu?

- ☑ In the View menu
- ☐ In the Format menu
- ☐ In the Tools menu
- ☐ In the Edit menu

**4** Which of these allows you to rename a document before saving it?

- ☐ Save
- ☐ Save in
- ☑ Save as
- ☐ Save as type

**5** Tick any of the items below which may not be a proper indent.

- ☐ First-line indent
- ☐ Left indent
- ☐ Right indent
- ☐ Hanging indent

**6** Which button on the Standard Toolbar would you most likely use to undo a typing error?

- ☑ ↰
- ☐ ABC✓
- ☐ ✂
- ☐ 🖌

**7** When you open the Toolbar Menu, what do the ticks indicate?

- ☐ The option has not been selected.
- ☐ The option is not available.
- ☐ The option may be chosen.
- ☑ The option is already available.

**8** What unit of measurement is used for letter (font) size?

- ☐ Millimetres (mm)
- ☑ Points (pt)
- ☐ Inches (ins)
- ☐ Other

**9** How many ways can you align text margins using the Formatting Toolbar?

- ☐ 1
- ☐ 2
- ☐ 3
- ☑ 4

**10** How many of the following describe the functioning of the Clipboard?

- ☑ A temporary store of information
- ☐ A permanent store of information
- ☑ A temporary store of graphics
- ☐ A permanent store of graphics
- ☑ A temporary store of text
- ☐ A permanent store of text

**11** What function may this key have?

Enter ↵

- ☐ It moves text around.
- ☐ It gives an upper character.
- ☐ It gives the upper case letter.
- ☑ It enters a blank line.

## Module 4     Self Check Exercises – Solutions

**1** What kind of information is commonly put into a spreadsheet cell? (*Tick all possible answers.*)

- ☑ Text
- ☑ Numbers
- ☑ Mathematical Formula
- ☐ Cell Addresses

**2** How would you identify the active cell on your spreadsheet?

- ☑ Darkened border
- ☐ Flashing border
- ☐ The contents of the cell are darkened.
- ☐ The contents of the cell flash.

**3** Which best describes a range of cells?

- ☐ A single column of cells
- ☐ A single row of cells
- ☑ A rectangular block of cells

**4** Which of these represents a correct cell reference?

- ☐ A
- ☐ 5
- ☑ B6
- ☐ D:7

**5** Which of these represents a correct range reference?

- ☐ A1
- ☑ A1:B6
- ☐ 6:B
- ☐ C:7/D:8

**6** What is a row header?

- ☑ A reference number to the left of the row
- ☐ A reference letter to the left of the row

**7** What appears in a selected cell immediately after clicking the **Paste Function** button?

- ☐ A formula
- ☑ An equal sign
- ☐ A cell reference
- ☐ A range reference

**8** Which of the following would best apply to a cell containing the formula =(A3+1)?

- ☑ The contents of this cell equals that in cell A3 plus 1.
- ☐ The contents of cell A equals 3 plus 1.
- ☐ The contents of cell A3 must start with +1.
- ☐ None of the above.

**9** If, having typed 'Monday' in A1, you drag the *fill handle* across to the right, what will happen?

- ☐ Monday will be copied into each of the other cells as well.
- ☑ The other days of the week will appear in the cells.

**10** What icons from the Standard Toolbar are not matched to a correct label explaining their function?

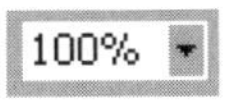

- ☑ `100% ▾` Perform a percentage calculation. 
- ☑ `A↓Z` Perform an Ascending alphabetical sort. 
- ☐ `Σ` Perform an Addition operation.

**11** Having selected a **Paste Function**, what appears next in the selected cell?

- ☐ A numeric value
- ☑ A formula
- ☐ The name of the function
- ☐ Nothing

# Module 5    Self Check Exercises – Solutions

**1** Which of these would you click to include a field in a query?

- ☐ Yes
- ☐ Include
- ☐ ✓
- ☑ >

**2** What is the name of the database application you are using for this exercise?

- ☑ Microsoft Access
- ☐ Microsoft Excel
- ☐ Microsoft PowerPoint

**3** Which of these items do you need to create in your database if you wish to include an additional new category of information?

- ☑ A field
- ☐ A record
- ☐ A file
- ☐ A folder

**4** In a database, what is shown in a table?

- ☑ All records in a particular database
- ☐ All fields related to a particular record

**5** Which of the following does a single form in a database display?

- ☑ Fields from a particular table or query
- ☐ The records in a database

**6** Tick the statement(s) that is/are true of a query?

- ☑ A query may present a set of complete records.
- ☑ A query may present a set of modified records.

**7** Columns in a database table correspond to which of the following?

- ☑ Fields
- ☐ Records

**8** In any given database, at least one field is usually assigned as which of the following?

- ☐ A field name
- ☐ A wild card
- ☑ A primary key

**9** If you can see all the records and fields on your computer screen, which of these are you most likely to be viewing?

- ☐ The query
- ☐ The form
- ☑ The table

**10** You wish to search a database for all dates after 15th Nov. 1987. Which formula would you use?

- ☐ >=15/11/87
- ☑ >15/11/87
- ☐ <=15/11/87
- ☐ <15/11/87

**11** Tick which data items will be matched with the formulae: **=B\* and =Sm?th**.

- ☑ Smith
- ☑ Brennan
- ☐ O'Brien
- ☑ Smyth

**12** Match the wildcard characters to their functions.

**o\***        Finds the words with letters o to w inside.

**t[!ow]n**   Finds words beginning with o.

**b[o-w]ts**  Excludes the words with the letters o to w inside.

**13** Tick the *inaccurate* statements.

The form wizard allows you to...

- ☐ select any number of fields for display.
- ☐ select all fields for display.
- ☑ display not more than a limited number of fields.

**14** Which is the correct statement?

- ☐ You may save a query as a filter.
- ☑ You may save a filter as a query.

# Module 6    Self Check Exercises – Solutions

**1** What is the function of *slide transitions*?

☐ They enable the slide show to progress automatically.

☑ They facilitate the creation of animations between slides.

**2** Which of these icons would you select to use Word Art?

☐ 🅰

☑ 🄰

☐ 📄

**3** Which of these would you use to set uniform text formats in a set of slides?

☐ A Text Box

☑ An AutoLayout Area

☐ An AutoShape

**4** Which of these would you normally use to obtain a slide background?

☐ Insert Object

☑ Apply Design

☐ Slide Sorter View

☐ Slide Transition

**5** Which two settings can be specified in the Transitions window?

☑ Effect

☐ Frequency

☐ Timing

☑ Size

**6** Is it possible to move text from one slide to another without using the normal copy/paste function?

☑ Yes

☐ No

**7** Having inserted a graphic from a Clip Art collection, is it possible to change the colours?

☑ Yes

☐ No

**8** Which tab icon is correctly matched to its function?

☐ ⌐ Aligns the left of the text to the tab.

☑ L Aligns the left of the text to the tab.

☐ ⊥ Centres the text on the page.

**9** Tick the icons that could be used to add a co-worker box to an organisation chart.

☑ ⊟⊢

☐ ⊤⊟

☐ ⊟⊣

☐ ⊟

☑ ⊣⊟

**10** Is it correct to say that in a PowerPoint presentation, you may hide slides in a presentation sequence?

☑ Yes

☐ No

**11** Tick the items that can be animated.

☑ A slide

☑ A title

☑ Other text

**12** By pressing the keys **Ctrl** and **S** during your work, what function are you performing?

☐ Re-start

☐ Sort

☑ Save

## Module 7    Self Check Exercises – Solutions

**1**  In how many of these activities could you engage while using a browser?

&#9745;  View images

&#9745;  Listen to music

&#9745;  Watch a video

&#9745;  Use a search engine

**2**  Which of the following is used for exchanging information over the Internet?

&#9744;  DOS

&#9744;  C

&#9745;  HTTP

&#9744;  Word

**3**  Match these abbreviations to their functions.

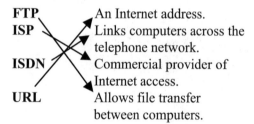

FTP — Allows file transfer between computers.
ISP — Commercial provider of Internet access.
ISDN — Links computers across the telephone network.
URL — An Internet address.

**4**  Place these components of an e-mail address in correct order, in a line, from left to right.

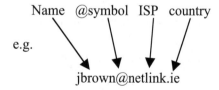

Name  @symbol  ISP  country

e.g.

jbrown@netlink.ie

**5**  What function is performed by the Outbox?

&#9745;  It is a temporary store for composed e-mail.

&#9744;  It provides a template for composing e-mail.

&#9744;  It stores a record of sent e-mail.

&#9744;  It retains a 'carbon copy' of the e-mail that has been sent.

**6**  You would choose Forward on the Toolbar to perform which of these functions?

&#9744;  To send an e-mail in the normal manner

&#9744;  To send a carbon copy of an e-mail to someone

&#9745;  To send a received e-mail to another address

&#9744;  To send a copy of an e-mail to a folder

**7**  Does a computer always need a modem to access the internet?

&#9744;  Yes

&#9745;  No

**8**  Place in order in a line, left to right, these components of a Web address.

web abbreviation**.name.category/country**

e.g.          www.ncte.com

or            www.scoilnet.ie

**9**  Match these icons on the Browser's Standard Toolbar to their functions.

Allows you to search the Internet.

Lists the sites you visited over a time.

Opens Outlook Express.

Brings you to the Browser's start page.

Loads a new copy of the current page.

Lists sites whose addresses you have stored.

Cancels the current search.

Returns you sequentially through the pages you are browsing.

# Module 2    Practical Exercises – Solutions

## Exercise 1

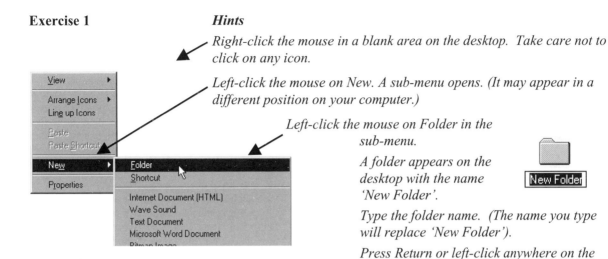

*Hints*

*Right-click the mouse in a blank area on the desktop. Take care not to click on any icon.*

*Left-click the mouse on New. A sub-menu opens. (It may appear in a different position on your computer.)*

*Left-click the mouse on Folder in the sub-menu.*

*A folder appears on the desktop with the name 'New Folder'.*

*Type the folder name. (The name you type will replace 'New Folder').*

*Press Return or left-click anywhere on the desktop to finish.*

## Exercises 2 to 6

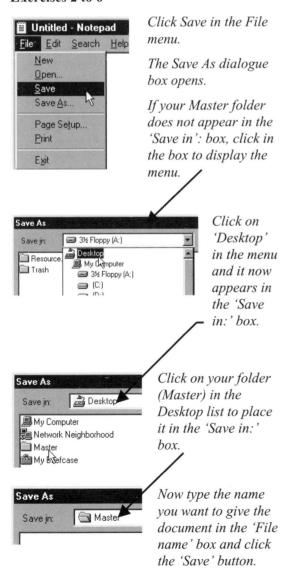

*Click Save in the File menu.*

*The Save As dialogue box opens.*

*If your Master folder does not appear in the 'Save in': box, click in the box to display the menu.*

*Click on 'Desktop' in the menu and it now appears in the 'Save in:' box.*

*Click on your folder (Master) in the Desktop list to place it in the 'Save in:' box.*

*Now type the name you want to give the document in the 'File name' box and click the 'Save' button.*

## Exercises 7

*Open the Master folder by double-clicking it.*

*Click New in the File menu.*

*Click Folder in the sub-menu.*

## Exercise 8

**Hint**: *Click on a file icon. Drag it to the Slave folder). Release the mouse button.*

| Answers |
|---|
| 1  No difference. Both use the same amount of memory. |
| 2  Addresses, Information, Small/Big Clip Art, My House. |
| 3  \slave |
| 4  My House |
| 5  (Will vary from person to person) |
| 6  3 different types – Word (3), Notepad (1), Bitmap (1). |

## Exercise 9

4  1.44Mb (Megabytes)

5  One, called 'Slave'.

6  About 0.4Mb (400kb). Some people's files may be larger or smaller.

## Module 3     Practical Exercises – Solutions

### Exercise 1

*Insert Clip Art and resize.*

*Use the* **Return/Enter** *key to add blank lines.*

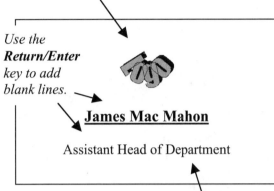

**James Mac Mahon**

Assistant Head of Department

*Change Font size and Style as required. Centre align.*

### Exercise 2

*1. Insert Clip Art and resize.*

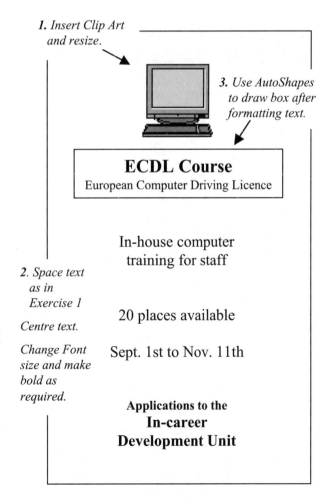

*3. Use AutoShapes to draw box after formatting text.*

**ECDL Course**
European Computer Driving Licence

In-house computer training for staff

*2. Space text as in Exercise 1*

*Centre text.*

*Change Font size and make bold as required.*

20 places available

Sept. 1st to Nov. 11th

**Applications to the In-career Development Unit**

### Exercise 3

*Enter text and divide into paragraphs without indents at first. Set Font size and make Bold as required.*

**Indents**

To indent means to increase or decrease the margin for part of the text in a document, as in the following examples.

*Select each piece of text in turn.*

*Apply the required indent to each.*

    A **first-line indent** gives a wider margin to the first line than to the other lines in a paragraph.

    A **paragraph indent** means that the margin for an entire paragraph is wider than for the rest of the text in the document.

**A hanging indent** reduces the margin for the first line of a paragraph so that it 'overhangs' to the left of the rest of the paragraph.

*Progress to the next piece of text.*

1   It can be used to draw attention to the beginning of a paragraph, as in the paragraph above.

2   It can be used to number a list, as in these two paragraphs.

### Exercise 4

*Insert WordArt*

**Social Committee**

| Date | Event | Eligible Staff |
|------|-------|----------------|
| 1st Sept. | Tennis Tournament | Non-smokers |
| 16th Nov. | Halloween Party | Non-drinkers |
| 23rd Dec. | Christmas Party | All welcome |
| 31st Dec. | New Year Party | Available |
| 3rd Jan. | Keep Fit Classes | Volunteers |

Left paragraph indent                    Centre Tab                    Right Tab

## Exercise 5

<u>Hints:</u> *Choose Font. Make Bold. Centre Align. Bullet other text. Insert arrows from AutoShapes. Format ⇒ Page Border.*

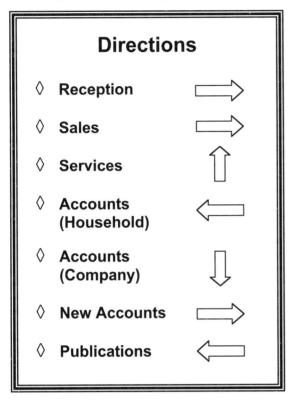

## Exercise 6

<u>AutoShapes:</u> *Select / Format / Colour / Position / Resize*

<u>Text format:</u> *Font / Size / Colour / Align*

<u>Borders and Shading:</u> Format ⇒ *Page Border*

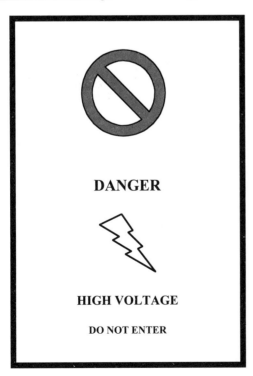

## Exercise 7

<u>Step 1:</u> *Type document 1 / Type document 2 / File ⇒ New document (or button) / Select text / Edit ⇒ Copy / Position cursor / Edit ⇒ Paste*

<u>Step 2:</u> *Format text / Bold-Italic / Line spaces / Hanging Indent / Right Align*

<u>Remember:</u> *To select text, you may click and drag over the text or click and drag along the text's left-hand margin.*

*Type text into new document.*
*(File ⇒ New document or New button)*

Protecting Data: 'Appropriate security measures shall be taken against unauthorised access to, or alteration, disclosure or destruction of, the data and against their accidental loss or destruction…'

Data Protection Act

'Access to your computer should be restricted to authorised staff. Systems should be password protected; information on your screen should be hidden from callers to your office; access to information should be restricted on a 'need-to-know' basis in accordance with a defined policy; all waste paper, printouts, etc., should be carefully disposed of.'

Guidlines to Data Controllers

*Centre align.*
*Change font size.*
*Make Bold.*

*Insert blank lines. (Return key)*

**Data Protection**

It is essential that any data relating to individuals, to which you have access or which you store on a computer, be adequately protected. Note the following:

*Select and indent.*

Under the *Data Protection Act* there are certain legal obligations.

*Guidelines for Data Controllers* have been issued by the Data Protection Commissioner.

**Protecting Data:** 'Appropriate security measures shall be taken against unauthorised access to, or alteration, disclosure or destruction of, the data and against their accidental loss or destruction…'

*Data Protection Act*

*Hanging indents*

'**Access** to your computer should be restricted to authorised staff. Systems should be password protected; information on your screen should be hidden from callers to your office; access to information should be restricted on a 'need-to-know' basis in accordance with a defined policy; all waste paper, printouts, etc., should be carefully disposed of.'

*Guidelines to Data Controllers*

*Right align and italic.*

## Module 4     Practical Exercises – Solutions

| | A | B | C | D | E | F | G | H | I | J |
|---|---|---|---|---|---|---|---|---|---|---|
| 1 | Munster Office First Quarterly Report | | | | | | | | | |
| 2 | | | | | | | | | | |
| 3 | | | | | | | | | | |
| 4 | | | September | October | November | Average | Total Unit Sales | Target | % Achieved | % of Total Units |
| 5 | | | | | | | | | | |
| 6 | | | | | | | | | | |
| 7 | | Telephones | 116 | 79 | 56 | 83.67 | 251 | 350 | 71.71 | 14.25 |
| 8 | | Answer Mach. | 47 | 50 | 35 | 44.00 | 132 | 150 | 88.00 | 7.49 |
| 9 | | Calculators | 9 | 38 | 17 | 21.33 | 64 | 300 | 21.33 | 3.63 |
| 10 | | Shredders | 297 | 225 | 120 | 214.00 | 642 | 200 | 321.00 | 36.44 |
| 11 | | Laminators | 79 | 56 | 34 | 56.33 | 169 | 220 | 76.82 | 9.59 |
| 12 | | Binding Mach. | 83 | 88 | 38 | 69.67 | 209 | 250 | 83.60 | 11.86 |
| 13 | | Mini recorders | 57 | 69 | 7 | 44.33 | 133 | 100 | 133.00 | 7.55 |
| 14 | | Transcribers | 57 | 69 | 36 | 54.00 | 162 | 100 | 162.00 | 9.19 |
| 15 | | | 745 | 674 | 343 | | 1762 | 1670 | | 100 |
| 16 | | | | | | | | | | |
| 17 | | | | | | | | | | |
| 18 | | Total Number of Units Sold | | | | | 1762 | | | |
| 19 | | Total Number for Target Units | | | | | 1670 | | | |
| 20 | | Unit Throughput as % of Target | | | | | 105.51 | | | |

*Note:*

*On completion of all the exercises, your spreadsheet should look like this, except for row 15. This is a reference row and has not been requested in the exercises.*

### Exercises 1 and 2

*There is no assistance for these exercises.*

### Exercise 3

- Type the formula =**SUM(C7:E7)** in **G7** and press **Return**.
- Select **G7** again and drag the fill handle down to **G14**.
  The figures in the Target column are given; they are not calculated.

### Exercise 4

To tidy up (format) numbers:

- Select the numbers to be formatted.
- Select Cells from the Format menu.
- Select the Number Tab.
- Set the decimal places to 2.
- Click OK.

| % Achieved |
|---|
| 71.71428571 |
| 88 |
| 21.33333333 |
| 321 |
| 76.81818182 |
| 83.6 |
| 133 |
| 162 |

### Exercise 5

We need to use a <u>Relative</u> Reference, i.e., the total number of each of the units sold.

- Select cell **G15**.
- Click **Autosum**.
- Select cell **I7** and enter the formula =**(G7/H7*100)**.
- Press **Return**.
- Select cell **I7** again.
- Use the **Fill** handle to enter data in the rest of the column.

### Exercise 6

Here, we need to use an <u>Absolute</u> Reference – to the total number of units sold.

- Select cell **G15**.
- Click **Autosum**.

- Select cell **J7** and enter the formula =**(G7/$G$15*100)**.
- Press **Return**.
- Select cell **J7** again.
- Use the **Fill** handle to enter data in the rest of the column.

### Exercise 7

Check by using Autosum on the column.
It should give you **100%**. See cell **J15** above.

### Exercise 8

The % option multiplies the cell value by 100.

In this instance, we want to format the percentage numbers to two decimal places and not calculate/convert to percentage values.

### Exercise 9

Cell G18: =SUM(G7:G15)  Ans. 1762
Cell G19: =SUM(H7:H14)  Ans. 1670
Cell G20: =(G18/G19)*100 Ans. 105.51

### Exercise 10

- Select cells **C7** to **E7**.
- Hold down **Ctrl** for the second selection, **C4** to **E4**.
- Click the **Charting** icon on the Toolbar.
- Choose the first Columnar chart.
- In the **Data Range** dialogue box, choose **Next**.
- Click the **Titles** tab and…
  - Enter a **Chart Title**.
  - Enter **First Quarter** in the X Axis box.
  - Enter **Units Sold** for the Y Axis box.
- Click the **Legend** tab and unclick **Show Legend**.

- After **Next**, choose the **Chart Location** and **Finish**.

### Exercise 11

*There is no assistance for this exercise.*

# Module 5    Practical Exercises – Solutions

## Exercise 1

Open **Access**, select **Blank Database** and click
**OK**. In the next Dialogue box, name your file,
decide where to save it and click **Create**. The
**Database** window opens.

Click **New**,
select **Design
View** and
click **OK**.
The Table
window
opens.

Enter the
**Field Names**,
choosing an
appropriate
**Data Type**
for each field.

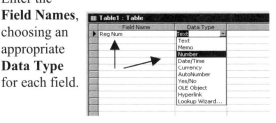

## Exercise 2

Click the **Forms** tab in the **Database** window.
• Click **New**
• Choose **Table** or **Query**. In this instance it
  will be 'Staff Location'.
• Click **Form Wizard**.
• Select the **fields** you require.
  – Select the **background**.
  – Follow instructions. Then click **Finish**.

## Exercise 3

Here you should use a simple sort.
• Select the **Surname** column.
• Click the **Apply Filter** button on
  the Toolbar in the filter window.

## Exercise 4

Again, a simple sort is required here.
• Highlight the **Registration No.** column.
• Click the **Ascending Sort** icon.

## Exercise 5

• Go to **Records** on the **Menu Bar**.
• Filter.
• Advanced Filter/Sort (Clear the grid if
  necessary).
• In the first Field Box, click **Reg. Number**.
• Then **Ascending** in the **Sort** box below.
• In the second Field Box, click **Sex**.
• Then **F** in the **Criteria** box below.
• Click the **Apply Filter** icon.

## Exercise 6

The filter/sort in exercises 4 and 5 present
tables with all the information about every
employee. To select fields for display, a
**Query** is helpful.

• Click the **Query** tab.
• Click **New**
• Choose **Simple Query Wizard**
• Select the Table on which to base the
  Query.
• Select the **Fields** for display.
  – Reg. Number
  – Sex
  – Surname
• Give the Query a title.
• Click **Finish**.
• Reopen the Query and go to **Design** view.
• In the **Reg. No.** field, choose **Ascending**
  as the Sort option.
• Click the **Run** button on the toolbar.

## Exercise 7

A **Filter by Selection** would allow you to
display only male employees, only female
employees or only Ireland employees,
depending on which of these fields you
choose to select by.

An **Advance Filter/Sort** using the field
**Country** with the criterion **Ireland,** along
with **Ascending** in the **Sort** option for the **Sex**
field, would display the appropriate table.

A **Query** would be useful if you had to select fields
for display. Remember, you have to reopen the
Query, go to **Design** view and set the appropriate
sort, **Ascending**, in the **Sex** field and the criterion
**Ireland** in the **Country** field.

## Exercise 8 and 9

*There is no assistance for these exercises.*

## Exercise 10

Apply the criterion  **>=24/06/99**

# Module 6    Practical Exercises – Solutions

## Exercise 1

Open PowerPoint. **Blank Presentation** is already selected in the opening dialogue box. Click **OK**.

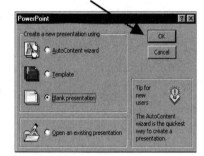

- In the **New Slide** dialogue box, the first design is already selected. Click **OK**.

- Click in the box and add the **Title**.

- Click in the next box and add the **Sub Title**.

## Exercise 2

- Click **Apply Design** in the **Format** menu.

- Select **high voltage** and click **Apply**.

## Exercise 3

- Insert the logo as you would insert Clip Art in a Word document.

- For the animation…

    ◆ Click in the **Title** text box on the slide.

    ◆ Click the **Animation** icon on the toolbar.

    ◆ Click the required animation in the **Animation** dialogue box.

- Repeat as above for the next text.

## Exercise 4

Repeat as above for new slides, entering text and background.

For the footer…

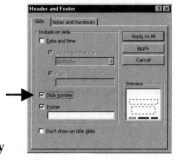

- Click **Header and Footer…** in the **View** menu.

- Click **Slide Number**.

- Click the **Apply to all** button.

## Exercise 5

Format all three slides as follows.

- Centre align all the titles.

- Remove the bullets in Slide 2.

- Bullet the text in Slide 3.

## Exercise 6

- Choose **Outline** from the **View** menu and click the **Summary Slide** icon at the left of the screen.

- Enter any other bulleted sub-text required.

- Select **Slide** from the **View** menu.

- Click **WordArt** on the **Drawing** Toolbar and click an item as for a Word document.

- Resize the WordArt on the slide as required.

- Click the WordArt item on the slide, click the **Animation** button and then click **Custom Animation**. In the next dialogue box… Click **Animation Order**. In **Entry animation and sound**, click **Fly From Right**.

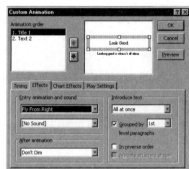

- Click the **Timing** tab and then click **automatically** at bottom right.

- Enter **5** in the little box to set the time delay.

- Click **OK**.

## Exercise 7

Create/Format a new slide as before.

- Click the **Insert Chart** button.

- Select cells and enter your own data in the sample Demo spreadsheet.

- Select **Chart Type** from the **Chart** menu.

- Select a chart type and click **OK**.

## Exercise 8

- Begin with a completely blank presentation.

- Select **Background** in the **Format** menu.

- Continue to make the slide as before.

- Use the **Rotate** button on the **Drawing** Toolbar to rotate the WordArt.

# Module 7     Practical Exercises – Solutions

## Exercise 1
- To create a folder, see Module 2, Ex. 1.
- To open the site **www.blackrock-edu.ie**:
  1. Double-click the Internet Explorer icon.
  2. Type the address in the address box and press **Return**.
- The information required is available on the Home Page. (To open a Word document, see Module 3, Section 1.1.)

## Exercise 2
To save the Home Page:

1  With the Home Page open, select **Save** in the **File** menu.
   In the **Dialogue Box**, type a name for the document.  Select the folder to save in: **Internet Samples**

2  Search the site for the picture: Right-click on the image, left-click Save Picture As and continue as above.

## Exercise 3
Try the link in the menu on the Home Page. **Other Centres** should be listed as a link. Right-click on the map you find and follow the same sequence as in Exercise 2.

## Exercise 4
Type **www.yahoo.com** into the **Address** box and press the **Return** key.
- In the **Search** box, type 'newspapers of the world' and press **Return**.
- Search for the Top 250 link or start a new search with Top 250 Newspaper Sites.
- Click **Favourites** in the **Menu** bar, and then click **Add to Favourites**.  Check that the Name is suitable and click **Create in**. Choose either the **Favourites** folder itself or another suitable one.

Answers may vary from time to time depending on the sites and links.

## Exercise 5
Open any search engine as in Exercise 4 above (or click **Search** and choose any other).

1  **www.latimes.com**  It has three editions (may vary with time).

2  Finding the address:
  - Choose a search engine, e.g., Yahoo!
  - Type 'irish government' in the search box.

- Choose **Regional>Countries>Irish>Government**
- Choose **Government of Ireland/Ria...**
- Now look in the Address box.

## Exercise 6
Follow the steps in Module 7, section 3.4 to 3.8, and send the email to **friend1@isp.ie**.

## Exercise 7
Click **Compose Message** (or **New Mail**). Type the address, **friend2@isp.ie** in the **To** box.
Type *My Conquest*…. In the **Message** box, click in the blank text area.  Click **Sent Items.** Double-click **friend1@isp.ie.** Select the text. Click **Edit**, then **Copy**.  Close the letter.

You are now returned to the friend2 letter. Click **Edit**, then **Paste**.

## Exercise 8
On the **Toolbar…**

1 Click **Address Book**.  2 Click **New Contact**. 3 Under **Name** click in **Display**.  4 Enter the person's name.  5 Under **E-Mail Addresses** click in **Add New**.  6 Enter the e-mail address. Click **Add.**

- Go to the **Inbox.**
  1  Double-click the letter from Friend 2.
  2  On the **Menu Toolbar** (letter), click **Tools**.
  3  Click **Add to address book.**

  Follow on from 3 above.

## Exercise 9
Go to the **Inbox** and double-click the e-mail to open it on the screen.

On the **Menu Toolbar**, click **Reply to Author** and type your reply.

## Exercise 10
There are two options.
- Compose a letter as normal. Enter the two addresses in the **To** box, separated by a semi-colon.
- Enter the first address in the **To** box and the second address in the **Cc** box.

## Exercise 11
The solutions here require you to combine the skills you have learnt in Modules 2 and 7. *There is no assistance offered here.*

# Glossary

Glossary

# Glossary

**Adventure Game**  A computer game in which the player explores an environment and solves puzzles in order to proceed.

**ASCII** (American Standard Code for Information Interchange)  Text saved in ASCII format can be used by most word processors without the need for translators, but any layout or styles are lost.

**Backup**  To keep a copy of a file or files for safekeeping in the case of loss or damage to the original.

**Bar Code**  A pattern of black and white lines that can be scanned and read by computer as seen at supermarket checkouts.

**Bit** (**BI**nary Digi**T**)  One of the two digits (0 or 1) used in the binary counting system used by computers.  Bits are commonly used in sets of 8, called Bytes.

**Bit Map**  The arrangement of a collection of dots to form a picture on a computer screen.  When bit-mapped images are enlarged, the individual dots can be seen and appear jagged, in contrast to *Draw* illustrations which are sharp at all sizes.

**Browse**  To work through a program or presentation, often at random.

**Browser**  A program to allow the user to view pages on the World Wide Web.

**Byte**  A set of (usually) 8 Bits.  A byte can represent a single character of the alphabet or a 'normal' number.

**Cache Memory**  A special type of memory between the CPU and the main memory chips that stores frequently used data to save time, thus increasing the speed of the computer.

**CAD**  See Computer Aided Design

**CAM**  See Computer Aided Manufacture

**CD ROM** (Compact Disk Read Only Memory)  A storage medium with the same size and appearance as normal music CDs, used for storing large amounts of information.  The data is optically encoded and read by a laser beam.

**Cell**  A single 'box' on a spreadsheet.  Each cell has its own unique address derived from the letter of the column (A, B, C…) and the number of the row (1, 2, 3…) as in B3 etc.

**Centring**  Aligning text or objects to be centred on the page between the margins.

**Central Processing Unit** (CPU)  The principal part of a computer.  It performs all the activities required by the instructions input from the keyboard or mouse, for example, and displays the result on the screen.  Also used to describe the actual microprocessor chip that actually does the work, or the box in which it is contained.

**Click**  Pressing (and releasing) the mouse button to give a command to the computer.

**Clip Art**  Collections of professionally drawn illustrations from which the user can select and use in his/her own work.

**Command Line Interface**  A method of controlling the computer by typing in commands at the keyboard, now largely superseded by Graphical User Interfaces such as the Mac OS and Windows.

**Computer Aided Design** (CAD) 1. The use of computer systems or applications in design, from simple products to a whole aircraft.

2. A specialised program that allows the user to simplify the production of complex drawings and designs.

**Computer Aided Learning** (CAL) The use of the computer to provide usually inter-active instruction to the student.

**Computer Aided Manufacture** (CAM) The use of computer systems or applications to process the fabrication and assembly of products.

**Computer Based Training** (CBT) The use of the computer to provide usually interactive instruction to the student as with CAL, but often used for more specialised purposes.

**Computer Graphics**  Illustration drawn on or by a computer.

**Configure**  To set up hardware or software so that it operates as required.

**Control Panel**  On a computer, a piece of software that can be used to set various options such as the number of colours displayed on the screen, the Printer to be used, and so on.

**Copy and Paste**  A technique where data is copied from one location and pasted into another, as with text in a document.  The original data remains in place when a copy is made, unlike Cut and Paste.

**Corruption**  Damage to computer files that may render them unusable, caused by mal-

Glossary

function, mechanical failure, magnetic fields etc.

**CRM** See Customer Relationship Management.

**Cursor** An icon on the screen that shows where the next action will begin, such as where typed text will appear. Often used interchangably with Pointer.

**Customer Relationship Management**

Support systems that monitor and direct a company's interaction with its client base, from contract management to call management. May include on-line ordering, software updates, etc.

**Cut and Paste** A technique for transferring data from one location to another, as with Copy and Paste. When cut, the original data is removed and pasted into its new position, unlike Copy and paste.

**Cybernetics** The study and use of computers to control various processes, such as the machines used in car assembly plants.

**Data** A term used for an item or items of information.

**Data Compression** A technique for reducing the space occupied by files to maximise storage or for transmission over a network, for example. Compressed files have to be decompressed before they can be used.

**Data Protection Act** An Act of the Oireachtas governing the use and control of data stored on computer systems.

**Database** A large collection of information. A computer database brings the computer's speed and versatility to finding, sorting and presenting information in a variety of ways.

**Decision Support Systems** Systems that supply various analytical tools to evaluate information, usually subsidiary applications to a management information system. (q.v.)

**Default** A setting that is used in the absence of any instructions to the contrary. Default settings can be thought of as 'factory' settings which remain in force unless changed by the user.

**De-Install** To remove unwanted software from the computer's Hard Disk.

**Desktop** A term used to describe the computer screen on which icons represent items as if they were arranged on a 'real' desktop.

**Desktop Publishing** (DTP) The use of per-sonal computers, page layout programs, laser printers, scanners etc. to produce high quality documents etc. as distinct from sending the original material to a commercial printer.

**Dictionary** A list of words in its memory which the computer uses to check spelling, as in a word processing document. Words not in the original list can be added to create a User Dictionary.

**Digital** Commonly used to describe data in digital format, i.e a string of ones and zeros, that can be used by a computer to reconstruct the original image, whether it be text, sound, video etc.

**Digitiser** A piece of equipment that converts, for example, drawings on paper into a digital format that can be used by the computer. A scanner, for example, converts an illustration on paper into a digital file that can then be edited and manipulated on the computer.

**Directory** A collection of files and/or folders stored under a common name. Also know as a Folder. A Directory or Folder can contain sub-directories or folders as well as files and can be empty.

**Disk Drive** A mechanical device that consists of either a metal (hard) or plastic (floppy) magnetic disk on which data is stored.

**Disk Format** The electronic structure of a disk that determines the type of computer on which it can be used.

**Dot Matrix Printer** A printer that forms letters from a pattern (matrix) of dots. The dots are commonly formed by pins striking the paper through an inked ribbon.

**Download** To transfer data from a remote computer – as on the Internet – to your own computer.

**Dragging** Pointing to an object, holding down the mouse button and moving the mouse to perform an action on the screen, then releasing the mouse button.

**Drawing** In computer terms, producing illustrations from a variety of lines and shapes, in contrast to Painting which produces illustrations from collections of dots.

**DSS** See Decision Support Systems.

**EIS** See Executive Information Systems

**Electronic Mail** (E-Mail) Messages sent from user to user over a computer network, particularly the Internet. It is quick, cheap and usually informal. Other documents or files can be attached to E-mail messages.

**Encryption** A method of encoding data for security purposes so that it can only be accessed by authorised users.

**Error Message** A message displayed on the screen when something goes wrong or a problem occurs. There may also be buttons to click which offer various options towards resolving the problem.

**Ethernet** A networking system – the standard for many LANs. The computers are connected by cable to a central hub which directs the signals to the other com-puters.

**Executive Information Systems** Programmes that select and organise data into categories of information and reports.

**Export** The ability to send or save a file from one application in a format that can be used in another.

**Field** A part of a database record that contains a single item of information, such as a person's surname or a telephone number.

**File** Can be a set of data, such as a document, or a program such as a word processor.

**Flat File Database** A database held as a single computer file, in contrast to a Relational Database which can use several files.

**Font** The set of characters and numbers of a particular design and style that determines the overall appearance of text, more correctly described as a Typeface. Examples are Arial and Times New Roman.

**Format** The structure of a file depending on the application that produced it. Microsoft Word files, for example, are stored in a different format form files produced by other word processors, making them mutually incompatible unless special translators are used.

**Formatting** The process of preparing a disk electronically before it can be used on a computer. Many disks are available pre-formatted.

**Formula** An instruction used in a spreadsheet to perform a calculation, such as adding up a series of numbers.

**Function** A preset formula used in a spreadsheet which saves the user from having to devise and insert the formula. For example, SUM(A3..A15) calculated the sum of the numbers from cells A3 to A15.

**Graphical User Interface** (GUI) A system of pictures or icons on the screen to allow the user to control the computer by clicking on them with the mouse, in contrast to typing in commands from the keyboard.

**Graphics** Drawings, illustrations, diagrams, photographs etc.

**Hacking** A term used to describe (usually) unlawful attempts to gain access to protected computer systems.

**Hard Copy** Computer file printed out on paper as distinct from the 'invisible' copy on the computer's Hard Disk.

**Hardware** The physical computer equipment and peripherals, such as keyboards, scanners, monitors and so on as distinct from the computer programs or *software*.

**Help System** A series of files included with many application packages which the user can call on for assistance on screen.

**Highlight** To select and object or text, as in a word processor, so that an action can be performed on it.

**Icon** A small picture or symbol used to represent a feature or activity on the screen. Clicking on an icon with the mouse is a way of giving a command to the computer.

**Import** To include a file from an outside source in an application. For example, to take a piece of clip art into a document or records from one database into another.

**Information Technology** The use of technology such as computers, telecommunications and other electronics technology to process information

**Inkjet Printer** A type of printer that sprays tiny drops of ink onto the paper to build up an image. Inkjet printers give high quality but are slower and more expensive to run than laser printers.

**Input Device** A device such as a keyboard, scanner etc. for entering data in the computer.

**Install** To transfer software from the medium on which it has been bought – floppy disc, CD ROM etc – to the computer's hard disk.

**Interactive** The ability of the user to interact with a program such as a computer program to alter and select its progress in contrast to, for example, a film or TV program over which the user has no control.

**Interface** The system used to aid the transfer of data from one environment to another. The human interface between the user and the CPU includes the keyboard, mouse and monitor; a modem is the interface between a computer and the telephone system, for example.

**Justification** Aligning text so that it lines up neatly at the left or right margins, or both, or in the centre of the page.

Glossary

**Key** In a database, a special field such as an ID number, used to identify a record.

**LAN** (Local Area Network) A computer network confined to a local area, such as a single building or group of buildings close together.

**Laser Printer** A printer that uses electrostatic charges to transfer toner powder to paper in the manner of a photocopier, giving very high quality.

**Line Break** The end of a line in a word processing document. Lines usually 'break' between words, but a hyphen can be inserted to break the line within a word, for a neater appearance.

**Liquid Crystal Display** A type of display used in laptop computers, for example, where the size, weight and power requirements of standard monitors are not appropriate.

**Logging Off** The process of disengaging from a system to which you have logged on.

**Logging On** The process of gaining access to a protected system, usually involving entering a user identification or password.

**Macro** A series of commonly used actions that are recorded in such a way that a single click activates the sequence without having to perform them again separately.

**Mail Merge** Combining data such as names and addresses from a database file with a document such as a letter in a word processor so that individualised documents can be printed.

**Management Information Systems** monitor information for the various management levels of an organisation. Used extensively to assist in decision making. See also Decision Support Systems.

**Memory** Electronic chips that can store information on the computer while it is

being used. Devices that store information when the computer is switched off, such as Hard or Floppy disks, is sometimes referred to as secondary memory.

**Menu** A list of actions or choices from which the user makes a choice. Commonly displayed on a Menu Bar. When clicked, the menu drops down and displays the list.

**Merge** To combine two or more files to form a single file.

**MIDI** (Musical Instrument Digital Interface) A way of allowing music data to be sent to or from a computer by a musical instrument. The interface allows the music to

be recorded on a computer as a series of codes which can later be used to reconstruct the sounds.

**MIS** See Management Information Systems.

**Modem** (Short for **M**odulator/**Dem**odulater) A device that enables computer signals to be transmitted to remote computers using the telephone system. It does this by superimposing the computer signals on an audible tone: it *modulates* the tone, which is then demodulated by the remote computer.

**Monitor** The screen on which the computer displays information. It 'monitors' what the CPU is doing and displays the results for the user.

**Mouse** A hand-controlled input device for giving instructions to the computer. A ball in the base of the mouse rolls along the surface of the mouse mat or desk and causes the pointer on the screen to move in sympathy. A button or buttons can be clicked to perform further actions.

**Multimedia** Presenting information using text, sound, animation, graphics and video. Because of the large size of multimedia files, multimedia programs are commonly distributed on CD ROM.

**Network** Usually used to describe a number of computers connected together so that data can be exchanged between them. A network can consist of a small number of computers in the same building or a worldwide system such as the Internet.

**Non-breaking Space** In a word processor, a special space character that ensures that a line does not break between, for example, 'Mr' and 'John'. 'Mr John' then goes to the next line without a break.

**Operating System** A collection of programs that controls the entire computer and the way the user operates it. Major Operating Systems are DOS, UNIX, Windows and the Mac OS. All these are mutually incompatible, in that applications designed for one will not run on the others, but files can often be exchanged between computers using different operating systems.

**Output Device** A device such as a Monitor or Printer on which the output of the CPU is displayed or made available.

**Painting** In computer terms, producing illustrations using thousands of dots or *bits*, each of which can, if necessary, be treated individually. 'Paint' illustrations are commonly described as bit-mapped.

**Palette** A selection, usually of colours, available to the user.

**Password** A security feature requiring a word or series of characters that must be entered before access is granted.

**Peer-to-Peer Network** A simple computer network in which the computers exchange files directly with one another.

**Peripheral** A piece of equipment such as a printer, scanner or external Hard Drive that can be attached to a computer.

**Pixel** A single 'dot' on a computer monitor. Monitors commonly display an area of 600 X 800 pixels. Each pixel's colour and brightness is controlled by the computer to produce the complex images you see on the monitor.

**Point** To move the mouse so that the pointer rests on an object on the screen, such as an icon.

**Pointer** An icon such as a arrowhead that moves around the screen mimicing the movement of the mouse. The pointer can change shape according to its function. Often referred to as the Cursor.

**Port** A socket on the computer into which external cables or devices can be plugged.

**Printer Port** The socket on the computer to which the printer is connected.

**Program** A set of instructions, written in a programming language, used by the computer to perform an action.

**Prompt** Usually a flashing symbol on the screen or a sound to indicate to the user that the computer is expecting some kind of input, such as text to be entered or an action to be performed.

**RAM** (Random Access Memory) A kind of memory chip in which the computer stores and retrieves data. RAM needs a constant supply of power so any data in it is lost when the computer is switched off.

**Read Me File** A file often included with software containing details of last-minute instructions or details of changes too late to be included in the printed documentation, if any.

**Record** The basic unit in a database system, containing various fields, equivalent to a paper catalogue card.

**Relational Database** A computer database that uses several related files. For example, a company might keep a list of customers in one file and a list of products in another and addresses in another. The database can

extract and combine data from the different files as the user requires.

**RGB** (Red, Green, Blue) The method used by computer monitors to display colours by adding these three colours in various intensities.

**ROM** (Read Only Memory) A kind of memory chip containing permanent data which is retained when the computer is switched off. The computer cannot alter the contents of RAM; it can only 'read' it.

**RTF** (Rich Text Format) A format for exchanging text between different word processors without losing the layout or style content, in contrast to ASCII which loses it.

**Run** To Run a program is to start it operating.

**Scroll Bar** A bar usually along the side or bottom of the screen or window to enable the contents to be moved up or down or from side to side when the window is too small to display all of it at once.

**Scrolling** Moving the contents of a window to view parts that are hidden because of the small size of the window.

**Server** A computer that acts as a storage or processing unit for other computers on a network. A single expensive resource can be made available to several users over the network by using a server.

**Software** A computer program of any kind. word processors, database packages, graphics manipulation packages, games, and so on are all examples of software.

**Software Piracy** The illegal copying and use of software, whether for personal or commercial use or for sale.

**Sort** To arrange items in alphabetical or numerical order, or in some other order.

**Speech Recognition** The ability of a computer to recognise spoken words and act on them.

**Speech Synthesis** The production of 'human' speech electronically, as when a computer 'reads' text aloud.

**Spell Check** A program that checks the spelling in a document against a built-in dictionary and facilitates the correction of errors.

**Spreadsheet** An application program commonly used to display and manipulate financial or statistical information. The program can perform calculations on the information and produce graphs and diagrams.

**Synthesiser** In music, a piece of equipment used to generate sounds artificially instead of using musical instruments.

**System Software** The set of programs that the computer uses to operate, as distinct from programs such as word processors used by the user.

**Thesaurus** A special dictionary that allows the user to select from a list of words with the same or similar meaning.

**Toolbar** A bar containing a selection of buttons which, when clicked, perform an action or make certain options available.

**Touch Screen** A special screen that responds to the user's finger touching the surface, replacing the mouse or keyboard in kiosk type public information systems, for example.

**Touchpad** An input device that, for example, replaces the mouse on laptop computers.

**Trackball** An input device for controlling the computer; essentially an 'upside down' mouse with the ball on top instead of underneath.

**Turtle** A small computer-controlled wheeled device used to demonstrate the computer's ability to perform external operations. Commonly used with LOGO to draw simple lines with an attached pen on a sheet of paper taped to the floor.

**Twisted Pair** A type of cable used to connect computers in a network.

**Upload** To transfer data from you own computer to a remote computer over a network, e.g. the Internet.

**User Friendly** Term used to describe hardware or software that is not difficult to use.

**Video Clip** A short section of video, film or animation incorporated in another presentation.

**Virtual Memory** The use of an area of the Hard Disk when there is not enough 'real' memory (RAM) available. As the computer can access RAM much faster that it can the Hard Disk, the use of Virtual Memory slows down the operation the computer considerably.

**Virtual Reality** Computer-generated scenes designed to give the user the impression of being actually in the scene, usually achieved by wearing a special headset.

**Virus** A software program written with malicious intent. A virus interferes with the normal operation of the computer and may display a harmless message on the screen or cause serious corruption of files, for example, depending on the virus.

**VRAM** (Video RAM) A type of memory used by the computer to store data needed for the monitor display. The number of colours that can be displayed depends on the size of the monitor and the amount of VRAM installed.

**WAN** (Wide Area Network) A computer network in which the computers are geographically remote from each other such as the ATM system used by banks, or even world-wide as in the Internet.

**Wildcard** A symbol – often an asterisk – used when searching for data when the exact format is unknown. Thus to search for words ending in ...mac one would enter '*mac'.

**Window** A clearly defined area on the screen in which information is displayed. Several Windows can open at a time and they can be individually moved and resized. It is usual that only one Window can be active at a time, the others being visible but inactive.

**Wizard** Term used to describe a feature in some applications that helps the user through a series of tasks by displaying a series of choices on the screen for the user to choose from.

**Word Processor** A computer program used to prepare, edit, format and produce documents in a more sophisticated way than is possible, for example, on a typewriter.

**Word Wrap** A facility in word processors to insert a line break and move on to the next line automatically.

**Write Protect** The action of preventing the computer from saving on, for example, a floppy disk. Data on a write-protected disk cannot be altered by the computer, thus protecting it against accidental corruption or erasure.

**WYSIWYG** Pronounced 'wizzy-wig'. Describes a screen display that accurately matches the eventual paper version produced on the printer. Literally, 'What-You-See-Is-What-You-Get'.

# Index

Index

# Index

Print
  In *Internet and Email*: printing a page, 351; printing frames, 351
  In *Presentation*: printing, 321; print range, 321; print what, 321
  In *Spreadsheets*, 211; clear print area, 211; set print area, 211; options, 212; part of a spreadsheet, 210; preview, 210; a spreadsheet, 211
  In *Using the Computer*: a document, 108; print preview, 108
  In *Word Processing*: layout, 123; to file, 145; view, 123
Printer
  In *Basic Concepts*: types, 35
  In *Using the Computer*: renaming, 107
  In *Word Processing*: choosing, 145
Printing
  In *Using the Computer*, 107–109; monitoring, 109; setting up, 107
  In *Word Processing*, 143–145; print preview, 143
Priority
  In *Internet and Email*, 366
Privacy
  In *Basic Concepts*: data privacy, 57
Program
  In *Basic Concepts*, 41
Projection
  In *Presentation*, 289
Properties
  In *Using the Computer*: file/folder, 98
Public domain
  In *Basic Concepts*: software, 41
Query
  In *Database*, 241, 262, 268; create, 269; create in design view, 269, 272; criteria in, 271; run button, 271; saving, 268, 273; simple query wizard, 269; wildcard, 274
RAM
  In *Basic Concepts*, 37, 43
Record
  In *Database*, 238, 240, 259: advanced filter/sort, 259; in a form, 259; in a table, 259; navigation button, 259; sorting, 259
  In *Basic Concepts*, 38
Recycle bin
  In *Using the Computer*: emptying, 97
Redo
  In *Word Processing*, 135
Reference
  In *Spreadsheets*: absolute reference, 217; range of references, 217
Rename
  In *Using the Computer*: file, 96; printer, 107
Replace
  In *Spreadsheets*, 209; replace with box, 209
Report
  In *Database*, 241, 275; designing, 275; page footer, 277; page header, 277; previewing, 277; printing, 277; reprinting, 279
Restarting
  In *Using the Computer*, 71

ROM
  In *Basic Concepts*, 37
Rotate
  In *Presentation*: an object, 316
Rows
  In *Spreadsheets*: adding, 204; header, 200, 203; height, 205
Save
  In *Before You Begin*, 14–15
  In *Internet and Email*: a web address, 345; a web graphic, 350; a web page, 350; saving test, 348
  In *Presentation*: a presentation, 298; in other formats, 298
  In *Spreadsheets*: save, 199
  In *Using the Computer*, 84–90; again, 87; button, 86; for the World Wide Web, 88; in different formats, 87
  In *Word Processing*: a document, 121
Save As
  In *Internet and Email*: save as type, 350
  In *Spreadsheets*, 199
  In *Using the Computer*, 87
  In *Word Processing*: button, 121; window, 121
Scale
  In *Spreadsheets*: scaling, 212
Scanner
  In *Before You Begin*, 33
Screen
  In *Basic Concepts*: screen saver, 106; touch screen, 32
  In *Before You Begin*, 18; screen tips; see also: monitor
Search
  In *Basic Concepts*: search engine, 47
  In *Internet and Email*, 352; customise settings, 354; detailed searching, 355; human editors, 352; meta search engines, 352; search assistant, 354; search button, 353; search button settings, 354; search engine tips, 355
  In *Spreadsheets*: by column, 209; by row, 209
  In *Using the Computer*: advanced, 93for files, 91; wildcard searches, 92
Security
  In *Using the Computer*: and deleting, 97
Select
  In *Before You Begin*: text, 9; graphics, 9; in table, 9
  In *Using the Computer*: files, 94
  In *Word Processing*: selecting labels, 186; text, 126; text to indent, 171
Send
  In *Internet and Email*: group mail, 376; messages to many, 364; options, 358, 361; send and receive mail, 360; send/receive button, 360; send/receive message settings, 358; sent items folder, 364
Separate
  In *Spreadsheets*: separator, 207, 224
Server
  In *Basic Concepts*, 45